Japan's Pre-War Perspective of Southeast Asia
Focusing on Ethnologist Matsumoto Nobuhiro's Works during 1919–1945

Petra Karlová

早稲田大学エウプラクシス叢書――010

早稲田大学出版部

Japan's Pre-War Perspective of Southeast Asia
Focusing on Ethnologist Matsumoto Nobuhiro's Works during 1919-1945

KARLOVÁ Petra, PhD, is a research associate at the Global Education Center Academic Writing Program, Waseda University.

First published in 2018 by
Waseda University Press Co., Ltd.
1-9-12 Nishiwaseda
Shinjuku-ku, Tokyo 169-0051
www.waseda-up.co.jp

© 2018 by Petra Karlová

All rights reserved. Except for short extracts used for academic purposes or book reviews, no part of this publication may be reproduced, stored in a retrieval system or transmitted in any form whatsoever—electronic, mechanical, photocopying or otherwise—without the prior and written permission of the publisher.

ISBN978-4-657-17808-4

Printed in Japan

Contents

List of tables and charts
Acknowledgements
Foreword

Introduction 1
1. Background: Significance of Matsumoto Nobuhiro's work ... 1
2. Matsumoto Nobuhiro's life history ... 10
3. Key concepts: Southeast Asia and ethnology ... 16
   3.1. Southeast Asia and South Seas ... 16
   3.2. Ethnology ... 20

Chapter 1: Discovering the ethnology of Southeast Asia during 1919–1923 25
1. Introduction ... 25
2. Matsumoto's study of ethnology ... 28
   2.1. Influence of Kawai Teiichi on Matsumoto's study of ethnology ... 29
   2.2. Influence of Yanagita Kunio on Matsumoto's study of ethnology ... 34
   2.3. Influence of Japanese historians on Matsumoto's study of ethnology ... 42
   2.4. Influence on Matsumoto's methodology ... 47
      2.4.1. The ethnological methodology ... 48
      2.4.2. The methodology of historical science ... 50
3. Matsumoto Nobuhiro's ideas regarding Southeast Asia ... 55
   3.1. Southeast Asian culture as a primitive culture ... 57
   3.2. Matsumoto's application of ethnological theories to Southeast Asian culture ... 61
4. Conclusion ... 66

Chapter 2: Giving importance to Southeast Asia during 1924–1932 67

1. Introduction 67
2. Influence of sociologist ethnology on Matsumoto's ideas regarding Southeast Asia 71
    2.1. The relationship of Marcel Mauss and Marcel Granet with Matsumoto Nobuhiro 72
        2.1.1. Matsumoto Nobuhiro's relationship with Marcel Mauss 73
        2.1.2. Matsumoto's relationship with Marcel Granet 74
    2.2. The sociological influence on Matsumoto Nobuhiro's writings 76
        2.2.1. The idea of the social benefit of primitive culture 78
        2.2.2. The theory of the gift and potlatch 79
        2.2.3. The theory of the seasonal festivals 82
        2.2.4. The theory of the unity of religious and political power 87
3. Influence of evolutionist ethnology on Matsumoto's ideas regarding Southeast Asia 90
    3.1. Influence of the theory of totemism and exogamy 93
    3.2. Influence of the theme of taboo 96
    3.3. Influence of the theory of spiritual power 97
    3.4. Influence of the theme of fertility 100
4. Influence of diffusionist ethnology on Matsumoto's ideas regarding Southeast Asia 102
    4.1. Influence of the theory of Austroasiatic languages 103
        4.1.1. Significance of Wilhelm Schmidt and Jean Przyluski concerning Matsumoto's adoption of the theory of Austroasiatic languages 103
        4.1.2. Matsumoto's adoption of the theory of the Austroasiatic languages 106
    4.2. Influence of the theory of Southern Pacific influence 111
    4.3. Influence of the ideas of Southern culture on Japan 116
        4.3.1. Matsumoto's concept of the South Seas 120
        4.3.2. Southward theory and contradiction in Matsumoto's works 122

5. Conclusion 127

Chapter 3: Visiting the South Seas during 1933–1940 131
1. Introduction 131
2. Significance of Matsumoto Nobuhiro's research trips in the establishment of Southeast Asian studies in Japan 134
   2.1. Significance of Matsumoto Nobuhiro's research trip to French Indochina 135
      2.1.1. Matsumoto Nobuhiro's research trip to French Indochina 136
      2.1.2. Significance of Matsumoto's research trip to French Indochina 139
   2.2. Significance of Matsumoto Nobuhiro's research trip to the Southern Pacific Islands 145
      2.2.1. Matsumoto Nobuhiro's research trip to the Southern Pacific Islands 146
      2.2.2. Significance of Matsumoto Nobuhiro's research trip to the Southern Pacific Islands 149
   2.3. Significance of Matsumoto Nobuhiro's research trip to China 151
      2.3.1. Matsumoto Nobuhiro's research trip to China 151
      2.3.2. Significance of Matsumoto Nobuhiro's research trip to China 154
3. Conclusion 159

Chapter 4: Ideas for establishing Southeast Asian studies during 1933–1945 161
1. Introduction 161
2. Concepts of South Seas and Southeast Asia 166
3. Influence of diffusionist ethnology on Matsumoto's works 167
   3.1. Matsumoto's ideas regarding Indochinese peoples' origins in China 170
   3.2. Matsumoto's ideas regarding Southeast Asian peoples' relation with Japan 174
   3.3. Matsumoto's research on Southeast Asian languages 178

4. Orientalism in Matsumoto's ideas regarding the people of
   Southeast Asia   183
   4.1. Matsumoto's hierarchy of Southeast Asian people
        based on dichotomy of the powerful and the weak   186
   4.2. Matsumoto's hierarchy in Indochina based on the
        dichotomy of the civilized and primitive   193
   4.3. Exotism and similarity in Matsumoto's ideas regarding
        Southeast Asian and Southern Pacific people   201
        4.3.1. Exotism   202
        4.3.2. Similarity   203
        4.3.3. Significance of similarity between Japan and
               Southest Asia   206
5. Influence of the climate theory on Matsumoto's ideas
   regarding the people of Indochina   208
   5.1. Watsuji Tetsuro's climate theory   210
   5.2. Matsumoto's application of the climate theory for
        interpretation of Indochinese people   211
        5.2.1. Contradictions in Matsumoto's application of the
               climate theory on Vietnamese people   213
6. Conclusion   217

Chapter 5: Political influence on Southeast Asian studies during
1933–1945 219
1. Introduction   219
2. Influence of Japan's Southern Advance Theory   221
   2.1. Japan's Southern Advance and Southern Advance Theory   221
   2.2. Influence of Japan's Southern Advance Theory
        on Matsumoto's works   227
3. Influence of Pan-Asianism on Matsumoto's research on
   Southeast Asia   232
   3.1. Concept of Pan-Asianism   232
   3.2. Matsumoto's reluctance toward Pan-Asianism   234
   3.3. Pan-Asianist elements in Matsumoto's works on Indochina   238
   3.4. Matsumoto's contribution to the Pan-Asianist policy
        toward Southeast Asia   244

4. Conclusion　　　　　　　　　　　　　　　　　　　　247

Conclusion 251

Bibliography 261
    Matsumoto Nobuhiro 松本信広 (works in the chronological order)
    Other authors (works in alphabetic order)

The list of Japanese personal names 293

Index 296

List of tables and charts

Table 1:	Matsumoto Nobuhiro's life chronology	11
Table 2:	Nan'yō, Nankai, and Southeast Asia	18
Table 3:	Ethnological schools	21
Table 4:	Matsumoto Nobuhiro's hierarchy of people in Indochina according to his evaluation of their culture	201
Table 5:	Summary of Matsumoto Nobuhiro's development and formation as the founder of Southeast Asian studies in 1919–1945	252
Chart 1:	Influence on Matsumoto's ideas regarding Southern culture in France	116

Acknowledgements

This book could not have been completed without the support of the following people. First, the author wishes to express her deepest gratitude to Professor Shiraishi Masaya of Waseda University for his guidance and support during her research. The author would also like to thank Professor Gotō Ken'ichi, Professor Hayase Shinzō, and Professor Shimao Minoru for their valuable contribution in examining this thesis. The author is indebted to Professor Shimao for mediating the contact with Professor Chikamori Masashi of Keio University who provided responses to author questions during her interviews on Matsumoto Nobuhiro and invited her to participate in the symposium and social gathering on the 50th anniversary of the foundation of the Keio Institute of Cultural and Linguistic Studies at Keio University (October 13, 2012).

Furthermore, the author wishes to thank the Japanese Ministry of Education, Culture, Sports, Science and Technology for providing scholarship to cover her school fees and living expenses in Tokyo from April 2008 to September 2012. This book could not have been written without the support of NPO Terashima Bunko, particulary Terashima Jitsuro who employed the author as a visiting researcher and enabled her to proceed with her research while working there. The author is also grateful to the Waseda University Global Education Center (the writing center) and Professor Tanaka Aiji and Professor Sadoshima Saori for employing her as a tutor (teaching assistant and associate) and a Research Associate subsequently, which enabled her to earn money to pay for her living expenses and developed her academic writing skill. The author wishes to extend gratitude to all tutors who helped her with editing her Ph. D. thesis and revising it for this book.

The author also received great support from many colleagues and friends in and outside of Waseda University. The author would like to thank all zemi fellows, especially Bernardette Bravo Canave, Delilah Ruth Russel, Odaira Takeshi, Shimabayashi Takaki, and Edgar Santiago Pelaez Mazariegos for their inspiring comments, questions, and encouragement. Furthermore, it is necessary to thank all tutors of the Waseda University writing center for sharing concerns and the joy of writing an academic paper. In addition, the author cannot forget the warm support of her friends Toshikawa Yuki, Rafael Boada, Jhang Hyejin, Aurelijus Zykas, Kawakami Reiko, Kawashima Yūko, and many others. The author is also indebted to all the members of the Japan Karate Association Taishijuku who supplied her with endurance and a strong spirit during the practice and friendly gatherings. Finally, the author wants to express her gratitude to her family for understanding and supporting her lasting passion for research on Japan and Vietnam.

Foreword

Japan's attitude toward Asian countries during the prewar and war period continues to be a significant topic in international discussions. In praticular, the problem of interpreting this part of history has affected Japan's relations with China and South Korea. Comparatively, Japan's relations with Southeast Asian countries appear to be smooth and friendly due to the Japanese contribution to their economic development. However, this does not mean that the Japanese exploitation of Southeast Asia has been forgotten. Many Southeast Asian materials discussing this period still address Japanese as "imperialists," "colonialist," and "fascists." Furthemore, international academic cooperation with regard to examining Japan's involvement in Southeast Asia during World War II demonstrates the importance of this issue. Various international conferences presenting the results of this research were recently held in relation to the 70th anniversary of the end of World War II.[1]

Owing to the effort of the scholars of Japan, Southeast Asia, and other countries, the political history of Japan's relation with Southeast Asia has been clarified to a large extent. The existing research from this perspective (Yano Tooru, Goto Ken'ichi, Tachikawa Kyoichi,

---

1. "Historical, Social, and Cultural Issues in Relations between Japan and Vietnam" (13-15 November 2013, International Research Center for Japanese Studies, Vietnam), "Indochina, Thailand, Japan and France during World War II: Overview of Existing Literature and Related Documents for Future Development of Research" (6-7 December 2014, Waseda University, Japan), and "Vietnam-Indochina-Japan's relation during the Second World War: Document and Interpretation" (18-19 September 2015, University of Social Sciences & Humanities (USSH), Vietnam).

Nguyễn Văn Khánh, Bi Shi Hong, etc.)[2] argues that Japan was interested in Southeast Asia due to its natural resources and market. Furthemore, Japan mainly used Southeast Asia for its military purposes during the Greater East Asian War.

In contrast, this book suggests that the Japanese had other approaches to Southeast Asia during that time. It uses the case of ethnologist Matsumoto Nobuhiro to demonstrate that there were Japanese who were interested in Southeast Asian culture.

In contradiction with the political history, the research on ideational and cultural history in the background of Japan's relations with Southeast Asia has been scarcely conducted. Nonetheless, clarifying the history of the Japanese government's moves toward Southeast Asia and the work of the Japanese scholars researching the region during this period in necessary. Indeed, they, as specialists, were expected to provide objective knowledge regarding Southeast Asia based on scientific research.

This book focuses on the Japanese ethnologist Matsumoto Nobuhiro (松本信広, 1897-1981). He received a doctoral degree from Sorbonne University for his two theses, one of which examined Southeast Asian languages (1928), and contributed to the founding of Southeast Asian studies in Japan in the 1930s. He is known as the founder of these studies, together with Yamamoto Tatsuro (1910-2001). Tracing the development and formation of Matsumoto's ideas regarding Southeast Asia during 1919-1945 clarifies the Japanese image of Southeast Asia produced by a leading scholar and Matsumoto's role in founding Southeast Asian studies in Japan.

This book is written on the basis of a qualitative research of the data collected from papers and books (Waseda University Library, Keio University Library, Toyo Bunko, and the National Diet Library), unstructured interviews with Matsumoto's student Chikamori Masashi at Keio University (August 23, 2012; October 13, 2012; and De-

---

2. The Japanese and Vietnamese names are mentioned in the traditional order: the surname first, (middle name), and then the given name. The Japanese characters of the Japanese names can be found in the list of the Japanese names on page 381.

cember 10, 2012), and the observation of the symposium and social gathering on the 50th anniversary of the foundation of the Keio Institute of Cultural and Linguistic Studies at Keio University (October 13, 2012). The content analysis was applied to the relevant writings of Matsumoto Nobuhiro, his teachers (Kawai, Teiichi Yanagita Kunio, Tanaka Suiichiro, Hashimoto Matsukichi, Kato Shigeshi, Marcel Granet, Marcel Mauss, and Jean Przyluski), his teachers' teachers (Wilhelm Wundt and James George Frazer), and other scholars who influenced Matsumoto (Wilhelm Schmidt and Watsuji Tetsuro). Thereafter, the content of Matsumoto's writings was compared with the content of other writers' writings and was analyzed in relation to the historical background from 1919 to 1945. Since the author is a historian, the research was conducted from the historical perspective; thus, it has limitations in discussing ethnological theories.

Thise book comprises five chapters. Chapter 1 traces how and why Matsumoto started studying Southeast Asian culture in connection with his interest in evolutionist ethnology during 1919-1923. Chapter 2 examines the influence of sociologist, evolutionist, and diffusionist ethnology on Matsumoto's works when he began stressing on Southeast Asia during 1924-1932. Chapter 3 investigates his trips to the South Seas region (French Indochina, South Seas Islands, and China) during 1933-1940 and their significance in the establishment of Southeast Asian studies in Japan. Chapter 4 analyzes Matsumoto's ideas regarding Southeast Asia, shaped by various theories,during the founding of Southeast Asian studies in 1933-1945. Finally, Chapter 5 examines the political influence of Japan's Southern Advance Theory and Pan-Asianism on Matsumoto's writings about Southeast Asia during 1933-1945.

Introduction

1. Background: Significance of Matsumoto Nobuhiro's work

Matsumoto Nobuhiro (1897-1981) was the founder of Southeast Asian studies and an important personality in Japan—Vietnam relations. He brought a significant amount of literature on Southeast Asia and Vietnam to Japan,[1] created an enabling environment for research on Southeast Asia in Japan, and published his research on Southeast Asia. His pioneering work on Southeast Asian studies gained the appreciation of many Japanese scholars such as those specializing in Vietnam studies (Suenari Michio,[2] Frédéric Roustan,[3] Shimao Minoru,[4]

---

1. Iwai, Daie "Nagata Yasukichi shūshū Annam bon mokuroku," *Shigaku*, dai 14 kan, dai 2 gō, Mita Shigakkai, 1935, pp. 101 (283)-109 (291); Yamamoto, Tatsurō "Betonamu kenkyū shiryō no shōkai to shuppan," *Nihon minzoku bunka no kigen, dai 3 kan*, Geppō dai 3 gō, Kōdansha, 1978, pp. 3-5; Wada, Hironari "Matsumoto Nobuhiro kyōju jūrai no Vetonamu shahon sanshu ni tsuite - Nihon-Chūgoku no kindaika to Vetonamu," *Shigaku*, dai 35 kan, dai 4 gō, Mita Shigakkai, 1963, pp. 431-434; *Keiō gijuku toshokan zō Matsumoto bunko mokuroku*, Keiō gijuku daigaku Mita jōhō sentā, 1991; Wada, Masahiko "Matsumoto Nobuhiro hakase jūrai no Annan hon ni tsuite - Keiō gijuku toshokan Matsumoto bunko shozō Annan hon kaidai" (Jō), *Shigaku*, dai 62 kan, dai 1/2 gō, Mita Shigakkai, 1992, pp. 165-183; Wada, Masahiko "Matsumoto Nobuhiro hakase jūrai no Annan hon ni tsuite - Keiō gijuku toshokan Matsumoto bunko shozō Annan hon kaidai" (Ka), *Shigaku*, dai 63 kan, dai 1/2 gō, Mita Shigakkai, 1993, pp. 165-183; Hayashi, Masako "Betonamu hon ni tsuite - 'Tōyō bunko zō Betonamu hon shomoku' ni miru Nihon tono kakawari," *Atomi gakuen joshi daigaku bungaku fōramu*, 9, Atomi gakuen joshi daigaku, 2011, pp. 188-127.

and Kawamoto Kunie[5]), those specializing in Southeast Asian studies (Japan Society for Southeast Asian Studies[6]), those specializing in Asian history (Yoshikai Masato[7]), anthropologists (social anthropologist Shimizu Akitoshi[8] and cultural anthropologists Yamashita Shinji[9] and Suzuki Masataka[10]), folklorists (Ito Seiji[11] and Ito Mikiharu[12]), and historians (Koyama Shiro[13]). Furthermore, Matsumoto is also known as a pioneer in advocating Southern genealogy among the Japanese mythologists (Obayashi Taryo[14] and Hirafuji Kikuko[15]).

Matsumoto studied at the Boys Junior High School (Futsūbu

2. Suenari, Michio *Betonamu bunka jinruigaku. Bunken kaidai. Nihon kara shiten*, Fūkyōsha, 2009, p. 224.
3. Roustan, Frédéric "From Oriental Studies to South Pacific Studies: The Multiple Origins of Vietnamese Studies," *Journal of Vietnamese Studies*, Vol. 6, Issue 1, 2011, pp. 1-42.
4. Shimao, Minoru "Betonamu. Tōnan Ajiashi he no teii to tenkai," *Tōnan Ajia shi. Kenkyū no hatten*, Tōnan Ajia Gakkai 40 shūnen, Kinen jigyō iinkai, Yamakawa shuppansha, 2009, pp. 110-113.
5. Kawamoto, Kunie "Gengo bunka kenkyūjo sanjūnen," *Keiō gijuku daigaku gengo bunka kenkyūjo hōkokushū*, Keiō gijuku daigaku gengo bunka kenkyūjo, dai 24 gō, 1992, pp. 1-2.
6. Tōnan Ajia Gakkai *Tōnan Ajia shi. Kenkyū no hatten*, Tōnan Ajia Gakkai 40 shūnen, Kinen jigyō iinkai, Yamakawa shuppansha, 2009, p. 12.
7. Yoshikai, Masato "One Century of Bronze Drum Research in Japan," *Transacktions of the International Conference of Eastern Studies*, No. XLIX, Vol. 419, The Tōhō Gakkai, 2004, pp. 23-40. "Rekishigakusha to 'Minami Shina'," *Shōwa - Ajiashugi no jitsuzō. Teikoku Nihon to Taiwan, 'Nanyō', 'Minami Shina*, ed. by Matsuura, Masataka, Minerva shobō, 2007, pp. 54-77.
8. Shimizu, Akitoshi *Anthropology and Colonialism in Asia and Oceania*, ed. by J. v. Bremen and A. Shimizu, Richmond, Surrey: Curzon, 1999, p. 149, 165, note 28.
9. Yamashita, Shinji *The Making of Anthropology in East and Southeast Asia*, New York: Berghahn Books, 2004, pp. 104-105.
10. Suzuki, Masataka "Chiiki kenkyū to Keiō gijuku - Jinbunshakaigaku no shiza kara," *Mita Hyōron*, 10/ No. 1182, 2014, pp. 32-37.
11. Itō, Seiji "Matsumoto Nobuhiro - 'Nampōsetsu' no kaitakusha," *Bunka jinruigaku gunzō*, Nihonhen (3), Kyōto: Akademia shuppankai, 1988, p. 234.
12. Itō, Mikiharu "Nihon shinwa to Ryūkyū shinwa," *Nihon shinwa to Ryūkyū*, Kōza Nihon no shinwa, dai 10 kan, Yūseidō shuppan, 1977, p. 2-5.
13. Kōyama, Shirō *Shigaku*, dai 51 kan, dai 1 gō, Mita Shigakkai, 1981, pp. 237-238.

gakkō, 普通部)[16] and the University of Keio Gijuku (Keiō Gijuku 慶応義塾). After his graduation from Keio University, he was employed as a teacher at the Boys Junior High School. Subsequently, from 1924 to 1928, he studied Oriental studies at Sorbonne University in France, where he received his doctoral degree. After his return to Japan, he became an associate professor at his Alma Mater Keio University (promoted to the rank of professor in 1930). In 1935, he became a founding member of the Japan Ethnological Society (Minzokugakkai 日本民族学会). In 1939, he became a researcher along with Yamamoto Tatsuro at the Research Institute for South Asian Culture (Minami Ajia Kenkyūjo 南亜細亜研究所). Furthermore, in 1965, he became the chairman of Mita Historical Society at Keio University (Mita Shigakkai 三田史学会), a founding member, and the third chairman of the Japan Society for Southeast Asian Historical Studies (Tōnan Ajia Shigakkai 東南アジア史学会, the present Japan Society for Southeast Asian Studies Tōnan Ajia Gakkai 東南アジア学会).[17]

Matsumoto received several awards for his academic works. His book *The Peoples and Cultures of Indochina*[18] was awarded by the Scholar Promotion Fund of Keio University[19]. His book was listed

---

14. Ōbayashi, Taryō "Nihon shinwa no kenkyū," *Kokubungaku kaisetsu to kinkanshō*, 37-1, 1972, p. 163. Ōbayashi, Taryō "Kaisetsu," *Nihon minzokugaku no kigen I: shinwa-densetsu*, Kōdansha, 1978, pp. 162-164.
15. Hirafuji, Kikuko "Shakaigakuteki kenkyū - Matsumoto Nobuhiro no shinwa kenkyū ni okeru Furansu shakaigakuha no eikyō," *Shinwagaku to Nihon no kamigami*, Kōbunkan, 2004, pp. 33-41; Hirafuji, Kikuko "Shokuminchi teikoku Nihon no shinwagaku," *Shūkyō to fashizumu*, Suiseisha, 2010, pp. 311-347; Ōbayashi, Taryō "Nihon shinwa no kenkyū," *Kokubungaku kaisetsu to kinkanshō*, 37-1, 1972, p. 163.
16. A grammar school that belonged to Keio Gijuku and was affiliated with Keio University.
17. *Ine-fune-matsuri: Matsumoto Nobuhiro sensei tsuitō ronbunshū*, Kyōshuppan, 1982. *Matsumoto Nobuhiro shinpen zakki*, Matsumoto Chie, 1982. Sakurai, Yumio "Tōnan Ajia shi no yonjūnen," *Tōnan Ajia shi. Kenkyū no hatten*, Tōnan Ajia Gakkai 40 shūnen, Kinen jigyō iinkai, Yamakawa shuppansha, 2009, p. 12.
18. Matsumoto, Nobuhiro *Indoshina no minzoku to bunka*, Iwanami shoten, 1942.

among the recommended readings by the Japan Publishing Culture Association in 1943.[20] Furthermore, he received the academic Keio Gijuku Award for his paper *Ethnology and Fukuzawa Sensei* in 1951.[21] In 1955, the French government presented him with an award for his contribution to the Japanese-French cultural exchange, called *Les palmes académiques*.[22] His contribution to the study of Japan's historical relations with Southeast Asia was so well known that the Japanese government dispatched him to Hong Kong to start an introductory course for establishing Japanese studies at the Hong Kong Chinese University.[23] Matsumo's lecture in Hong Kong was realized owing to his relationship with two scholars of Keio University, namely Kani Hiroaki (*1932) and Trần Kinh Hoà (陳荊和, Chin Kei Wa, 1917–1995) who worked as teachers in Hong Kong.[24]

Matsumoto dedicated his working life mainly to his Alma Mater, Keio University, where he was a professor from 1930. He was the dean of Keio University Faculty of Letters, director of the Keio Institute of Cultural and Linguistic Studies (Keiō gijuku daigaku gengo bunka kenkyūjo 慶應義塾大学言語文化研究所, 1962, its predecessor was the below-mentioned Linguistic Institute), president of the Mita Historical Society of Keio University, and member of the Science Council of

---

19. *Ine-fune-matsuri: Matsumoto Nobuhiro sensei tsuitō ronbunshū*, Kyōshuppan, 1982, p. 694.
20. Takeda, Ryūji "*Indoshina no minzoku to* bunka (Matsumoto Nobuhiro, Iwanami shoten shokō," *Shigaku*, dai 22 kan, dai 4 gō, Mita Shigakkai, 1943, p. 119 (489).
21. *Ine-fune-matsuri: Matsumoto Nobuhiro sensei tsuitō ronbunshū*, Kyōshuppan, 1982, p. 694.
22. Ibid.
23. Kani, Hiroaki "Matsumoto Nobuhiro sensei to Honkon kōkogaku" "Matsumoto Nobuhiro sensei wo shinobu," *Kodaigaku Jānaru*, dai 194 gō, Nyū saiensusha, 1981, pp. 27–30.
24. Ibid., Kawamoto, Kunie "Shiki ni mukau keigan – Chin Kei Wa hakushi wo itamu," *Keiō gijuku daigaku gengo bunka kenkyūjo kiyō*, dai 28 gō, Keiō gijuku daigaku gengo bunka kenkyūjo, 1996, pp. 12, 16. "Chin Kei Wa zenshochō keireki, kenkyū jisseki ichiran," *Sōdai Ajia kenkyū*, dai 15 gō, Sōka daigaku Ajia kenkyūjo, 1994, pp. 148-149. Ōsawa, Kazuo "Dainan jitsuroku to Matsumoto Nobuhiro," *Ine-fune-matsuri: Matsumoto Nobuhiro sensei tsuitō ronbunshū*, Kyōshuppan, 1982, p. 689.

Japan.[25] In addition, he co-initiated the foundation of the Linguistic Institute (Keiō gijuku gogaku kenkyūjo 慶応義塾語学研究所, 1942), Asia Research Institute (Ajia kenkyūjo 亜細亜研究所, 1943), and Keio Institute of Cultural and Linguistic Studies.[26] All these institutes were also related to Southeast Asian studies, and the Keio Institute of Cultural and Linguistic Studies became the center of Southeast Asian studies in Japan during the postwar period. He became The professor emeritus of Keio University in 1969.[27] Due to his contributions, he is often commemorated on important anniversaries at Keio University.[28] His students (especially Ito Seiji) and colleagues from various disciplines published their memories of his work:[29] for example, Ito Seiji wrote many paper's on Matsumoto's various contributions. Chikamori shared his memories with Matsumoto during the research in Kujūku Village in the 1950s,[30] and Kawamoto Kunie wrote regarding Matsumoto's contribution to the establishment of the Keio Institute of Cultural and Linguistic Studies.[31]

---

25. "Kōkogaku nyūsu", *Kōkogaku jānaru*, 189 gō, 1981, p. 32
26. *Ine-fune-matsuri: Matsumoto Nobuhiro sensei tsuitō ronbunshū*, Rokkō-shuppan, 1982, p. 694. Kawamoto, Kunie "Gengo bunka kenkyūjo sanjūnen," *Keiō gijuku daigaku gengo bunka kenkyūjo hōkokushū*, Keiō gijuku daigaku gengo bunka kenkyūjo, dai 24 gō, 1992, pp. 1-2.
27. *Ine-fune-matsuri: Matsumoto Nobuhiro sensei tsuitō ronbunshū*, Kyōshuppan, 1982, p. 695.
28. "Mita no shigakusha profīru," *Shigaku*, dai 60 kan, dai 2/3 gō, Mita Shigakkai, 1991, p. 343; Kawakita, Nobuo "Keiō gijuku daigaku bungakubu kyōin tantō kamoku ichiran," *Shigaku*, dai 60 kan, dai 2/3 gō, Mita Shigakkai, 1991, p. 183 (357); Kawamoto, Kunie "Gengo bunka kenkyūjo sanjūnen," *Keiō gijuku daigaku gengo bunka kenkyūjo hōkokushū*, Keiō gijuku daigaku gengo bunka kenkyūjo, dai 24 gō, 1992, pp. 1-12; Itō, Seiji "Minzokugaku, Fōkuroa, Tōyō shigaku no hazamade" (Dainikai zadankai, Mitashigaku no hyakunen wo kataru), *Shigaku*, dai 60 kan, dai 2/3 gō, Mita Shigakkai, 1991, pp. 253-263; Esaka, Teruya "Mita no kōkogaku" (Dainikai zadankai, Mitashigaku no hyakunen wo kataru), *Shigaku*, dai 60 kan, dai 2/3 gō, Mita Shigakkai, 1991, pp. 245, 249, 250; *Gengo bunka kenkyūjo sōritsu 50 shūnen kinen kōenkai - kinen shimpojiumu*, 2012nen 10gatsu 13nichi. Suzuki, Masataka "Chiiki kenkyū to Keiō gijuku - Jinbunshakaigaku no shiza kara," *Mita Hyōron*, 10/ No. 1182, 2014, pp. 32-37.

In this manner, Matsumoto's ideas formed the foundations for the future generation of Japanese researchers. Matsumoto is said to have instigated interest in Southeast Asia in his students.[32] Among his students are Kawamoto Kunie, a Vietnam specialist; Takeda Ryuji, a specialist in Vietnamese history; Chikamori Masashi, an ethnoarchaologist; Ito Seiji, a folklorist; Kani Hiroaki, a scholar in Oriental history; Esaka Teruya, an archaeologist; and Matsubara Hidekichi, a scholar in French literature. All the aforementioned scholars became professors at Keio University. Among them, in particular, Kawamoto Kunie's work is the most appreciated since he contributed to the development of Vietnamese studies in Japan through his research and guidance. Kawamoto is noted for educating a well-known scholar of Vietnamese history at Keio University, Shimao Minoru.[33]

In this manner, Matsumoto influenced many different scholars, especially in the beginning of their studies; however, nobody continued his research. Out of all of Matsumoto's students, Chikamori's ethnoarchaological[34] research is closest to Matsumoto's legacy. This is because Matsumoto combined ethnology and history in his research on

---

29. Itō, Seiji "Hito to gakumon, Matsumoto Nobuhiro," *Shakai jinruigaku nenpō*, Tōkyō toritsu daigaku shakai jinrui gakkai, dai 12 kan, 1986, pp. 117-131; "Matsumoto Nobuhiro - 'Nampōsetsu' no kaitakusha," *Bunka jinruigaku gunzō*, Nihonhen (3), Kyōto: Akademia shuppankai, 1988, pp. 225-242; "Minzokugaku, Fōkuroa, Tōyō shigaku no hazamade" (Dainikai zadankai, Mitashigaku no hyakunen wo kataru), *Shigaku*, dai 60 kan, dai 2/3 gō, Mita Shigakkai, 1991, pp. 253-263; "Matsumoto Nobuhiro to gakumon," *Keiō gijuku daigaku gengo kenkyūjo hōkokushū*, Keiō gijuku daigaku, dai 24 kan, 1992; "Sumiyaki chōsha no hanashi - Yanagita Kunio to Matsumoto Nobuhiro," *Shigaku*, dai 75 kan, dai 2/3 gō, 2007, pp. 211-231. Kawamoto, Kunie "Gengo bunka kenkyūjo sanjūnen," *Keiō gijuku daigaku gengo bunka kenkyūjo hōkokushū*, Keiō gijuku daigaku gengo bunka kenkyūjo, dai 24 gō, 1992, pp. 1-12. Ōsawa, Kazuo "Dainan jitsuroku to Matsumoto Nobuhiro," *Ine-funematsuri: Matsumoto Nobuhiro sensei tsuitō ronbunshū*, Kyōshuppan, 1982, 679-691. Chikamori, Masashi "Matsumoto Nobuhiro no 'Genmin no kenkyū'," Keiō gijuku *daigaku daigakuin shakaigaku kenkyū kiyō. Ningen to shakai no tankyū. Kujūkuri chōsa*, Keiō gijuku daigaku daigakuin shakaigaku kenkyūka, 2013, pp. 235-239. Esaka, Teruya "Mita no kōkogaku" (Dainikai zadankai, Mitashigaku no hyakunen wo kataru), *Shigaku*, dai 60 kan, dai 2/3 gō, Mita

Southeast Asia, and Chikamori combined ethnology and archaeology in his research of the Southern Pacific Islands.[35] However, the main difference was that Matsumoto's research was a combination of ethnology and Oriental history on Southeast Asia. Thus, none of his stu-

> Shigakkai, 1991, pp. 69-78 (243-252). Yawata, Ichirō "Kaisetsu," *Nihon minzoku bunka no kigen: Tōnan Ajia bunka to Nihon*, dai 3 kan, geppō dai 3 gō, Kōdansha, 1978, pp. 1-3. Shimizu, Junzō "Kaisetsu," *Nihon minzoku bunka no kigen II : Kodai no fune / Nihon go to Nampogo*, Kōdansha, 1978, pp. 403-408. Kōyama, Shirō "Fuhō," *Shigaku*, dai 51 kan, dai 1 gō, Mita Shigakkai, 1981, pp. 237-238. Mabuchi, Tōichi "Odayaka de fukutsu no daisempai" *Nihon minzoku bunka no kigen*, dai 2 kan, geppō dai 2 gō, Kōdansha, 1978, pp. 1-3. Iwata, Keiji "Kaisetsu," *Nihon minzoku bunka no kigen: Tōnan Ajia bunka to Nihon*, Kōdansha, 1978, pp. 447-454. Yamamoto, Tatsurō "Betonamu kenkyū shiryō no shōkai to shuppan," *Nihon minzoku bunka no kigen, dai 3 kan*, Geppō dai 3 gō, Kōdansha, 1978, pp. 3-5.

30. Chikamori, Masashi "Matsumoto Nobuhiro no 'Genmin no kenkyū'," *Keiō gijuku daigaku daigakuin shakaigaku kenkyū kiyō. Ningen to shakai no tankyū. Kujūkuri chōsa*, Keiō gijuku daigaku daigakuin shakaigaku kenkyūka, 2013, pp. 235-239.
31. Kawamoto, Kunie "Gengo bunka kenkyūjo sanjūnen," *Keiō gijuku daigaku gengo bunka kenkyūjo hōkokushū*, Keiō gijuku daigaku gengo bunka kenkyūjo, dai 24 gō, 1992, pp. 1-12.
32. Roustan, Frédéric "From Oriental Studies to South Pacific Studies: The Multiple Origins of Vietnamese Studies," *Journal of Vietnamese Studies*, Vol. 6, Issue 1, 2011, p. 20. Interview with Chikamori Masashi, 23 August 2012, Keio University, Tokyo.
33. Kawamoto, Kunie *Vetonamu bōkoku shi ta* (1966), *Betonamu no uta to rekishi* (1967), *Minami Betonamu seiji han no shōgen* (1974), *Shōkai Betonamu go jiten* (2011)
34. Ethnoarchaeology is an interdisciplinary discipline combining ethnography and archaeology. It emerged in the 1960s as an ethnographic study of living cultures to provide ethnological analogies for the interpretation of archaeological data. David, Nicolas and Kramer, Carol *Ethnoarchaeology in Action*. Cambridge World Archaeology, Cambridge University Press, 2001, pp. 2, 6, 10, 43. "Ethnoarchaeology," *Encyclopedia of Cultural Anthropology*, Vol. 2, edited by Levinson, David and Ember, Melvin, New York: Henry Holt and Company, 1996, pp. 396-399.
35. Chikamori, Masashi *Sangoshō no minzoku kōkogaku - Renneru shima no bunka to tekiyō* (1988), *Sangoshō no keikan shi - Kukku shotō chōsa no ronshū* (2008), *Sangoshō to ningen - Porineshia no fīrudonōto* (2012).

dents took over his research. This was because ethnology in its development separated from Oriental history and gave preference to more convincing evidences from archaeology. In this sense, Matsumoto's research became outdated. From this perspective, Matsumoto's contribution to the Japanese academia lays in his foundation work for various academic disciplines, especially Southeast Asian and Vietnamese studies. Owing to the interdisciplinary character of Matsumoto's work, the study of Southeast Asia became known to the scholars of other fields.

Japanese scholars appreciated Matsumoto's specific contribution to the study of Southeast Asia. Historian Yoshikai Masato wrote regarding Matsumoto's leading role in the research on Southeast Asian bronze drums during the prewar period.[36] Cultural anthropologist Suenari Michio praised his ethnological work regarding the peoples of Vietnam.[37] However, the passages concerning Matsumoto by these authors are limited to one page.

Interestingly, the content of Matsumoto's research is comprehensively discussed mostly by the scholars of Japanese mythology, such as Obayashi Taryo, Hirafuji Kikuko, and Ushijima Iwao.[38] This means that Matsumoto's research on Southeast Asia was also important for the development of Japanese mythology. These scholars highlighted the

---

36. Yoshikai, Masato "One Century of Bronze Drum Research in Japan," *Transacktions of the International Conference of Eastern Studies*, No. XLIX, Vol. 419, The Tōhō Gakkai, 2004, pp. 31–32.
37. Suenari, Michio *Betonamu bunka jinruigaku. Bunken kaidai. Nihon kara shiten*, Fūkyōsha, 2009, p. 224.
38. Ōbayashi, Taryō "Nihon shinwa no kenkyū," *Kokubungaku kaisetsu to kinkanshō*, 37-1, 1972, p. 163. Ōbayashi, Taryō "Kaisetsu," *Nihon minzokugaku no kigen I: shinwa-densetsu*, Kōdansha, 1978; Hirafuji, Kikuko "Shakaigakuteki kenkyū - Matsumoto Nobuhiro no shinwa kenkyū ni okeru Furansu shakaigakuha no eikyō," *Shinwagaku to Nihon no kamigami*, Kōbunkan, 2004; Hirafuji, Kikuko "Shokuminchi teikoku Nihon no shinwagaku," *Shūkyō to fashizumu*, Kōbunkan, 2004, pp. 311–347; Ōbayashi, Taryō "Nihon shinwa no kenkyū," *Kokubungaku kaisetsu to kinkanshō*, 37-1, 1972, p. 163; Ushijima, Iwao "Matsumoto Nobuhiro, Mishina Sōei, Oka Masao ni okeru Nihon shinwa no kenkyū," *Kokubungaku kaisetsu to kinkanshō*, 37-1, 1972, pp. 174–177.

significance of Matsumoto's research in arguing in favor of the Southern origin of the Japanese myths. Furthermore, cultural anthropologist Yamashita mentioned Matsumoto as a "historical ethnologist of Indochina" who sought "Japan's homeland in Southeast Asia."[39]

Thus, according to many of the previous researchers including Matsumoto's students and colleagues (Yamashita, Hirafuji, Obayashi, Ito Seiji, Ito Mikiharu, Esaka, Iwata, etc.), Matsumoto was an advocator of Southward Theory, claiming that Japanese origins came from the South, especially in Southeast Asia or the Southern Pacific Islands. However, Chikamori claimed that Matsumoto Nobuhiro did not believe in the Southern origin of the Japanese nation and that Matsumoto's evaluation was a result of the fact that the origins of the Japanese nation were a big issue during his era.[40] From the late 19th century, Western scholars proposed various biased hypotheses regarding the Japanese origins.[41] Thus, the Japanese made efforts to formulate their own theories on this issue of national importance.

Chikamori argued that Matsumoto explored the common basic culture (archaeo-civilization) instead of the Southern origin.[42] However, Chikamori admitted that he is not familiar with Matsumoto's pre-war ideas.[43] In fact, the reference to archaeo-civilization appeared in Matsumoto's writing in 1956 in his book *The Japanese Myths*. In this book he reconsidered his ideas on the Japanese myths. According to the preface of this book, Matsumoto borrowed the concept of archeo-civilization from Marcel Mauss's student André Varagnac during the

---

39. Yamashita, Shinji *The Making of Anthropology in East and Southeast Asia*, New York: Berghahn Books, 2004, pp. 104–105.
40. Interview with Chikamori Masashi, 23 August 2012, Keio University, Tokyo.
41. In 1879, American zoologist and orientalist Edward Sylvester Morse presented a hypothesis based on the evidences from his excavation in Ōmori shell mound that the Japanese ancestors were cannibals.
42. Interview with Chikamori Masashi, 23 August 2012, Keio University, Tokyo.
43. Interview with Chikamori Masashi, 23 August 2012, Keio University, Tokyo. Chikamori, Masashi "Matsumoto Nobuhiro no 'Genmin no kenkyū'," Keiō gijuku *daigaku daigakuin shakaigaku kenkyū kiyō. Ningen to shakai no tankyū. Kujūkuri chōsa*, Keiō gijuku daigaku daigakuin shakaigaku kenkyūka, 2013, p. 235.

postwar period.[44] Furthermore Matsumoto's teacher Yanagita Kunio mentioned regarding the basic culture (*kisō bunka* 基層文化) after the war.[45] This was because the postwar perspective of Southeast Asia criticized the bias of the prewar research; thus, labeling the native people of Southeast Asia as "primitive" was not suitable for scholars anymore. They had to come up with new concepts for addressing other peoples' culture. Since this book focuses on Matsumoto's writings during 1919–1945, it dose not analyze the concepts of archaeo-civilization and basic culture. However, it discusses them together with other postwar ideas in the concluding chapter. On the other hand, it examines the concept of common primitive culture that was the predecessor of these concepts. It also considers the argument of Southern origins in relation to Matsumoto's works.

2. Matsumoto Nobuhiro's life history

This section overviews Matsumoto Nobuhiro's life history, specitically focusing on the period 1919–1945, which is the scope of this thesis. In clarifies the manner in which his upbringing and early scholastic endeavors influenced his academic career. The following table provides a brief overview of Matsumoto Nobuhiro's life.

---

44. "At present, the people of the new generation are active in the Parisian academic circles. For example, people who listened to Mauss's lectures, such as Varagnac, etc., they advocate a new academic discipline "archeo-civilization," indicating the direction where the folkloristic should advance." Matsumoto, Nobuhiro "Hashigaki," *Nihon no shinwa*, Ibundō, 1956.
45. "In the popular tradition [studies], there are people arguing cultural sedimentation (gesunkene Kultur) that was proposed by German Naumann etc. Namely, that the culture of the upper class gradually sunk into the layer of common people and is spread among all the people of the country. This fact surely exists. On the contrary, basic culture is taken in consideration; in fact the flows of these two cultures are constantly negotiating with each other." Yanagita, Kunio "Minkan denshō," *Minzokugaku jiten*, 1969 (first edition 1951), p. 579.

Table 1: Matsumoto Nobuhiro's life chronology[46]

October 11, 1897	Born in Tokyo
1910	Enrolled in the Keio Gijuku Boys Junior High School (慶応義塾普通部) and with Kawai Teiichi who taught him ethnology
1915-1920	Enrolled in Keio University (慶応義塾大学), majored in history
1918	Went on a school trip to Korea, Manchuria and China with the Alpine Club
1918	Met with the founder of folklore studies, Yanagita Kunio
1920	Employed as a lecturer at the Keio Gijuku Boys Junior High School
1924-1928	Majored in Oriental Studies at Sorbonne University, Paris; met with Marcel Mauss, Marcel Granet, and Jean Przyluski
1928	Published his theses The Japanese and the Austro-Asiatic Languages: A Comparative Study of Vocabulary and The Essay on the Japanese Mythology in Paris
1928	Became an associate professor at the Keio University Faculty of Letters
1930	Became professor at the Keio University Faculty of Letters
1931	Published *The Research of the Japanese Myths*
1932	Published *Theories of Ancient Culture*
1933	Went on a research trip to Indochina thanks to his friend Émile Gaspardone at the École Française d'Extrême-Orient in Hanoi
1935	Participated in the foundation of the Japan Ethnological Society (日本民族学会)
1937	Went on a research trip to the Southen Pacific Islands with the Japan Society of Oceanian Ethnography
1938	Began teaching ethnology at Keio University

---

46. Based on chronology in *Ine-fune-matsuri: Matsumoto Nobuhiro sensei tsuitō ronbunshū*, Kyōshuppan, 1982, pp. 693-5.

1938, 1939	Went on research trips to China as a member of the archaeological mission at the Chinese continent of Keio University
1939	Became a researcher at the Research Institute for South Asian Culture (南亜細亜研究所) along with Yamamoto Tatsuro
1941	Published Jiangnan Survey
1942	Co-founded the Keio University Linguistic Institute (慶応義塾大学語学研究所)
1942	Published *The Peoples and Cultures of Indochina, Introduction to the Annamese Language, South Seas Books Catalogue*
1943	Received an award from the Keio University Scholar Promotion Fund for his book *The Peoples and Cultures of Indochina*
1943	Co-founded the Keio University Asia Research Institute (慶応義塾大学亜細亜研究所)
1947	Started research on boats with Yanagita Kunio
1951	Again started teaching ethnology at Keio University
1955	Received an award for his contribution to Japanese-French cultural exchange, Les palmes académiques from the French government
1956	Published *The Japanese Myths*
1956–1957	Organized a research mission to Thailand, Laos, and Cambodia to investigate the rice cultivation culture of Southeast Asian people
1962	Co-founded the Keio University Institute of Cultural and Linguistic studies (慶応義塾大学言語文化研究所)
1963	Became a member of the Science Council of Japan (日本学術会議)
1965	Published *Indochina Research*
1965	Became the president of the Mita Historical Society (三田史学会)
1966	Published *Southeast Asia*

1967	Taught an introductory course of Japanese studies at the Hong Kong Chinese University
1968	Published *Collection of Papers on East Asian Peoples*
1969	Published *Small History of the Vietnamese People*
1969	Became the professor emeritus of Keio University
1973 or 1974	Visited the Rennel Island in the Solomon Archipelago, where his student Chikamori Masashi conducted an archaeological research
1981, 8 March	Passed away in the Keio University Hospital in Tokyo

Matsumoto Nobuhiro was born on October 11, 1897, in Shiba Ward (today's Minato Ward), Tokyo, in a family of entrepreneurs.[47] Being the youngest of four brothers, Nobuhiro was given the opportunity to pursue his interests, whereas older sons were expected to follow into their father's footsteps.[48] In 1910, he enrolled in the Boys Junior High School, a grammar school attached to Keio University. From 1915, he studied at Keio University, where he majored in history.[49]

During his studies, Matsumoto learnt evolutionist ethnology from Kawai Teiichi (1870–1955)[50] and received guidance in folklore studies from Yanagita Kunio (1875–1962). Owing to his interest in ethnology, Matsumoto began focusing on Southeast Asian people in the early 1920s.

In 1924, he left for Paris as a self-financed student at Sorbonne University, where he obtained doctorate in 1928.[51] In Paris, Matsumoto studied sociologist ethnology under famous scholars of the French School of Sociology: Marcel Mauss (1972–1950) and Marcel Granet

---

47. *Ine-fune-matsuri: Matsumoto Nobuhiro sensei tsuitō ronbunshū*, Kyōshuppan, 1982, p. 693.
48. *Matsumoto Nobuhiro shinpen zakki*, Matsumoto Chie, 1982, p. 38.
49. *Ine-fune-matsuri: Matsumoto Nobuhiro sensei tsuitō ronbunshū*, Kyōshuppan, 1982, p. 693.
50. Kawai, Teiichi "Tetsugaku to kyōiku," *Ōsaka kōen*, Keiō gijuku shuppankyoku, 1913, pp. 160–164.
51. *Matsumoto Nobuhiro shinpen zakki*, Matsumoto Chie, 1982, p. 41.

(1884-1940). In addition, Matsumoto was influenced by diffusionist ethnology from his guiding professor, Jean Przyluski (1885-1944). Przyluski conducted research on Indochina and encouraged Matsumoto to focus on Southeast Asia.

After Matsumoto returned to Tokyo, he became a professor at the Keio University Faculty of Letters. He also rejoined Yanagita's group in conducting research on Japanese folklore. In the early 1930s, Matsumoto published his rewritten two doctoral theses from Sorbonne University[52] into two works: *The Research in Japanese Mythology* (1931) and *Theory of Ancient Culture* (1932).[53] Both books contained discussions on Southeast Asia and argued the existence of Southern genealogy in Japanese culture.

His friendship with scholars from École Française d'Extrême-Orient, such as Émile Gaspardone (1895-1982) and Henri Maspero (1882-1945),[54] helped him conduct a successful research trip to French Indochina from August to October 1933. In Indochina, Matsumoto collected extensive material on Southeast Asia, including rare Vietnamese chronicles, and observed the mountain ethnic minorities in Tonkin.[55] This trip to Indochina was significant because it enabled Matsumoto to establish himself as a founder of Southeast Asian studies. Matsumoto incorporated this new knowledge on Southeast Asia into his course of ethnology that he began to teach at Keio University in 1938.[56]

52. Matsumoto wrote two doctoral theses, the main thesis *Le japonais et les langues austroasiatiques: étude de vocabulaire comparé* (1928) and the supplementary thesis *Essai sur la mythologie Japonaise* (1928) and, as it was required by Sorbonne University.
53. Matsumoto, Nobuhiro *Nihon shinwa no kenkyū*, Dōbunka, 1931; "Kodai bunkaron," *Gendai shigaku taikei*, Vol. 10, Kyōritsusha shoten, 1932.
54. Maspero, Anri "Senshin jidai no Shina ni okeru saihōbunka no eikyō" *Shina kenkyū*, Keiō gijuku Mochidzuki kikin Shina kenkyūkai hen, Iwanami shoten, 1930, pp. 399-401; Matsumoto, Nobuhiro "Indoshina inshōki (I and II)" in *Mita hyōron*, Mita hyōron hakkōjo, No. 437 and No. 440, January and April 1934.
55. Matsumoto, Nobuhiro "Indoshina inshōki (I and II)" in *Mita hyōron*, Mita hyōron hakkōjo, No.437 and No. 440, January and April 1934; "Annan ryokōki (daiisshin)," *Minzokugaku*, dai 5 kan, dai 5 gō, Minzokugakkai, 1933, p. 87.

Matsumoto went on further research trips to the Southern Pacific Islands in 1937 and to Southern China in 1938 and 1939. However, he did not bring as much material from there as he did from French Indochina.

The growing importance of Southeast Asia for Japanese national policy from the late 1930s provided Matsumoto with new opportunities to develop Southeast Asian studies. During the Greater East Asian War, Matsumoto not only produced a huge amount of academic work on Southeast Asia but also contributed to the foundation of research institutes related to Southeast Asia and to the propagation of Southeast Asian studies. During this period, he published a book titled *The Peoples and Cultures of Indochina* (1942).

After the war, he explored Southeast Asian boats in relation to his research on ancient boats with Yanagita Kunio from 1947.[57] In the years between 1956 and 1957, inspired by Yanagita's research on the rice culture,[58] Matsumoto organized a research mission to Thailand, Laos, and Cambodia to investigate the rice cultivation culture of Southeast Asian people.[59] During this time, Matsumoto developed the Rice Cultivation Culture theory that was discussed in relation to the Laurel Forest Culture theory. Such ideas became popular among scholars investigating

---

56. Kawakita, Nobuo "Keiō gijuku daigaku bungakubu kyōin tantō kamoku ichiran," *Shigaku*, dai 60 kan, dai 2/3 gō, Mita Shigakkai, 1991, p. 205 (379).
57. Itō, Seiji "Matsumoto Nobuhiro sensei no omoide to kodai fune no kenkyū" "Matsumoto Nobuhiro sensei wo shinobu," *Kodaigaku Jānaru*, dai 194 gō, Nyū saiensusha, 1981, pp. 27-30; Esaka, Teruya "Matsumoto Nobuhiro sensei tono chōsa kaiko," "Matsumoto Nobuhiro sensei wo shinobu," *Kodaigaku Jānaru*, dai 194 gō, Nyū saiensusha, 1981, pp. 27-28. Ishii, Kenji "Kodai suitei fune yasei gō no omoide," *Nihon minzoku bunka no kigen*, dai 2 kan, geppō dai 2 gō, Kōdansha, 1978, pp. 3-6. "Minzokugaku kōkogaku kenkyūshitsu no Kujūkuri chōsa," *Keiō gijuku daigaku daigakuin shakaigaku kenkyū kiyō. Ningen to shakai no tankyū. Kujūkuri chōsa*, Keiō gijuku daigaku daigakuin shakaigaku kenkyūka, 2013, pp. 231-232.
58. Matsumoto, Nobuhiro "Kaisetsu" *Nihon bunka no kigen* (3). *Minzokugaku* 1, Heibonsha, 1971, p. 40.
59. Matsumoto, Nobuhiro *Tōnan Ajia no inasaku bunka no sōgō chōsa shuisho*, Nihon minzoku kyōkai, 1957.

the common basic culture.⁶⁰

In 1962, Matsumoto played an important role in the foundation of the Keio Institute of Cultural and Linguistic studies at Keio University,⁶¹ one of the important centers for Southeast Asian studies in Japan. After he became a professor emeritus of Keio University in 1969, he continued conducting lectures at various universities.⁶² He visited Rennel Island in the Solomon Archipelago at the age of 77 since Keio University researchers, including Chikamori Masashi, conducted ethnoarchaeological research there during 1973–1974.⁶³ He passed away at the Keio University Hospital in Tokyo at the age of 83 on March 8, 1981.⁶⁴

3. Key concepts: Southeast Asia and ethnology

This book examines Matsumoto Nobuhiro's ideas regarding Southeast Asia that were based on his ethnological research. Therefore, clarifying the concept of Southeast Asian studies and ethnology before progressing to the analysis of Matsumoto's writings is necessary.

3.1 Southeast Asia and South Seas

Southeast Asian studies *Tōnan Ajia kenkyū* 東南アジア研究) were

---

60. Itō, Seiji "Matsumoto Nobuhiro – 'Nampōsetsu' no kaitakusha," *Bunka jinruigaku gunzō*, Nihonhen (3), Kyōto: Akademia shuppankai, 1988, p. 238.
61. Kawamoto, Kunie "Gengo bunka kenkyūjo sanjūnen," *Keiō gijuku daigaku gengo bunka kenkyūjo hōkokushū*, Keiō gijuku daigaku gengo bunka kenkyūjo, dai 24 gō, 1992, pp. 1–12.
62. *Ine-fune-matsuri: Matsumoto Nobuhiro sensei tsuitō ronbunshū*, Kyōshuppan, 1982, p. 695.
63. Itō, Seiji "Hito to gakumon, Matsumoto Nobuhiro," *Shakai jinruigaku nenpō*, Tōkyō toritsu daigaku shakai jinrui gakkai, dai 12 kan, 1986, p. 130. Arima, Makiko "Hito, Matsumoto Nobuhiro," *Kikan jinruigaku*, 5-1, Shakaishisōsha, 1974, p. 155.
64. *Ine-fune-matsuri: Matsumoto Nobuhiro sensei tsuitō ronbunshū*, Kyōshuppan, 1982, p. 695.

officially established in the 1950s when the Western regional concept of Southeast Asia came into general use. Prior to that, the study of Southeast Asia was called South Seas studies (*Nanyō kenkyū* 南洋研究). However, Shimao Minoru of Japan Society for Southeast Asian Studies argued that Southeast Asian studies and Vietnamese studies in Japan were launched by Yamamoto Tatsuro (山本達郎, 1910–2001) and Matsumoto Nobuhiro in the 1930s.[65]

Indeed, there are some cases of using the naming of Southeast Asia in the pre-war period despite the established theory that it is a post-war concept. In fact, the Japanese naming of Southeast Asia (*Tōnan Ajiya* 東南アジヤ) appeared for the first time in a Japanese geography textbook in 1919 when Japan noticed the chances in Southeast Asian market and natural resources during World War I. According to Shimizu, it was not imported from the West because the term Southeast Asia was rarely used during that time. The Japanese introduced the name Southeast Asia in 1919. However, it came into common use only after 1943, with the creation of the geographical concept of Southeast Asia when Western powers established "South East Asia Command" during World War II.[66] This was because countries of Southeast Asia were known as colonies under the rule of various Western countries (except Thailand) rather than as a region. For example, Vietnam was perceived as a part of French Indochina. This occurred after World War II when Southeast Asian studies were officially established in the 1950s in connection with the independence movements in Southeast Asia. Nevertheless, Matsumoto's and Yamamoto's contribution to Southeast Asian studies during 1933–1945 indicates that a significant body of research has already existed before World War II.

---

65. Shimao, Minoru "Betonamu. Tōnan Ajiashi he no teii to tenkai," *Tōnan Ajia shi. Kenkyū no hatten*, Tōnan Ajia Gakkai 40 shūnen, Kinen jigyō iinkai, Yamakawa shuppansha, 2009, p. 110.
66. Shimizu, Hajime "Kindai Nihon ni okeru 'Tōnan Ajiya' chiiki gainen no seiritsu (I)," (Shō-chūgakkō chiri kyōkasho ni miru), *Ajia keizai*, 28/6, Ajia kenkyūjo, 1987, pp. 2, 11. *Nanshin-ron*: Its Turning Point in World War I," *The Developing Economies* 15/4, December 1987, p. 390. Ishii, Yoneo "Tōnan Ajia no shiteki ninshiki no ayumi," *Tōnan Ajia no rekishi*, Kōbundō, 1991, p. 11.

Therefore, in the 1930s, Japan's Southeast Asian studies came into existence when the naming of Southeast Asian studies (*Tōnan Ajia kenkyū* 東南アジア研究) had not been commonly used yet because the Japanese awareness of Southeast Asia was generally low.

To address this region, there existed two prewar geographical concepts of South Seas — the Japanese *Nan'yō* (南洋) and the Chinese *Nankai* (南海).[67] *Nan'yō* represented the region to the south of Japan, comprising both insular and continental Southeast Asia (especially Indochina), islands in Southern Pacific, Oceania, and Australia during Matsumoto's time. Alternatively, *Nankai* reached more to the West because it originally referred to the areas south of China: Indochina Peninsula (French Indochina and Thai), Burma and Malay Peninsula, Andaman and Nicobar Islands and Ceylon in the West, Indonesian Archipelago in the South, and Philippines in the East.[68] See Table 2 below.

Table 2: Nan'yō, Nankai, and Southeast Asia[69]

Nan'yō	Nankai	Southeast Asia
Indochina, insular Southeast Asia, Southern Pacific Islands, Oceania, Australia	Region from Indochina Peninsula (**French Indochina**, and Thai), Burma and Malay Peninsula, Andaman and Nicobar Islands and Ceylon in the West, Indonesian Archipelago in the South, and Philippines in the East	Myanmar, Thailand, **Laos**, **Cambodia**, **Vietnam**, Malaysia, Singapore, Indonesia, Brunei, and the Philippines
Japanese concept	Chinese concept	Western concept
Pre-war concept		Post-war concept

---

67. Ishida, Mikinosuke *Nankai ni kansuru Shina shiryō*, Seikatsusha, 1945, pp. 2–3.

In particular, the term *Nan'yō* was used frequently. It was originally defined as a separate region from the East/Orient (*Tōyō* 東洋) and the West/Occident (*Seiyō* 西洋), but its meaning has changed throughout the history. During the Tokugawa era, it was almost limited to Indochina with which Japan had trade relations. During the Meiji era, it mainly indicated islands in Southeast Asia and Oceania, where the Japanese people migrated to. However, after Japan occupied South Seas Islands (Marshall Islands, the Carolinas, the Marianas, and the Palau Islands) during World War I, it also included continental Southeast Asia. Simultaneously, the Japanese divided the concept of the South Seas into the Inner South Seas (*Uchi Nan'yō* 内南洋) under the Japanese control and Outer South Seas (*Soto Nan'yō* 外南洋) under the rule of Western Powers.[70] The Outer South Seas were called "Front South Seas" (*Omote Nan'yō* 表南洋) and Inner South Seas were called "Back South Seas" (*Ura Nan'yō* 裏南洋).[71] Compared with *Nan'yō*, the Chinese concept *Nankai* has not been examined much. In short, in the 1930s, when Southeast Asian studies emerged, the most used geographical term in relation to Southeast Asia was the Japanese South Seas *Nan'yō*. Nonetheless, *Nankai* appears in Matsumoto's writings as often as *Nan'yō*.

68. Ishii, Yoneo "Tōnan Ajia no shiteki ninshiki no ayumi," *Tōnan Ajia no rekishi*, Kōbundō, 1991, p. 3. Shimizu, Hajime "Kindai Nihon ni okeru 'Tōnan Ajiya' chiiki gainen no seiritsu (I)," (Shō-chūgakkō chiri kyōkasho ni miru), *Ajia keizai*, 28/6, Ajia kenkyūjo, 1987, p. 8. Yamashita, Shinji *The Making of Anthropology in East and Southeast Asia*, New York: Berghahn Books, 2004, p. 107. Ishida, Mikinosuke *Nankai ni kansuru Shina shiryō*, Seikatsusha, 1945, pp. 2–3.
69. Ibid.
70. Yano, Tooru *Nanshin no keifu. Nihon no Nan'yō shikan*, Chikurashobō, 2009, pp. 262–263. Shimizu, Hajime "Kindai Nihon ni okeru 'Tōnan Ajiya' chiiki gainen no seiritsu (I)," (Shō-chūgakkō chiri kyōkasho ni miru), *Ajia keizai*, 28/6, Ajia kenkyūjo, 1987, pp. 9–11.
71. Shimizu, Hajime "Kindai Nihon ni okeru 'Tōnan Ajiya' chiiki gainen no seiritsu (I)," (Shō-chūgakkō chiri kyōkasho ni miru), *Ajia keizai*, 28/6, Ajia kenkyūjo, 1987, pp. 10–11.

3.2. Ethnology

Ethnology is an academic discipline that studies the culture of various ethnic groups. Adam František Kolár, a Slovak historian, coined this term in 1783.[72] The meaning of the term has changed during the course of its history. As a research on the culture of different people, ethnology emerged from the discussions on human origins based on evolutionism in the first half of the 19th century. In its early stage, ethnology developed in close relation with physical anthropology, ancient history, and folklore studies before it became an independent discipline.[73] In Japan, ethnology became an independent academic discipline in 1935.[74] Approximately during this time, Matsumoto became the founder of Southeast Asian studies. Thus, Matsumoto's ideas regarding Southeast Asia during 1919–1933 were formed when the borders of ethnology with other academic disciplines were ambiguous. Consequently, this book discusses Matsumoto's ethnological research that overlapped with history and folklore studies.

This book applies the commonly used classification of ethnologists for evaluating Matsumoto's prewar work. In regard to the scope of the book that covers the period 1919–1945, three categories of prewar ethnology are considered: evolutionist, diffusionist, and sociologist ethnology.[75] (See Table 3)

---

72. "Ethnography and ethnology," *The Dictionary of Anthropology*, edited by Barfield, Thomas, Cambridge, Mass.: Blackwell Publishers, 1997, p. 157.
73. **Physical anthropology** examined human skeletal remains to clarify the origins of mankind. **Ancient history** detected the traces of the beginnings of human civilization in the ancient written documents. **Ethnology**, especially unilinear ethnology, researched various ethnic groups to reconstruct the origins of the human culture from the analysis of their primitive culture based on the belief that the primitive stage was common for all the ethnic groups. **Folkloristics, or folklore studies**, researched folklore, which is a popular tradition of common people (usually of one ethnic group), namely of peasants or artisans, supposed to be transmitted from generation to generation from immemorial.
74. "Nihon minzoku gakkai setsuritsu shuisho," *Minzokugaku kenkyū*, dai 1 kan, dai 1 gō, Nihon minzoku gakkai, Sanseidō, 1935, pp. 219–222.

Table 3: Ethnological schools

Ethnological schools	Based on the evolutionist theory	Research hypothesis
Evolutionist ethnology	Unilinear evolutionism	Common primitive culture
Sociologist ethnology	Unilinear evolutionism	Common primitive society
Diffusionist ethnology	Multilinear evolutionism	Genealogy, cultural influence

Before discussing the ethnological schools, This book focuses on the evolutionist theories to clarify the background. There were two theories of evolutionism in general: unilinear evolutionism arguing that all peoples had one common origin, and multilinear evolutionism argued that all the people have a common origin, and multilinear evolutionism argued that different people have different origins. Thus, unilinear evolutionists considered the difference in the stages of evolution of people and suggested that all people can become civilized. In contrast, multilinear evolutionists considered the differences in separate origin; they believed that only some people can be civilized, whereas other people are closer to the apes. In other words, they assumed that all the people do not undergo the same evolutionary stages and considered primitive people as a different (and lower) species from civilized people.

Evolutionist ethnology (prevailing in the 19th century — the early 20th century) developed from the unilinear evolutionist presumption that all people, including people considered to be civilized, evolved from a primitive stage. Therefore, evolutionist ethnologists surmised that all people are equally innovative. They mainly focused on the primitive culture (life condition of primitive people) by deducing it

---

75. *The Routledge Dictionary of Anthropologists*, London, New York: Routledge, 1997. King, Victor T. and Wilder, William D. *The Modern Anthropology of South-East Asia. An Introduction*, London and New York: Routledge Curzon, 2005 (first edition 2003).

from similarities in the primitive stage of different people. They examined the contemporary culture of primitive people, and compared it with the ancient culture of civilized people from old documents or old habits of civilized people that persisted in the contemporary era. Accordingly, they identified cultural elements for constructing the picture of a common primitive culture. Such research was considered to contribute to the clarification of the ancient history of mankind that could not be reconstructed from the historical documents or archaeological excavations.

Similar to evolutionist ethnology, sociologist ethnology (prevailing in the 1920s, especially in France) was based on the unilinear evolutionist belief that all people shared a common primitive culture; however, but it focused on the study of primitive society of different people in general. Thus, sociologist ethnologists inferred the existence of the common primitive society for the entire mankind. While evolutionist ethnologists believed that the development of culture was affected by the natural environment of the people, sociologist ethnologists believed that culture was mainly determined by society. Similar to evolutionist ethnologists, sociologist ethnologists compared contemporary primitive society with the ancient society of civilized people.

In contrast to the concept of unity of mankind in evolutionist and sociologist ethnology, diffusionist ethnology (dominant from the 1930s) introduced the concept of cultural diffusion. It was based on the presumption that there existed a limited number of cultural centers from which culture spread among other peoples in different regions.[76] From this point of view, diffusionism got inspiration from multilinear evolutionism because it implied various trajectories of evolution for different people. Briefly, it presupposed the existence of different cultures, not one common primitive culture, for the entire mankind, although it admitted that some people can have a common

---

76. *The Routledge Dictionary of Anthropologists*, London, New York: Routledge, 1997, pp. 40-41. *Encyclopedia of Cultural Anthropology*, Vol. 2, edited by Levinson, David and Ember, Melvin, New York: Henry Holt and Company, 1996, p. 343.

origin. Hence, the common culture in diffusionist interpretation meant cultural traits specific to only certain people, not shared by the entire mankind. This discourse became possible due to many new findings in linguistics, archaeology, and physical anthropology[77], which questioned the evolutionist theories of psychological unity of the mankind. Consequently, diffusionist ethnologists focused more on individual people and examined relations among them. They classified the relations into 1) genealogy when a common origin could be found between two ethnic groups with a common culture or 2) cultural diffusion or influence when a common culture could be found between two ethnic groups of different origins. In other words, they believed that only some ethnic groups had a same origin and that similarities between two different cultures were the result of cultural diffusion from a cultural center; thus, only some people were innovative.

Previous research has emphasized the influence of sociologist ethnology on Matsumoto's work (Hirafuji Kikuko and Ito Seiji) and has interpreted Matsumoto's argument as Japan's Southern genealogy or its origins in Southeast Asia, which corresponds to diffusionist ethnology (Yamashita Shinji and Ito Seiji). This book characterizes Matsumoto as an evolutionist, sociologist, and diffusionist ethnologist in each period from 1919 to 1945. Other theories in Matsumoto's works on Southeast Asia, such as cultural evolutionism, social Darwinism, Orientalism, climate theory, Japan's Southern Advance Theory, and Pan-Asianism are explained in the corresponding chapters.

---

77. *The Routledge Dictionary of Anthropologists*, London, New York: Routledge, 1997, p. 41.

Chapter 1:
Discovering the ethnology of Southeast Asia during 1919-1923

1. Introduction

This chapter discusses the emergence of Matsumoto Nobuhiro as an ethnologist during 1919-1923 when he was a student at Keio Gijuku (1910-1920) and worked as a teacher at Keio Boys Junior High School (1920-1924). Exploring the beginnings of Matsumoto's ethnological career is important because Matsumoto's Southeast Asian studies emerged from his ethnological study of Southeast Asia. Therefore, this chapter inquires why Matsumoto became an ethnologist under the influence of his teachers and how he discussed Southeast Asia in his ethnological writings during 1919-1923.

In general, the early 1920s was the age of evolutionism. The Japanese adopted Western civilization, which was considered to occupy the top tier of civilization from the viewpoint of cultural evolution theory.[1] This adoption aimed to reach an equal footing with the Western powers. In addition, the Japanese considered territorial expansion to be indispensable to their progress and their national power. This was in accordance with social Darwinism, a theory arguing that only the fittest could persevere in the struggle for survival.[2] Thus, the Japanese adopted cultural evolutionism and social Darwinism as basic theories for the formation of their relations with nations and regions

---

1. Cultural evolutionism was a theory based on a hypothesis that culture evolves through stages, beginning from a primitive stage and advancing to a civilized stage. Therefore, culture evolutionists tended to hypothesize on the stage of certain cultures that they discussed.

abroad.

Evolutionism formed the basis of Matsumoto's thinking because Matsumoto received western education at Keio Gijuku. He studied at Keio Gijuku from junior high school to university, a period covering a decade. The framing philosophy of Keio Gijuku was based on the ideas of Fukuzawa Yukichi (1835-1901), who preached the adoption of Western civilization and democracy. On the one hand, Fukuzawa argued for the equality of all people. On the other hand, he emphasized that Japan had to become westernized to be treated equally with Western countries. Thus, Matsumoto was raised in an environment wherein westernization was considered to be a decisive factor in achieving equal treatment. Consequently, despite being taught democracy, Matsumoto still considered Western people to be superior because they were more westernized than the Japanese. In other words, he believed that the degree of westernization determined peoples' superiority. Therefore, he considered the Japanese to be more superior than the non-Western people because they absorbed Western civilization. His bias is demonstrated through an analysis of Matsumoto's writings about Southeast Asia in this book, especially in Chapter 4.

Based on the evolutionist belief, the Japanese began building their relations with the Asia-Pacific Region. After World War I, Japan received the League of Nations mandate over the islands in the Southern Pacific,[3] in addition to the Ryukyu Islands (1879) and Taiwan (1895). During this period, Japanese called all the regions lying to be South of Japan as the South Seas (Nanyō, 南洋) and indicated them as the "Southern Region" (Nampō, 南方). After acquiring this former German territory, the Japanese government founded the South Seas Development Company (1921) and the South Seas Bureau (1922) for administrative purposes.[4] However, in these early stages of the Japanese ex-

---

2. Social Darwinism was a theory developed from Darwin's argument that natural selection determines the outcome of competition. It was applied to human society arguing that competition or the struggle for survival is inevitable and is necessary for human progress.
3. Japan expanded its control to the South of the Marshall Islands, Carolinas, Marianas, and Palau Islands in 1919.

ploration of the South, priority was placed on the economic exploitation of the newly acquired territories. Interestingly, Japan gave much more political attention to the Asian continent (mainly countries like China and Korea), and consequently, the region of the South Seas was perceived to be far less important. Therefore, in the early 1920s, Japanese knowledge regarding the South Seas remained limited; therefore, the region of Southeast Asia, remained completely unknown to the Japanese people.

Considering the lack of Japanese people's interest in Southeast Asia, Matsumoto was provided a rare opportunity to study about Southeast Asia through Western ethnology, which compared the culture of various ethnic groups, including that of Southeast Asian people. Under the influence of evolutionism, ethnology emerged in significance in connection with cultural history, physical anthropology, and folklore studies. Especially from the late 1870s, Japanese scholars had to clarifying Japanese origins since they were confronted with various biased theories on Japanese people produced by the Western scholars.[5] Therefore, it became an issue of national importance to interpret Japanese origins from the Japanese perspective and in the context of mankind's early history.

Since the discourse on Japanese origins was considered to be essential, it was joined by modern educated young men from wealthy families, such as Matsumoto Nobuhiro.[6] These young intellectuals were not concerned about their future and could spend their time pursuing their interests. Thus, through their participation in the discussion of Japanese origins, they contributed to the development of ethnology although ethnology was yet to be established as an independent academic discipline in the 1920s.

---

4. Shimizu, Akitoshi *Anthropology and Colonialism in Asia and Oceania*, Richmond, Survey, Curzon 1999, p. 144.
5. In 1879, American zoologist and orientalist Edward Sylvester Morse presented a hypothesis based on the evidences from his excavation in Ōmori shell mound that the Japanese ancestors were cannibals.
6. Itō, Seiji "Matsumoto Nobuhiro – 'Nampōsetsu' no kaitakusha," *Bunka jinruigaku gunzō*, Nihonhen (3), Kyōto: Akademia shuppankai, 1988, p. 228.

Matsumoto began studying ethnology and folklore studies during his studies at Keio University in the late 1910s. He majored in history at Keio University. He met excellent teachers of ethnology and folklore studies, such as Kawai Teiichi and Yanagita Kunio. Among previous researches, Matsumoto's disciples, Ito Seiji,[8] Chikamori Masashi,[9] etc., and mythologists, such as Obayashi Taryo[10] and Hirafuji Kikuko,[11] claimed Yanagita Kunio's importance in Matsumoto's research in general. However, this research reveals that also other teachers, especially Kawai Teiichi, played a significant role in the formation of Matsumoto Nobuhiro's ideas regarding Southeast Asia.

The following sections examine the beginnings of Matsumoto's research on Southeast Asia. First, this chapter clarifies the influence of Japanese scholars on Matsumoto's study of ethnology, including Matsumoto's methodology. Second, it discusses Matsumoto's ideas regarding Southeast Asia.

2. Matsumoto's study of ethnology

This section demonstrates through the analysis of Matsumoto's writings in 1919–1923 that Matsumoto became an armchair[12] ethnologist in 1920. It shows that Matsumoto learnt ethnology based on uni-

---

7. *Ine-fune-matsuri: Matsumoto Nobuhiro sensei tsuitō ronbunshū*, Rokkōshuppan, 1982, p. 693.
8. Itō, Seiji "Hito to gakumon, Matsumoto Nobuhiro," *Shakai jinruigaku nenpō*, Tōkyō toritsu daigaku shakai jinrui gakkai, dai 12 kan, 1986, p. 119. Itō, Seiji "Matsumoto Nobuhiro – 'Nampōsetsu' no kaitakusha," *Bunka jinruigaku gunzō*, Nihonhen (3), Kyōto: Akademia shuppankai, 1988, p. 231. "Matsumoto Nobuhiro to gakumon," *Keiō gijuku daigaku gengo kenkyūjo hōkokushū*, Keiō gijuku daigaku, dai 24 kan, 1992, p. 13.
9. Interview with Chikamori Masashi, 23 August 2012, Keio University, Tokyo.
10. Ōbayashi, Taryō "Kaisetsu," *Nihon minzokugaku no kigen I: shinwa-densetsu*, Kōdansha, 1978, p. 406.
11. Hirafuji, Kikuko "Shakaigakuteki kenkyū – Matsumoto Nobuhiro no shinwa kenkyū ni okeru Furansu shakaigakuha no eikyō," *Shinwagaku to Nihon no kamigami*, Kōbunkan, 2004, p. 38.

linear evolutionism. Since Matsumoto did not study abroad during 1919–1923 and no foreign teacher of ethnology lived in Japan during that time, it means that he studied ethnology from his teachers in Japan. Kawai Teiichi and Utsushikawa Nenozo (1884–1947) taught ethnology at Keio University. Kawai held classes of ethnopsychology (*minzoku-shinrigaku* 民族心理学) from 1921 to 1944.[13] Utsushikawa lectured on anthropology (*jinruigaku* 人類学) from 1919 to 1927.[14] In addition, Matsumoto received personal lectures on ethnology from folklorist Yanagita Kunio. However, Matsumoto's connection with Utsushikawa could not be demonstrated through Matsumoto's writings, so it is not discussed here. Furthermore, Matsumoto stated that Kawai Teiichi, Yanagita Kunio, and Kato Shigeshi contributed to the formation of his early ideas.[15]

This section examines the influence of Matsumoto's teachers on his study of evolutionist ethnology. First, it discusses the influence of his teachers of ethnology, Kawai Teiichi and Yanagita Kunio. Then, it clarifies the influence of his teachers of history, Kato Shigeshi and Hashimoto Masukichi, because Matsumoto combined ethnology with history.

2.1. Influence of Kawai Teiichi on Matsumoto's study of ethnology

Matsumoto's relationship with Kawai Teiichi was crucial to facilitate Matsumoto's interest in ethnology. This was primarily because Kawai Teiichi (1870–1955) studied under the German ethnologist Wil-

---

12. Matsumoto can be called armchair scholar because he studied ethnology mainly from his teachers' lectures and from books and rarely did field work despite becoming a disciple of Yanagita Kunio who was a well-known field worker in folkloristics. Later, he went for research trips in the 1930s, but his works reveal little about his field work. As shown in Chapter 3, his knowledge about Southeast Asian people came more from books rather than from his direct observation or interaction with these people.
13. Kawakita, Nobuo "Keiō gijuku daigaku bungakubu kyōin tantō kamoku ichiran," *Shigaku*, dai 60 kan, dai 2/3 gō, Mita Shigakkai, 1991, pp. 190, 195, 200.
14. Ibid., pp. 189, 192.
15. Matsumoto, Nobuhiro "Ko Hashimoto Masukichi kyoju no tsuioku," *Shigaku*, dai 219 kan, dai 4 go, Mita Shigakkai, 1957, p. 103 (467).

helm Wundt (1832-1920).[16] Furthermore, Kawai Teiichi maintained a personal relationship with Matsumoto even before Matsumoto began his studies at Keio University. Accordingly, Matsumoto was exposed to Kawai's ideas regarding mankind for many years.

Matsumoto met Kawai when he enrolled in Keio Boys Junior High School in 1910. During that time, Kawai was the director of the school, and Matsumoto was impressed by his speech on his first day there.[17] Matsumoto's memoirs present evidence that Matsumoto was attracted to Kawai's personality: "Director Kawai was good-natured and also had a strict hand. Thus, thanks to his policy and power, the spirit of the Boys Junior High School was simple and sturdy."[18] Matsumoto appreciated Kawai for his knowledge gained through his studies in Germany: "Sensei [Kawai] studied in Germany, and we think that it was he who built up the essence and the system of Boys Junior High School."[19] Therefore, Kawai Teiichi occupied an important place in Matsumoto's life even before Matsumoto's entry into Keio University in 1915.

Matsumoto's close relationship with Kawai continued when Matsumoto studied and worked at Keio University. This fact is proven by Matsumoto's contribution to the collection of papers published on Kawai's 60th birthday in 1931. In this collection, Matsumoto published his paper *Problems of the Austroasiatic languages*. This indicates that he discussed the topic of Southeast Asian languages.[20] At the end of his paper, Matsumoto expressed his tribute for Kawai as follows: "I dedicate this paper as my congratulation to Professor Kawai and I pray for his happiness. I have studied for ten years under him from Boys Junior High School till my graduation at Faculty of Letters, and I became interested in the issues of the mankind for the first time

---

16. Keiō gijuku *hyakunenshi*. Chūkanzen. Keiō gijuku daigaku, 1960, p. 320.
17. Matsumoto, Nobuhiro *Matsumoto Nobuhiro shinpen zakki*, Matsumoto Chie, 1982, p. 12.
18. Ibid., p. 14.
19. Ibid., p. 15.
20. Matsumoto, Nobuhiro "Ōsutoroajiago ni kan suru shomondai," *Kawai kyōju kanreki kinen ronbunshū*, Kawaikyōju kanreki shukugakai, 1931, p. 481-522.

thanks to his lecture 'ethno-psychology' [*minzoku shinrigaku*, 民族心理学]; I am really happy to be able to express my gratitude to him."[21] In short, Matsumoto began studying ethnology after Kawai's lectures on ethnopsychology[22] at Keio University.

Matsumoto's interest in Kawai's ethnology is evident from his early writings. In his first paper *The Record from Travel to Sayama*, Matsumoto wrote as follows: "The habit of the mountain worship in Japan that is a land of volcanoes, especially its development in Musashino is an interesting research topic in ethno-psychology."[23] Then, Matsumoto cited Wilhem Wundt's ethno-psychology in his further writings. In *The Mountain Legends in Fudoki*[24], Matsumoto mentioned that "Wilhelm Wundt in his *Ethno-Psychology* talks about the rituals of praying for the fertility as a form of early deity worship…"[25] Further, Matsumoto drew on Wundt's work in all his writings in 1919–1923, including his graduation thesis *The Research of the Family in Ancient China*.[26] Thus, Matsumoto's writings indicate that Matsumoto studied Wilhelm Wundt's ethnology under Kawai's guidance.

Kawai Teiichi studied ethnopsychology during his stay at the Jena University and the Leipzig University in Germany from 1899 to 1905.[27] This means that he received Wilhelm Wundt's direct guidance in the

---

21. Matsumoto, Nobuhiro "Ōsutoroajiago ni kan suru shomondai," *Kawai kyōju kanreki kinen ronbunshū*, Kawaikyōju kanreki shukugakai, 1931, pp. 519–520.
22. Kawai Teiichi's lecture is mentioned as "psychology" (心理学) in the sylabus in 1910–1920 and as "ethno-psychology" (民族心理学) in 1921–1944. Kawakita, Nobuo "Keiō gijuku daigaku bungakubu kyōin tantō kamoku ichiran," *Shigaku*, dai 60 kan, dai 2/3 gō, Mita Shigakkai, 1991, pp.185, 195, 200 (359, 369, 374).
23. Matsumoto, Nobuhiro "Sayama kikō," *Tōkōkō*, I, Keiō gijuku taiikukai sangakubu nenpō, Shuppan kagaku sōgō kenkyūjo, 1919, p. 124.
24. Fudoki (風土記) ancient records from the Japanese provinces. Matsumoto drew on the local myths, rituals, and poems contained in these records.
25. Matsumoto, Nobuhiro "Fudoki ni arawaretaru santake densetsu," *Tōkōkō*, II, Keiō gijuku taiikukai sangakubu nenpō, Shuppan kagaku sōgō kenkyūjo, 1920, p. 40.
26. Matsumoto, Nobuhiro "Shina kodai seishi no kenkyū" (1921), *Tōa minzoku bunkaronkō*, Seibundō shinkōsha, 1968, p. 441.

German environment. The conception of German ethnology during that time was shaped by Adolf Bastian's ideas of psychic unity of mankind,[28] which included refusal of Darwinism.[29] This ethnological thinking was called "universalism" because it implied the existence of a universal primitive culture for all people, regardless of their contemporary stage of culture. Furthermore, Wilhelm Wundt was a representative of universalism as indicated in his argument in *Elements of Folk Psychology*: "Though of diverse origins, people may nevertheless belong to the same group as regards the mental level to which they have attained."[30] Thus, Kawai adopted evolutionist ethnology based on universalism from Wundt and taught its principles to Matsumoto in his lectures on ethnopsychology.

Universalism in ethnology was based on the hypothesis of the unilinear evolution of mankind. The typical method of evolutionist ethnology was to compar various ethnic groups. It aimed to find a universal primitive culture by examining similarities among various ethnic cultures. Universalism was advocated by many Western ethnologists, including Tylor, Frazer, and Yanagita Kunio. Therefore, Matsumoto's adoption of universalism from these scholars is discussed in Section 2.2.

Matsumoto recognized his adoption of unilinear evolutionism in 1921. In his graduation thesis *The Research of the Family in Ancient China*, Matsumoto claimed that "Nobody believes that the trajectory

---

27. *Kawai kyōju kanreki kinen ronbunshū*, Kawaikyōju kanreki shukugakai, 1931, p. 6.
28. In his theory of the psychic unity of mankind, Adolf Bastian argued that all peoples, regardless their ethnicity, have common elementary ideas (*Elementargedanken*) and therefore the primitive thinking is same for all peoples. Bastian, Adolf, *Ethnische Elementargedanken in der Lehre vom Menschen* (1895), https://archive.org/details/ethnischeelemen00bastgoog
29. Penny, Glenn H. *Objects of Culture. Ethnology and Ethnographic Museums in Imperial Germany*, Chapel Hill and London: The University of North California Press, 2002, pp. 18–22.
30. Wundt, Wilhelm *Elements of Folk Psychology. Outlines of a Psychological History of the Development of Mankind*, London: George Allen & Unwin Ltd., 1916 (German edition in 1912), p. 5.

of the human evolution is only one, that the condition of the social organization through which civilized nations have gone exists among the uncivilized ethnic groups of the mankind now. Of course, activities of the races take different form according to their different goals and circumstances, and their trajectories of the evolution are different. However, the thinking existing among the races is generally same for all ethnic groups; it is no doubt that there is a limited universality that peoples develop on the common trajectory."[31] Using this as a basis, Matsumoto compared similar cultures of different contemporary primitive people, such as the primitive people of Australia, India, Africa, Cambodia, Kamchatka, Northern America, Southwest China, Tonkin, Melanesia, Oceania, Tibet, Uyghur, Morocco, New Guinea, and contemporary Arabian and Semitic people, in addition to ancient Japanese and Chinese people in his writings.[32] Although Matsumoto was aware about the differences among different people, he researched the similarities among people and advocated universalism based on unilinear evolutionism.

As a result of the adoption of universalism, Matsumoto focused on the similarities, and not on the differences, among people; these were discussed by social Darwinism based on multilinear evolutionism. Consequently, unlike Matsumoto's teachers of history,[33] Matsumoto did not discuss the struggle for survival of social Darwin-

---

31. Matsumoto, Nobuhiro "Shina kodai seishi no kenkyū" (1921), *Tōa minzoku bunkaronkō*, Seibundō shinkōsha, 1968, p. 412.
32. Matsumoto, Nobuhiro "Shina kodai seishi no kenkyū" (1921), *Tōa minzoku bunkaronkō*, Seibundō shinkōsha, 1968, pp. 419, 437, 439. "Shina kosei to tōtemizumu" (1921-1922), *Tōa minzoku bunkaronkō*, Seibundō shinkōsha, 1968, pp. 454, 462, 472, 473, 478, 479, 482-5. "Kodai Shina minzoku no sosen saishi," *Shigaku*, dai 1 kan, dai 4 gō, Mita Shigakkai, 1922, pp. 50, 67.
33. Social Darwinism is expressed in the following works of Matsumoto's teachers: Tanaka, Suiichirō "Seiji to fujin," *Ōsaka kōen*, Keiō gijuku shuppankyoku, 1913, p. 356. Tanaka, Suiichirō "Chūkōron," *Ōsaka kōen*, Keiō gijuku shuppankyoku, 1913, p. 114. Hashimoto, Masukichi *Tōyōshi kōza ikki*, Jitaiko gokanmatsu, Ji taiko, Kokushi kōshūkai, 1926, p. 1. Kanokogi, Kazunobu, *Bunmei to tetsugaku seishin*, Keiō gijuku shuppankyoku, 1915, p. v. *Sentō-teki jinseikan*, Bunsendō shobō, 1943 (first edition 1917), p. 335.

ism in his writings in 1919–1923. This fact is apparent from Matsumoto's graduation thesis *The Research of the Family in Ancient China*. In this thesis, he indicated the peaceful life of primitive people as follows: "… even though there is a hypothesis that the primitive society was always in state of fighting, this does not correspond to the relatively peaceful situation of the barbarians now."[34] Therefore, due to Kawai's influence, Matsumoto studied Wundt's ethnology based on universalism that claimed a common culture for all primitive people, and this was not based on social Darwinism.

However, it is impossible to trace the detailed influence of Kawai's ideas on Matsumoto's ideas in his writings. This is because the syllabus of Kawai's lectures in ethnopsychology is unavailable and because Kawai did not publish any works on ethnology. As Kawai's work *Philosophy and Education* and his class of education at Keio University suggested, Kawai's main field was education.[35] Therefore, Kawai could not provide full guidance in ethnology to Matsumoto. Thus, it can be inferred was that Kawai introduced ethnology to Matsumoto by teaching him the basics of evolutionist ethnology, especially those forwarded by Wilhelm Wundt.

In sum, although Kawai was not Matsumoto's supervisor at Keio University, he significantly impact Matsumoto's research in general. Kawai's contribution to Matsumoto's education comprised introducing Matsumoto to the basic ideas of evolutionist ethnology, namely universalism of the German scholar Wilhelm Wundt. Further discussion on Matsumoto's adoption of Wundt's ethnological approach is provide in Section 2.4.1.

2.2. Influence of Yanagita Kunio on Matsumoto's study of ethnology

In addition to Kawai's guidance in ethnology, Matsumoto's study

---

34. Matsumoto, Nobuhiro "Shina kodai seishi no kenkyū" (1921), *Tōa minzoku bunkaronkō*, Seibundō shinkōsha, 1968, pp. 440–441.
35. Kawai, Teiichi "Tetsugaku to kyōiku," *Ōsaka kōen*, Keiō gijuku shuppankyoku, 1913, pp. 118–164. Kawakita, Nobuo "Keiō gijuku daigaku bungakubu kyōin tantō kamoku ichiran," *Shigaku*, dai 60 kan, dai 2/3 gō, Mita Shigakkai, 1991, pp. 183, 185, 195 (357, 359, 369).

of ethnology was influenced by Yanagita Kunio's guidance in folklore studies. During that time, Yanagita Kunio (1875–1962) was known as a writer of Japanese folklore who conducted extensive field work in the Japanese countryside. He made several travels to Europe to study folklore studies there[36] and worked on introducing this new academic discipline in Japan. During this period, there was no clear distinction between ethnology and folklore studies, and both disciplines were based on the evolutionist perspective of culture. Thus, due to these historical circumstances, Matsumoto studied ethnology from Yanagita Kunio although Yanagita focused on the Japanese folk culture.

Matsumoto became Yanagita's student due to his interest in the mountains in 1918. Matsumoto was a member of the Keio University Alpine Club and met Yanagita regarding a lecture on life in the mountains for the Alpine Club.[37] From that time, Matsumoto began visiting Yanagita's house, and subsequently, Yanagita became Matsumoto's long-life teacher. Yanagita lent back numbers of journals on folklore studies and relevant books to Matsumoto and encouraged him to study folklore.[38] However, Matsumoto joined Yanagita on his field work only once — in the summer of 1920 when they trekked through Tohoku.[39] Therefore, Yanagita's guidance to Matsumoto mainly included providing the theory of folklore studies that shared similarities with ethnology.

Matsumoto's connection with Yanagita is apparent from the publication of their papers in the same journal of the Keio University Al-

---

36. Matsumoto, Nobuhiro "Ko Orikuchi Shinobu hakase to 'kodai kenkyū'," *Nihon oyobi Nihonjin*, 7(9), Kanaobun'endō, 1956-09, p. 101.
37. Matsumoto, Nobuhiro "Yanagita Kunio 'Kainan shōki' to 'Kaijō no michi' - minzoku to minzoku ni tsuite" *Nihon minzoku bunka no kigen I: shinwa-densetsu*, Kōdansha, 1978, p.332.
38. Matsumoto, Nobuhiro "Tōhoku no tabi," *Teihon Yanagita Kunioshū*, Geppō 1, Chikumashobō, 1962, p. 3.
39. Matsumoto, Nobuhiro "Sayama kikō," *Tōkōkō*, I, Keiō gijuku taiikukai sangakubu nenpō, Shuppan kagaku sōgō kenkyūjo, 1919, pp. 123-127. "Iwate no Kōgen yori," (1920) *Nihon minzoku bunka no kigen I: shinwa-densetsu*, Kōdansha, 1978, pp. 364-373. "Tōhoku no tabi," *Teihon Yanagita Kunioshū*, Geppō 1, Chikumashobō, 1962, pp. 360-363.

pine Club. Matsumoto published his writings about the mountain belief *The Mountain Legends in Fudoki* and *The Research of Mount Tai* in *Tōkōkō* (the journal of the Keio University Alpine Club).[40] simultaneously, Yanagita contributed his long paper on Musashino (*Miscellaneous Talks on Musashino*) to this journal.[41] Yanagita's influence on Matsumoto's paper is apparent from the fact that these two papers by Matsumoto examined the issue of mountain beliefs, a topic in folklore studies. Moreover, in *The Mountain Legends in Fudoki*,[42] Matsumoto discussed the Japanese legends, such as a legend that traced the origins of the celestial god of Kabire Pass[43], a material for folklore studies. In this manner, Matsumoto's early ethnological papers used folklore material.

Matsumoto's work *The Mountain Legends in Fudoki* reflected the undifferentiated coexistence of ethnology and folklore studies in this period.[44] Thus, Matsumoto began receiving Yanagita's guidance when Yanagita was exploring his way in folklore studies by studying European ethnology and folklore studies. Yanagita's paper *What is ethnology?* expressed Yanagita's effort to define "ethnology" in relation to Western research.[45] Yanagita's opinion on the naming of ethnology proves his outlook on the situation facing Western and Japanese aca-

---

40. Matsumoto, Nobuhiro "Fudoki ni arawaretaru santake densetsu," *Tōkōkō*, II, Keiō gijuku taiikukai sangakubu nenpō, Shuppan kagaku sōgō kenkyūjo, 1920, pp. 23-40. Matsumoto, Nobuhiro "Taizan no kenkyū," *Tōkōkō*, III, Keiō gijuku taiikukai sangakubu nenpō, Shuppan kagaku sōgō kenkyūjo, 1921, pp. 34-40.
41. Yanagita, Kunio "Musashino zatsuwa," *Tōkōkō*, I, Keiō gijuku taiikukai sangakubu nenpō, Shuppan kagaku sōgō kenkyūjo, 1919, pp. 18-37. "Zoku Musashino zatsuwa," *Tōkōkō*, II, Keiō gijuku taiikukai sangakubu nenpō, Shuppan kagaku sōgō kenkyūjo, 1920, pp. 1-18.
42. Matsumoto, Nobuhiro "Fudoki ni arawaretaru santake densetsu," *Tōkōkō*, II, Keiō gijuku taiikukai sangakubu nenpō, Shuppan kagaku sōgō kenkyūjo, 1920, p. 23.
43. Kabire Pass (賀毘禮峰) is a mountain pass on the Tokaidō in the Niigata Prefecture in Japan.
44. Ethnology became established as a separate academic discipline in 1935 when the Japan Ethnological Society was formed by Japanese ethnologists. "Nihon minzoku gakkai setsuritsu shuisho," *Minzokugaku kenkyū*, dai 1 kan, dai 1 gō, Nihon minzoku gakkai, Sanseidō, 1935, pp. 219-222.

demic circles: "For example the most influential scholars in what we call folklore studies (*minzokugaku*, 民俗学), such as Tsuboi Shogoro sensei and Professor E. B. Tylor, did not use the word ethnology at all; they called the discipline anthropology while it had the same content as ethnology in France; from the beginning to the end they spoke and wrote under the name of anthropology."[46] Therefore, Yanagita not only taught Matsumoto about Japanese folklore but also introduced him to Western ethnological research.[47]

Yanagita shared with Matsumoto his knowledge regarding the works of English ethnologists Edward Burnett Tylor and James George Frazer, the leading scholars of universalism based on the belief in unilinear evolution. This was because Yanagita respected them as founders of folklore studies and considered their works as the basis of folklore research.[48] Concertely, Yanagita transmitted Matsumoto Tylor's theory of remnants, which formed the foundations of ethnology in general. Yanagita was aware of the significance of Tylor's theory: "Sir James Frazer who adopted the daring theory of his teacher Tylor, indicated most politely the so-called barbarian remnants in civilization and he put the same method in the third volume of *Folklore of the Old Testament*. This is a method by which we can know the previous era of many peoples of today and of the past from now on."[49] According to Matsumoto, Yanagita bought Frazer's *The Golden Bough* from the bookstore Maruzen that offered the service of importing foreign books.[50]

Thus, Yanagita respected Tylor's and Frazer's research because he

---

45. Yanagita, Kunio "Ethnology to ha nanika" (1926), *Teihon Yanagita Kunioshū*, dai 25-kan, Chikumashobō, 1964, pp. 232–47.
46. Ibid., p. 234.
47. Yanagita's paper well reflected ambiguous existence of ethnology due to its connections with other disciplines and diverse development in various countries. See note 73 in previous chapter for definitions of the relevant academic disciplines.
48. Ibid., pp. 234, 254.
49. Yanagita, Kunio "Ethnology to ha nanika" (1926), *Teihon Yanagita Kunioshū*, dai 25-kan, Chikumashobō, 1964, p. 254.

was interested in their theory of remnants. Tylor and Frazer contributed to the development of unilinear evolutionism and universalism because they applied the theory of remnants on different people. Thus, Yanagita also became a universalist by adopting the theory of remnants.

In his theory, Tylor defined the remnants[51] as "processes, customs, and opinions, and so forth, which have been carried on by force of habit into a new state of society different from that in which they had their original home, and they thus remain as proofs and examples of an older condition of culture out of which a newer has been evolved."[52] Thus, according to Tylor, remnants meant phenomena of the previous culture remaining in the following stages of the cultural development. On the basis of this theory, Tylor claimed that the historical development of the people can be traced from these remnants.[53] In addition, based on universalism, he argued that the stages of different races can be compared if there are similarities between their cultures.[54]

Matsumoto's dedication to Tylor's theory of remnants is clearly expressed in Matsumoto's writings. In his graduation thesis *The Research of the Family in Ancient China*, Matsumoto wrote as follows: "The thinking and activities of the archaic peoples is practiced in the thinking and the activities of many uncivilized peoples today. To do research on the archaic thinking, ideas and system based on the knowledge about the contemporary uncivilized people is one method on which the researcher in ancient history should be based."[55] He applied Tylor's theory of remnants in his paper *The Family in Ancient*

---

50. Matsumoto, Nobuhiro "Ko Orikuchi Shinobu hakase to 'kodai kenkyū'," *Nihon oyobi Nihonjin*, 7(9), Kanaobun'endō, 1956-09, p. 101.
51. Tylor used the term "survival" for remnants. However, this word would be confusing with the term "the struggle for survival" of social Darwinism. Therefore, the author of this thesis chose to use the term "remnants" from the Japanese word 残存 (zanson) used in Matsumoto's writings.
52. Tylor, Edward Burnet *Primitive Culture*, Vol. 1, London: John Murray, 1873, p. 16.
53. Ibid., p. 17.
54. Ibid., p. 7.

China and Totemism: "Therefore, please allow me to follow the traces of totemism through the family names [姓] as the remnants of the system in the previous period in the society of that time and through the legends related to them."[56] Thus, Matsumoto thought that the remnants of primitive culture can be found both among the contemporary primitive people and in the legends.

Matsumoto applied Tylor's theory of remnants for the first time on the Japanese culture under Yanagita's influence in 1920. Yanagita's interpretation of the theory of remnants can be found in his writing *Miscellaneous Talks on Musashino*, which was published in *Tōkōkō*. In this paper, Yanagita explained how to trace the ancient elements in the present people and how to reconstruct the past condition of Musashino from its present appearance.[57] Matsumoto followed Yanagita's example for researching the remnants in Japanese folklore. In his paper *The Mountain Legends in Fudoki*, he wrote as follows: "The simple ideas of ancient men about mountains were recorded as traces in various legends remaining in ancient records. Thus, a good material about the thinking of ancient men is stored especially in Fudoki selected by Emperor Gemmei's court in the sixth year of Wadō Era [713]. Let me take two legends and let me try to research the beliefs of ancient people related to the mountains."[58] Matsumoto published his paper in *Tōkōkō* and mediated the publication of Yanagita's paper in the same journal.[59]

Matsumoto became interested in mountain beliefs because he became acquainted with Yanagita's opinions about the life of the Japa-

---

55. Matsumoto, Nobuhiro "Shina kodai seishi no kenkyū" (1921), *Tōa minzoku bunkaronkō*, Seibundō shinkōsha, 1968, p. 425.
56. Matsumoto, Nobuhiro "Shina kosei to tōtemizumu" (1921–1922), *Tōa minzoku bunkaronkō*, Seibundō shinkōsha, 1968, p. 461.
57. Yanagita Kunio "Musashino zatsuwa," *Tōkōkō*, I, Keiō gijuku taiikukai sangakubu nenpō, Shuppan kagaku sōgō kenkyūjo, 1919, pp. 32–33.
58. Matsumoto, Nobuhiro "Fudoki ni arawaretaru santake densetsu," *Tōkōkō*, II, Keiō gijuku taiikukai sangakubu nenpō, Shuppan kagaku sōgō kenkyūjo, 1920, p. 23.
59. Matsumoto, Nobuhiro *Matsumoto Nobuhiro shinpen zakki*, Matsumoto Chie, 1982, p. 25. *Tōkōkō*, II, Keiō gijuku taiikukai sangakubu nenpō, Shuppan kagaku sōgō kenkyūjo, 1920, p. 28.

nese people in the mountains.[60] Yanagita was concerned with the relationship of country people with their natural environment in general. This is apparent from his first work *The Tales of Tōno* (1910) and from his paper *Miscellaneous Talks on Musashino* that he published in the same journal with Matsumoto's writings about the mountains.

Matsumoto's interest in the relationship of people with the mountains can be found in his early writings. In his travel notes *From Kōgen in Iwate*, he indicated the crucial role of mountains in the religious life of common people. For example, he called the mountains "sacred mountains which are the core of the beliefs of inhabitants in this plain" or "mountains ruling the beliefs of villagers."[61] He elaborated his ideas regarding the mountain beliefs in his two papers *The Mountain Legends in Fudoki* and *The Research of Mount Tai*; in these papers, he compared the Japanese and Chinese mountain beliefs with the culture of other ethnic groups.[62] These writings revealed that under Yanagita's influence, Matsumoto considered mountain beliefs to be an important topic in folklore studies and ethnology.

Matsumoto's personal ties with Yanagita grew so important that Matsumoto never left the circles of folklore studies. Matsumoto maintained correspondence with Yanagita even when one of them stayed in Europe. This is apparent from Yanagita's diary entry made in Switzerland where Yanagita mentions receiving Matsumoto's letters.[63] After Yanagita returned from Europe, he started teaching folklore studies (under the name of anthropology) at Keio University due to Matsumoto's efforts in 1924. It was historically the first course in folk-

---

60. Matsumoto, Nobuhiro "Yanagita Kunio 'Kainan shōki' to 'Kaijō no michi' – minzoku to minzoku ni tsuite" *Nihon minzoku bunka no kigen I: shinwa-densetsu*, Kōdansha, 1978, p.332.
61. Matsumoto, Nobuhiro "Iwate no Kōgen yori" (1920), *Nihon minzoku bunka no kigen I: shinwa-densetsu*, Kōdansha, 1978, pp. 364, 369, 374.
62. Matsumoto, Nobuhiro "Fudoki ni arawaretaru santake densetsu," *Tōkōkō*, II, Keiō gijuku taiikukai sangakubu nenpō, Shuppan kagaku sōgō kenkyūjo, 1920, pp. 23–40. Matsumoto, Nobuhiro "Taizan no kenkyū," *Tōkōkō*, III, Keiō gijuku taiikukai sangakubu nenpō, Shuppan kagaku sōgō kenkyūjo, 1921, pp. 34–40.
63. Yanagita, Kunio "Suisu nikki" (1922), *Teihon Yanagita Kunioshū*, dai 3 kan, Chikuma shobō, 1963, pp. 290, 302.

lore studies at Keio University.⁶⁴ After Matsumoto returned from France, he took over Yanagita's course. However, its conception was based more on ethnology rather than on folklore studies.⁶⁵ Despite their complicated relationships⁶⁶ and the separation of folklore studies from ethnology in the 1930s, Matsumoto cherished this precious connection until Yanagita's death in 1962.

According to Chikamori Masashi, Yanagita never officially recognized Matsumoto as his disciple, but Matsumoto considered Yanagita to be his true mentor.⁶⁷ Matsumoto's close relationship with Yanagita is evident not only from Yanagita's diary but also from the fact that Matsumoto contributed to the journal in the 2nd volume out of the 31 volumes of Yanagita's collection in 1962.⁶⁸

Through Yanagita, Matsumoto became acquainted with other Japanese scholars of folklore studies, especially with Yanagita's friend and rival Orikuchi Shinobu (1887–1953). Matsumoto can be seen in the picture (1924) taken in Orikuchis's house together with Orikuchi, Yanagita, and other folklorists such as Nevski or Kidaichi Kyosuke.⁶⁹ Matsumoto regularly met Orikuchi at Keio University Faculty of Letters because Orikuchi taught Japanese literature from 1923.⁷⁰ Matsumoto's frequent contact with Orikuchi is also suggested by the

---

64. Itō, Seiji "Hito to gakumon, Matsumoto Nobuhiro," *Shakai jinruigaku nenpō*, Tōkyō toritsu daigaku shakai jinrui gakkai, dai 12 kan, 1986, p. 121.
65. Arima, Makiko "Hito, Matsumoto Nobuhiro," *Kikan jinruigaku*, 5-1, Shakaishisōsha, 1974, p. 156 (an interview with Matsumoto Nobuhiro), p. 156.
66. Matsumoto, Nobuhiro "Origuchi san no koto" *Nihon minzoku bunka no kigen I: shinwa-densetsu*, Kōdansha, 1978, p. 394.
67. Chikamori used to pay a New Year's visit to Matsumoto's house on the 2nd of January because Matsumoto attended Yanagita's house on the 1st of January. Interview with Chikamori Masashi, 23 August and 13 October 2012, Keio University, Tokyo.
68. Matsumoto, Nobuhiro "Tōhoku no tabi" *Teihon Yanagita Kunioshū*, Geppō 1, Chikumashobō, 1962, pp. 2-4.
69. Matsumoto, Nobuhiro *Matsumoto Nobuhiro shinpen zakki*, Matsumoto Chie, 1982, p. 7.
70. Kawakita, Nobuo "Keiō gijuku daigaku bungakubu kyōin tantō kamoku ichiran," *Shigaku*, dai 60 kan, dai 2/3 gō, Mita Shigakkai, 1991, pp. 193, 197, 203, 209 (367, 371, 377, 383).

multiple articles written about him by Matsumoto.[71] From Matsumoto's paper on Orikuchi's work, it seems that Orikuchi adopted Tylor's and Frazer's theories like Yanagita.[72] Therefore, Matsumoto also learnt about them from Orikuchi. However, Orikuchi's influence is not so obvious in Matsumoto's writings, so it is omitted from this book.

In sum, Yanagita became Matsumoto's long-life teacher when Yanagita was conducting research on European ethnology and folklore studies. Thus, Matsumoto deepened his knowledge of evolutionist ethnology that he received from Kawai by studying the theory of ethnology and folklore studies from Yanagita. Yanagita's ideas persistently influenced Matsumoto's research because Matsumoto kept his personal relationship with Yanagita until Yanagita's death, although Matsumoto became the founder of Southeast Asian studies and Yanagita became the founder of folklore studies in Japan.

2.3. Influence of Japanese historians on Matsumoto's study of ethnology

Kawai's and Yanagita's influence on Matsumoto's ethnology was most significant. However, Matsumoto adopted an ethnological approach to history because some of his teachers, such as Kato Shigeshi (1880–1946) and Hashimoto Masukichi (1880–1956), were influenced by cultural evolutionism in their historical research and researched ancient culture. Originally, Matsumoto chose to study history because he admired the personality of Tanaka Suiichiro (1873–1923), the head of the department of history at Keio University, who was famous for his research on Oriental history.[73] However, Tanaka was not concerned

---

71. Matsumoto, Nobuhiro "Ko Orikuchi Shinobu hakase to 'kodai kenkyū'," *Nihon oyobi Nihonjin*, 7(9), Kanaobun'endō, 1956-09, pp. 100-105. "Orikuchi san no koto," *Kokubungaku*, 18/1, January 1973. "Mita no Orikuchi Shinobu" (zadankai), *Mita hyōron*, dai 730 gō, Mita hyōron hakkōjo, October 1973.
72. Matsumoto, Nobuhiro "Ko Orikuchi Shinobu hakase to 'kodai kenkyū'," *Nihon oyobi Nihonjin*, 7(9), Kanaobun'endō, 1956-09, pp. 100-105.
73. Itō, Seiji "Matsumoto Nobuhiro – 'Nampōsetsu' no kaitakusha," *Bunka jinruigaku gunzō*, Nihonhen (3), Kyōto: Akademia shuppankai, 1988, p. 227-228. "Matsumoto Nobuhiro to gakumon," Keiō gijuku *daigaku gengo kenkyūjo hōkokushū*, Keiō gijuku daigaku, dai 24 kan, 1992, p. 13.

with ancient history like Matsumoto. Therefore, Matsumoto followed Kato and Hashimoto who were lesser-known researchers of Oriental history.

In general, historians in Matsumoto's era believed in social Darwinism. For example, Hashimoto framed his lecture on the ancient Orient with the theory based on the survival of the fittest by arguing that although peace is ideal for human life, it can never be completely attained because wars are inevitable since they serve as "a trial of the survival of the fittest."[74] Therefore, Matsumoto's teachers of history were followers of Darwinism that emphasized the differences between the people; in contrast, Matsumoto believe in universalism. Nevertheless, Matsumoto and his teachers of history shared the theory of cultural evolutionism that there were stages in the cultural evolution of differenct people.

Through his teachers of history such as Kato Shigeshi and Hashimoto Masukichi, Matsumoto was influenced by cultural evolutionism. For example, Hashimoto, Matsumoto's teacher of Oriental history, indicated the importance of Oriental history from the perspective of cultural evolution. In his lecture on ancient Oriental history, he wrote as follows: "...only when we clarify the history of the people of the Asian genealogy which was neglected in contrast to the history of the people of the European genealogy, that a larger reality can be seen, where we, the Asian people are also involved in the cultural development of the world..."[75] Hashimoto taught Matsumoto about China not only in the classroom but also on a school trip to Korea, Manchuria, and China in the summer of 1918.[76] Further, Matsumoto studied the de-

---

74. Hashimoto, Masukichi *Tōyōshi kōza ikki*, Jitaiko gokanmatsu, Ji taiko, Kokushi kōshūkai, 1926, p. 1.
75. Ibid., pp. 3-4.
76. *Ine-fune-matsuri: Matsumoto Nobuhiro sensei tsuitō ronbunshū*, Rokkōshuppan, 1982, p. 693. Itō, Seiji "Matsumoto Nobuhiro – 'Nampōsetsu' no kaitakusha," *Bunka jinruigaku gunzō*, Nihonhen (3), Kyōto: Akademia shuppankai, 1988, pp. 228. Matsumoto, Nobuhiro "Ko Hashimoto Masukichi kyoju no tsuioku," *Shigaku*, dai 219 kan, dai 4 go, Mita Shigakkai, 1957, p. 104 (468).

velopment of Chinese culture in Kato Shigeshi's classes of history of Chinese society.[77] Since the study of the Chinese history demanded the use of Chinese documents, Matsumoto developed his interest in ancient Chinese writings as the sources of Chinese culture under Hashimoto's and Kato's guidance. Therefore, he later considered the Chinese-written Vietnamese documents to be important for studying Vietnamese culture.

The influence of Hashimoto's and Kato's teaching on ancient Chinese history appears in Matsumoto's writings. Concretely, Matsumoto wrote four papers on the ancient Chinese culture: his graduation thesis *The Research of the Family in Ancient China*, *The Family in Ancient China and Totemism*, *Ancestor Worship of People in Ancient China* and *Research of the Shrine and the Millet* in the early 1920s.[78]

Hashimoto's and Kato's opinions appeared in Matsumoto's graduation thesis *The Research of the Family in Ancient China*. Matsumoto discussed them as a part of the existing research on the family (姓) in ancient China.[79] He mentioned Hashimoto's theory that the institution of the family (姓) appeared in China distinguish between the tribes due to differences in the customs, languages, etc. Furthermore, Matsumoto mentioned Kato's theory on the institution of the family (姓). This theory was developed to clarify kinship relations in a large kinship group formed by many hamlets.[80]

However, compared with the influence of these two teachers,

---

77. Kawakita, Nobuo "Keiō gijuku daigaku bungakubu kyōin tantō kamoku ichiran," *Shigaku*, dai 60 kan, dai 2/3 gō, Mita Shigakkai, 1991, pp. 188-189 (362-363). Matsumoto, Nobuhiro *Matsumoto Nobuhiro shinpen zakki*, Matsumoto Chie, 1982, p. 40.
78. Matsumoto, Nobuhiro "Shina kodai seishi no kenkyū," *Mita hyōron*, dai 3, 4, 5 gō, Mita hyōron hakkōjo, 1921, pp. 411-452. "Shina kosei to tōtemizumu," *Shigaku*, dai 1 kan, dai 1 gō, 1921, dai 2 gō, Mita Shigakkai, 1922, pp. 453-490. "Kodai Shina minzoku no sosen saishi," *Shigaku*, dai 1 kan, dai 4 gō, Mita Shigakkai, 1922, pp. 49-71. "Shashoku no kenkyū," *Shigaku*, dai 2 kan, dai 1 gō, Mita Shigakkai, 1922, pp. 493-513.
79. Ibid., pp. 417-425.
80. Matsumoto, Nobuhiro "Shina kodai seishi no kenkyū" (1921), *Tōa minzoku bunkaronkō*, Seibundō shinkōsha, 1968, pp. 417-418.

Kato's influence was more important. Matsumoto's memories of Hashimoto show that his personal relationship with him was rather difficult.[81] On the other hand, Matsumoto mentioned that Kato's lectures inspired him and provided him with many materials on Chinese society for his graduation thesis.[82] Nonetheless, Matsumoto criticized the detailed discussion of both his teachers as "insufficient" and "too abstract."[83] Since Matsumoto adopted ethnological theory of exogamy in his thesis,[84] he gave preference to ethnology in historical research. Therefore, the role of Matsumoto's teachers of history was introducing him to evolutionist theories related to Chinese ancient history, which were discussed together with ethnological theories since ethnology in this period was evolutionist ethnology.

Another contribution of Japanese historians to the formation of Matsumoto's ideas regarding primitive culture was that they introduced the works of Western sinologists to Matsumoto. Among them, Matsumoto was especially fascinated by the ideas of French sinologists Édouard Chavannes (1865-1918) and Marcel Granet (1884-1940) who were influenced by evolutionist ethnologist James George Frazer. Frazer was also active in the French academic circles and had personal contacts with French ethnologists and sociologists.[85] Matsumoto's interest in Chavannes' and Granet's work suggests that Matsumoto pre-

---

81. Matsumoto, Nobuhiro "Ko Hashimoto Masukichi kyoju no tsuioku," *Shigaku*, dai 219 kan, dai 4 go, Mita Shigakkai, 1957, p. 104 (468).
82. Matsumoto, Nobuhiro "Shina kodai seishi no kenkyū" (1921), *Tōa minzoku bunkaronkō*, Seibundō shinkōsha, 1968, p. 451, Note 1. "Ko Hashimoto Masukichi kyoju no tsuioku," *Shigaku*, dai 219 kan, dai 4 go, Mita Shigakkai, 1957, p. 103 (467).
83. Ibid., pp. 418-419, 424.
84. Ibid., p. 424, 440-450.
85. "Frazer, James George" *Alumni Cantabrigienses: A Biographical List of All Known Students, Graduates and Holders of Office at the University of Cambridge, from the Earliest Times to 1900*, compiled by J. A. Venn, Part II, Volume II, Cambridge the University Press, 1944, p. 570-571. Yanagita Kunio praised Frazer's wife after meeting Frazer in Switzerland. (Yanagita, Kunio "Ethnology to ha nanika" (1926), *Teihon Yanagita Kunioshū*, dai 25-kan, Chikumashobō, 1964, p. 235.)

ferred an ethnological approach in historical research. Since Hashimoto criticized the French sinological school,[86] the books of French sinologists were introduced to Matsumoto probably by Kato who lectured on Chinese society.

The references made in Matsumoto's writings in the early 1920s showed that Matsumoto drew from Chavannes' monumental books *The Memoirs of Sima Qian* (1895) and *Mount Tai* (1910).[87] *The Memoirs of Sima Qian* contained the translation of the Chinese classical book *The Records of the Grand Historian* (史記) and Chavannes' commentary to it. *Mount Tai* examined the history of Chinese cult worship practiced at Mount Tai. From *The Memoirs of Sima Qian*, Matsumoto used Chavannes' definition of the family (姓) as a large family system in his graduation thesis *The Research of the Family in Ancient China*.[88] Furthermore, Matsumoto adopted Chavannes' ideas regarding Chinese religious thinking from *Mount Tai* (1910) in his papers *The Research of Mount Tai* and *Research of the Shrine and the Millet*. Thus, Matsumoto used Chavannes' works as a source for his ethnological papers on the primitive culture in ancient China.

From Granet's works, Matsumoto was significantly influenced by the book *Festivals and Songs of Ancient China* (1919).[89] As Chavannes' student, Granet explored ancient China. However, he focused on the sociological phenomena since he was also a disciple of sociologist Émile Durkheim.[90] Therefore, he believed in the common cultural basis of different races and he mentioned about Southeast Asian customs. Among others, Granet focused on the mating customs: "The

---

86. Itō, Seiji "Matsumoto Nobuhiro – 'Nampōsetsu' no kaitakusha," *Bunka jinruigaku gunzō*, Nihonhen (3), Akademia shuppankai, Kyōto, 1988, p. 233.
87. Chavannes, Édouard *Les mémoires historiques de Se-Ma Ts'ien*, Société asiatique, Ernest Leroux, Paris, 1895. *Le T'ai chan: essai de monographie d'un culte chinois: appendice: Le dieu du sol dans la Chine antique*, E. Leroux, Paris, 1910.
88. Matsumoto, Nobuhiro "Shina kodai seishi no kenkyū" (1921), *Tōa minzoku bunkaronkō*, Seibundō shinkōsha, 1968, p. 412.
89. Granet, Marcel *Fêtes et chansons anciennes de la Chine*, second edition, Librarie Ernest Leroux, Paris, 1929 (first edition 1919).

plays of love songs are of general use in the majority of aboriginal populations of Southwest China and Tonkin, and in Tibet, they have existed in the ancient Japan."[91] Matsumoto adopted Granet's idea of connecting the seasonal festivals with the Japanese custom of *utagaki* (love songs banquet)[92] in his paper *The Mountain Legends in Fudoki*: "In ancient Sukhotai Land, single men and women freely choose their spouse, and after living one year together, they were permitted to freely decide the course of their action. Considering the above mentioned examples, *utagaki* was not simply a habit that was practiced only in ancient Japan, but was discovered to be practiced among many uncivilized men."[93] Thus, Matsumoto adopted Granet's argument that customs such as the Japanese custom of *utagaki* is typical for primitive people, including Southeast Asian people.

In summary, Hashimoto and Kato influenced Matsumoto's ethnology through their teachings about ancient China. However, only Kato probably played a role in introducing the works of French sinologists influenced by ethnology (Chavannes and Granet) by which Matsumoto was most fascinated.

2.4. Influence on Matsumoto's methodology

The discussion on the influence of the Japanese scholars on Matsumoto's ethnology showed that Matsumoto's ethnology was in-

---

90. Matsumoto, Nobuhiro "Furansu ni okeru Shina kenkyū," *Shina kenkyū* Keiō gijuku Mochidzuki Kikin Shina kenkyūkai-hen, Iwanamishoten, 1930, pp. 386–389. "Granet, Marcel," *Encyclopedia of religion*, second edition, Macmillan Reference USA, Detroit, 2005, pp. 3654–3655.
91. Granet, Marcel *Fêtes et chansons anciennes de la Chine*, second edition, Librarie Ernest Leroux, Paris, 1929 (first edition 1919), p. 146.
92. *Utagaki* (歌垣) is an ancient Japanese custom associated with fertility and celebrating the beginning of spring and autumn. Japanese peasants would gather together on the tops of mountains to sing, dance, eat and drink. Songs and poems from utagaki were recorded in the collection *Manyōshū* (cca 759).
93. Matsumoto, Nobuhiro "Fudoki ni arawaretaru santake densetsu," *Tōkōkō, II*, Keiō gijuku taiikukai sangakubu nenpō, Shuppan kagaku sōgō kenkyūjo, 1920, p. 38.

fluenced by ethnology, folklore studies, and cultural history. Since ethnology and folklore studies, used the same approach at this time, Matsumoto combined two methodological approaches in his research on primitive culture: ethnological and historical approach. Historians discussed ethnological theories because there were no written records about prehistoric times, and archaeologists presented only a few discoveries during that time. The following subsections specifically discuss Matsumoto's application of ethnological and historical methods.

2.4.1. The ethnological methodology

Matsumoto's ethnological methodology was based on his belief in unilinear evolutionism and universalism that he adopted from Yanagita and Kawai; they followed Western evolutionist ethnologists such as Tylor, Frazer, and Wundt. Consequently, Matsumoto believed in universality of the primitive culture for all people; like Western evolutionist ethnologists, he compared the ancient culture of the civilized people (in Matsumoto's case: Japanese and Chinese) with the contemporary culture of the primitive people. Thus, Matsumoto adopted comparative research as an ethnological methodology. Furthermore, he borrowed ethnological interpretations of the primitive culture by Western scholars' theories deduced from this comparative research. Due to his belief in the universality of the primitive mind, he assumed that ethnological interpretations of the primitive culture could be applied to the culture of any primitive people.

First, Matsumoto advocated the need for comparative research for historical study in his graduation thesis *The Research of the Family in Ancient China*: "Therefore, we can research the character of the peoples of ancient China, and by comparison with the similarities of the present uncivilized ethnic groups, we can clarify the insufficiencies in the legends, writings, customs, systems etc. existing in ancient China."[94] In the same paper, Matsumoto claimed that "In the research of the social system of ancient Chinese people, it is necessary to con-

---

94. Matsumoto, Nobuhiro "Shina kodai seishi no kenkyū" (1921), *Tōa minzoku bunkaronkō*, Seibundō shinkōsha, 1968, p. 412.

sider the comparison with the system of the different races which are at the same stage of the mental development with them [Chinese] and clarify the true character [of the Chinese social system]."[95]

He compared the cultures of different people in his other papers. For example, he compared Sumatran contemporary culture with the ancient Japanese custom *utagaki*. In his paper *The Mountain Legends in Fudoki*, he wrote, "In Sumatra, the Rechihi tribe believes that the Sun is man, the Earth is woman, and think that the Earth will bear fruits by the relation of the two, thus they place a big flat stone under the fig tree and they organize a festival every year ... The fact that *utagaki* has a religious meaning probably comes from the important element that is an agriculture festival."[96]

The quoted arguments of Matsumoto demonstrate that his comparison was superficial. He did not explicitly state which elements of the Sumatran custom correspond to which elements of the Japanese custom. In fact, Matsumoto's comparison was an association based on the matching of somewhat similar customs of different cultures. This practice using rationalist deduction and induction was common for many evolutionist scholars in Matsumoto's era.

Second, Matsumoto adopted ethnological theories interpreting primitive culture. He especially adopted Frazer's theory of totemism (*Tōtemizumu*, トーテミズム, belief in totem) in his paper *The Family in Ancient China and Totemism*. He learnt about the existence of totemism among Southeast Asian people and used this theory for claiming the existence of totemism in ancient China.[97] Matsumoto's adoption of the Western ethnological theories is discussed in Section 4.2.

As a result of Kawai's influence, Matsumoto called this ethnological approach "psychological research." He borrowed it from Wilhelm Wundt's ethnopsychology. He claimed that this method could appro-

---

95. Ibid., p. 425.
96. Matsumoto, Nobuhiro "Fudoki ni arawaretaru santake densetsu," *Tōkōkō*, II, Keiō gijuku taiikukai sangakubu nenpō, Shuppan kagaku sōgō kenkyūjo, 1920, p. 39.
97. Matsumoto, Nobuhiro "Shina kosei to tōtemizumu" (1921–1922), *Tōa minzoku bunkaronkō*, Seibundō shinkōsha, 1968, pp. 484–5.

priately to examine cultural history in *The Research of the Family in Ancient China*: "...it is necessary to research about the ideas of the archaic people towards the soul in its place related to ancestor worship. In starting a psychological research like this, we can learn about the origin and significance of the clan system."[98] In the same thesis, Matsumoto criticized previous works for not conducting the psychological research: "I must say that it is unfortunate that existing research on the family [姓], which did not use this psychological research and this comparative method, could not clarify its meaning."[99] Thus, due to Kawai's mediation of Wundt's ethnology, Matsumoto considered ethnological approach to ancient history to be better than the orthodox historical approach.

Furthermore, Matsumoto adopted the interpretation of the ancient or primitive culture from Yanagita as shown in Matsumoto's writings about the mountain beliefs in Section 2.2. Using Tylor's theory of remnants, Yanagita interpreted the culture of the ancient Japanese people from their daily customs in his folklore studies. Yanagita believed that this theory could explain why Japanese customs in the countryside retained its ancient form.

However, contrary to Yanagita, Matsumoto researched primitive culture mainly from books. Though he could not collect material on foreign people by himself, he did not base his research findings from field work as Yanagita did, but on the written accounts of different primitive people worldwide. Therefore, Matsumoto became an armchair ethnologist like Frazer and not a field worker like Yanagita who researched Japanese folklore.

2.4.2. Methodology of historical science

Matsumoto received training in the methodology of historical science from his supervisor Tanaka Suiichiro at Keio University Faculty of Letters. Matsumoto attended Tanaka's lectures on historical re-

---

98. Matsumoto, Nobuhiro "Shina kodai seishi no kenkyū" (1921), *Tōa minzoku bunkaronkō*, Seibundō shinkōsha, 1968, pp. 425.
99. Ibid., pp. 426.

search methods, modern historical readings on the Orient, and the modern history of China. He appreciated Tanaka's teaching efforts even though there were only four students, including Matsumoto, in the class. In addition, he joined the regular meetings of an academic organization called the Mita Historical Society founded by Tanaka.[100] Owing to Tanaka's guidance, he studied modern historical science introduced to Japan by Ludwig Riess (1861-1928) because Tanaka was one of Riess' students.[101] Consequently, Matsumoto learnt methods of historical science based on the evidences drawn from historical documents.

Due to this historical training, Matsumoto used historical records in his ethnological research. He drew from the Japanese annals *Nihonshoki*, *Fudoki*[102] in his paper *The Mountain Legends in Fudoki*. For example, he indicated his source as *Nihonshoki*: "In *Nihonshoki*, Vol. 11, it is written that, Shōmu Emperor watched *utagaki* at Suzaku Gate."[103] Furthermore, he referred to Chinese historical records such as *Records of the Grand Historian* (史記) and *the Classic of History* (書経).[104] For example, Matsumoto drew from *Records of the Grand Historian* in his paper *The Family in Ancient China and Totemism*: "The same legend is mentioned in *Zhou Records of the Great Historian*."[105] Thus, Matsumoto

---

100. Matsumoto, Nobuhiro "Tanaka hakushi wo itamu," *Mita hyōron*, dai 316 gō, Mita hyōron hakkōjo, December 1923, pp. 26-27. *Matsumoto Nobuhiro shinpen zakki*, Matsumoto Chie, 1982, p. 40.
101. "Mita no shigakusha profīru," *Shigaku*, dai 60 kan, dai 2/3 gō, Mita Shigakkai, 1991, p. 343. Matsumoto, Nobuhiro "Shigakusha to shite Tanaka Suiichirō sensei," *Shigaku* 45/4, Mita Shigakkai, 1973, p. 50 (410).
102. Matsumoto, Nobuhiro "Fudoki ni arawaretaru santake densetsu," *Tōkōkō, II*, Keiō gijuku taiikukai sangakubu nenpō, Shuppan kagaku sōgō kenkyūjo, 1920, pp. 23, 33, 35.
103. Ibid., p. 35.
104. Matsumoto, Nobuhiro "Taizan no kenkyū," *Tōkōkō, III*, Keiō gijuku taiikukai sangakubu nenpō, Shuppan kagaku sōgō kenkyūjo, 1921, p. 3. "Shina kodai seishi no kenkyū" (1921), *Tōa minzoku bunkaronkō*, Seibundō shinkōsha, 1968, p. 412.
105. Matsumoto, Nobuhiro "Shina kosei to tōtemizumu" (1921-1922), *Tōa minzoku bunkaronkō*, Seibundō shinkōsha, 1968, p. 470.

used the historical records of legends as material for primitive culture in his ethnological research.

This means that Matsumoto's concern for the primitive culture prevailed in his historical research. This is also made clear from Matsumoto's criticism on Tanaka's history: "His view on the history was beyond the trends of the time, he sympathized rather with the old style of historical perspective than with the historical philosophy [rekishi tetsugaku, 歴史哲学], but he did not impose it to students."[106] Therefore, Matsumoto considered Tanaka's work to be old fashioned since its pure historiography was completely based on historical documents.

Moreover, as an ethnologist, Matsumoto questioned the credibility of the historical records,[107] as it was already argued by Ito Seiji.[108] This is apparent in his statement in his graduation thesis *The Research of the Family in Ancient China*: "Many of Chinese classic texts are of relatively recent period, and there are many forgeries among them, thus, they largely lack the credibility."[109] Matsumoto's teacher Yanagita shared his distrust in written documents. Yanagita criticized historians for using unreliable documents in his paper *Miscellaneous Talks on Musashino*: "... senseis who research the history of Musashino should not easily agree with such kind of quick conclusion; they give too much weight to the oral tradition or old records of the locality.

---

106. Matsumoto, Nobuhiro "Tanaka hakushi wo itamu," *Mita hyōron*, dai 316 gō, Mita hyōron hakkōjo, December 1923, p. 27.
107. This doubt was typical for ethnology as Wilhelm Schmidt suggested in his book: "Nevertheless, it still holds good what Ratzel n his day already emphasized, that history is not dependent upon the existence of written sources." Schmidt, Wilhelm *The Culture Historical Method of Ethnology. The Scientific Approach to the Racial Question*, translated by S. A. Sieber, New York: Fortuny's, 1939, p. 17. (*Handbuch der Methode der kulturhistorischen Ethnologie*, 1937).
108. Itō, Seiji "Matsumoto Nobuhiro – 'Nampōsetsu' no kaitakusha," *Bunka jinruigaku gunzō*, Nihonhen (3), Kyōto: Akademia shuppankai, 1988, pp. 233–234.
109. Matsumoto, Nobuhiro "Shina kodai seishi no kenkyū," *Mita hyōron*, dai 3, 4, 5 gō, Mita hyōron hakkōjo, 1921, p. 411.

Only few old records are older than 200 years, many of them are oral tradition written three or four generations ago. Moreover, there is rare evidence that there is no mistake in the oral tradition, it is so to speak, a reference, which means that there should be other materials for presumption..."[110] Due to doubts about the credibility of the written documents, Yanagita conducted his research from the material collected through his field work from the existing customs among the people in the Japanese countryside.

However, Matsumoto collected his material only from the works of other scholars and from old documents. Therefore, he thought that the comparison with the contemporary culture of the primitive people recorded in other scholars' work could make up for the deficiency of the old documents: "... by comparison with the similarities of the present uncivilized ethnic groups, we can clarify the insufficiencies in the legends, writings, customs, systems etc. existing in ancient China."[111] Therefore, Matsumoto combined the material from the old documents with the material on the contemporary primitive people in his writings.

As a result of Matsumoto's adoption of the ethnological methods, Matsumoto's approach to the research on ancient history differed from those of historians Tanaka, Hashimoto, and Kato Shigeshi. In this sense, his graduation thesis *The Research of the Family in Ancient China* represented an exception in the historical circles of Keio University because Matsumoto adopted the ethnological theory of exogamy from Endo Ryukichi's theory of totem clans based on Frazer's theory of totemism.[112] This approach adopted by Matsumoto was criticized by orthodox historians at Keio University. Namely, Hashimoto argued the impossibility of reconstruction of the ancient past due to the lack of supportive material, and refused the application of totemism to explain the ancient Chinese family.[113] This was because, unlike

---

110. Yanagita, Kunio "Musashino zatsuwa," *Tōkōkō*, I, Keiō gijuku taiikukai sangakubu nenpō, Shuppan kagaku sōgō kenkyūjo, 1919, p. 30.
111. Matsumoto, Nobuhiro "Shina kodai seishi no kenkyū" (1921), Tōa *minzoku bunkaronkō*, Seibundō shinkōsha, 1968, p. 412.
112. Ibid., pp. 417–425.

Matsumoto, Hashimoto did not believe in universalism; therefore, he denied ethnological methods based on the hypothesis of the universal primitive culture. However, despite this rejection, Matsumoto continued to apply the ethnological comparative method and the theory of totemism in his further writings. This was because Tylor and Frazer's ethnology was generally accepted among the Japanese scholars of ethnology and folklore studies, including Matsumoto's teachers Kawai and Yanagita.

Nevertheless, with Hashimoto's opposition, Matsumoto rarely discussed Chinese history after his graduation; this was because Hashimoto became the leading personality in this field at Keio University after Tanaka's sudden death in 1923.[114] According to Ito Seiji, Matsumoto tried to avoid conflicts with Hashimoto who disliked sinology influenced by ethnology.[115] This reason is also confirmed by Matsumoto's statement in his paper *Reminiscences of Late Professor Hashimoto Masukichi*: "...at this point, I was aware that this historic theory cannot receive Hashimoto sensei's support, moreover, in fact, doctor [Hashimoto] strongly rejected the existence of totemism in China, so after that, as for writing a paper concerning ancient history of China, I had to quail in order to prevent sensei's severe refutation."[116]

In conclusion, Matsumoto emerged as an ethnologist since he gave preference to his ethnological methodology for examining history over the existing historical methodology. From the ethnological methodology based on universalism, Matsumoto adopted comparative

---

113. Hashimoto, Masukichi *Tōyōshi kōza ikki*, Jitaiko gokanmatsu, Ji taiko, Kokushi kōshūkai, 1926, pp. 132-134. Matsumoto, Nobuhiro "Ko Hashimoto Masukichi kyoju no tsuioku," *Shigaku*, dai 219 kan, dai 4 go, Mita Shigakkai, 1957, p. 104 (468).
114. Matsumoto, Nobuhiro "Ko Hashimoto Masukichi kyoju no tsuioku," *Shigaku*, dai 219 kan, dai 4 go, Mita Shigakkai, 1957, p. 104.
115. Itō, Seiji "Matsumoto Nobuhiro – 'Nampōsetsu' no kaitakusha," *Bunka jinruigaku gunzō*, Nihonhen (3), Kyōto: Akademia shuppankai, 1988, p. 233.
116. Matsumoto, Nobuhiro "Ko Hashimoto Masukichi kyoju no tsuioku," *Shigaku*, dai 219 kan, dai 4 go, Mita Shigakkai, 1957, p. 104.

research, combining it with Western scholars' ethnological theories, and supplemented it with material from historical documents. The reason was that he shared Yanagita's doubt about the credibility of the historical documents. Thus, by following Yanagita and Kawai, Matsumoto became an evolutionist ethnologist despite majoring in history and being criticized by historians.

3. Matsumoto Nobuhiro's ideas regarding Southeast Asia

The previous sections suggested that Matsumoto discussed Southeast Asia from the perspective of cultural evolutionism and universalism. Matsumoto's ideas regarding Southeast Asia can be traced from his early writings in 1919–1923. During this time, Southeast Asia was an unexplored region for the Japanese people. Therefore, Matsumoto could not gain sufficient knowledge about Southeast Asia due to the lack of sources in Japan. Matsumoto majored in Oriental history; this did not cover Southeast Asia at all.[117] Furthermore, none of his teachers had any linkage to Southeast Asia. Nevertheless, Matsumoto began discussing Southeast Asia in his papers on the ancient Japanese and Chinese cultures.

During 1919–1923, Matsumoto did not use geographical terms such as the South Seas or Southeast Asia in his writings. He only mentioned some examples of the primitive people in Southeast Asia, such as the Reichihi tribe in Sumatra in his paper *The Mountain Legends in Fudoki*[118] and the Mán, Thái, Noi, and Lolo tribes living in Indochina in his paper *The Family in Ancient China and Totemism*.[119] Matsumoto discussed these Southeast Asian people among many other people in

---

117. Hashimoto, Masukichi *Tōyōshi kōza ikki*, Jitaiko gokanmatsu, Ji taiko, Kokushi kōshūkai, 1926.
118. Matsumoto, Nobuhiro "Fudoki ni arawaretaru santake densetsu," *Tōkōkō, II*, Keiō gijuku taiikukai sangakubu nenpō, Shuppan kagaku sōgō kenkyūjo, 1920, p. 39.
119. Matsumoto, Nobuhiro Shina kosei to tōtemizumu" (1921–1922), *Tōa minzoku bunkaronkō*, Seibundō shinkōsha, 1968, pp. 484–5.

comparison with ancient Japanese and Chinese people.[120] In this respect, he was not especially interested in Southeast Asia.

Matsumoto only focused on the primitive people of Southeast Asia, namely on the culture of the tribes that comprised marginalized people, living in relative isolation from the influence of the majority culture. Hence, he did not discuss the culture of the majority races in Southeast Asia, such as the Vietnamese, Cambodians, or Laotians who were considered to be semi-civilized. Consequently, Matsumoto's image of Southeast Asia was limited to the marginalized people who he considered to be primitive.

The absence of the geographical naming of Southeast Asia reflects Japan's situation in the early 1920s. Japan only received the South Pacific Mandate in 1919. Therefore, the public interest in the region of South Seas was still low, and mainly low-class Japanese migrated to these areas. Advocators of Japan's Southern Advance Theory (*Nanshinron*, 南進論) called for Japanese economic expansion southward, and some Japanese companies started their business there.[121] (Japan's Southern Advance Theory is discussed in Chapter 4.) However, Matsumoto was indifferent to economic issues in general. Moreover, Matsumoto's teacher Yanagita had just begun his discussion on Japan's connection with Southern regions (Yanagita's opinions on the Southern culture is discussed in Chapter 2 Section 4.3.). Therefore, although Japan showed economic concern for the South Seas, this region had not been the object of the academic research yet; thus, Matsumoto's discussion regarding Southeast Asia was rare in this period.

Since no Japanese scholars looked at Southeast Asia at this time, Matsumoto drew information about Southeast Asia from Western

---

120. Matsumoto, Nobuhiro "Shina kodai seishi no kenkyū" (1921), *Tōa minzoku bunkaronkō*, Seibundō shinkōsha, 1968, pp. 419, 437, 439. "Shina kosei to tōtemizumu" (1921-1922), *Tōa minzoku bunkaronkō*, Seibundō shinkōsha, 1968, pp. 454, 462, 472, 473, 478, 479, 482-5. "Kodai Shina minzoku no sosen saishi," *Shigaku*, dai 1 kan, dai 4 gō, Mita Shigakkai, 1922, pp. 50, 67.
121. Yano, Tooru *Nanshin no keifu*, Chūōkōronsha, 1975. *Nihon no Nan'yō shikan*, Chūōkōronsha, 1979.

scholars. In his paper *The Family in Ancient China and Totemism*, (1921-1922) he cited a French scholar's arguments concerning Southeast Asia: "In general, customs similar to totemism are practiced among races of Indochina even now. According to Henri Maspero's research, the tribes Thai and Noi have a custom of a taboo concerning the names of the family and the objects of the same names."[122] Furthermore, Matsumoto learned about Southeast Asian culture from Marcel Granet's book *Festivals and Songs of Ancient China* (1919) because he closely observed the mating customs in his paper *The Mountain Legends in Fudoki* where he discussed the Japanese custum *utagaki* (Section 2.3). Therefore, Matsumoto's writings indicate that Matsumoto drew on findings from French scholars on Southeast Asian culture.

This section examines how Matsumoto discussed Southeast Asian peoples in his writings. First, it shows that Matsumoto focused on primitive culture in Southeast Asia and then discusses Matsumoto's application of the Western ethnological theories to his ideas regarding Southeast Asian culture.

3.1. Southeast Asian culture as a primitive culture

This section examines how Matsumoto discussed Southeast Asia in his ethnological writings. It shows that Matsumoto perceived that Southeast Asian people were primitive because he considered their marital custom to be promiscuous and their religious thinking to be naïve.

Matsumoto often used the word "primitive" or "uncivilized" in his writings, but he did not specify its meaning in relation to other stages in the human evolution. He followed the practice of many ethnologists who discussed only the primitive culture without defining its stage in the evolutionary process. Among them, eminent ethnologist James George Frazer, who was one of Matsumoto's most cited authors, did not present any sequence of stages in his works. Frazer was obviously concerned with the lower stages of the development since he used the

---

122. Matsumoto, Nobuhiro "Shina kosei to tōtemizumu" (1921-1922), *Tōa minzoku bunkaronkō*, Seibundō shinkōsha, 1968, pp. 484-5.

terms "primitive," "barbarous," "ruder", and "savage."[123] Similar to Western ethnologists, Matsumoto used the term "primitive" for indicating the lower stages of the human evolution.

Matsumoto's writings suggest that Matsumoto considered Southeast Asian culture to be primitive. In his paper *The Mountain Legends in Fudoki*, he introduced his comparison of the ancient Japanese culture with the culture of other primitive people in these words: "I do not have space to compare *utagaki* broadly with the customs of uncivilized peoples [*mikaijin*, 未開人] to build an argument now, so I will just mention a few examples."[124] Then, he noted the marital custom of people in ancient Sukhotai (Thai kingdom): "In ancient Sukhotai Land, single men and women freely chose their spouse, and after living together for one year, they were permitted to freely decide the course of their action. Considering the above mentioned examples, *utagaki* is not simply habit that was practiced only in ancient Japan, but it is a common habit broadly discovered among many uncivilized peoples [*mikaijin*, 未開人]."[125] Furthermore, he added the custom of the contemporary people in Sumatra, which is cited in Section 2.4.1.[126]

The three quotations in Matsumoto's paper indicated that Matsumoto considered Southeast Asian people to be uncivilized, primitive people in his comparison with the ancient Japanese culture. Thus, he borrowed the method of the Western ethnologists who used the comparison with the contemporary primitive people for reconstructing the ancient culture of the contemporary civilized people in accordance with universalism. In Matsumoto's writing, the customs of ancient Japan, ancient Sukhotai, and the contemporary Rechihi tribe in Sumatra suggested a promiscuous relationship between men and women from the perspective of the contemporary modern people,

---

123. Frazer, James George *The Golden Bough. A study in magic and religion*, Wordsworth Reference, 1993, pp. XI, 2, 6, 10, 48, etc.
124. Matsumoto, Nobuhiro "Fudoki ni arawaretaru santake densetsu," *Tōkōkō, II*, Keiō gijuku taiikukai sangakubu nenpō, Shuppan kagaku sōgō kenkyūjo, 1920, p. 36.
125. Ibid., p. 38.
126. Ibid., p. 39.

with different marriage norms. In this manner, Matsumoto's idea had origins in the hypothesis of evolutionist scholars that the primitive people were promiscuous.

In addition, Matsumoto considered Southeast Asian people to be naïve because he borrowed the Western scholars' opinion that naivety was a typical feature of primitive culture. Matsumoto's belief in the naivety of the primitive people is apparent from his vocabulary. He indicated the naivety of the ancient Japanese people in *The Mountain Legends in Fudoki*: "Naïve ideas of ancient people [*kodaijin no sobokuna kangae*, 古代人の素朴な考え] concerning mountains were recorded as traces in various legends remaining in ancient records."[127] In *Ancestor Worship of People in Ancient China*, he mentioned the ancient Chinese people as follows: "From the naïve psychology [*sobokuna shinri kara*, 素朴な心理から], they called the soul by names *hun* [魂], *hunqi* [魂気] or *zhiqi* [知気]."[128] Moreover, Matsumoto suggested that considering this primitive thinking, naivety is a common opinion held by modern Japanese people in their early beginnings. This is clear from his words in *The Research of Mount Tai*: "Now we laugh at the stupid superstitions of the ancient people, then maybe generations of few thousand years later will laugh at many ancestral idols of our present time."[129]

From the afore mentioned quotations in three of Matsumoto's writings, it can be concluded that Matsumoto considered primitive people to be naïve because of their religiosity. This was not an unusual perception of an educated Japanese man who believed in evolutionism. This opinion was based on the Western scholars' argument that science was superior to religion and symbolized the top of the human cultural evolution. Thus, in Matsumoto's era, many scholars argued

---

127. Matsumoto, Nobuhiro "Fudoki ni arawaretaru santake densetsu," *Tōkōkō, II*, Keiō gijuku taiikukai sangakubu nenpō, Shuppan kagaku sōgō kenkyūjo, 1920, p. 23.
128. Matsumoto, Nobuhiro "Kodai Shina minzoku no sosen saishi," *Shigaku*, dai 1 kan, dai 4 gō, Mita Shigakkai, 1922, p. 49.
129. Matsumoto, Nobuhiro "Taizan no kenkyū," *Tōkōkō, III*, Keiō gijuku taiikukai sangakubu nenpō, Shuppan kagaku sōgō kenkyūjo, 1921, p. 40.

the naivety of religious thinking. Frazer, Matsumoto's favorite ethnologist, even applied this approach to Christianity.[130] Thus, it was common for believers in evolutionism in Matsumoto's era to surmise cultural inferiority of contemporary Southeast Asian peoples due to this perceived naivety stemming from their religious thinking.

Matsumoto's ethnological study indecated that Matsumoto was concerned with the primitive spirit of the primitive people within the realm of religiosity. Consequently, he did not discuss the national spirit although it was usual during his time. For example, Fukuzawa Yukichi,[131] the founder of Keio Gijuku, or Matsumoto's teachers such as Tanaka and Kanokogi Kazunobu discussed the Japanese national spirit. Matsumoto's teachers had an idea that the national spirit existed at the level of the nation-state, which was considered to be important during Matsumoto's era. However, Matsumoto did not reflect on Tanaka's ideas or Kanokogi's ideas regarding the national spirit in his writings, but this did not mean he was unimpressed by them.[132] This is because Matsumoto focused on the study of people who did not have any notion of the nation-state. In contrast to his non-ethnologist teachers, Matsumoto perceived the spirit to encompass the entire humanity in the primitive stage of the human evolution.

In summary, Matsumoto discussed Southeast Asian people because he considered them to be the holders of primitive culture. Based on universalism, he believed that this comparison with Southeast Asian culture could contribute to an improved understanding on the ancient culture of Japan and China. Thus, due to this ethnological approach, Matsumoto's image of Southeast Asia was limited to its primitive culture of marginalized people, which he considered to be culturally inferior to the contemporary Japanese and Chinese people.

---

130. Frazer, James George *Folk-lore in the Old Testament: studies in comparative religion, legend and law*, 1919.
131. Fukuzawa, Yukichi *An Outline of a Theory of Civilization*, New York: Columbia University Press, 2008, p. 22.
132. Matsumoto, Nobuhiro *Matsumoto Nobuhiro shinpen zakki*, Matsumoto Chie, 1982, p. 39.

3.2. Matsumoto's application of ethnological theories to Southeast Asian culture

This section discusses Matsumoto's application of the Western ethnological theories to Southeast Asian culture for its interpretation. Matsumoto's adoption of Western ethnological theories has been already suggested by previous research, which indicated the importance of Western scholars in Matsumoto's work. Ito Seiji[133] and Chikamori Masashi[134] claimed the importance of French scholar Lucien Lévy-Bruhl. Furthermore, Chikamori Masashi argued the importance of British scholar James George Frazer.[135] Therefore, this section examines the influence of Lévy-Bruhl's and Frazer's theories on Matsumoto's ideas regarding Southeast Asian people. In addition, it mentions the influence of Wilhelm Wundt's theories since Matsumoto was influenced by Wundt's ethnology as it has been discussed in Section 2.1.

According to Ito Seiji[136] and Chikamori Masashi[137], Matsumoto was interested in the interpretation of the primitive culture by French sociologist Lucien Lévy-Bruhl (1857–1939). Matsumoto studied Lévy-Bruhl's ideas upon the recommendation of Russian folklorist Nevsky to whom Matsumoto was introduced to by Yanagita.[138] As suggested by the titles of Lévy-Bruhl's books *The Mental Functions in the Inferior Societies* and *The Primitive Mentality*[139], Lévy-Bruhl developed a theory regarding the mentality of the primitive people in the inferior stage of

---

133. Itō, Seiji "Matsumoto Nobuhiro – 'Nampōsetsu' no kaitakusha," *Bunka jinruigaku gunzō*, Nihonhen (3), Kyōto: Akademia shuppankai, 1988, p. 230. "Matsumoto Nobuhiro to gakumon," *Keiō gijuku daigaku gengo kenkyūjo hōkokushū*, Keiō gijuku daigaku, dai 24 kan, 1992, p. 120.
134. Interview with Chikamori Masashi, 13 October 2012 and 10 December 2012, Keio University, Tokyo.
135. Ibid.
136. Itō, Seiji "Matsumoto Nobuhiro – 'Nampōsetsu' no kaitakusha," *Bunka jinruigaku gunzō*, Nihonhen (3), Kyōto: Akademia shuppankai, 1988, p. 230. "Matsumoto Nobuhiro to gakumon," Keiō gijuku *daigaku gengo kenkyūjo hōkokushū*, Keiō gijuku daigaku, dai 24 kan, 1992, p. 120.
137. Interview with Chikamori Masashi, 13 October 2012 and 10 December 2012, Keio University, Tokyo.

cultural development. According to his theory, primitive people do not perceive the world like the civilized people despite having the same senses and cerebral structure because their mentality is mystic and pre-logic.[140] This corresponds to Matsumoto's ideas that Southeast Asian people have a naïve culture. However, Matsumoto did not refer to Lévy-Bruhl's works in his writings. Therefore, Lévy-Bruhl's concrete influence on Matsumoto is not clear.

In contrast, the influence of Frazer's and Wundt's interpretation of the primitive culture can be traced in many of Matsumoto's writings. Matsumoto absorbed the theories of Frazer and Wundt because they were important for Matsumoto's teachers Yanagita and Kawai.

In particular, Frazer's influence was significant for Matsumoto's ethnology. This was because Matsumoto was influenced by Frazer's ideas during his studies at Sorbonne University (1924-1928) under the scholar of the French School of Sociology who considered Frazer as their teacher. (The influence of Matsumoto's studies in France on Matsumoto's ideas regarding Southeast Asia is discussed in Chapter 2.) Moreover, Matsumoto's continuous reference to Frazer shows persisting importance of Frazer's ideas for Matsumoto even in the 1930s and 1940s.[141] Accordingly, Matsumoto's adoption of Frazer's ethnological theories helped classify Matsumoto as an evolutionist ethnologist.

In relation to the primitive culture of Southeast Asian people, Matsumoto adopted the theory of animism, totemism, and magic from Frazer and Wundt. Matsumoto studied about animism (belief in souls) and totemism (belief in totem) from Frazer's books *The Golden Bough* (1890-1915) and *Totemism and Exogamy* (1910) and Wundt's book *Elements of Folk Psychology. Outlines of a Psychological History of*

---

138. Matsumoto, Nobuhiro "Tōhoku no tabi," *Teihon Yanagita Kunioshū*, Geppō 1, Chikumashobō, 1962, p. 3. Itō, Seiji "Hito to gakumon, Matsumoto Nobuhiro," *Shakai jinruigaku nenpō*, Tōkyō toritsu daigaku shakai jinrui gakkai, dai 12 kan, 1986, p. 120.
139. Lévy-Bruhl, Lucien *Les fonctions mentales dans les sociétés inférieures* (1910), *La mentalité primitive* (1922).
140. Lévy-Bruhl, Lucien *Les fonctions mentales dans les société inférieures*, Paris: Librarie Félix Alcan, 1922 (7th edition), pp. 37, 457.

the Development of Mankind (1912).

First, Matsumoto discussed the culture of the contemporary primitive people of Southeast Asia in relation to animism. In his writing *The Mountain Legends in Fudoki* (1920), Matsumoto indicated that animism was practiced among primitive people: "The ancient people considered the soul the same as the breath, and thought that it floated in the heaven after the death."[142] Against this backdrop in the general belief of primitive people in souls, Matsumoto refered to the belief of a Sumatran tribe in the same paper (see the quotation on page 49).[143] However, Matsumoto did not engage in a detailed analysis of this Southeast Asian belief. This means that he only associated it with the concept of animism provided by Western ethnologists. In this manner, Matsumoto thought that animism existed among the contemporary primitive people of Southeast Asia because their belief somehow corresponded to the ethnological concept of animism.

Second, Matsumoto indicated totemism (belief in totem) among the contemporary primitive people of Southeast Asia. For example, Matsumoto wrote in *The Family in Ancient China and Totemism* as follows: "In general, customs similar to totemism are practiced among races of Indochina even now. According to Henri Maspero's research, the tribes Thai and Noi have a custom of taboo concerning the names of the family and the objects of the same names. The family Lau cannot eat bamboo shoots ... And this taboo cannot be removed even by

---

141. Matsumoto, Nobuhiro "Chamu no yashizoku to 'yashi no mi' setsuwa," *Minzokugaku*, dai 5 kan, dai 6 gō, 1933, p. 449; "Nihon shinwa ni tsuite," *Iwanami kōza Nihon rekishi*, Iwanami shoten, 1934, p. 13; "Furansu ni okeru minzokugakuteki kenkyū," *Nihon minzokugaku kenkyū*, (ed. by Yanagita), Iwanami shoten, 1935, pp. 383, 386; "Jōdai Indoshina no kōkogakuteki kenkyū ni tsuite - Korani joshi kizō dozoku hyōhon wo chūshin ni" (1937), *Indoshina minzoku to bunka*, Iwanami shoten, 1942.11, p. 165; "Annan shiryō ni arawareru Indoshina sanchi minzoku," *Andō kyōju kanreki Shukuga kinenronbunshū*, Andō kyōju kanreki Shukuga kinenkaihen, Sanseidō, 1940, p. 1010.
142. Matsumoto, Nobuhiro "Fudoki ni arawaretaru santake densetsu," *Tōkōkō, II*, Keiō gijuku taiikukai sangakubu nenpō, Shuppan kagaku sōgō kenkyūjo, 1920, p. 24
143. Ibid., p. 39.

purification. Further, families of Thai and Noi people have ruling power over the tiger. Then, they have taboo of the cat meat or of hunting. Further, they call the dead tiger their grandfather and must conduct funeral rites for him."[144] Thus, Matsumoto indicated totemism among the contemporary primitive people of Southeast Asia by citing Western researchers' findings concerning Southeast Asian culture. In this respect, he believed that the contemporary primitive people of Southeast Asia followed totemism because it was argued by Western ethnologists. He namely believed in Frazer's arguments on totemism as it is shown in his paper *The Family in Ancient China and Totemism*: "There is no doubt that Frazer's theory considering sufficiently the material about totemism is most credible in the dispute of this kind."[145] By highlighting totemism of these Southeast Asian people in his paper *The Family in Ancient China and Totemism*, Matsumoto attempted to demonstrate the existence of totemism in ancient China.[146]

Third, Matsumoto borrowed Frazer's theory on magic. In his book *The Golden Bough*, Frazer presented his theory of sympathetic and contagious magic and argued that the belief in magic was an error "deduced immediately from elementary process of reasoning."[147] Matsumoto adopted this theory of magic in his paper *The Family in Ancient China and Totemism*: "It is because the uncivilized people believe in the close relation of the name and the object of the same name. For bringing growth to the animals and plants that they eat, they appeal to the magical methods. These methods are sympathetic or imitative magic and contagious magic."[148] Since evolutionist ethnologists considered belief in magic to be a typical feature of the primitive people, Matsumoto surmised that contemporary Southeast Asian

---

144. Matsumoto, Nobuhiro "Shina kosei to tōtemizumu" (1921-1922), *Tōa minzoku bunkaronkō*, Seibundō shinkōsha, 1968, pp. 484-5.
145. Ibid., p. 454.
146. Ibid., p. 461, 490.
147. Frazer, James George *The Golden Bough. A study in magic and religion*, Wordsworth Reference, 1993, pp. 19, 54-56.
148. Matsumoto, Nobuhiro "Shina kosei to tōtemizumu" (1921-1922), *Tōa minzoku bunkaronkō*, Seibundō shinkōsha, 1968, p. 459.

primitive people believed in magic.

However, Matsumoto did not understand the theories of Western ethnologists properly. For example, he claimed to have adopted the theory of totemic clans in his graduation thesis *The Research of the Family in Ancient China*: "I finally followed the theory of totemic clans."[149] However, he did not discuss the belief in totems in this thesis at all. Instead, he mentioned many theories by Western scholars on exogamy (*izoku kekkon*, 異族結婚)[150]: "Therefore, I will discuss various theories related to exogamy, and I will introduce Morgan's and Frazer's theories."[151] Thus, Matsumoto mistook exogamy for totemism in his graduation thesis. This is because, according to Frazer, exogamy was considered to be a typical feature of the primitive people who followed totemism.[152] This means that Matsumoto did not have sufficient understanding of Frazer's theories on totemism and exogamy.

In summary, Matsumoto believed that ethnological theories could emphasize the naïve culture of the primitive people, including contemporary Southeast Asian people. Therefore, he adopted the theories of animism, totemism, and magic, interpreting the culture of these primitive people mainly from Frazer and Wundt. However, he matched the data on Southeast Asian customs with these ethnological concepts based on a few similarities and without any further analysis since he did not understand the Western ethnologists' theories sufficiently.

---

149. Matsumoto, Nobuhiro "Shina kodai seishi no kenkyū" (1921), *Tōa minzoku bunkaronkō*, Seibundō shinkōsha, 1968, p. 425.
150. Frazer defined exogamy as "the rule which obliges a man to marry a woman of a different clan from his own". Frazer, James George *The Golden Bough. A study in magic and religion*, Wordsworth Reference, 1993, p. 152.
151. Matsumoto, Nobuhiro "Shina kodai seishi no kenkyū" (1921), *Tōa minzoku bunkaronkō*, Seibundō shinkōsha, 1968, p. 440.
152. Frazer, James George *Totemism and Exogamy. A Treatise on Certain Early Forms of Superstition and Society*, Vol. IV, Macmillan and Co., London, 1910, p. 8.

4. Conclusion

The analysis of Matsumoto's writings in 1919–1923 revealed that Matsumoto discovered the culture of Southeast Asia people when he began studying evolutionist ethnology in relation to the issue of Japanese origins as a student of history at Keio University. He learnt evolutionist ethnology (Frazer, Tylor, and Wundt) and Oriental history influenced by ethnology (Chavannes and Granet) through his Japanese teachers (namely Kawai, Yanagita, and Kato). He was especially attracted to Frazer's works and French sinologists' works influenced by Frazer since this kind of ethnology was popular among the Japanese folklorists at that time. Consequently, Matsumoto began conducting research on Southeast Asia because he wanted to compare the ancient Japanese and Chinese cultures with the culture of contemporary Southeast Asian people to clarify Japanese and Chinese origins. From the perspective of evolutionist ethnology, his study established connection between Southeast Asian culture and the Japanese and Chinese cultures in the primitive stage of evolution.

Chapter 2:
Giving importance to Southeast Asia during 1924–1932

1. Introduction

During 1924–1932, Matsumoto's ideas regarding Southeast Asia were formed during his studies at Sorbonne University (1924–1928), which significantly influenced his entire scholarship, and through, Yanagita's influence. His study in France was a natural step. Matsumoto mentioned that he was gradually advancing in the direction of the French School of Sociology that followed Frazer's ethnology,[1] as shown in the previous chapter. Matsumoto's study at the Sorbonne University was a unique experience since Matsumoto was introduced to the Western academic circles and had access to knowledge unavailable in Japan. In particular, he broadened his knowledge of Southeast Asia through his encounters with scholars well versed in the subject.

In 1924, Matsumoto arrived in France to discover many new things. In the 1920s, Europe was recovering from the damages of World War I. Yet, France, being one of the key members of the Triple Entente, was on the winning side and entered an era of academic prosperity. Thus, in 1924, when French academic circles represented one of the world's most influential centers in Oriental research.[2] Matsumoto was enrolled as a self-financed student in Oriental studies at Sorbonne University where he attended lectures at École Nationale des Langues

---

1. Matsumoto, Nobuhiro "Ko Orikuchi Shinobu hakase to 'kodai kenkyū'," *Nihon oyobi Nihonjin*, 7(9), Kanaobun'endō, 1956–09, p. 102.
2. Matsumoto, Nobuhiro *Matsumoto Nobuhiro shinpen zakki*, Matsumoto Chie, 1982, p. 41.

Orientales Vivantes and École Practique des Hautes Etudes of the Sorbonne University.[3] During his studies there, Matsumoto witnessed the foundation of the Institute of Ethnology with the support of the Ministry of Colonies at Sorbonne University in 1925.[4] This was an event of great importance for Matsumoto as an ethnologist because it represented a significant step in the establishment of ethnology as an academic discipline in France.

Matsumoto's stay coincided with the golden age of the French School of Sociology. Marcel Mauss, the leader of the school, published his famous work *The Gift* in 1923–1924. This writing, in which Mauss compared societies of the primitive people with the ancient European societies, considerably influenced the ethnological circles and academic circles in general. Matsumoto studied sociological research under Marcel Mauss and his disciple Marcel Granet. He was especially inspired by Mauss' analysis of the Southern Pacific society and Granet's analysis of ancient Chinese society in relation to Southeast Asia.

In the French ethnologist circles, Matsumoto came in contact with scholars conducting research on Southeast Asia because France had established a research institute École Française d'Extrême-Orient (EFEO) in Indochina in 1901.[5] One of the researchers of Indochina, Jean Przyluski, became Matsumoto's supervisor. Przyluski transmitted to Matsumoto his deep interest in Indochina. Moreover, since French scholars conducted a local research in foreign areas under Western

---

3. Matsumoto, Nobuhiro "Furansu ni okeru Shina kenkyū," *Shina kenkyū*-Keiō gijuku Mochidzuki kikin Shina kenkyūkai-hen, Iwanamishoten, 1930, pp. 386, 389. Matsumoto, Nobuhiro *Le japonais et les langues austroasiatiques: étude de vocabulaire comparé*, P. Geuthner, Paris, 1928, p. 1. Matsumoto, Nobuhiro *Nihon shinwa no kenkyū*, Dōbunkan, 1931, p. 2.
4. Matsumoto, Nobuhiro "Pari yori," *Minzoku*, dai 2 kan, dai 1 gō, Minzoku hakkōjo, 1926, p. 141.
5. EFEO was founded in December 1898, but its title was decided in January 1900 and its institutional stability was assured by a French presidential decree of 21 April 1901. Clémentine-Ojha, Catherine and Manguin, Pierre-Yves *A Century in Asia. The History of École française d'Extrême-Orient 1898-2006*, Edition Didier Millet, EFEO, 2007, p. 18.

(mainly French) rule, they also brought back various specimens with them. Therefore, Paris provided Matsumoto with numerous occasions to see artifacts from distant countries, including those of Southeast Asia that were exhibited in museums, such as the Guimet Museum or the National Archaeological Museum.[6]

Hence, Matsumoto was able to study under the leading scholars of Oriental studies, including Indochina studies, and see objects from Southeast Asia and other regions with his own eyes. In short, his studies in Paris provided Matsumoto a chance to develop more as an ethnologist, with a special interest in Southeast Asia under the influence of the French School of Sociology.

In the meantime, the Japanese awareness of the South Seas grew slowly due to the Japanese territorial acquisition of the Southern Pacific Islands called the South Seas islands (Nanyō shotō, 南洋諸島) in 1919. (Japan's Southern advance is separately discussed in Chapter 4 that focuses on political influence on Matsumoto's works.) The first research center specializing in ethnography of the South Seas under the Japanese Empire was established in Taiwan (Taihoku Imperial University) in 1928. Coincidently, Matsumoto's teacher Utsushikawa Nenozo (1884-1947) was charged with introduceing ethnological studies there.[7] Therefore, Matsumoto ended his studies at Sorbonne University at the time when the South Seas studies in Japan was about to evolve.

Matsumoto's French education was unique in Japan because he was the first Japanese scholar in Oriental studies and ethnology to be awarded an academic degree in France.[8] He immediately became an associate professor of Oriental history at the Keio University Faculty

---

6. Matsumoto, Nobuhiro *Le japonais et les langues austroasiatiques: étude de vocabulaire comparé*, P. Geuthner, Paris, 1928, p. 1.
7. Itō, Seiji "Matsumoto Nobuhiro – 'Nampōsetsu' no kaitakusha," *Bunka jinruigaku gunzō*, Nihonhen (3), Akademia shuppankai, Kyōto, 1988, p. 232. Ōbayashi, Taryō "Kaisetsu," *Nihon minzokugaku no kigen I: shinwa-densetsu*, Kōdansha, 1978, p. 401. Hirafuji, Kikuko "Shakaigakuteki kenkyū – Matsumoto Nobuhiro no shinwa kenkyū ni okeru Furansu shakaigakuha no eikyō," *Shinwagaku to Nihon no kamigami*, Kōbunkan, 2004, pp. 33–41.

of Letters in 1928 and started teaching Oriental history (from 1928) and sociology (from 1930).[9] However, as indicated by Chikamori Masashi,[10] hardly anybody understood Matsumoto's aspirations concerning ethnology and Southeast Asia. This was because the academic situation in Japan differed from that in France. In contrast to the situation in France, ethnology had not been officially established in Japan yet. Moreover, while it was quite common to research about Indochina in France, Southeast Asia remained almost unexplored by Japanese scholars. Only a few Japanese scholars, such as Utsushikawa or Yanagita, became interested in the the South Seas Region. They focused on the Southern regions under Japanese control, such as the Ryukyu Islands, Taiwan, and the Southern Pacific Islands under the Japanese mandate. Due to these conditions in 1924–1932, Matsumoto could neither teach ethnology that he learnt at the Sorbonne University yet nor broadly share his interest in Southeast Asia.

As a result of this situation in Japan, Matsumoto employed the Japanese geographical concept of the South Seas in his research on Southeast Asia. Among the previous researchers who discussed Matsumoto, Hirafuji Kikuko, in her paper The Sociological Research - the Influence of the French School of Sociology in Matsumoto's Research of the Mythology, argued that Matsumoto focused on the Southern genealogy of the Japanese myths while being influenced by the French School of Sociology.[11] In his paper *Matsumoto Nobuhiro - a Pioneer of Southward Theory*, Ito mentioned that Matsumoto became gradually interested in Indochina under Przyluski's influence.[12] Fur-

---

8. Kōyama, Shirō "Fuhō," *Shigaku*, dai 51 kan, dai 1/2, Mita Shigakkai, 1981, p. 237. Itō, Seiji "Matsumoto Nobuhiro to gakumon," Keiō gijuku *daigaku gengo kenkyūjo hōkokushū*, Keiō gijuku daigaku, dai 24 kan, 1992, p. 14.
9. Kawakita, Nobuo "Keiō gijuku daigaku bungakubu kyōin tantō kamoku ichiran," *Shigaku*, dai 60 kan, dai 2/3 gō, Mita Shigakkai, 1991, p. 199 (373).
10. Interview with Chikamori Masashi, 23 August and 13 October 2012, Keio University, Tokyo.
11. Hirafuji, Kikuko "Shakaigakuteki kenkyū – Matsumoto Nobuhiro no shinwa kenkyū ni okeru Furansu shakaigakuha no eikyō," *Shinwagaku to Nihon no kamigami*, Kōbunkan, 2004, pp. 34, 38.

thermore, Ito claimed that Matsumoto began exploring the South Seas myths upon Marcel Mauss' recommendation in his several writings about Matsumoto.[13] Furthemore, Ito argued that Matsumoto planned to write a supplementary doctoral thesis on mythology by including a comparison with the Northern culture, but Utsushikawa instigated him to change it and include the Southern culture.[14] Thus, according to the previous research, Matsumoto was influenced by both the French and the Japanese scholars in his study of the South Seas.

However, previous research did not discuss these influences in detail and did not establish the connection between these influences and Matsumoto's ethnological research on Southeast Asia. Since Matsumoto discussed Southeast Asia as a part of the Japanese concept of the South Seas, this chapter examines influences under which Matsumoto conducted research on the South Seas, especially on Southeast Asia, during 1924–1932. It explores the influence of sociologist ethnology, evolutionist ethnology, and diffusionist ethnology on Matsumoto's ideas regarding Southeast Asia.

2. Influence of sociologist ethnology on Matsumoto's ideas regarding Southeast Asia

The influence of the French School of Sociology on Matsumoto's research has been emphasized by many previous researchers. Matsumoto was aware of this sociological influence as it is obvious from the foreword of his book *The Research of the Japanese Myths*: "I

---

12. Itō, Seiji "Matsumoto Nobuhiro – 'Nampōsetsu' no kaitakusha," *Bunka jinruigaku gunzō*, Nihonhen (3), Kyōto: Akademia shuppankai, 1988, p. 231.
13. Itō, Seiji "Hito to gakumon, Matsumoto Nobuhiro," *Shakai jinruigaku nenpō*, Tōkyō toritsu daigaku shakai jinrui gakkai, dai 12 kan, 1986, p. 122. "Matsumoto Nobuhiro – 'Nampōsetsu' no kaitakusha," *Bunka jinruigaku gunzō*, Nihonhen (3), Kyōto: Akademia shuppankai, 1988, p. 236. "Matsumoto Nobuhiro to gakumon," *Keiō gijuku daigaku gengo kenkyūjo hōkokushū*, Keiō gijuku daigaku, dai 24 kan, 1992, p. 14.
14. Itō, Seiji "Matsumoto Nobuhiro – 'Nampōsetsu' no kaitakusha," *Bunka jinruigaku gunzō*, Nihonhen (3), Kyōto: Akademia shuppankai, 1988, p. 232.

published this thesis *The Research in Japanese Mythology* in the series 'French Studies', because I received the influence of Professor Yanagita Kunio, and at the same time I have also received lectures from professors such as Granet, Mauss and Przyluski ... It gives me a great pleasure that in this book I can present to readers some research methods of their sociologiststyle in mythology, especially the French academic style."[15]

As Matsumoto's statement suggested, the sociologist style was a typical feature of the ethnology produced by the scholars of the French School of Sociology. As sociologists, Matsumoto's French teachers Mauss and Granet specialized in the study of primitive societies. They were followers of Frazer's evolutionist ethnology based on uniliniear evolutionism. Therefore, they believed in universalism of the primitive culture. Since the foundations of Matsumoto's ethnology were formed by universalism and unilinear evolutionism, the ideational basic of Mauss and Granet was similar to that of Matsumoto at that time. In addition, Matsumoto's ethnological research focused on society, which was a new approach used by French sociologists of this period.

This section examines the sociological influence on Matsumoto's writings during 1924–1932. First, it discusses Matsumoto's relationships with the scholars of the French School of Sociology, especially Mauss and Granet. Then, it analyzes the influence of Mauss' theories on Matsumoto's writings during 1924–1932. The influence of Matsumoto's supervisor Jean Przyluski is discussed in Section 4 because Przyluski taught Matsumoto diffusionist ethnology although Przyluski presented works influenced by sociologist ethnology.

2.1. The relationship of Marcel Mauss and Marcel Granet with Matsumoto Nobuhiro

The sociological influence on Matsumoto's ethnology concretely comprised the direct influence of the French scholars who taught Matsumoto during his studies at Sorbonne University in 1924–1928.

---

15. Matsumoto, Nobuhiro *Nihon shinwa no kenkyū*, Dōbunkan, 1931, p. 2.

Most notable among these scholars were Marcel Mauss (1872-1950), the leader of the French School of Sociology at that time, and Mauss' disciple Marcel Granet (1884-1940).

2.1.1. Matsumoto Nobuhiro's relationship with Marcel Mauss

Matsumoto studied primitive culture under Mauss' guidance. Matsumoto considered Mauss as "the foremost person in the research of religions of primitive peoples."[16] Mauss taught this subject at the École Practique des Hautes Études of Sorbonne University where Matsumoto studied.[17] Matsumoto became Mauss' admirer after he started attending his lectures from 1924 upon Granet's recommendation.[18] He claimed that Mauss' lectures were among the most useful classes for his research on ancient culture.[19]

Moreover, Matsumoto attended Mauss' lectures at the Institute of Ethnology.[20] As Durkheim's eminent disciple, Mauss naturally became the leader of the sociological circles. Like other scholars such as Lévy-Bruhl and Paul Rivet, he played a significant role in these circles; this was because as a sociologist, he used the results of ethnographic and ethnological research as sources for his sociological research. Consequently, Mauss' work was of great interest for ethnologists. Therefore, Matsumoto closely noted the fact that Mauss presented the guidelines for the collection of research material: "Mauss promptly accepted assignments to make the collection guidelines for ethnography, and he held lectures on it in the research institute every year; but they [the guidelines] were not published."[21] Thus, Matsumoto studied various

---

16. Matsumoto, Nobuhiro "Gendai Furansu ni okeru Tōyōgaku," *Fransu no shakaigakka. Gendai ni okeru shokeikō*, Fransu gakkai, 1930, p. 596.
17. Matsumoto, Nobuhiro "Furansu ni okeru Shina kenkyū," *Shina kenkyū*-Keiō gijuku Mochidzuki kikin Shina kenkyūkai-hen, Iwanamishoten, 1930, p. 390.
18. Matsumoto, Nobuhiro *Matsumoto Nobuhiro shinpen zakki*, Matsumoto Chie, 1982, p. 41.
19. Matsumoto, Nobuhiro "Preface," *Essai sur la mythologie Japonaise*, Paris: P. Geuthner, 1928.
20. Matsumoto, Nobuhiro "Annan ryokōki (daisanshin)," *Minzokugaku*, dai 5 kan, dai 10 gō, Minzokugakkai, 1933, p. 101 (935).

approaches ranging from sociology to ethnology.

Matsumoto considered Mauss' research as a general model for the research on primitive culture, including Japanese culture. In his paper *Folklore Research in France*, Matsumoto emphasized the importance of Mauss' research for ethnology: "Of course Mauss' guidelines cannot be simply applied to the research of social phenomena of a country with a high civilization like Japan, but as I mentioned above, there are many primitive elements remaining in the society of the civilized peoples. And especially when observing the social phenomena historically, the standard of the ethnological observation is a good lesson for reference."[22]

As a universalist, Mauss compared various ethnic groups to clarify the common basics of human society. In his famous work *The Gift*, Mauss particularly examined the primitive society of the contemporary Polynesian, Melanesian, and North West American people and compared them with ancient Semitic, Greek, Roman, Hindu, Germanic, and Celtic customs to clarify the gift as a social phenomenon that is applicable to the entire mankind.[23] Thus, from Mauss' approach, Matsumoto thought that Mauss' ideas were relevant for the research on the primitive stage of any culture, including Japanese and Southeast Asian cultures. Therefore, Matsumoto adopted Mauss' theories in his ethnological writings, as is discussed in Section 2.2.

2.1.2. Matsumoto's relationship with Marcel Granet

Matsumoto practiced Mauss' research methods under his teacher Granet, who had a close relationship with Mauss. Matsumoto described Granet's relationship with Mauss in his paper *Folklore Research in France* (1935): "Granet is Mauss' friend, he applies Mauss' method most accurately in his research of China."[24] Thus, Matsumoto

---

21. Matsumoto, Nobuhiro "Furansu ni okeru minzokugakuteki kenkyū," *Nihon minzokugaku kenkyū*, (ed. by Yanagita), Iwanami shoten, 1935, pp. 365-6.
22. Ibid., p. 377.
23. Mauss, Marcel *The Gift*, translated by W. D. Halls, London: Routledge, 1990.
24. Matsumoto, Nobuhiro "Furansu ni okeru minzokugakuteki kenkyū," *Nihon minzokugaku kenkyū*, (ed. by Yanagita), Iwanami shoten, Tokyo, 1935, p. 382.

was aware that Granet adopted Mauss' sociological methodology in his ethnological research on ancient China.

Matsumoto was interested in Granet's research because it was related to the study of ancient China, a subject that Matsumoto researched in the early 1920s, from an ethnosociological perspective. Before his studies at Sorbonne University, Matsumoto read Granet's writings *Ancient Festivals and Songs of China*[25] and *The Sorolal Polygyny and the Sororate in Feudal China*.[26] In his writings, Granet discussed Chinese culture in comparison with Southeast Asian culture. Matsumoto drew from them for his writings about the mountain beliefs and the culture of ancient China in the early 1920s.[27] Therefore, Matsumoto immediately visited Granet after his arrival to Paris and asked for his permission to attend his lectures.[28]

Matsumoto considered Granet to be a special person because Granet studied sociology under its founder Émile Durkheim like Mauss, and at the same time, was also a student of Édouard Chavannes, who was considered to be the founder of French sinology.[29] Granet researched Far Eastern religions as a chair of geography, history, and institutions of the Far East at the École Nationale des Langues Orientales Vivantes.[30] In Granet's course of Far Eastern religions,

---

25. Granet, Marcel *Fêtes et chansons anciennes de la Chine*, second edition, Paris: Librarie Ernest Leroux, 1929 (first edition 1919).
26. Granet, Marcel *La Polygénie sororale et le sororat dans la Chine féodale*, Paris: Leroux, 1920.
27. Matsumoto, Nobuhiro "Fudoki ni arawaretaru santake densetsu," *Tōkōkō, II*, Keiō gijuku taiikukai sangakubu nenpō, Shuppan kagaku sōgō kenkyūjo, 1920, pp. 23-40. "Shina kodai seishi no kenkyū," *Mita hyōron*, dai 3, 4, 5 gō, Mita hyōron hakkōjo, 1921, pp. 411-452. "Marcel Granet; La Polygynie sororale et la Sororate dans la Chine féodale: Études sur les former anciennes de la polygamie chinoise, Paris, 1920," *Shigaku*, dai 1 kan, dai 4 gō, Mita Shigakkai, 1922, pp. 625-626.
28. Matsumoto, Nobuhiro *Matsumoto Nobuhiro shinpen zakki*, Matsumoto Chie, 1982, p. 41.
29. Matsumoto, Nobuhiro "Furansu ni okeru Shina kenkyū," *Shina kenkyū* Keiō gijuku Mochidzuki kikin Shina kenkyūkai-hen, Iwanamishoten, 1930, p. 386-389. "Granet, Marcel," *Encyclopedia of religion*, second edition, Detroit: Macmillan Reference USA, 2005, pp. 3654-3655.

Matsumoto studied about the religious ceremonies from the Chinese documents. Studying from old documents was a requirement that French teachers at Sorbonne University imposed on their students who were studying about Oriental culture.[31] The study of old documents was typical for Granet, as Matsumoto wrote: "Granet makes the effort to make conclusions from documents limited exclusively on China. Therefore, Granet's research has a close relationship to the interpretation of the documents, and I think that this is Granet's strong point."[32] In short, from Granet, Matsumoto learnt how to discover important data about ancient Oriental culture from written documents which was different from Yanagita's field work approach.

In summary, Matsumoto learnt from Mauss and Granet the sociological approach to ethnological research on the primitive culture based on universalism. In addition, Mauss' and Granet's ethnology contributed to the development of Matsumoto's interest in contemporary Southeast Asia, Southern Pacific, and ancient China.

2.2. The sociological influence on Matsumoto Nobuhiro's writings

This section discusses Mauss and Granet's sociological influence on Matsumoto Nobuhiro's writings during 1928-1932. Among the previous researchers, Ito Seiji,[33] Obayashi Taryo,[34] Hirafuji Kikuko,[35] Furuno

---

30. Matsumoto, Nobuhiro "Gendai Furansu ni okeru Tōyōgaku," *Fransu no shakaigakka. Gendai ni okeru shokeikō*, Fransu gakkai, 1930, p. 596.
31. Matsumoto, Nobuhiro "Furansu ni okeru minzokugakuteki kenkyū," *Nihon minzokugaku kenkyū*, (ed. by Yanagita), Iwanami shoten, Tokyo, 1935, p. 390.
32. Ibid., p. 383.
33. Itō, Seiji "Matsumoto Nobuhiro sensei wo shinonde," *Minzoku kenkyū*, dai 46 kan, dai 1 gō, Minzokugakkai, 1981, p. 126. "Hito to gakumon, Matsumoto Nobuhiro," *Shakai jinruigaku nenpō*, Tōkyō toritsu daigaku shakai jinrui gakkai, dai 12 kan, 1986, pp. 117-131. "Matsumoto Nobuhiro – 'Nampōsetsu' no kaitakusha," *Bunka jinruigaku gunzō*, Nihonhen (3), Kyōto: Akademia shuppankai, 1988, pp. 225-242. "Minzokugaku, Fōkuroa, Tōyō shigaku no hazamade" (Dainikai zadankai, Mitashigaku no hyakunen wo kataru), *Shigaku*, dai 60 kan, dai 2/3 gō, Mita Shigakkai, 1991, pp. 253-263. "Matsumoto Nobuhiro to gakumon," Keiō gijuku *daigaku gengo kenkyūjo hōkokushū*, Keiō gijuku daigaku, dai 24 kan, 1992, p. 13.

Kiyoto,[36] and Ushijima Iwao[37] indicated the influence of the French School of Sociology on Matsumoto's research. Namely, Ito wrote in his article *Matsumoto Nobuhiro and His Academic Achievements* as follows: "The French School of Sociology at that time was at its height; moreover, it has listed prominent authorities of Jean Przyluski, Marcel Granet, Henri Maspero, etc. Matsumoto sensei had contacts with them and received a decisive influence from them."[38] Ethnologist Ōbayashi linked Matsumoto's name with the French School of Sociology in his *Commentary*: "Matsumoto was an ethnologist and an Orientalist connected to the line of the French School of Sociology of Mauss, Granet, etc."[39] Furthermore, mythologist Hirafuji examined Matsumoto's research in relation to the influence of the French School of Sociology in her writing *The Sociological Research - the Influence of the French School of Sociology in Matsumoto's Research of the Mythology*.[40]

Among the previous researchers, only Hirafuji specified the influence of the French School of Sociology on Matsumoto's research. She characterized the influence from a sociological perspective, which ex-

---

34. Ōbayashi, Taryō "Nihon shinwa no kenkyū," *Kokubungaku kaisetsu to kinkanshō*, 37-1, 1972, p. 163. "Kaisetsu," *Nihon minzokugaku no kigen I: shinwa-densetsu*, Kōdansha, 1978, pp. 401–406.
35. Hirafuji, Kikuko "Shakaigakuteki kenkyū - Matsumoto Nobuhiro no shinwa kenkyū ni okeru Furansu shakaigakuha no eikyō," *Shinwagaku to Nihon no kamigami*, Kōbunkan, 2004, pp. 33–41; "Shokuminchi teikoku Nihon no shinwagaku," *Shūkyō to fashizumu*, Kōbunkan, 2004, pp. 311–347.
36. Furuno, Kiyoto "Nihon shinwagaku no shinkenkyū - Matsumoto Nobuhiro shi no kingyō shōkai," *Minzoku*, dai 4 kan, dai 1 gō, Minzoku hakkōjo, 1928, pp. 153–154.
37. Ushijima, Iwao "Matsumoto Nobuhiro, Mishina Sōei, Oka Masao ni okeru Nihon shinwa no kenkyū," *Kokubungaku kaisetsu to kinkanshō*, 37-1, 1972, pp. 174–177.
38. Itō, Seiji "Matsumoto Nobuhiro to gakumon," Keiō gijuku *daigaku gengo kenkyūjo hōkokushū*, Keiō gijuku daigaku, dai 24 kan, 1992, p. 13.
39. Ōbayashi, Taryō "Kaisetsu," *Nihon minzokugaku no kigen I: shinwa-densetsu*, Kōdansha, 1978, p. 401.
40. Hirafuji, Kikuko "Shakaigakuteki kenkyū – Matsumoto Nobuhiro no shinwa kenkyū ni okeru Furansu shakaigakuha no eikyō," *Shinwagaku to Nihon no kamigami*, Kōbunkan, 2004, pp. 33–41.

amined the primitive culture from the viewpoint that myths are associated with rites.[41] This aspect of the French sociological influence on Matsumoto's research is discussed in Section 2.2.3. However, other sociological ideas appeared in Matsumoto's writings during 1928-1932. Therefore, this section examines Matsumoto's adoption of sociological theories in relation to his ideas regarding Southeast Asia to evaluate the significance of the sociological influence on Matsumoto's research on Southeast Asia.

2.2.1. The idea of the social benefit of primitive culture

Under Mauss and Granet's guidance, Matsumoto gained insight about the social benefit of the primitive culture for civilized people. Mauss claimed the significance and benefit of primitive customs for the existing modern society in his essay *The Gift*: "As we shall note that this morality and organization still function in our own societies, in unchanging fashion and, so to speak, hidden, below the surface, and as we believe that in this we have found one of the human foundations on which our societies are built, we shall be able to deduce a few moral conclusions concerning certain problems posed by the crisis in our own law and economic organization."[42] Mauss' words indicated a contradiction because he argued that the morality and organization of the primitive customs remained under the surface of the modern society although they had disappeared in the modern world of being outdated. This is because Mauss believed in the theory of remnants, according to which some elements of the primitive culture were preserved unchanged in the modern culture. On this basis, he claimed the importance of the primitive culture for the modern society.

A similar appreciation of primitive society can be found in Matsumoto's writings. In his paper *The Utility of the Folklore Studies*, Matsumoto argued as follows: "... what meaning does the clarification of the ancient customs have? ... By reviving the research of these festi-

---

41. Ibid., pp. 34, 36, 37, 38.
42. Mauss, Marcel *The Gift*, translated by W. D. Halls, London: Routledge, 1990, p. 4.

vals and rites, we can discover the material that will be the remedy for correction of several problems, such as the decline of the religious heart which is the malady of the present society."[43] Thus, like Mauss, Matsumoto believed that the primitive culture could provide helpful hints for the modern society. Since Matsumoto studied the Southeast Asian culture in relation to the Japanese culture, he believed that the study of Southeast Asian primitive culture could be useful for the modern Japanese people.

2.2.2. The theory of the gift and of the potlatch

Like many people in France at that time, Matsumoto became deeply impressed by Mauss' book *The Gift* (1923–1924). Among various Mauss' theories of religion of the primitive people, Matsumoto adopted Mauss' theory of the gift, including the concept of the potlatch.

In his book *The Gift*, Mauss presented a study of the gift as a social phenomenon and discussed ideas of the primitive people related to it. Mauss defined the gift as a "total social phenomenon" because it reached all spheres of social life. Hence, according to Mauss, the gift meant a special form of performing total services and the distribution of goods.[44] In the same book, Mauss introduced the concept of the potlatch, a festival gathering during which gifts were exchanged.[45] According to Mauss, the potlatch of the American Indians represented a highly developed type of total services because it comprised rites, legal and economic services, and promotion of tribal members in political rank, among others. In this potlatch, the distribution of wealth served as a tool of political power.[46] Mauss indicated that the social and political power exercised during the potlatch included spiritual power that resided in wealth.[47]

---

43. Matsumoto, Nobuhiro "Minzokugaku no kōyō," *Minzokugaku*, Minzokugakkai, dai 5 kan, dai 1 gō, 1933, p. 16.
44. Mauss, Marcel *The Gift*, translated by W. D. Halls, London: Routledge, 1990, p. 3.
45. Ibid., pp. 6–7, 18, 21, 35–39, 42–46.
46. Ibid., p. 6.
47. Ibid., p. 8.

From his French teachers Mauss and Granet, Matsumoto learnt that the social phenomena of the primitive people, such as potlatch, are universal for many people. For example, he was drawn to Granet's statement in his book *Dances and Legends of Ancient China* that the idea of the potlatch also existed in ancient China.[48] Under the influence of his French teachers, Matsumoto claimed the existence of customs related to the gift and the potlatch in his book *The Research of the Japanese Myths*.[49]

Matsumoto employed Mauss' theory of the gift for interpretaing of the Japanese and Ainu legends in his paper *A Study of a Legend of Hospitality towards Strangers*[50] and in the first chapter of his book *The Research of the Japanese Myths*.[51] In these writings, Matsumoto focused on the customs of hospitality among ancient Japanese and Ainu people that he drew from Japanese documents (*Hitachi Fudoki*, 713) and from the works of Japanese folklorists, for example, Kindaichi Kyosuke's *The Legends of Ainurak*.[52] He indicated similarities among Japanese, Ainu, and American Indian customs of gift giving. The American Indian customs were similar to those mentioned by Mauss.[53] This means that Matsumoto's application of the gift theory was matching the material available in Japan with the theory and examples mentioned by Mauss. A difference from Mauss' discourse was that Matsumoto discussed the gift giving not only among the people but also in relation to the god because the Japanese legend encompassed this topic.[54] In this

---

48. Matsumoto, Nobuhiro "Furansu ni okeru minzokugakuteki kenkyū," *Nihon minzokugaku kenkyū*, Iwanami shoten, Tokyo, 1935, p. 383. Granet, Marcel *Danses et légendes de la Chine ancienne*, Les Presses universitaires de France, Paris, 1926, pp. 57, 58, 606, 611, 613–615, 619.
49. Matsumoto, Nobuhiro *Nihon shinwa no kenkyū*, Dōbunkan, 1931, p. 26.
50. Matsumoto, Nobuhiro "Gaisha kantai densetsu kō," *Shigaku*, dai 9 kan, dai 1 gō, Mita Shigakkai, 1930, p. 26.
51. Matsumoto, Nobuhiro *Nihon shinwa no kenkyū*, Dōbunkan, 1931, pp. 1–40.
52. Ibid., p. 1, 12.
53. He cited same books like Mauss in his The Gift, for example Franz Boas's Tsimshian Mythology (1909-1910), Waldemar Joechelson's The Koryak (1908), Waldemar Bogoras' The Chukchee (1904-1905). Matsumoto, Nobuhiro *Nihon shinwa no kenkyū*, Dōbunkan, 1931, p. 18, 24, 31.

manner, Matsumoto showed the existence of gift giving as a total social phenomenon among ancient Japanese and Ainu people.

In addition, Matsumoto adopted Mauss' concept of the potlatch in his writings.[55] In *The Research of the Japanese Myths*, Matsumoto difined potlatch as a banquet organized by the chief to distribute the wealth: "...the chief invites all the people, organizes a big banquet and shares the property. This is a habit known among the American Indians as potlatch. If one does not distribute the offerings and the property, one cannot hold new privileges. In these tribes, the property is accumulated in order to be divided."[56] This indicates that Matsumoto adopted Mauss' concept of the potlatch as Mauss defined it from the case of the American Indians. Matsumoto claimed the existence of the potlatch among Ainu based on the comparison of the potlatch in the Tsimshian tribe in North Western America with the story in Ainu's poem "The Song Sung by the Owl God Itself."[57] Matsumoto drew the material on the Tsimshian tribe from Boas's *Tsimshian Mythology* which was also cited in Mauss' *The Gift*, and he referred to Chiri Yukie's *Collection of Ainu Mythology* for the material on Ainu.[58] In short, he matched an Ainu legend with the custom of the American Indians discussed in Mauss' *The Gift* to demonstrate the existence of the potlatch among the Ainu.

Matsumoto argued that Ainu tales contained an important aspect of the potlatch, "the competition for the total gift among the people," because the hero of the tale organized a banquet and became the chief of the village.[59] From his statement, it seems that Matsumoto focused

---

54. Ibid., p. 40.
55. Matsumoto, Nobuhiro "Ainu no potoracchi" (1930), *Nihon minzoku bunka no kigen I: shinwa-densetsu*, Kōdansha, 1978, pp. 327-330.
56. Matsumoto, Nobuhiro *Nihon shinwa no kenkyū*, Dōbunkan, 1931, p. 19. Another reference to Mauss' *The Gift* is in other chapters on pp. 95, 126.
57. Matsumoto, Nobuhiro "Ainu no potoracchi" (1930), *Nihon minzoku bunka no kigen I: shinwa-densetsu*, Kōdansha, 1978, pp. 327-330.
58. Ibid., pp. 327, 329.
59. Matsumoto, Nobuhiro "Ainu no potoracchi" (1930), *Nihon minzoku bunka no kigen I: shinwa-densetsu*, Kōdansha, 1978, p. 328.

on the aspect of competition described in Mauss' *The Gift*: "In certain kinds of the potlatch, one must expend all that one has, keeping nothing back. It is a competition to see who is the richest and also the most madly extravagant."[60] However, Matsumoto did not describe this kind of competition; he only indicated that the hero became rich and organized a banquet. Nevertheless, Matsumoto followed Mauss' concept of the potlatch as an occasion where a man receives social and political status.[61] In this respect, he wanted to emphasize that the hero of the Ainu tale only became chief of the village when he organized the banquet.[62]

In summary, Matsumoto used Mauss' theory of the gift and the potlatch for the interpretation of Japanese and Ainu culture by combining some data from Mauss' *The Gift* with the data available in Japan. Matsumoto's application of these theories was somewhat different from Mauss' original theory because of the character of the Japanese material that Matsumoto used. Matsumoto did not apply these theories on Southeast Asian peoples because neither Mauss nor other French scholars discussed them in relation to these theories.

2.2.3. The theory of the seasonal festivals

Matsumoto was influenced by the sociological theory of seasonal festivals in which Mauss argued that rituals were associated with myths. Matsumoto mentioned about adopting Mauss' theory that myths had their origins in the rites that were preserved in the seasonal festivals.[63] He recollected about this theory in his "Commentary" in the book *The Origins of the Japanese Culture*: "Marcel Mauss who lectured on the religion of uncivilized people at the École des Hautes

---

60. Mauss, Marcel *The Gift*, translated by W. D. Halls, London: Routledge, 1990, p. 37.
61. Ibid., p. 6.
62. Matsumoto, Nobuhiro *Nihon shinwa no kenkyū*, Dōbunkan, 1931, pp. 38-39.
63. Matsumoto, Nobuhiro "Kaisetsu" *Nihon bunka no kigen* (3). *Minzokugaku* 1, Heibonsha, 1971, p. 13. Matsumoto's opinion on the relation of the myths and the rites: Matsumoto, Nobuhiro *Essai sur la mythologie Japonaise*, Paris: P. Geuthner, 1928, pp. 50, 76, 90.

Études of Sorbonne claimed importance of comparison of the Japanese myths with the Polynesian myths, and together with Marcel Granet argued that the myths are in fact rites, that the myths cannot exist without performed rites."[64] Thus, Matsumoto intentionally followed Mauss' and Granet's theory that rites were closely connected with myths.

This influence of Mauss' and Granet's theory of the seasonal festivals has been already indicated by Hirafuji in her writing *The Sociological Research - the Influence of the French School of Sociology in Matsumoto's Research of the Mythology*.[65] Hirafuji examined Matsumoto's research on the Japanese myth in relation to Matsumoto's evaluation of the French influence on his writing in 1978.[66] She emphasized, "When we look at Matsumoto Nobuhiro's research of the myths, we can see a strong influence of Mauss' ideas of the French School of Sociology especially in establishing relations between the myths and rites."[67] However, she discussed this issue briefly. This section explores the influence of the theory of seasonal festivals and examines its relation to Matsumoto's ideas regarding Southeast Asia.

In fact, Matsumoto learnt about the significance of the social phenomenon of the seasonal festivals (*kisetsu sai,* 季節祭) before his study in France. Matsumoto encountered this research technique for the first time in Granet's book *Ancient Festivals and Songs of China* in Japan.[68] He also read about it in the book *The Melanges of History of Religions* where Mauss mentioned that the rituals of the festivals could be studied from the myths with which they were connected.[69] Thus,

---

64. Matsumoto, Nobuhiro "Kaisetsu" *Nihon bunka no kigen* (3). *Minzokugaku* 1, Heibonsha, 1971, p. 13.
65. Hirafuji, Kikuko "Shakaigakuteki kenkyū – Matsumoto Nobuhiro no shinwa kenkyū ni okeru Furansu shakaigakuha no eikyō," *Shinwagaku to Nihon no kamigami*, Kōbunkan, 2004, pp. 33-41.
66. Ibid., p. 34.
67. Ibid., p. 35.
68. Granet, Marcel *Fêtes et chansons anciennes de la Chine*, second edition, Paris: Librarie Ernest Leroux, 1929 (first edition 1919). Matsumoto, Nobuhiro "Fudoki ni arawaretaru santake densetsu," *Tōkōkō, II*, Keiō gijuku taiikukai sangakubu nenpō, Shuppan kagaku sōgō kenkyūjo, 1920, p. 38.

Matsumoto knew about this theory before his studies in France and was trained in the application of this theory during his studies at Sorbonne University under Mauss and Granet's guidance.

Matsumoto's focus on the connection between the myths and the rites can be found in his doctoral thesis *The Essay on the Japanese Mythology* and in his book *The Research of the Japanese Myths*. In his thesis *The Essay on the Japanese Mythology*, Matsumoto interpreted some parts of the Japanese myths by making comparisons with Japanese customs. For example, he argued that Amaterasu Ōmikami in the Japanese myths was perceived to be both a priestess and a goddess at the same time because Japanese priests disguise themselves as gods during the festivals.[70] He also indicated the relation of the seasonal festivals with the myths in his book *The Research of the Japanese Myths*.[71] He explained his reasons for this most clearly in his article *Woman That Does Not Laugh*: "When we examine the actions taken during a festival by associating a myth with a seasonal festival as much as possible, we can understand the numerous links of its reasons which were unknown until now."[72] Therefore, he believed that the interpretation of the myth from the comparison with the rite could contribute to the understanding of the primitive people's thinking in relation to the myth and festival.

Matsumoto focused on three kinds of festivals: the harvest festival in autumn, mating festival in spring, and requiem festival in winter. First, he discussed the harvest festival to explain the legend of Mount Tsukuba in *Hitachi Fudoki*. The legend praised the merit of treating a god visiting Mount Tsukuba. Matsumoto connected the legend with

---

69. Mauss, Marcel and Hubert, Henri *Mélanges d'histoire des religions*, Paris: Félix Alcan, 1909, p. III. Matsumoto, Nobuhiro "Ōshūjin no Kyokutō kenkyū," *Shigaku*, dai 8 kan, dai 1 gō, MitaShigakkai, 1929, p. 23.
70. Matsumoto, Nobuhiro *Essai sur la mythologie Japonaise*, P. Geuthner, Paris, 1928, pp. 76–77.
71. Matsumoto, Nobuhiro *Nihon shinwa no kenkyū*, Dōbunkan, 1931, pp. 4, 48, 51, 177, 219, 271, 272.
72. Matsumoto, Nobuhiro "Warazaru onna" (1932), *Nihon minzoku bunka no kigen III: Tōnan Ajia to Nihon*, Kōdansha, 1978, pp. 423.

the custom of the offerings given to the god during the harvest festival (*niinamesai*, 新嘗祭). He surmised that the ancient Japanese people considered the harvest festival as an occasion to give lavishly.[73] This argument obviously comes from Mauss' theory of the gift and potlatch because the shared commonality in the legend of Mount Tsukuba and the harvest festival was the act of giving to the god and every participant of the festival.[74]

Second, Matsumoto discussed the spring festival based on Granet's book *Ancient Festivals and Songs of China*.[75] From Granet's book, Matsumoto learnt about the existence of the custom where men and women exchange love songs during the spring festival in ancient China and in contemporary Southeast Asia. Matsumoto accepted Granet's opinion that a similar mating festival was practiced in ancient Japan as *utagaki* or *kagai* (singing banquet).[76] Furthermore, he learnt about the Southeast Asian ritual of young people going around the pillar from Jean Przyluski.[77] Matsumoto introduced this custom to the Japanese readers in his paper *Spring Festival of Miao Tribe and the Pillar*.[78]

Matsumoto applied this idea of the spring festival of combining the customs of song exchange and going around the pillar in his book *The Research of the Japanese Myths*. Concretely, he suggested that a pillar might have been built on the place where *utagaki* was held in ancient Japan. Furthermore, he claimed that this custom of going around a pillar was described in the Japanese myth of Izanagi and Izanami, and on this basis, he suggested that this custom was recorded

---

73. Matsumoto, Nobuhiro *Nihon shinwa no kenkyū*, Dōbunkan, 1931, p. 4.
74. Ibid., p. 40.
75. Ibid., pp. 160-164, 205-206.
76. Ibid., pp. 40, 160, 161. Granet, Marcel *Fêtes et chansons anciennes de la Chine*, second edition, Librarie Ernest Leroux, Paris, 1929 (first edition 1919), p. 147, 278-279.
77. Matsumoto, Nobuhiro "La Marche Autour de la Colonne," *Essai sur la mythologie Japonaise*, P. Geuthner, Paris, 1928, p. 124.
78. Matsumoto, Nobuhiro *Nihon shinwa no kenkyū*, Dōbunkan, 1931, pp. 197, 204-208. "Miao zoku no haru no matsuri to hashira," *Minzoku*, dai 5 kan, dai 3 gō, Minzokugakkai, March 1933, pp. 190-192.

in the myth because it was practiced during *utagaki*.⁷⁹ Thus, in his application of the theory of connection between the ritual and the myth, Matsumoto linked the contemporary Southeast Asian ritual with the ancient Japanese custom of *utagaki* and with the Japanese myth of Izanagi and Izanami because of the similarity between the spring festivals of Japan and Southeast Asia.

Third, Matsumoto interpreted the Japanese myth of the celestial cavern from its association with the requiem festival (*chinkonsai*, 鎮魂祭) in his doctoral thesis *The Essay on the Japanese Mythology* and in his book *The Research of the Japanese Myths*. Matsumoto discussed the part of the myth in which the sun goddess emerges from the celestial cave and brings sunlight to the Earth. First, Matsumoto rejected Revon's hypothesis that this part described the end of the solar eclipse.⁸⁰ Instead, he presented a hypothesis emphasizing the return of the sunlight at the end of the winter in connection with the requiem festival held in winter.⁸¹ Matsumoto literarily wrote in his book *The Research of the Japanese Myths* as follows: "It is sure that the ancient Japanese believed that the winter festival and the myth of Goddess' revival are associated."⁸² He demonstrated it by indicating the similarity of the dance in the myth of the celestial cavern and that in the requiem festival.⁸³ Thus, this is the only case when Matsumoto presented his original hypothesis, which he interpreted from the comparison of a myth with a festival.

Although Matsumoto emphasized the importance of the seasonal festivals several times, he often did not discuss them in detail. An exception is found only in the case of the requiem festival.⁸⁴ The insuffi-

---

79. Matsumoto, Nobuhiro *Nihon shinwa no kenkyū*, Dōbunkan, 1931, pp. 205-206.
80. Matsumoto, Nobuhiro *Essai sur la mythologie Japonaise*, P. Geuthner, Paris, 1928, p. 81. *Nihon shinwa no kenkyū*, Dōbunkan, 1931, p. 102.
81. Matsumoto, Nobuhiro *Essai sur la mythologie Japonaise*, Paris: P. Geuthner, 1928, pp. 81-90. *Nihon shinwa no kenkyū*, Dōbunkan, 1931, pp. 102-108.
82. Matsumoto, Nobuhiro *Nihon shinwa no kenkyū*, Dōbunkan, 1931, p. 106.
83. Matsumoto, Nobuhiro *Essai sur la mythologie Japonaise*, P. Geuthner, Paris, 1928, pp. 86-88. Matsumoto, Nobuhiro *Nihon shinwa no kenkyū*, Dōbunkan, 1931, p. 107.

cient discussion on the seasonal festivals was not missed by Matsumoto Yoshio, Matsumoto's colleague at Keio University, who demanded more evidences from the seasonal festivals in his criticism of Matsumoto Nobuhiro's book *The Research of the Japanese Myths*.[85] Moreover, despite comparing the festivals with the Japanese myths, Matsumoto Nobuhiro did not use the data from his observations of the Japanese festivals.[86] In contrast, Matsumoto Nobuhiro drew on the festivals from Japanese documents and from the research conducted by Japanese and Western scholars.

In summary, the examination of the influence of Mauss' theory of the seasonal festivals on Matsumoto's ideas showed that Matsumoto applied this theory in combination with other ideas proposed by Western scholars. Matsumoto combined the theory of seasonal festivals with Mauss' theory of the gift in his discussion of the harvest festival, Granet's idea of *utagaki*, and Przyluski's opinion of the Southeast Asian ritual of young people going around the pillar in his discussion of the spring festival. In addition, he presented his original idea on the relation of the Japanese myth with the rituals in his discussion of the requiem festival. Thus, among others, Matsumoto mentioned Southeast Asian culture in his application of Mauss' theory of seasonal festivals.

2.2.4. The theory of the unity of religious and political power

Matsumoto was influenced by the theory of the unity of religious and political power. This theory was presented by Frazer, and other Western scholars such as Mauss and Granet, adopted it. Under their influence, the theory of the unity of religious and political power formed the framework of Matsumoto's supplementary doctoral thesis

---

84. Matsumoto, Nobuhiro *Nihon shinwa no kenkyū*, Dōbunkan, 1931, pp. 4, 6, 7, 26, 40, 48, 51, 118, 127, 177, 205, 206, 207, 219, 261.
85. Matsumoto, Yoshio "Nihon shinwa no kenkyū (Matsumoto Nobuhiro cho, Dōbunkan hakkō)," *Shigaku*, dai 11 kan, dai 1 gō, Mita Shigakkai, 1932, p. 138.
86. For example, Matsumoto described the festival of Hayachine Shrine that he observed in Iwate. Matsumoto, Nobuhiro "Iwate no Kōgen yori," (1920) *Nihon minzoku bunka no kigen I: shinwa-densetsu*, Kōdansha, 1978, pp. 36

The Essay on the Japanese Mythology.

The concept of the unity of religious and political power among the primitive people was introduced by Frazer in his book *The Golden Bough*. Frazer demonstrated this through the cases of the king-magician and king-god among various people.[87] His ideas were adopted by many western scholars, including Matsumoto's teachers. For example, Mauss admitted the influence of Frazer's theory of kings-priests-gods on his ideas in *The Mélanges of History of Religions* (1909): "Mr. Frazer drew attention to these interesting characters - at the same time kings, priests and gods which appear in many religions and whose periodic death or murder is a true sacrifice, of the kind we call the sacrifice of the god."[88] Furthermore, Mauss discussed the political and religious power of giving in his writing *The Gift*.[89]

Under these influences, Matsumoto adopted this theory of the unity of religious and political power in his doctoral thesis *The Essay on the Japanese Mythology*, which he wrote under Granet's guidance.[90] In his doctoral thesis, Matsumoto sought to examine the organization of the Japanese mythology by analyzing politico-religious centers in ancient Japan.[91] From the analysis of the Japanese myths, Matsumoto discovered the existence of three centers of the religious tradition (Izumo, Yamato, and Kyushu). Matsumoto characterized each of these religious cults by the description of their gods. Then, he analyzed the relationship among the gods of each religious center. On this basis, he argued that the Yamato clan with the solar cult incorporated the myths of two other centers, Izumo and Kyushu, because Yamato clan

---

87. Frazer, James George "Priestly Kings," "Magicians as Kings," "Incarnate Human Gods," *The Golden Bough. A study in magic and religion*, Wordsworth Reference, 1993, pp. 9-11, 83-106.
88. Mauss, Marcel and Hubert, Henri *Mélanges d'histoire des religions*, Félix Alcan, Paris, 1909, p. II.
89. Mauss, Marcel *The Gift*, translated by W. D. Halls, London: Routledge, 1990, pp. 30, 37, 71.
90. Matsumoto, Nobuhiro *Essai sur la mythologie Japonaise*, P. Geuthner, Paris, 1928, preface.
91. Ibid., p. 1.

subjugated them politically.[92] Finally, he concluded that the spread of the Yamato cult of the sun goddess resulted from the integration of conquered cults due to the unification of the country.[93] Thus, Matsumoto adopted the theory of the unity of religious and political power in his research on the religious political organization of ancient Japan after the unification of Japan by the Yamato clan.

In addition, Matsumoto also adopted the concept of the priest-king, which reflected the unity of religious and political power. First, in his *The Essay on the Japanese Mythology*, Matsumoto indicated the existence of the "the priest-governor" on the basis of Japanese historical documents. He wrote that the hereditary priest of Izumo Shrine guarded the sacred fire and the sacred water at the same time when he ruled Izumo Province as a governor in ancient Japan.[94] Then, Matsumoto applied the concept of the priest-king to the interpretation of the role of the shamaness (*miko*, 巫女) of the solar cult. Based on the hypothesis of the existence of the priest-king in primitive cultures, Matsumoto claimed that the shamaness who controlled the sun worship was both a religious and political chief of the tribe and that the myth of the sun goddess (Amaterasu Ōmikami) was probably created in that period.[95] However, Matsumoto did not discuss the political aspects of this shamanness. He only indicated the separation of the worship of the sun goddess from the imperial court during the reign of Sujin Tenno (97–29 BC) based on the information gathered from the Japanese annals *Nihonshoki*.[96] Interestingly, Matsumoto did not apply this concept to Southeast Asia until 1940 although he already knew about one case of king shamans in Southeast Asia from Frazer's book *The Goldern Bough*.[97]

In summary, during 1924–1932, Matsumoto used sociological theories for interpreting Japanese legends, myths, and customs. He rarely applied the sociological theories to the Southeast Asian culture be-

---

92. Ibid., pp. 37, 70, 71, 100, 109.
93. Ibid., pp. 1, 109, 112.
94. Ibid., 1928, pp. 61–62.
95. Matsumoto, Nobuhiro *Nihon shinwa no kenkyū*, Dōbunkan, 1931, p. 262.
96. Ibid., p. 263.

cause the French sociologists did not focus on this region. Granet discussed Southeast Asian customs, but was more concerned with ancient Chinese society. Therefore, sociologists contributed to Matsumoto's interest in Southeast Asia in 1924-1932; however, their inspiration did not make Matsumoto focus on Southeast Asia.

3. Influence of evolutionist ethnology on Matsumoto's ideas regarding Southeast Asia

The influence of unilinear evolutionism was apparent in the earliest period of Matsumoto's ethnological career, but it appears in Matsumoto's writings during 1924-1932. This was because unilinear evolutionism formed the basis of the ideas of Matsumoto's teachers at Sorbonne University: Marcel Mauss (1872-1950), Marcel Granet (1884-1940) and Jean Przyluski (1885-1944). These teachers was influenced by the British evolutionist ethnologist James George Frazer (1854-1941).

The French School of Sociology maintained a strong relationship with Frazer for many years. It began with personal contacts forged by Émile Durkheim (1858-1917), the founder of the French School of Sociology, with Frazer. Durkheim's eminent disciple Mauss researched the primitive society based on Frazer's theories of magic and totemism. Mauss expressed his indebtedness to Frazer in his common writing with his colleague Henri Hubert in *The Mélanges of History of Religions*: "Mr. Frazer drew attention to these interesting characters - at the same time kings, priests and gods which appear in many religions and whose periodic death or murder is a true sacrifice, of the kind we call the sacrifice of the god. [Frazer's] *The Golden Bough* explained to

---

97. "...there is a legend of two states 火舎 and 水舎 describing the contacts of the famous king of fire and king of water of Jarai, thus it is important material for ethnology ... The kings of these two countries are famous as existing magician-kings, they are described also in the Volume 2 of Frazer's The Golden Bough." Matsumoto, Nobuhiro "Annan shiryō ni arawareru Indoshina sanchi minzoku," *Andō kyōju kanreki Shukuga kinenronbunshū*, Andō kyōju kanreki Shukuga kinenkaihen, Sanseidō, 1940, pp. 1011-1012.

us the nature and the function of these persons which he described in a large collection."[98] Thus, Mauss adopted Frazer's notion of the king-priest which Mauss considered to be a significant sociological phenomenon in the evolution of human society. Mauss admired Frazer's work to the extent that he translated some of his writings into English and sent them to Frazer to receive his comments in the 1920s.[99] Thus, Mauss respected Frazer as his teacher especially after his teacher and uncle Émile Durkheim passed away in 1917. Since Mauss' ideas inspired Granet, both Mauss and Granet were strongly influenced by Frazer's theories.

Matsumoto shared Granet's opinion about Frazer's concept of totemism. Granet argued that totemism existed in ancient China in his work *Dances and Legends of Ancient China* (1926)[100] and analyzed the ancient Chinese culture based on Frazer's theory of exogamy in this book. Matsumoto believed in the existence of totemism in China.[101] First, Matsumoto proposed a hypothesis on the existence of totemism and exogamy in China in his papers *The Research of the Family in Ancient China* and *The Family in Ancient China and Totemism*. With Granet's support, Matsumoto confirmed his hypothesis in his paper *The Clan 'Coconut tree' and the Popular Tale 'Coconut' of Cham People*: "Of course, there are some sources on totemism in China, and I too advocate the theory that totemism existed in China."[102]

In addition, Matsumoto learnt another interpretation of totemism from his guiding professor Jean Przyluski's paper *Totemism and Vegetalism in India*.[103] In this work, Przyluski concluded that totemism is a

---

98. Mauss, Marcel, Hubert, Henri, *Mélanges d'histoire des religions*, Félix Alcan, Paris, 1909, p. II.
99. Liebersohn, Harry *The Return of the Gift*, Cambridge University Press, 2010, pp. 149, 195, 200.
100. Granet, Marcel *Danses et légendes de la Chine ancienne*, Les Presses universitaires de France, Paris, 1926, pp. 38, 52, 602, 606.
101. Matsumoto, Nobuhiro "Kodai bunkaron," *Gendai shigaku taikei*, Kyōritsusha shoten, 1932, p. 136.
102. Matsumoto, Nobuhiro "Chamu no yashizoku to 'yashi no mi' setsuwa," *Minzokugaku*, dai 5 kan, dai 6 gō, 1933, p. 449.

result of the geographical influence. For example, tropical zones let to the emergence of plant totems as a reflection of its enormous vitality of flora there.[104] Przyluski's interpretation was a large divergence from the sociologist thinking that considered the influence of society to be the most important factor in the formation of culture.

Matsumoto noticed this difference between Przyluski and the French sociologists, but he still chose to introduce Przyluski's theory in his writing *Theories of Ancient Culture*. Hence, Matsumoto evidently did not insist on the sociological perspective of totemism. Although Matsumoto did not fully accept it, he respected Przyluski's opinion as an interesting hypothesis: "The above mentioned Przyluski's idea is completely opposite to Durkheimist thinking in examining the religions of the oldest human races; it is a new theory reversing the flag. But, I feel a bit anxious because this important issue was discussed only on several pages. Southern Asia has specific geographical features and human races, so it is difficult to do research on the history of their religion only by one method; thus I must admit, and I agree that it is original to apply Przyluski's new interpretation of totemism and vegetalism."[105] In other words, Matsumoto acknowledged the theory of Mauss and Granet as well as that of Przyluski because he thought that diversity of Southeast Asia required a variety of approaches. According to Shiraishi Masaya, specialist in Vietnamese studies, civilization includes social interaction among the people and interaction of the people with the natural environments.[106] In this sense, Matsumoto's adoption of both theories corresponds to Shirai-

---

103. Przyluski, Jean "Totemisme et vegetalisme dans l'Inde," *Revue de l'Historie des Religions*, 1927 in Matsumoto, Nobuhiro *Nihon shinwa no kenkyū*, Dōbunkan, 1931, p. 208. "Kodai bunkaron," *Gendai shigaku taikei*, Kyōritsusha shoten, 1932, pp. 51–53.

104. Przyluski, Jean "Totemisme et vegetalisme dans l'Inde," *Revue de l'Historie des Religions*, 1927 in Matsumoto, Nobuhiro *Nihon shinwa no kenkyū*, Dōbunkan, 1931, p. 208. "Kodai bunkaron," *Gendai shigaku taikei*, Kyōritsusha shoten, 1932, p. 52.

105. Matsumoto, Nobuhiro *Nihon shinwa no kenkyū*, Dōbunkan, 1931, p. 208. "Kodai bunkaron," *Gendai shigaku taikei*, Kyōritsusha shoten, 1932, p. 52–53.

shi's definition.

In short, Matsumoto continued applying Frazer's theories because they were used by leading scholars of the French School of Sociology: Mauss, Granet, and Przyluski. The following sections examine the significance of Frazer's theories for Matsumoto's interest in Southeast Asia during 1924–1932 when Matsumoto was influenced by sociologist ethnology.

3.1. Influence of the theory of totemism and exogamy

Frazer's theories of totemism and exogamy belonged to the principal theories discussed by the scholars of the French School of Sociology. In addition, since Matsumoto had employed the theories of totemism and exogamy in his graduation thesis at Keio University, he had the chance to develop his understanding of these theories under the guidance of his French teachers.

As a result of the French sociologists' influence, Matsumoto learnt about sociological aspects of totemism and exogamy. Matsumoto's statement in his book *The Research of the Japanese Myths* suggested that Matsumoto understood the meaning of totemism as a social phenomenon connected with religious ideas: "When we consider the origins of legends, we can trace the life of the ancient villages in them to a very distant antiquity. As we can find in the traces of the old social life such as totemism, potlatch, etc. in Ainu's legends, the legends of Fuji and Tsukuba from Hitachi Fudoki also give the modern people glimpses of the ancient religious ideas that the ancient Japanese had."[107] Thus, under Mauss' and Granet's influence, Matsumoto thought that totemism could be discussed as a social phenomenon in Japan. However, Matsumoto did not discuss it in this way. He just claimed the existence of totemism as he did in his other writings during 1919–1923.

Concerning the existence of totemism, Matsumoto proposed a

---

106. Consultation with Shiraishi Masaya, Professor of the Waseda University Graduate School of Asia Pacific Studies, 24 November 2014, Waseda University.
107. Matsumoto, Nobuhiro *Nihon shinwa no kenkyū*, Dōbunkan, 1931, p. 39.

theory that its traces could be found in the Japanese legend of Princess Toyotama. In more concrete terms, he suggested that the killing of an animal in the legend was an expression of totemism in his book *The Research of the Japanese Myths*: "... it can explain important aspects in legends, such as the legend of Princess Toyotama. That is, to acquire the animal crest means to kill and send off the animal. ...this is a variation of a story where the outer soul was expressed in the form of an animal, a story about acquiring an totem-emblem through of which a young man can succeed [in the society]."[108] His claims were based on comparing the legend of Princess Toyotama with the Ainu legend of the owl god, which he interpreted as an expression of totemism.[109] In Section 2.2.2, Matsumoto indicated the similarities between an Ainu tale and a North American Indian tale that had totemism. Thus, Matsumoto's reason for suggesting totemism in the Japanese legend Princess Toyotama was the similarity found in both tales in the phenomenon of killing an animal. This means that Matsumoto did not try to find evidence for the belief in the totem in the legend of Princess Toyotama to demonstrate totemism in this legend. Rather, he matched the Japanese legend with an Ainu tale on which totemism could be proved due to similarities with a North American Indian tale.

Besides totemism, Matsumoto indicated exogamy (*izoku kekkon*, 異族結婚) in the legend of Princess Toyotama. In his book *The Research of the Japanese Myths*, Matsumoto discussed a tale in which a young man fails to hunt down an animal, and the animal escapes back to its country where animals live like people. The young man follows him to this country, heals an injured woman of a different tribe who is in fact the animal, and becomes rich because of marrying the woman and returns home.[110] Matsumoto interpreted the legend as a form of exogamy after he mentioned about the existence of exogamy among the Tsimshian tribe in America in the same book.[111] Thus, he concluded that the marriage of Princess Toyotama was an exogamic tie be-

---

108. Matsumoto, Nobuhiro *Nihon shinwa no kenkyū*, Dōbunkan, 1931, pp. 96–97.
109. Ibid., p. 96.
110. Ibid., p. 97.
111. Matsumoto, Nobuhiro *Nihon shinwa no kenkyū*, Dōbunkan, 1931, p. 95.

cause of this comparison with North American Indian culture. Matsumoto did not examine the phenomenon of exogamy in itself in the legend of Princess Toyotama, but he referred to the similarity with the Indian culture, which was considered to have exogamy by Western scholars.

Furthermore, Matsumoto employed the theory of plant totems that was discussed by his teacher Jean Przyluski in his paper *The Clan 'Coconut tree' and the Popular Tale 'Coconut' of Cham People*.[112] This paper was a study of totemism in Indochina, and it was the only study in which Matsumoto exclusively dealt with totemism. In the paper, he indicated the use of coconut and betel palms as plant totems among the Cham people. In fact, Matsumoto used Frazer's accounts of totemism in Indochina (*Totemism and Exogamy*) as pointers, and he connected them with Wilhelm Schmidt's theory of the Austroasiatic languages. Since the Austroasiatic languages are spread in Indochina, Matsumoto suggested that totemism was typical for the area inhabited by the Austroasiatic people.[113] First, Matsumoto argued that totemism might have existed in Đông Sơn culture in Indochina although the people of this culture had reached a relatively high stage of civilization based on Przyluski's opinion.[114] Then, Matsumoto attempted to prove the existence of plant totems among the Cham people through an analysis of their legends, which told about the existence of two clans—the Betel Palm clan and the Coconut Palm clan.[115] The common characteristic of these legends was that they focused on the significance of the plants that Matsumoto took as an evidence of totemism. Thus, Matsumoto combined Przyluski's interpretation of Frazer's theory of totemism with Schmidt's theory of Austroasiatic languages in this research.

In summary, Matsumoto discussed totemism and exogamy in the Japanese culture in connection with non-Japanese cultures, including Southeast Asian cultures. However, he did not examine totemism in

---

112. Matsumoto, Nobuhiro "Chamu no yashizoku to 'yashi no mi' setsuwa," *Minzokugaku*, dai 5 kan, dai 6 gō, 1933, pp. 449–465.
113. Ibid., p. 449.
114. Ibid., p. 455.
115. Ibid., pp. 456, 457, 459.

the Japanese culture but rather explored the similarities between the Japanese culture and the non-Japanese primitive cultures, including those of Southeast Asia.

3.2. Influence of the theme of taboo

Among Frazer's theories, Matsumoto Nobuhiro also adopted the theory of taboo. Frazer presented his discussion regarding taboo in four of his chapters from *The Golden Bough*. Frazer defined taboo as a negative application of magic in reference to his theory of the sympathetic and contagious magic.[116] Frazer divided the taboo according to its target: "tabooed acts," "tabooed persons," "tabooed things," and "tabooed words."[117] However, the scholars of French School of Sociology did not emphasize this topic much. Mauss only made a passing reference to taboo in *The Gift*.[118]

The theory of taboo appeared for the first time in Matsumoto's graduation thesis *The Research of the Family in Ancient China* in relation to totemism that contained the taboo of killing the totem animal.[119] After his studies in Paris, Matsumoto applied the theory of taboo in his book *The Research of the Japanese Myths* wherein he presented two opinions on taboo. First, he discussed the case of breaking the taboo in the exogamic couple, which resulted in the separation of the couple in the legend of Princess Toyotama. Matsumoto explained that the man broke his wife's taboo by seeing her in her animal form or by breaking the rule of her totem.[120] Then, he presented an opinion on taboo concerning fire and the realm of the dead in the leg-

---

116. Frazer, James George *The Golden Bough. A study in magic and religion*, Wordsworth Reference, 1993, p. 19.
117. Frazer, James George "Tabooed Acts," "Tabooed Persons," "Tabooed Things," "Tabooed Words," *The Golden Bough. A study in magic and religion*, Wordsworth Reference, 1993, pp. 194–262.
118. Mauss, Marcel *The Gift*, translated by W.D. Halls, Routledge, London, 1990, p. 20.
119. Matsumoto, Nobuhiro "Shina kosei to tōtemizumu" (1921–1922), *Tōa minzoku bunkaronkō*, Seibundō shinkōsha, 1968, p. 454, 482, 485.
120. Matsumoto, Nobuhiro *Nihon shinwa no kenkyū*, Dōbunkan, 1931, p. 87, 215.

end of Izanagi and Izanami: "... he lighted the fire in the place where it was forbidden, this is the opposition to taboo..."[121] However, Matsumoto did not specify the mentioned taboos. Thus, Matsumoto indicated taboos in general without any further discussion.

3.3. Influence of the theory of spiritual power

Matsumoto adopted the theory of spiritual power, which was originally suggested by Frazer's theory of magic. In his book *The Golden Bough*, Frazer described the belief in magic according to a man's ability to possess a special power, such as controlling natural forces. Frazer claimed that this belief in the special power is universal for people in the lower stages of human evolution.[122] Although Frazer did not use the term "spiritual power" to address this special power, his concept of the belief in spiritual power spread among the Western scholars. The term "spiritual power" appeared in the ideas of Matsumoto's French teachers who adopted Frazer's theory of the belief in magic and spiritual power. For example, in his book *The Gift*, Mauss claimed that he found the existence of the concept of the spiritual power, which plays an essential role in the social life of the native people of Polynesia, Melanesia, and the Indians of the American Northwest.[123] Concretely, Mauss wrote that the spiritual power, which he called *mana*, was an essential element in potlatch, the seasonal festival, because it was the source of authority and wealth.[124]

Matsumoto adopted the concept of the spiritual power in his interpretation of the legends in Japan. Matsumoto presented it as a belief in a special power possessed by people with high morality, contained in the fishing instruments, and possessed by god's descendants.

First, he mentioned the primitive belief in the spiritual power

---

121. Ibid., p. 150.
122. Frazer, James George *The Golden Bough. A study in magic and religion*, Wordsworth Reference, 1993, pp. 54-91: Chapters "Sympathetic Magic," "Magic and Religion," "The Magical Control of the Weather," "Magicians as Kings".
123. Mauss, Marcel *The Gift*, translated by W. D. Halls, Routledge, London, 1990, pp. 8, 10-13, 30, 38-39, 48, 75.
124. Ibid., pp. 8, 10.

stemming from moral virtues in the Ainu legend of the owl god and in the Japanese legend of Princess Toyotama in his book *The Research of the Japanese Myths*. Matsumoto claimed that the Ainu hero received the spiritual power of the animal god because of his moral qualities (*dōtokuteki seishitsu*, 道徳的性質), and this spiritual power (*reiryoku*, 霊力) made the hero a rich man and a chief of the village.[125] Matsumoto explained that the hero possessed a high moral character because the owl god let the hero kill him, thereby letting the hero win the hunting competition.[126] Hence, according to Matsumoto, the Ainu people believed that the spiritual power was transferred from the animal god to the hero.

Furthermore, he implied from the legend of Princess Toyotama that the ancient Japanese people also thought that the spiritual power came from moral excellence.[127] Matsumoto explained that the hero possessed the spiritual power because of his moral virtues, which was proven by the fact that he became rich and won against his older brother: "Also in Princess Toyotama Legend greedy Umisachihiko became poor and subjugated, and Yamasachihiko acquired treasures from a different tribe and became the winner. A loyal person that is a bounteous person, in the tradition of tribal spirit will become the winner in the end rather than a selfishly motivated person."[128] From these points, Matsumoto conjectured that the ancient Japanese people believed that the hero obtained spiritual power due to his moral qualities. Connected to giving.

Second, from the Japanese legend of Princess Toyotama, Matsumoto highlighted that there existed a belief that the spiritual power resided in fishing and hunting tools. In his book *The Research of the Japanese Myths*, Matsumoto argued that the ancient Japanese people believed that the success of a hunt was determined by spiritual pow-

---

125. Matsumoto, Nobuhiro *Nihon shinwa no kenkyū*, Dōbunkan, 1931, pp. 96, 98, 99. Matsumoto, Nobuhiro "Ainu no potoracchi" (1930), *Nihon minzoku bunka no kigen I: shinwa-densetsu*, Kōdansha, 1978, p. 330.
126. Matsumoto, Nobuhiro *Nihon shinwa no kenkyū*, Dōbunkan, 1931, p. 97.
127. Ibid., pp. 44–45.
128. Ibid., pp. 98–99.

ers, which was also contained in their fishing or hunting tools.[129] However, as seen from his other cases, Matsumoto neither explained the basis of this Japanese belief nor provided any evidence demonstrating this belief in the spiritual power of the fishing hook, which was an important tool in the legend of Princess Toyotama. Thus, Matsumoto only presented another hypothesis of the ancient Japanese belief in the spiritual power.

Third, Matsumoto presented a theory that the ancient Japanese believed in the existence of the spiritual power coming from the descendants of a god or a deity. In his study of the Japanese legend of Princess Toyotama in *The Research of the Japanese Myth*, Matsumoto indicated that Princess Toyotama was believed to possess spiritual power since she descended from a sea god. Through this hereditary process, the same power was also transmitted to her offspring.[130] In addition, Matsumoto claimed that Princess Toyotama was a shamaness (*miko*, 巫女) because she had spiritual abilities (*reinō shutoku*, 霊能取得).[131] According to Matsumoto, this meant that the hero of the legend could win against his older brother because he could acquire spiritual power through his wife, Princess Toyotama.[132] Hence, Matsumoto assumed that the ancient Japanese people believed in the transmission of the spiritual power from the wife to the husband. Matsumoto connected the concept of the belief in spiritual power with the theory of exogamy since he concluded that the ancient Japanese people believed in acquiring spiritual power through exogamic marriages (a marriage with a woman of a different tribe). Ultimately, Matsumoto presented three hypotheses concerning the Japanese ancient belief on how the hero in the legend of Princess Toyotama obtained spiritual power in his book *The Research of the Japanese Myth*.

Moreover, in the writing *Theories of Ancient Culture*, Matsumoto offered a different interpretation of the origin of spiritual power in the

---

129. Ibid., pp. 44–45.
130. Matsumoto, Nobuhiro *Nihon shinwa no kenkyū*, Dōbunkan, 1931, pp. 50–51, 155.
131. Ibid., pp. 50–51.
132. Ibid., pp. 44–45.

same story of Princess Toyotama. In this version, Matsumoto argued that the hero became rich and secured victory over his brother because he received "the magical power" (*juryoku*, 呪力) from the sea god.[133] Matsumoto used term "spiritual power" (*reiryoku*, 霊力) as well as "magical power" (*juryoku*, 呪力) to indicate the same belief that the ancient people had in special powers. In this manner, he tried to imagine various interpretations of the ancient Japanese belief in spiritual power without bringing up evidence on such beliefs. However, despite using various terms and different explanations of the special powers, he always indicated only one effect: to become rich and politically influential. At this point, Matsumoto's theory reflects Mauss' definition of the spiritual power in *The Gift*.

3.4. Influence of the theme of fertility

From Frazer's theories, Matsumoto adopted the theory of fertility based on the Western interpretation of the myth of Demeter, the goddess of agriculture. Frazer developed this theme in the three chapters of his book *The Golden Bough*.[134] Matsumoto further drew from the papers of various French scholars of European folklore studies (such as Salomon Reinach and Paul-Louis Couchoud) and applied this theory on the Japanese myth of the celestial cave in his book *The Research of the Japanese Myths*.[135]

In the chapter *The Ritual of Laughter and the Myth*, Matsumoto drew comparisons between the sun goddess and goddess Demeter on the basis of their similarities in approaching the theme of fertility. Both goddesses were regarded as the source of fertility, and it was believed that the world turned in chaos when they became angry. Therefore, much effort was made to recover their humor so that the world

---

133. Matsumoto, Nobuhiro "Kodai bunkaron," *Gendai shigaku taikei*, Kyōritsusha shoten, 1932, p. 154–155.
134. Frazer, James George "Demeter and Persephone," "The Corn-mother and the Corn-maiden in Northern Europe," "The Corn-mother in many Lands," *The Golden Bough. A study in magic and religion*, Wordsworth Reference, 1993, pp. 393–447.
135. Matsumoto, Nobuhiro *Nihon shinwa no kenkyū*, Dōbunkan, 1931, p. 111.

could emerge from darkness and restore life. According to the Japanese myth, the angry sun goddess hid in a celestial cave and could only be persuaded to come out with the dance of the goddess Amenouzume.[136] Matsumoto used this Western theory of fertility to explain the purpose of the dance of the goddess Amenouzume in the myth of the celestial cave.

Matsumoto gathered that the ancient Japanese people believed that the dance invoked the fertility of nature. In the chapter *The Ritual of Laughter and the Myth*, Matsumoto argued as follows: "Exposing the female genitals... is a way to recall wealth and fertility to the angry 'nature' ... In both the Greek myth and the Japanese myth, the laughter evocated by the dancer's conduct is ceremonial. Owing to this laughter, the life that was thought to be stopped was resurrected."[137] This idea did not originate from Matsumoto since the similarity between the myth of Demeter and the Japanese myth of the celestial cave was indicated by Salomon Reinach, a French specialist in the history of religions.[138] Matsumoto's originality lies in his presentation of these myths with an Ainu myth that contains a motive of repulsing a demon by a woman's naked body: "A myth where a woman exposes her bosom and thus brings the light to the world can be discovered also among Ainu tribes."[139] Thus, Matsumoto emphasized the common motive of recovering the fertile power in the Greek, Japanese, and Ainu myths.

In addition, Matsumoto mentioned this topic again in the paper *A Woman That Does Not Laugh*. However this time, he employed Frazer's motive of the goddess Demeter for the interpretation of a cruel queen in the Chinese legend of the King You of Zhou (周幽王). He argued that the topic *A Woman That Does Not Laugh* was probably borrowed from the story of an angry goddess that symbolized infertile

---

136. Matsumoto, Nobuhiro *Nihon shinwa no kenkyū*, Dōbunkan, 1931, p. 101-129. Frazer, James George "Demeter and Persephone," *The Golden Bough. A study in magic and religion*, Wordsworth Reference, 1993, pp. 393-394.
137. Matsumoto, Nobuhiro *Nihon shinwa no kenkyū*, Dōbunkan, 1931, p. 119.
138. Ibid., p. 111.
139. Ibid., p. 120.

nature.[140] This means that Matsumoto applied Frazer's theory of the goddess of fertility to the Chinese legend on the basis of a common motive of making a woman laugh. However, in this case of the Chinese legend, he did not prove the role of the queen as the goddess of fertility. In this way, Matsumoto's discussion concerning the Chinese legend mainly matched the legend with the popular topic of the goddess of fertility in the Western circles.

4. Influence of diffusionist ethnology on Matsumoto's ideas regarding Southeast Asia

This section examines the influence of diffusionism on Matsumoto's ideas regarding Southeast Asia before Matsumoto's trip to French Indochina in 1933. In the 20th century, evolutionist ethnology was challenged by the ideas of various diffusionist schools. Contrary to evolutionists, diffusionists did not believe in the universal cultural foundation of mankind because they imagined culture as something that spreads from a center to different people, implying various cultural foundations. Consequently, their interpretation of the similarities between the two different cultures resulted from the contacts between these cultures, where a more civilized culture influenced a less civilized culture.[141] Thus, in contrast with evolutionist ethnologists, diffusionist ethnologists argued that people differed by their origin and that similarities between different people were caused by influence from abroad.

First, this section examines the diffusionist influence of Schmidt and Przyluski's theory of Austroasiatic languages on Matsumoto's ideas regarding Southeast Asia in France. Second, it explores the influence of other Western diffusionist theories on the Southern Pacific culture. Third, this section discusss diffusionist influence on Matsu-

---

140. Matsumoto, Nobuhiro "Warazaru onna" (1932), *Nihon minzoku bunka no kigen III: Tōnan Ajia to Nihon*, Kōdansha, 1978, pp. 424–425.
141. Gaillard, Gérald "III The turn of the century. The Diffusionist Schools," *The Routledge Dictionary of Anthropologists*, London, Routledge, New York, 1997, pp. 40–41.

moto's ideas in Japan, especially Yanagita's influence, and indicates the contradictions in Matsumoto's ideas due to concurrent evolutionist and sociologist influences.

4.1. Influence of the theory of Austroasiatic languages

This section investigates the influence of the theory of Austroasiatic languages on Matsumoto's ideas regarding Southeast Asia. The theory of the Austroasiatic languages is a genealogical theory of many languages being distributed across continental Southeast Asia and India.[142] Matsumoto studied this theory from his advisor Jean Przyluski who adopted it from Austrian linguist and ethnologist Wilhelm Schmidt. The theory of the Austroasiatic languages played a central role in Matsumoto's doctoral thesis at Sorbonne University and significantly influenced Matsumoto's further writings.

4.1.1. Significance of Wilhelm Schmidt and Jean Przyluski for Matsumoto's adoption of the theory of Austroasiatic languages

Wilhelm Schmidt (1868-1954), founder of the Vienna Diffusionist School, introduced his theory of the Austroasiatic languages in his paper *The Mon-Khmer Peoples, a Link between the Peoples of Central Asia and Austronesia* in 1906.[143] This theory created a sensation in the linguistic and ethnological circles because it indicated the genealogical connection between India and Southeast Asia. In his linguistic research, Schmidt proved that the languages of Munda and Khasi in India, Mon-Khmer languages, and some languages of Indochina and Malay Peninsulas belong to the same language family or, in other words, have the same origin. Thus, Schmidt's theory of the Austroasiatic lan-

---

142. The Austroasiatic languages – language family of languages distributed in continental Southeast-Asia. They are also referred to as Mon-Khmer languages. This language family includes languages Munda, Khasi-Palaungic, Khmuic, pakanic, Vieto-Katuic, Bahnaric, Khmer, Pearic, Nicobarese, Aslian, Monic, Shompen.
143. Schmidt, Wilhelm "Die Mon-Khmer-Völker, ein Bindeglied zwischen Völkern Zentralasiens und Austronesiens," *Archiv für Anthropologie*, Braunschweig, new series, 5, 1906, pp. 59-109.

guages was related to Southeast Asia and had great importance for linguistics and ethnology in general.

Schmidt's theory of Austroasiatic languages was attractive for Matsumoto's teacher Jean Przyluski. Przyluski was the chair of Indochina studies at the College de France of Sorbonne University and researched about the influence of Austroasiatic people in India.[144] He also presented a research on Vietnamese folklore and Indian Buddhism. As Matsumoto suggested, "He [Przyluski] employs the folkloristic methods in his Indological research and explores ancient Buddhism."[145] Thus, Przyluski explored Indochina and India—two regions whose linguistic links Schmidt had proven in his research on the Austroasiatic languages.

As a result of Przyluski's interest in the Austroasiatic languages, he became a specialist in the field in France. This is apparent from his contribution to the French dictionary *The Languages of the World*. Przyluski wrote the part on the Austroasiatic languages in this dictionary, which was published by the Linguistic Society of Paris in 1924.[146]

In his research, Przyluski attempted to prove a wider influence of the Austroasiatic languages in India. In his paper *Non-Aryan Loans in Indo-Aryan*, Przyluski argued that Sanskrit "acquired important loans from the languages of the non-Dravidian populations."[147] He suggested that these non-Dravidian languages were Austroasiatic languages.[148] Thus, Przyluski clearly believed that the sphere of the Austroasiatic languages in India was not limited to the languages of Munda and Khasi but included the Aryan language—Sanskrit. In this sense, Pr-

---

144. Matsumoto, Nobuhiro "Furansu ni okeru minzokugakuteki kenkyū," *Nihon minzokugaku kenkyū*, (ed. by Yanagita), Iwanami shoten, Tokyo, 1935, p. 384. "Gendai Furansu ni okeru Tōyōgaku," *Furansu no shakaigakka. Gendai ni okeru shokeikō*, Fransu gakkai, 1930, p. 591.
145. Matsumoto, Nobuhiro "Furansu ni okeru minzokugakuteki kenkyū," *Nihon minzokugaku kenkyū*, (ed. by Yanagita), Iwanami shoten, 1935, p. 384.
146. Meillet *Les Langues du Monde*, É. Champion, Paris, 1924, pp. 385–403.
147. Przyluski, Jean "Non-Aryan Loans in Indo-Aryan," *Pre-Aryan and Pre-Dravidian in India*, translated by Prabodh Chandra Bagchi Culcatta, Culcutta University Press, Senate House, Culcutta, 1929 (French edition in 1923), p. 4.
148. Ibid., pp. 9, 14, 15, 17, 21, 24, 25, 30.

zyluski suggested that the Austroasiatic languages originally spread across the entire territory of India. Hence, Przyluski attempted to prove the existence of the Austroasiatic sphere in Southern and Southeast Asia.

Matsumoto was impressed by Przyluski's research on the influence of the Austroasiatic languages in India in the paper *Non-Aryan Loans in Indo-Aryan*. Its impact was so strong that Matsumoto introduced Przyluski's research to Japanese readers in his paper after returning to Japan. In his article *The Far Eastern Research of Europeans*, Matsumoto argued that Przyluski proved the existence of the vocabulary originating from the Austroasiatic languages in the vocabulary of Sanskrit.[149] In addition, Matsumoto introduced Przyluski's writings.[150] From Przyluski, Matsumoto learnt that the Austroasiatic influence was not limited only to the sphere of the language: "Moreover, in his paper *Totemism and Vegetalism in India*, Mr. Przyluski mentions about the influence that ancient tribes of the Austroasiatic genealogy exerted upon the Indian religion."[151] Therefore, Matsumoto's writings demonstrated Matsumoto's deep interest in Przyluski's claim of the Austroasiatic influence in India.

He actively informed Przyluski that he discovered similarities between the Japanese vocabulary and the vocabulary of the Austroasiatic languages. Przyluski, who was deeply concerned with the Austroasiatic languages at that time, encouraged Matsumoto to inquire about the similarities between the Austroasiatic languages and Japanese language.[152] Matsumoto's close relation with his professor is also suggested by the fact that he spent his summer holiday at Przyluski's summer house in Chamonney Valey.[153]

---

149. Matsumoto, Nobuhiro "Ōshūjin no Kyokutō kenkyū (I)," *Shigaku*, dai 8 kan, dai 1 gō, MitaShigakkai, 1929, pp. 24–25.
150. Matsumoto, Nobuhiro "Kodai bunkaron," *Gendai shigaku taikei*, Kyōritsusha shoten, 1932, pp. 46–52.
151. Ibid., p. 46.
152. Arima, Makiko "Hito, Matsumoto Nobuhiro," *Kikan jinruigaku*, 5-1, Shakaishisōsha, 1974, p. 156 (an interview with Matsumoto Nobuhiro).

4.1.2. Matsumoto's adoption of the theory of the Austroasiatic languages

Under Przyluski's influence and guidance, Matsumoto wrote a doctoral thesis *The Japanese and the Austroasiatic languages: A Comparative Study of Vocabulary*.[154] In the thesis, Matsumoto attempted to prove the affinity of the Japanese language with the Southern languages by comparing the roots of the words. He declared that he was able to prove the relationship between the Japanese people and the Austroasiatic people. He identified 113 common word roots: "... anyway, we can affirm that the Austroasiatic element played an important role in the formation of the Japanese language. In the anthropological, archeological and ethnological domains, the proof was already made that there are relations between the Japanese and Austroasiatic peoples; no surprise to these relations if they would have transmitted by a common linguistic element. ...we have successfully approached step by step 113 Japanese roots of Austroasiatic words, and this number is not absolute: new researches permit, without doubts, multiple examples. In these conditions, we are convinced about the broad relation of Japanese and Austroasiatic languages."[155]

However, his argument on the cause of the similarities between the Japanese and the Austroasiatic languages was contradictory because he claimed that there were the Japanese roots of words in the vocabulary of the Austroasiatic languages. Simultaneously, he emphasized the importance of the Austroasiatic element for the formation of the Japanese language.[156] His sentence on the Japanese roots of words in the Austroasiatic vocabulary was probably a mistake because Matsumoto never presented an argument regarding the Japanese influence on the Austroasiatic languages. He even found it difficult to support theories arguing the influence of Japan on the South Seas.[157] Neverthe-

---

153. Matsumoto, Nobuhiro "Furansu daigaku," *Sanshokuki*, dai 42 gō, Keiō gijuku Daigaku tsūshin kyōikubu, 1951, p. 2.
154. Matsumoto, Nobuhiro *Le japonais et les langues austroasiatiques: étude de vocabulaire comparé*, P. Geuthner, Paris, 1928.
155. Ibid., p. 96.
156. Ibid., p. 96.
157. Matsumoto, Nobuhiro *Nihon shinwa kenkyū*, Ibundō, 1956 (2nd edition), p. 48.

less, Matsumoto adopted Schmidt's theory of the Austroasiatic languages following the model of Przyluski's comparative research on the Sanskrit vocabulary with the vocabulary of the Austroasiatic languages. Therefore, Matsumoto claimed the influence of the Austroasiatic languages in Japan similar to Przyluski who claimed the influence of the Austroasiatic languages in India.

Nonetheless, Matsumoto misinterpreted Schmidt's theory in his doctoral thesis. This was because he compared the Japanese and Ryukyu languages with the Austroasiatic languages and the Austronesian (Malayo-Polynesian) languages[158] despite entitling the thesis *The Japanese and the Austroasiatic languages: A Comparative Study of Vocabulary*.[159] This means that, unlike Schmidt, he did not distinguish between the Austroasiatic languages in continental Southeast Asia and the Austronesian languages in insular Southeast Asia and the Pacific as separate language families. This fact was criticized by Schmidt at the Congress of German Linguists in Vienna in 1930. In this conference, Schmidt noted that Matsumoto used the term "the Austric languages" for indicating two groups of the Austroasiatic languages and the Austronesian languages.[160] Przyluski misinterpreted Schmidt's theory in his preface to Matsumoto's thesis.[161] Since the research on language genealogies was in its embryonic stage, various interpretations of the Austroasiatic language family existed. Thus, that Matsumoto adopted Przyluski's interpretation and included the Austronesian languages in the Austroasiatic languages following Przyluski's instruction.

---

158. Austronesian languages, or Malayo-Polynesian languages,are distributed in maritime Southeast Asia, Oceania and Madagascar. Few Austronesian speakers are also in continental Southeast Asia.
159. Matsumoto, Nobuhiro *Le japonais et les langues austroasiatiques: étude de vocabulaire comparé*, P. Geuthner, Paris, 1928, pp. 45-93.
160. Schmidt, Wilhelm "Nihongo to Ōsutorisshugo tono kankei" ("Die Beziehungen der austrischen Sprachen zum Japanischen"), *Indoshina no minzoku to bunka*, Iwanami shoten, transl. by Matsumoto Nobuhiro, 1942, p. 357.
161. Przyluski, Jean "Preface," in Matsumoto, Nobuhiro *Le japonais et les langues austroasiatiques: étude de vocabulaire comparé*, P. Geuthner, Paris, 1928, p. VII.

Moreover, Schmidt rejected the conclusion of Matsumoto's thesis *The Japanese and the Austroasiatic languages: A Comparative Study of Vocabulary* that the Austroasiatic languages played a significant role in the formation of the Japanese language. Schmidt declared that there was no genealogical relationship between the Japanese and Austroasiatic languages. In addition, Japanese linguist Kobayashi Hideo dismissed the results of Matsumoto's linguistic research due to the lack of evidences in 1928.[162] Matsumoto defended his thesis against Schmidt's criticism in his Japanese writing. He argued that Schmidt misunderstood his purpose and that he discussed only the relationship between the Japanese and the Austroasiatic, languages, and not their common genealogy.[163]

Obviously, Matsumoto did not know how to interpret the comparison of the Japanese and the Austroasiatic cultures due to the concurrent influence of evolutionist, sociologist, and diffusionist ethnologists. While evolutionists and sociologist ethnologists searched for common elements of the various cultures to clarify the cultural basis of the mankind, diffusionist ethnologists compared various cultures (languages) to clarify their genealogy and indicated the common origin of the compared languages. Consequently, Matsumoto interpreted the common culture through two ways. First, he compared various peoples' customs based on the evolutionist-sociologist hypothesis of the universal primitive culture. Second, he followed the hypothesis of cultural diffusion when he compared languages.

However, Matsumoto received support from some French schol-

---

162. Kobayashi, Hideo "Nihongo no shozoku mondai – Matsumoto Nobuhiro shi no kingi wo yomu," *Minzoku*, dai 4 kan, dai 1 gō, Minzoku hakkōjo, 1928, p. 165.
163. Matsumoto, Nobuhiro "Ōsutorikku gozoku ha hatashite sonzai nasuya," *Shigaku, dai 10 kan, dai 1 gō*, Mita Shigakkai, 1931, p. 96. Schmidt, Wilhelm "Die Beziehungen der austrischen Sprachen zum Japanischen," *Wien Beitrag zur Kulturgeschichte und Linguistik*, Vol. I, Wien, 1930, pp. 239-252 opt. cit. in Matsumoto, Nobuhiro "Kodai bunkaron," *Gendai shigaku taikei*, Kyōritsusha shoten, 1932, pp. 94-95. Matsumoto, Nobuhiro "Ōsutoroajiago ni kan suru shomondai," *Kawai kyōju kanreki kinen ronbunshū*, Kawaikyōju kanreki shukugakai, 1931, pp. 513-519.

ars. In addition to Przyluski, diffusionist ethnologist Paul Rivet (1876–1958) acknowledged Matsumoto's conclusion regarding the Austroasiatic influence on Japan. In his book *Sumerian and Oceanian*, Rivet discussed theories claiming the influence of Southern culture, including Przyluski's and Matsumoto's opinions.[164] Rivet wrote in relation to the result of Matsumoto's doctoral thesis as follows: "O. Gjerdman signalized a great number of lexical accords between Ainu and the Austronesian languages ... Furthermore, a Japanese scholar, Matsumoto brought evidence on similarities between the same languages and the Japanese language."[165] This means that Rivet disagreed with Schmidt's definition of the Austroasiatic and Austronesian languages. Hence, the opinion on the Austroasiatic influence encompassing Austronesia was shared by some scholars in the French ethnological and linguistic circles. Therefore, Matsumoto continued to claim the validity of his comparative research on the Japanese and the Austroasiatic languages.

Matsumoto republished his linguistic research from his doctoral thesis *The Japanese and the Austro-Asiatic languages: A Comparative Study of Vocabulary* in his paper "Problems of the Austro-Asiatic languages"[166] and in his writing *Theories of Ancient Culture*.[167] His only correction was that he decreased the number of the common root words of the Japanese and the Austroasiatic languages from 113 to 97.[168] He argued regarding the close relationship of the Japanese language with the Austroasiatic languages (*Ōsutoroajia go*, オーストロアジア語) without defining the relationship specifically: "From this table of correspondences, it is clear that the vocabulary of the Japanese language

---

164. Rivet, Paul *Sumérien et Océanien*, Librairie ancienne honoré champion, La Société de linguistique de Paris, Paris, 1929, p. 11.
165. Ibid., p. 9.
166. Matsumoto, Nobuhiro "Ōsutoroajiago ni kan suru shomondai," *Kawai kyōju kanreki kinen ronbunshū*, Kawaikyōju kanreki shukugakai, 1931, pp. 481–522.
167. Matsumoto, Nobuhiro "Kodai bunkaron," *Gendai shigaku taikei*, Kyōritsusha shoten, 1932, pp. 81–95.
168. Matsumoto, Nobuhiro "Ōsutoroajiago ni kan suru shomondai," *Kawai kyōju kanreki kinen ronbunshū*, Kawaikyōju kanreki shukugakai, 1931, p. 512. Matsumoto, Nobuhiro "Kodai bunkaron," *Gendai shigaku taikei*, Kyōritsusha shoten, 1932, p. 93.

has a close relationship with the vocabulary of the Austroasiatic language family. But what kind of conclusion can be drawn from it? Is it the common origin of the Japanese language and the Austric language family? At the present point, we cannot state it clearly. But, should we admit that both languages had contacts and mixed up, and the Japanese language borrowed the vocabulary from the Austric languages? It is also difficult to give a safe answer to it. Today the only proven fact is that the Southern elements played an important role in the formation of the Japanese language."[169] Thus, although Matsumoto did not know how to interpret the similarities between the Japanese language and Austroasiatic languages, he accepted the diffusionist interpretation of the Austroasiatic influence on the Japanese language because his teacher Przyluski and Rivet argued about the Austroasiatic influence.

However, Matsumoto did not agree with Przyluski's opinion on the Austroasiatic influence in India. He surmised the existence of the Austroasiatic elements in China. In his paper *Theories of Ancient Culture* (1932), he first focused on the archaeological fact that the stone implements found in China were not made by the ethnical Chinese.[170] Then, he claimed that he believed in the contacts of the Austroasiatic languages and Chinese language.[171] Finally, he followed Przyluski's opinion that the Southern culture influenced the Chinese culture: "According to Mr. Przyluski, the custom of the spring festival is a living topic in China's tales in which a girl throws a ball and chooses her spouse like this, and this is the influence of Southward [*Nampō*, 南方] peoples on the China's culture."[172] Thus, under Przyluski's influence, Matsumoto did not consider the theory of the Austroasiatic languages

---

169. Matsumoto, Nobuhiro "Ōsutoroajiago ni kan suru shomondai," *Kawai kyōju kanreki kinen ronbunshū*, Kawaikyōju kanreki shukugakai, 1931, p. 513. Matsumoto, Nobuhiro "Kodai bunkaron," *Gendai shigaku taikei*, Kyōritsusha shoten, 1932, p. 94.
170. Matsumoto, Nobuhiro "Kodai bunkaron," *Gendai shigaku taikei*, Kyōritsusha shoten, 1932, p. 5.
171. Ibid., p. 77.
172. Ibid., p. 109.

as a linguistic theory, but he imagined a zone of the Austroasiatic culture encompassing India, Southeast Asia, China, and Japan. Since he believed in the diffusionist theory of Southern influence, he surmised that the Austroasiatic culture spread from a center in Southeast Asia to India, China, and Japan. Thus, under Przyluski's influence, Matsumoto became a proponent of the Southward Theory advocating Japan's connection with the South, especially with Southeast Asia.

4.2. Influence of the theory of Southern Pacific influence

In addition to Przyluski's influence, Matsumoto was inspired by other diffusionist ethnologists' theories on the Southern Pacific influence. This section examines the influence of the French diffusionist Paul Rivet (1876-1958) and the American diffusionist Roland B. Dixon (1875-1934) on Matsumoto's ideas regarding Southeast Asia. Dixon's influence has been already mentioned by Hirafuji.[173]

During his studies at Sorbonne University, Matsumoto was exposed to Rivet's diffusionist ideas regarding the Southern Pacific. Rivet was the director of the anthropological department of the Parisian Museum of Natural Sciences.[174] At the time Matsumoto was in Paris in 1924-1928, Rivet presented writings about the diffusion of the Southern Pacific culture: *Melaneso-polynesians and Australians in America*,[175] *Australians in America*,[176] and *Malayo-Polynesians in America*.[177] It can be surmised that Matsumoto attended Rivet's lectures. This is because Rivet's works were the second foreign work that Matsumoto introduced to the Japanese readers after his return to Japan. First,

---

173. Hirafuji, Kikuko "Shakaigakuteki kenkyū – Matsumoto Nobuhiro no shinwa kenkyū ni okeru Furansu shakaigakuha no eikyō," *Shinwagaku to Nihon no kamigami*, Kōbunkan, 2004, p. 38.
174. Matsumoto, Nobuhiro "Ōshūjin no Kyokutō kenkyū (II)," *Shigaku*, dai 8 kan, dai 3 gō, MitaShigakkai, 1929, p. 43 (365).
175. Rivet, Paul *Les Mélaneso-polynésiens et les Australiens en Amérique*, Picard, Paris, 1924
176. Rivet, Paul *Les Australiens en Amérique*, Librairie ancienne Honoré Champion, Paris, 1925.
177. Rivet, Paul "Les Malayo-Polynésian en Amérique", *Journal de la Société des Américanistes de Paris*, Nouvelle Série, XVIII, 1926, pp. 143-145.

Matsumoto wrote about Przyluski's work on the Austroasiatic influence in India, and then he presented Rivet's works on the South Pacific influence in America in his paper *Far Eastern Research of Europeans (II)*.[178] Matsumoto mentioned about Rivet's research in his paper *The Japanese and the Austroasiatic Languages*.[179] In addition, he mentioned about the most recent book by Rivet, *Sumerian and Oceanian* (1929) in his article *Problems of the Austroasiatic languages*[180] and in his paper *Theories of Ancient Culture*.[181] Through his references to Rivet in his writings, Matsumoto focused on several of Rivet's works in 1929–1932 when he presented his research on the Austroasiatic languages.

First, Matsumoto became interested in Rivet's idea of the connection among Australia, Oceania, and the American continents. Rivet attempted to prove a close relationship of a North American language with the Austronesian languages in his booklet *Australians in America* and a close relationship of a South American language with Australian languages in his paper *Malayo-Polynesians in America* through the comparison of the vocabulary.[182] Matsumoto believed in Rivet's research findings as he wrote in his paper *Far Eastern Research of Europeans (II)*: "On 12 December 1924, the Nestor of the French linguistic circles Antoine Meillet reported about two of Rivet's researches in the Academie des Inscription et Belles-Lettres and supported his theory as valuable. As Rivet says, the existence of a close kinship relation between South Sea languages [*Nankai go*, 南海語] and the languages of

---

178. Matsumoto, Nobuhiro "Ōshūjin no Kyokutō kenkyū (II)," *Shigaku*, dai 8 kan, dai 3 gō, MitaShigakkai, 1929, pp. 43-60 (365-382).
179. Matsumoto, Nobuhiro "Nihongo to Ōsutoroajiago," *Shigaku zasshi*, dai 40 kan, dai 1 gō, Shigakkai, 1929, p. 111.
180. Matsumoto, Nobuhiro "Ōsutoroajiago ni kan suru shomondai," *Kawai kyōju kanreki kinen ronbunshū*, Kawaikyōju kanreki shukugakai, 1931, pp. 519.
181. Matsumoto, Nobuhiro "Kodai bunkaron," *Gendai shigaku taikei*, Kyōritsusha shoten, 1932, pp. 55-57.
182. Matsumoto, Nobuhiro "Ōshūjin no Kyokutō kenkyū (II)," *Shigaku*, dai 8 kan, dai 3 gō, MitaShigakkai, 1929, p. 43 (365). "Ōsutoroajiago ni kan suru shomondai," *Kawai kyōju kanreki kinen ronbunshū*, Kawaikyōju kanreki shukugakai, 1931, p. 519. "Kodai bunkaron," *Gendai shigaku taikei*, Kyōritsusha shoten, 1932, p. 55.

the American continent is difficult to believe quickly, but the mutual contacts among them should be confirmed; [Rivet's] research shed some light on the difficult issue of what are the origins of the American languages, we can say that it indicated the direction of the future research."[183] Matsumoto expressed his support for Rivet's conclusion in his paper *Theories of Ancient Culture*: "Rivet demonstrated that the North American language family has relations with Indonesia, Melanesia and Polynesia languages."[184] These statements suggest that Matsumoto considered South Sea languages (*Nankaigo*, 南海語) to be a broad language family that included the Austroasiatic languages and the languages of Oceania and Australia (that encompasses Austronesian languages). This is also visible from Matsumoto's incorporation of the Austronesian languages in the Austroasiatic language family in his doctoral thesis *The Japanese and the Austroasiatic languages: A Comparative Study of Vocabulary* (1928).

Second, Matsumoto discussed Rivet's idea regarding the connection between the Sumerian language and the Austronesian languages from Rivet's book *Sumerian and Oceanian*. Matsumoto presented Rivet's comparative research in his paper *Theories of Ancient Culture*.[185] Matsumoto agreed in general with Rivet's conclusion about the similarity between the Sumerian language and the South Sea languages (Australia, Tasmania, Melanesia, Indonesia, Mon-Khmer, etc.): "From these examples, we can see that the vocabulary of the Sumerian language is very similar to the vocabulary of the South Sea languages."[186] In his comparative research, Rivet included the Mon-Khmer languages from the Austroasiatic language family.[187] Thus, Matsumoto shared Rivet's argument that the South Sea languages (including Austroasiatic and Austronesian languages) expanded over a large territory since

---

183. Matsumoto, Nobuhiro "Ōshūjin no Kyokutō kenkyū (II)," *Shigaku*, dai 8 kan, dai 3 gō, MitaShigakkai, 1929, pp. 43–44 (365–466).
184. Matsumoto, Nobuhiro "Kodai bunkaron," *Gendai shigaku taikei*, Kyōritsusha shoten, 1932, p. 60.
185. Ibid., pp. 55–57.
186. Ibid., p. 57.
187. Ibid., p. 57.

they came in contact with the Sumerian language.

Matsumoto borrowed Przyluski's idea of the Austroasiatic zone spreading from India in the West to Japan in the East. Under Rivet's influence, Matsumoto imagined this cultural zone to be even broader, reaching as far as America. Consequently, Matsumoto perceived Southeast Asia with the Austroasiatic languages as a core of a larger South Sea culture that expanded in many directions in the ancient times.

Matsumoto's concern for the South Seas was supported by the leader of the French School of Sociology—Mauss. Mauss discussed Melanesian and Polynesian culture in his book *The Gift* and recommended Matsumoto to consider the comparison of the Japanese and the Oceanic myths. Matsumoto introduced this in the second edition of his book *The Research of the Japanese Myths*: "The comparative research of resemblance between the Japanese myths and the myths of Pacific islands was recommended to me in Paris by Marcel Mauss, the great master in the research of primitive religions..."[188]

However, there was an important difference between Mauss' and Matsumoto's approach to the South Seas. Mauss considered the Southern Pacific culture to be suitable for researching the basis for the modern society in general, as was discussed in Section 2. Matsumoto shared Mauss' opinion, but he discussed the Japanese contacts with the South Sea culture and emphasized the influence of South Sea culture under the various diffusionist influences. This means that Matsumoto's discussion of the South Sea languages was diffusionist in contrast to the sociological approach of Mauss. Nevertheless, Mauss encouraged Matsumoto to focus on Southern culture.

As a result of Mauss' recommendation, Matsumoto became interested in the Southern Pacific myths researched by the diffusionist scholar Dixon. Matsumoto read Dixon's book *Oceanic*[189] because it represented a basic reading on Southern Pacific mythology at that time. Moreover, Dixon, who was the professor of anthropology at

---

188. Matsumoto, Nobuhiro *Nihon shinwa kenkyū*, Ibundō, 1956 (2nd edition), p. 1.
189. Dixon, Roland Burrage *Oceanic*, Marshall Jones, Boston, 1916.

Harvard University, was the teacher of Matsumoto's teacher Utsushikawa Nenozo (1884-1947). Coincidently, Utsushikawa visited Matsumoto in Paris before he introduced ethnology at Taihoku Imperial University in Taiwan in 1928. During this time, Matsumoto helped Utsushikawa collect necessary literature on the South Seas in Paris.[190] Therefore, Utsushikawa also encouraged Matsumoto to study the South Seas and shared with him more information about Dixon's ideas. Thus, under Mauss' and Utsushikawa's influence, Matsumoto considered Dixon's work on Oceanic mythology to be significant.

In his book *Oceanic*, Dixon classified various Oceanic myths into two types: the genealogical (evolutionary) type and the creative type.[191] Furthermore, he divided Oceania into five different regions (Polynesia, Melanesia, Indonesia, Micronesia, and Australia) according to the characteristics of their mythology.[192]

From Dixon's book, Matsumoto adopted the classification of the myths into the genealogical or evolutionary type and the creative type and paraphrased the Oceanic myths in his book *The Research of the Japanese Myths*.[193] Against this theoretical background, Matsumoto singled out the similarities between the Japanese myth concerning the creation of the heaven and Earth and the Polynesian myth of the evolutionary type: "The first half of the Japanese myth of the creation of the world has similar points with this evolutionary myth of Polynesia."[194] This approach to the Japanese myth was later adopted by Obayashi Taryo.[195] In this sense, Dixon's book supported Matsumoto's

---

190. Matsumoto, Nobuhiro *Nihon shinwa no kenkyū*, Dōbunkan, 1931, p. 177. "Kodai bunkaron" *Gendai shigaku taikei*, Kyōritsusha shoten, 1932, p. 178. Itō, Seiji "Matsumoto Nobuhiro – 'Nampōsetsu' no kaitakusha," *Bunka jinruigaku gunzō*, Nihonhen (3), Akademia shuppankai, Kyōto, 1988, p. 232
191. Dixon, Roland Burrage *Oceanic*, Marshall Jones, Boston, 1916, pp. 2, 5, 18.
192. Ibid., pp. xi, xiv.
193. Matsumoto, Nobuhiro *Nihon shinwa no kenkyū*, Dōbunkan, 1931, pp. 178-179.
194. Ibid., p. 181.
195. Ōbayashi, Taryō "Sōzōgata shinwa," *Nihon shinwa no kigen*, Kadokawa shoten, 1961, pp. 58-64. Ōbayashi also compared the Japanese myths with Oceanian myths in Ōbayashi, Taryō "Tsuranaru Tōnan Ajia, Oceania," *Shinwa no keifu: nihon shinwa no genryū wo saguru*, Seidosha, 1986, pp. 221-315.

belief concerning the Southern influence on the Japanese culture although Dixon himself did not discuss it at all.

4.3. Influence of ideas regarding Southern culture in Japan

Before his studies in France, Matsumoto was exposed to diffusionist ideas regarding Southern culture in Japan. This section examines the influence of Japanese ideas regarding Southern culture on Matsumoto's writings.

First, Matsumoto's ideas regarding Southern culture were influenced by Yanagita's account of his experience in the eastern coast of Kyushu and the Ryukyu Islands. Yanagita traveled there from December 1920 to March 1921.[196] As a result of this research trip, Yanagita

Chart 1: Influences on Matsumoto's ideas regarding Southern culture in France

```
Schmidt ──── diffusionist theory of Austroasiatic languages
    │
    ▼
Przyluski ──── diffusionist theory of Austroasiatic languages
              diffusionist theory of Austroasiatic influence in India, China, Japan

Rivet ──── diffusionist ideas of Southern influence in America (Southern Pacific culture)

Dixon ──── classification of Southern myths (Oceanic culture)

diffusionist ethnology Southern culture
    │
    ▼
Utsushikawa ──── diffusionist theory of Southern culture

Mauss, Granet ──── sociologist theories, evolutionist theories
                   theory of Southern culture (Southern Pacific and Southeast Asia)

evolutionist theories (totemism, exogamy)
    │
    ▼
Frazer ──── evolutionist theories (totemism, exogamy)
```

→ Matsumoto's ideas regarding Southern culture

wrote several essays that were published first in a series of articles in the Asahi Newspaper in 1921 and were included in his book *Small Records from Seas in South* (*Nankai shōki*, 海南小記) in April 1925.[197] However, Yanagita's influence did not impact Matsumoto's writings in the early 1920s. This was because that Matsumoto focused on the culture of ancient China at that time. Matsumoto mentioned Ryukyu myths in relation to the Japanese myths for the first time in his French doctoral thesis in 1928.[198] Then, he compared a Ryukyu legend with a Japanese myth in his book *The Research of the Japanese myths*.[199] This means that Yanagita's ideas regarding Southern culture became significant for Matsumoto only after he received the influence of Western scholars who argued regarding the importance of Southern culture during 1924–1928.

Matsumoto wrote that the Okinawa trip considerably impacted Yanagita. According to Matsumoto's statement, Yanagita organized a research meeting in which he argued regarding the importance of Okinawa. In addition, Yanagita organized the Southern Islands Discussion Meeting (*Nantō danwakai*, 南島談話会) to deliver his research on Okinawa in 1922.[200] Matsumoto also wrote that Yanagita originally planned to go on this research trip with his friend Orikuchi Shinobu (1887–1953), but they did not meet on the way due to technical problems in their communication.[201] Thus, Matsumoto was present at Yanagita's research meetings concerning the travel to Okinawa and knew the details of Yanagita's journey.

Yanagita's ideas in *Small Records from Seas in South* significantly

---

196. Fukuta, Ajio *Yanagita Kunio no minzokugaku*, Yoshikawa kōbunkan, 1992, p. 257. *Yanagita Kunio: sasayakanaru mukashi shō kokyō shichijūnen shō*, ed. by Okaya Kōji, Nihontoshosentā, 1998, p. 245.
197. Ibid., pp. 245–246.
198. Matsumoto, Nobuhiro *Essai sur la mythologie Japonaise*, P. Geuthner, Paris, 1928, p.
199. Matsumoto, Nobuhiro *Nihon shinwa no kenkyū*, Dōbunkan, 1931, p. 188.
200. Matsumoto, Nobuhiro "Yanagita Kunio 'Kainan shōki' to 'Kaijō no michi' – minzoku to minzoku ni tsuite" *Nihon minzoku bunka no kigen I: shinwa-densetsu*, Kōdansha, 1978, p. 333.
201. Ibid., p. 333.

influenced the formation of Matsumoto's ideas regarding Southern culture. The most important opinion was Yanagita's argument on the migration across the ocean to the Japanese islands. According to his book *Small Records from Seas in South*, Yanagita believed in "great migration of the ancient oceanic people", which changed the culture of the Japanese islands by assimilating with the native people.[202] Based on this hypothesis, Yanagita examined various connections of the Japanese islands with the south. For example, he indicated that the sweet potato in Kyushu originally came from Southern China.[203]

However, despite this idea of Japan's connection with South, Yanagita did not argue regarding the Japanese origins abroad Japan. His interest in Southern culture was mainly interest in culture spread in the Southern parts of the Japanese Empire, such as Kyushu, Ryukyu, and Taiwan. For example, he proposed a theory that the origin of the Japanese tale of Potato Digger Millionaire was in Kyushu.[204] In this manner, Yanagita was a diffusionist looking for the Japanese origins in Southern Japan.

Matsumoto adopted Yanagita's idea regarding a transoceanic migration from the South. In his French doctoral thesis on mythology *Essay on the Japanese Mythology*, Matsumoto argued that the advent of the first Japanese emperor in Hyūga in the Japanese myths has "allusion to migrations of the Japanese people from South-East to North-East."[205] In this context, Matsumoto indicated "the influence of Southern civilization" in Kyushu where Hyūga was a religious political center.[206]

Second, in Yanagita's folklore circles, Matsumoto came in contact with Iha Fuyu (1876-1947), who founded the Japanese Ryukyu studies. Yanagita's relationship with Iha Fuyu was undoubtedly strengthened

---

202. Yanagita, Kunio *Kainan shōki*, Sōgensha, 1945 (first edition 1925), pp. iv-v.
203. Ibid., p. 4.
204. Matsumoto, Nobuhiro "Imohori chōsha" (1930), *Nihon minzoku bunka no kigen I: shinwa-densetsu*, Kōdansha, 1978, pp. 309-310.
205. Matsumoto, Nobuhiro *Essai sur la mythologie Japonaise*, P. Geuthner, Paris, 1928, p. 104.
206. Ibid., p. 104.

by their meeting in Naha in January 1921.²⁰⁷ Matsumoto's relationship with Iha was discussed by Sato Yoshiyuki who analyzed Iha's letters to Matsumoto.²⁰⁸ Matsumoto respected Iha as an influential scholar in Ryukyu studies. He noted Iha's research on the Okinawan dialect in his doctoral thesis *The Japanese and the Austro-Asiatic Languages: A Comparative Study of Vocabulary*.²⁰⁹ Furthermore, he drew on Ryukyu legends from Iha's book *Old Ryukyu* (1911) in his doctoral thesis *Essay on the Japanese Mythology*.²¹⁰ This reveals that Matsumoto obviously knew Iha's work in linguistics as well as in folklore studies to some extent.

Third, Matsumoto read books related to Taiwanese culture. In the *Essay on the Japanese Mythology*, he especially referred to Sakima Kōei's *Legends of Southern Islands*（南島説話, 1922）and Sayama and Onishi's *The Collection of Traditions of Taiwanese Aborigines*（生蛮伝説集, 1923）.²¹¹ In these books, Matsumoto drew from the legends of the marriage between a brother and a sister and the myth of the separation of the heaven from the Earth in the appendix "Analogies between the Japanese myths and the myths of southern peoples."²¹² Matsumoto mentioned the same Taiwanese legends in his Japanese book *The Research of the Japanese Myths*.²¹³ In other words, he used the legends and myths in these books on Taiwan to indicate their similarities with the Japanese ancient culture.

Fourth, Matsumoto was probably affected by the writings of journalist and politician Takegoshi Yosaburo (1865–1950), an advocator of Japan's Southern advance. Takegoshi graduated from Keio University.

---

207. Matsumoto, Mikio "Yanagita Kunio no Ryūkyū tabi," *Yanagita Kunio to umi no michi: "Kainan shōki" no genkei*, Yoshikawa kōbunkan, 2003, pp. 108.
208. Satō, Yoshiyuki "Iha Fuyu no Matsumoto Nobuhiro ate shokan. Meiji-Taishō no gengogaku, Sono 9," *Gakuen*, No. 821, 2009/3, pp. 102–109.
209. Matsumoto, Nobuhiro *Le japonais et les langues austroasiatiques: étude de vocabulaire comparé*, P. Geuthner, Paris, 1928, p. 11.
210. Matsumoto, Nobuhiro *Essai sur la mythologie Japonaise*, P. Geuthner, Paris, 1928, pp. 114–115.
211. Ibid., pp. 119, 122, 123, 125, 126.
212. Ibid., pp. 113–126.
213. Matsumoto, Nobuhiro *Nihon shinwa no kenkyū*, Dōbunkan, 1931, pp. 196–197.

In 1910, he published records from his travel to Dutch East Indies, French Indochina, and Yunnan in China, where he went in 1909, in his book *Records from Southern Countries*.[214] Here, he indicated that he could imagine prehistoric relationship between the Japanese and Malaysian people based on similarities between the two cultures.[215] Thus, Matsumoto could learn from Takegoshi about the Japanese connection with the South Seas in the ancient times.

In summary, Matsumoto came in contact with the research on Southern culture in Japan in the early 1920s before his studies in France. Although there existed some travel records from Southeast Asia, the Japanese research on Southern culture was generally limited to Okinawa and Taiwan, which were annexed to the Japanese Empire in the late 19th century. The research on these regions was the basis of South Sea studies in Japan because it was easy to access them in comparison with other Southern regions. Moreover, since Yanagita made the effort to promote Okinawa studies, these South Sea studies also had relations to Japanese folklore studies. Under this influence, Matsumoto began thinking about the significance of the Southern culture for Japan. Like Yanagita, Matsumoto believed that the Southern culture was brought across the sea to Kyushu. Therefore, he compared myths and legends from Japan with those from Ryukyu, Taiwan, Southeast Asia, and Southern Pacific. In short, Matsumoto and Yanagita can be considered to be followers of diffusionism since they both believed that the Southern culture was imported to the Japanese mainland.

4.3.1. Matsumoto's concept of the South Seas

The discussion on the diffusionist influence on Matsumoto's ideas showed that Matsumoto's ideas regarding Southeast Asia were inseparably linked with his ideas regarding the South Seas and the Southern culture. This was because Matsumoto interpreted the theory of Aus-

---

214. Takegoshi, Yosaburō *Nankokuki*, Nippon hyōronsha, 1942 (1st edition 1910), p.134.
215. Ibid., p. 272.

troasiatic languages, including those of Austronesian languages in connection with Southern Pacific areas and Southern Japan. This reflected the Japanese geographical context of the South Seas. Therefore, this section examines Matsumoto's use of the term of the South Seas in his writings.

During 1924–1932, Matsumoto used two geographical concepts including Southeast Asia: the Japanese concept *Nanyō* (南洋) and the Chinese concept *Nankai* (南海). For example, he wrote *Nanyō* in *Theories of Ancient Culture*: "However, as Dixon has surmised, the oral tradition of Thai ethnic in the mountains of Indochina is similar to the South Seas tradition [南洋伝統]."[216] Simultaneously, he used the term Nankai (南海): "Therefore, for research of civilization of ancient India, it is necessary to consider the South Seas [南海], especially folklore of manners and customs of Indochina's primitive people as a comparative source."[217] These quotations suggest that Matsumoto gave preference to the Chinese concept *Nankai* when he also covered the Indian Region in his discussion. In addition, he considered the South Sea languages (Nankaigo, 南海語) to be synonymous with Austroasiatic languages: "[Paul Rivet] argues that all South Sea languages [*Nankai go*, 南海語] of Australia, Tasmania, Melanesia, Indonesia, Mon-Khmer, etc. are similar."[218] This was because Khasi and Munda languages from Mon-Khmer languages are spoken in India. However, the Chinese concept *Nankai* did not originally include Australia, Tasmania, and Melanesia. Therefore, Matsumoto's concept of *Nankai* was the Japanese concept of *Nanyō* enlarged by the Indian Region.

Therefore, in his vocabulary regarding South Seas, Matsumoto mixed *Nanyō* (南洋) and *Nankai* (南海) and was ambiguous in distinguishing between Southeast Asia and the Southern Pacific Region. This was because while he held the Japanese and Chinese notions of the South Seas, he also adopted Western concepts of Austroasiatic languages encompassing Austronesian languages and the Western

---

216. Matsumoto, Nobuhiro "Kodai bunkaron," *Gendai shigaku taikei*, Kyōritsusha shoten, 1932, pp. 104–191.
217. Ibid., pp. 104–105.
218. Ibid., p. 55.

concept of the Oceanic Region. As a result, his concept of *Nankai* also included Australia that was not originally covered in this Chinese concept. Nevertheless, Matsumoto specifically focused on the South Seas in the sense that it was a region lying to be south of Japan.

4.3.2. Southward Theory and contradiction in Matsumoto's works

Due to his interest in the South Seas under the diffusionist influence, Matsumoto became an advocater of the Southward Theory (*Nampōron*, 南方論). This theory argued regarding the importance of the South Seas for Japan and the existence of Southern genealogy in the Japanese culture. During that time, the Southward Theory represented a minor stream in contradiction with the Northern theory that emphasized the Japanese contacts with the Asian continent, especially with China and Korea. However, Yanagita claimed the importance of the Southern culture. This was in accord with the diffusionist theories that Matsumoto learnt at the Sorbonne University. As explained in Section 4.1., Matsumoto argued regarding the Austroasiatic influence on the Japanese language. Hence, Yanagita's stance of Southward Theory enabled Matsumoto to apply his diffusionist knowledge from France in Japan.

Following Yanagita, Matsumoto took the opposite stance against the Northern influence. Yanagita who made the effort to establish the origins of the Japanese tradition in the Japanese territory disliked any reference to foreign influence on the Japanese culture, as indicated by Ito Seiji.[219] Matsumoto emphasized Yanagita's anti-foreign approach: "Yanagita avoided the discussion mentioning examples from abroad, avoided calling the tales of *Kojiki* and *Nihonshoki* myths and disliked

---

219. Matsumoto, Nobuhiro "Yanagita Kunio 'Kainan shōki' to 'Kaijō no michi' - minzoku to minzoku ni tsuite" *Nihon minzoku bunka no kigen I: shinwa-densetsu*, Kōdansha, 1978, pp. 336-338. Itō, Seiji "Matsumoto Nobuhito to imohiru chōsha no hanashi," *Nihon bunka no kigen*, dai 3 kan, Geppō dai 3 gō, 1978, pp. 5-8. Itō, Seiji "Sumiyaki chōsha no hanashi - Yanagita Kunio to Matsumoto Nobuhiro," *Shigaku*, dai 75 kan, dai 2/3 gō, 2007, pp. 211-231. Yanagita, Kunio "Kigenron kentō," *Minkan denshōron*, Kyōritsusha shoten, 1934, pp. 69-73.

calling the Japanese *Mikodō* [巫女道] by the name Shamanism from the continent."[220] Thus, Yanagita was critical toward the Northward Theory that advocated the influence of the Northern Asian continent on the Japanese culture.

Matsumoto became fully aware of Yanagita's opposition to the Northward Theory especially in 1930. In this year, Matsumoto presented a paper *The Tale of Potato Digger Millionaire*; in this paper, he compared a Japanese tale with a Korean tale. On the basis of the similarity between the Japanese and the Korean tales, Matsumoto claimed that "the old legend of Hachimangū genealogy has quite a deep and logical connection with Korea" and that "we may consider that these myths and legends were imported to Japan together with the crafts that arrived from the continent."[221] This study by Matsumoto was diffusionist because he claimed the Korean origins of the Japanese tale in his conclusion.

In this paper, Matsumoto proposed a hypothesis different from Yanagita's theory who argued that the origin of the tale of Potato Digger Millionaire is in Usa Hachimangū of Kyushu.[222] Yanagita responded in anger to Matsumoto's argument, which strongly impacted Matsumoto. Matsumoto described this episode in his paper *Yanagita Kunio's 'Notes from South Sea' and 'The Sea Route' - about the Race and the Folklore*[223], and Ito Seiji discussed this problem in his writings *Matsumoto Nobuhiro and the Tale of Potato Digger Millionaire*[224] and *The Tale of Charcoal Burner Millionaire - Yanagita Kunio and Matsumoto Nobuhiro*.[225] In addition, Ito mentioned that Matsumoto hesitantly told his

---

220. Matsumoto, Nobuhiro "Kaisetsu," *Nihon bunka no kigen*, dai 3 kan, "Minzokugaku 1," Heibonsha, 1971, p. 12.
221. Matsumoto, Nobuhiro "Imohori chōsha" (1930), *Nihon minzoku bunka no kigen I: shinwa-densetsu*, Kōdansha, 1978, p. 310.
222. Ibid., pp. 309-310.
223. Matsumoto Nobuhiro explained this Yanagita's opposition as the opposition of ethnology and folklore studies. Matsumoto, Nobuhiro "Yanagita Kunio 'Kainan shōki' to 'Kaijō no michi' - minzoku to minzoku ni tsuite" *Nihon minzoku bunka no kigen I: shinwa-densetsu*, Kōdansha, 1978, pp. 336-338.
224. Itō, Seiji "Matsumoto Nobuhito to imohori chōsha no hanashi," *Nihon bunka no kigen*, dai 3 kan, Geppō dai 3 gō, Kōdansha, 1978, pp. 5-8.

students that he was scolded by Yanagita.[226] Since Yanagita was Matsumoto's life-long teacher, Matsumoto had to accept Yanagita's opposition. Therefore, Matsumoto took a critical stance toward the Northward Theory and became prudent when claiming Japanese origins from abroad for maintaining a good relationship with Yanagita. Since then, we can find only Matsumoto's hypothesis arguing in favor of Southern influence on the Japanese culture.

Matsumoto criticized the Northward Theory in his paper *Theories of Ancient Culture*: "We should reconsider the attitude of researchers whose existing researches pay attention only to the relationship with the Northern continent, and there is only one thing to say: we should consider [the Japanese] contacts with the South Seas."[227] Thus, he claimed the importance of the contacts of the Japanese culture and the Southern culture while admitting the influence of the Northern culture.

Since the Northern theory mainly argued regarding the Chinese influence on the Japanese civilization, Matsumoto aimed at denouncing the importance of the Chinese influence by claiming the importance of the South Seas. In his book *The Research of the Japanese Myths*, Matsumoto wrote as follows: "I do not think that gods expressing a relatively high philosophical thinking, such as two gods Takamimusubi and Kamimusubi, were formed in Japan for the first time as a result of the Chinese influence. The god like Io in the New Zealand's myth exists as immortal and myriad of things and he is a supreme god. If such a god can exist, then it is not necessary to estimate that the Japanese spiritual ability at the time of creating the myth was so low; therefore, I cannot think that the ability to believe in higher gods like

---

225. Itō, Seiji "Sumiyaki chōsa no hanashi – Yanagita Kunio to Matsumoto Nobuhiro," *Shigaku*, dai 75 kan, dai 2/3 gō, 2007, pp. 211–231.
226. Itō, Seiji "Matsumoto Nobuhito to imohori chōsha no hanashi," *Nihon bunka no kigen*, dai 3 kan, Geppō dai 3 gō, 1978, p. 6.
227. Matsumoto, Nobuhiro "Ōsutoroajiago ni kan suru shomondai," *Kawai kyōju kanreki kinen ronbunshū*, Kawaikyōju kanreki shukugakai, 1931, p. 513. Matsumoto, Nobuhiro "Kodai bunkaron," *Gendai shigaku taikei*, Kyōritsusha shoten, 1932, p. 94.

Musubinokami did not develop until the reception of the Chinese thinking."[228] Thus, the comparison of the Japanese and Southern Pacific myths served Matsumoto as a counter-argument against the Northward Theory.

Yanagita's attitude toward the folklore studies significantly influenced Matsumoto's discussion on the Southern influence. Matsumoto did not specify Southern influence on the Japanese culture although he argued for it twice in his book *The Research of the Japanese Myths* published in Japan.[229] He described the Southern influence only in his doctoral thesis *An Essay on the Japanese Mythology* published in France: "The myth of god Hikohohodemi presents a local color that manifests influence of the southern civilization. ... Moreover it guards the maritime character. We cannot suppose that this myth was imagined by inhabitants of the Yamato Province, the site of the imperial power, a country surrounded by mountains. It is probable that the origins of this account come from a tradition transmitted by certain maritime tribes of Kyushu, probably the Hayatos, and that it was later assimilated by official myths and incorporated into the mythic history of the imperial family."[230] This quotation indicates that Matsumoto characterized the Southern influence as an influence of a maritime culture in his book published in France. In this manner, Matsumoto's diffusionist argument was generally limited on the proclamation of the Southern influence on the Japanese culture. Matsumoto did not examine the manner in which the Southern culture was transmitted to Japan or its influence on the Japanese culture.

Moreover, while indicating the maritime influence of South on Japan, Matsumoto argued that the myths are a result of the environment of the country: "...the myths of a nation are a specific product of its country and have close relations with the seasonal festival of the region."[231] He emphasized that the Japanese cults were compatible

---

228. Matsumoto, Nobuhiro *Nihon shinwa no kenkyū*, Dōbunkan, 1931, p. 177. "Kodai bunkaron" *Gendai shigaku taikei*, Kyōritsusha shoten, 1932, pp. 181-182.
229. Matsumoto, Nobuhiro *Nihon shinwa no kenkyū*, Dōbunkan, 1931, pp. 165, 273.
230. Matsumoto, Nobuhiro *Essai sur la mythologie Japonaise*, P. Geuthner, Paris, 1928, p. 212.

with the Japanese land.[232] He thought that the belief of the primitive people was formed by various cults of the natural gods or of the personified nature.[233]

These arguments reflected Yanagita's approach from evolutionist ethnology by which he interpreted Japanese folklore from the common people's relation with their natural environment. In addition, the argument of connection with seasonal festivals came from the sociologist ethnologists. Matsumoto also specified in his paper *Theories of Ancient Culture* that his teacher and sociologist ethnologist Granet preferred comparisons with various ethnic groups living in a region with a similar climate.[234] Thus, Matsumoto proposed a hypothesis based on evolutionist and sociologist ethnology that the oceanic character was the original Japanese trait coming from the Japanese natural environment.

This contradiction in interpreting the oceanic character of the Japanese culture was caused by the inconsistencies in Yanagita's ideas and by contradicting ideas of Matsumoto's French teachers Mauss, Granet, and Przyluski. Yanagita stood by his rule to interpret the Japanese folklore as a national culture in relation with the Japanese environment in accord with evolutionism. Although he believed in the existence of Japan's transoceanic connection with Southeast Asia, he claimed the origins of the Japanese culture in the Southern parts of the Japanese Empire. Thus, he argued regarding the Southern genealogy in the Japanese culture, but rejected the claim of its foreign origins. In addition, although Mauss suggested Matsumoto to compare the Japanese myths with Southern Pacific myths, he did not support the theory of Southern influence. In contrast, Przyluski was known for promoting Austroasiatic (that is Southern) influence. Thus, Mauss and

---

231. Matsumoto, Nobuhiro *Nihon shinwa no kenkyū*, Dōbunkan, 1931, p. 177. "Kodai bunkaron" *Gendai shigaku taikei*, Kyōritsusha shoten, 1932, p. 125.
232. Matsumoto, Nobuhiro *Nihon shinwa no kenkyū*, Dōbunkan, 1931, p. 177. "Kodai bunkaron" *Gendai shigaku taikei*, Kyōritsusha shoten, 1932, p. 125.
233. Matsumoto, Nobuhiro *Nihon shinwa no kenkyū*, Dōbunkan, 1931, p. 148.
234. Matsumoto, Nobuhiro "Kodai bunkaron" *Gendai shigaku taikei*, Kyōritsusha shoten, 1932, p. 125.

Granet believed in the similarity between the Japanese and Southern Pacific myths due to their hypothesis of the common primitive culture as a result of similar natural environments. However, Przyluski thought that the similarity meant there was a Southern influence on Japan. All these opinions caused contradictions in Matsumoto's writings since Matsumoto tried to follow the opinions of all his teachers.

Thus, as previous researches have already argued, Matsumoto became an advocator of the Southward Theory in opposition to the Northward Theory. However, the circumstances were complicated. First, Yanagita's critical attitude toward the Northward Theory played a key role in Matsumoto's advocation of the Southward Theory in Japan. Second, Matsumoto could become an advocator of the Southward Theory owing to his studies in Western diffusionist ethnology claiming the diffusion of Southern culture from Southeast Asia and from the Southern Pacific. Third, Matsumoto did not argue for the origins of the Japanese culture abroad because it was against the opinion of his main teacher Yanagita. Thus, Matsumoto had to compromise between his and Yanagita's ideas in his advocation of the Southward Theory, which is probably the cause for ambiguity of Matsumoto's arguments.

5. Conclusion

The analysis of Matsumoto's writings in 1924–1932 showed that he was influenced by sociologist, evolutionist, and diffusionist ethnology during this period. However, it was demonstrated that among these influences, Matsumoto focused on Southeast Asia mainly because of the diffusionist influence. This was because the diffusionist theories focused on the diffusion of Southern culture. This was a change in comparison with the situation in the previous period when Matsumoto cast only a cursory glance at Southeast Asia due to the influence of evolutionist ethnology.

As a result of diverse influences, Matsumoto became known both as a representative of sociologist ethnology and an advocate of the

Southward Theory in Japan. Torn between two approaches (sociologist and evolutionist ethnology on the one hand and diffusionist ethnology on the other hand), Matsumoto did not attempt to deepen his discussion in any of these directions. Unlike Yanagita, he did not further examine the connection between the Japanese culture and the Japanese natural environment although he adopted the sociological theory of the seasonal festivals. The insufficient influence of sociologist ethnology on Matsumoto's research is suggested by an argument of Matsumoto's colleague Mabuchi Tōichi (1909–1988), a social anthropologist who categorized Matsumoto as a cultural anthropologist.[235] Matsumoto did not try to clarify more about the Southern influence on the Japanese culture, for example, by inquiring what elements of Southern culture were imported and from where and how they were brought to Japan. Nonetheless, despite this reluctance, it is obvious from his discussion on Southern culture that Matsumoto believed in the significance of Southeast Asia and South Pacific for Japan because he continued to focus on the similarities between Japan and the South Seas.

Although Matsumoto has been known as a representative of sociologist ethnology, as for his prewar writings, the influence of sociological theories of his teachers Mauss and Granets is visible mainly during 1924–1932. This was because Matsumoto introduced the French sociological theories in his book *The Research of the Japanese Myths*[236] and did not apply them in his further works. In general, he failed to attract the attention of other Japanese ethnologists in his sociological discussions. Only Furuno Kiyoto (1899–1979), a young Tokyo University scholar, wished to share sociological ideas with Matsumoto due to his fascination with the research of the French School of Sociology.[237]

The dulled enthusiasm among Japanese ethnologists on this sub-

---

235. Mabuchi, Tōichi "Odayaka de fukutsu no daisempai," *Nihon minzoku bunka no kigen*, dai 2 kan, geppō dai 2 gō, Kōdansha, 1978, p. 2.
236. Matsumoto rewrote *Essai sur la mythologie Japonaise* (1928), expanded it by papers written after his return to Japan and published the compillation under the title *The Research of the Japanese Myths* (*Nihon shinwa no kenkyū*, 1931).

ject was also caused by the fact that not many Japanese mastered French language at that time. The delayed translation of French ethnologists' books in the Japanese language explains the Japanese disinterest in sociologist ethnology. Mauss' famous work *The Gift* (1923–1924) was published in Japanese in 1938.[238] The first translation of Granet's book to the Japanese was *Festivals and Songs of Ancient China* (1919) in 1943.[239] One of the reasons for the delay was the difficulty of the language. This is suggested by Yamada Yoshihiko, the translator of Mauss' *The Gift*, in the introductory remarks to Mauss' book.[240]

Another important reason for Japanese scholars' disinterest in social ethnology was the overwhelming influence of diffusionism. Hence, Matsumoto changed course and subscribed to mainstream diffusionist ethnology, which influenced the research of Western scholars on Indochina (this is discussed in chapters 3 and 4). In this sense, sociologist ethnology based on unilinear evolutionism became irrelevant because it was in contradiction with diffusionist ethnology based on multilinear evolutionism. Matsumoto could come back to sociologist and evolutionist ethnology only after World War II, when the situation in the academic circles changed again.

---

237. Arima, Makiko "Hito, Matsumoto Nobuhiro", *Kikan jinruigaku*, 5-1, Shakaishisōsha, 1974, p. 156 (an interview with Matsumoto Nobuhiro).
238. Mōsu, Maruseru (translation by Yamada Yoshihiko), *Taiheiyō minzoku no genshi keizai: kosei shakai ni okeru kōkan no keishiki to riyū,* Nikkōshoin, 1943.
239. Gurane, Maruseru (translated by Tsuda Itsuo), *Shina kodai no sairei to kayō*, Kōbundō shobō, 1938.
240. Yamada, Yoshihiko "Hanrei," Mōsu, Maruseru *Taiheiyō minzoku no genshi keizai: kosei shakai ni okeru kōkan no keishiki to riyū*, Nikkōshoin, 1943, p. 2.

Chapter 3:
Visiting the South Seas during 1933-1940

1. Introduction

The change in Japan's international situation in the 1930s influenced Matsumoto's academic career. While Japan appeared to play by the rules as a member of the international community in the 1920s, her imperialistic ambitions assumed frontstage in Japan's Northern and Southern advance, especially as her involvement in China intensified during the 1930s. (The influence of Southern Advance Theory is examined in Chapter 5.) Similarly, while Matsumoto studied in France in the 1920s, he conducted several field trips to Asia and the Pacific in the 1930s. These trips can be divided into three groups according to their destinations.

First, Matsumoto went on a research trip to French Indochina in summer 1933 and stopped by Hong Kong on his way back to Japan. This trip was financed by the Keio University Mochidzuki Foundation shortly after the conclusion of the Japan-French Trade Agreement (May 13, 1932), which was also applied to Japan-Indochina relations.[1] This was followed by a conclusion of the Customs Treaty between Japan and French Indochina in 1934.[2] Matsumoto boarded a ship Surabaya belonging to OSK Company, which began providing a direct connection between Kobe and Haiphong in Vietnam at the end of 1932.[3]

---

1. "Customs agreement conclusion between Japan and Indochina," National Archives of Japan, Showa Financial Historical Materials No. 4 Vol. 137, Reference code: A08072515300

The timing shows that Matsumoto went to Indochina when the Japanese began entering the Indochina market.

Second, Matsumoto visited the Southern Pacific Islands of Palau, Tenian, and Saipan under the administration of the Japanese and New Guinea under the Dutch in 1937. Japan continued occupying these islands, which it received under the mandate of the League of Nations after World War I, despite its withdrawal from the League on March 27, 1933. The reason was the growing involvement of Japanese companies in the region accompanied by the migration of Japanese people to make up for the labor shortage. While there were only 3,600 Japanese scattered over these islands in 1920, the Japanese population exceeded 50,000 in 1937. Moreover, Matsumoto visited the Southern Pacific Islands owing to the support of Nanyo Kohatsu K. K. (Nan'yō Kōhatsu Kaisha, 南洋興発会社), which prospered due to the cultivation of sugarcane in Micronesia.[4] Nanyo Kohatsu K. K. had close relations with a group of Japanese ethnologists, of which Matsumoto was a member. Hence, Matsumoto's trip to the Southern Pacific Islands was conducted during the time of Japanese colonization and economic expansion there. This means that Matsumoto had contacts with the people preaching Japan's Southern advance.

Third, Matsumoto participated in two research trips to China as part of the group dispatched by Keio University, with the support of the Keio University Mochidzuki Foundation in 1938 and in 1939. Matsumoto's reports from this travel clearly showed that Matsumoto could get access to the Chinese historical relics as a result of the Japanese occupation of the Chinese territory. Simultaneously, Matsumoto did not remain in the dark about the effects of the occupation as he

---

2. "Documents relating to customs treaty between Japan and French Indochina," Diplomatic Archives of the Ministry of Foreign Affairs, Documents relating to customs treaty between Japan and French Indochina, Reference code: B04013588500.
3. Matsumoto, Nobuhiro "Indoshina inshōki (I)," *Mita hyōron*, dai 437 gō, Mita hyōron hakkōjo, 1934, p. 24.
4. Matsumoto, Nobuhiro "Waga Nan'yō wo miru," *Mita hyōron*, dai 483 gō, Mita hyōron hakkōjo, 1937, p. 6.

witnessed the war damages on the historical sites when he visited Shanghai, Nanjing, and Hangzhou several months after the Marco Polo Bridge Incident (July 7, 1937), Nanjing Incident (December 13, 1937), and Battle of Shanghai (August 13 to November 26, 1937). In other words, Matsumoto's accessibility to these sites of academic interest was facilitated by the Japanese military's acquisition of Chinese territory following the Second Sino-Japanese War.

Due to the Japanese expansion, Matsumoto went on research trips to various locations, of which Indochina and the Southern Pacific Islands were connected to Japan's Southern advance. His research trips aimed to collect Western works on Southeast Asia and Vietnamese books published in French Indochina,[5] observe the native culture in the Southern Pacific Islands,[6] and join an excavation survey in China.[7] However, in China, things took an unexpected turn when Matsumoto was invited to join a Japanese team working on the requisition of specimens from Chinese museums.Though it was a departure from his original plans, Matsumoto spent time organizing Chinese research reports and classifying archaeological artifacts.[8] In addition, on these trips, Matsumoto met with the local inhabitants and observed their culture. Consequently, Matsumoto's ideas regarding Southeast Asia were based not only on the research produced by other scholars but also on his personal experiences.

Despite his various objectives and destinations, all of Matsumoto's trips were connected with his research on Southeast Asia. This was because Matsumoto adopted Heine-Geldern's diffusionist hypotheses that the contemporary inhabitants in continental Southeast Asia had their origins in China and that the ancestors of the inhabitants in maritime Southeast Asia and the Pacific came from continental South-

---

5. Matsumoto, Nobuhiro "Indoshina inshōki (I)," *Mita hyōron*, dai 437 gō, Mita hyōron hakkōjo, 1937, p. 26.
6. Matsumoto, Nobuhiro "Nan'yō guntō ryokō nisshi," *Shigaku*, dai 16 kan, dai 3 gō, Mita Shigakkai, 1937, p. 77.
7. Matsumoto, Nobuhiro "Kōnan hōkoki," *Shigaku*, dai 17 kan, dai 4 gō, Mita Shigakkai, 1939, p. 3.
8. Ibid., p. 4.

ast Asia in ancient times.[9] Moreover, Matsumoto shared Przyluski's diffusionist opinion that Southeast Asian culture influenced Chinese culture. This means that Matsumoto thought that the ancestors of contemporary Southeast Asian people influenced Han people when they resided in the Chinese territory in close contact with Han people. Then, the ancestors of contemporary Southeast Asian people were pushed by the expansion of Han people to Southeast Asia where they subjugated original inhabitants or forced them to move to the mountains or migrate to maritime Southeast Asia and the Pacific. Therefore, the locations of Matsumoto's trips corresponded to the places discussed by diffusionist theories related to Southeast Asia.

From the above discussion, it is clear that Matsumoto's ideas regarding Southeast Asia were developed by his research trips to French Indochina, the Southern Pacific Islands, and China under the dominance of diffusionist ethnology during 1933–1939. Therefore, this chapter examines the significance of Matsumoto's research trips in securing his position as the founder of Southeast Asian studies and his contribution to the Japanese academic circles.

2. Significance of Matsumoto Nobuhiro's research trips in the establishment of Southeast Asian studies in Japan

Ito Seiji claimed that Matsumoto's trip to Indochina represented the start of establishing Matsumoto's "position as a pioneer in Southeast Asian studies."[10] Ito mainly emphasized that Matsumoto brought Vietnamese annals to Japan,[11] which has been argued by many other researchers.[12] Likewise, Shimao Minoru indicated Matsumoto's contri-

---

9. Matsumoto, Nobuhiro "Indoshina minzoku," *Iwanami kōza Tōyō shichō*, I (Tōyō no minzoku, Tōyō no shakai), Iwanami shoten, 1935, p. 3. "Indoshina gengo no keitō," *Iwanami kōza Tōyō shichō*, I (Tōyō gengo no keitō), Iwanami shoten, 1934, p. 38.
10. Itō, Seiji "Matsumoto Nobuhiro to gakumon," Keiō gijuku *daigaku gengo kenkyūjo hōkokushū*, Keiō gijuku daigaku, dai 24 kan, 1992, p. 18. "Matsumoto Nobuhiro – 'Nampōsetsu' no kaitakusha," *Bunka jinruigaku gunzō*, Nihonhen (3), Kyōto: Akademia shuppankai, 1988, p. 234.

bution to the foundation of Southeast Asian studies in Japan in the 1930s,[13] and Frédéric Roustan discussed the importance of Matsumoto's trip to Indochina for Matsumoto's foundation of Vietnamese studies in the 1930s.[14] However, there are also other important aspects of Matsumoto's trips. Therefore, this section investigates the significance of Matsumoto's travels abroad in the 1930s from Matsumoto's writings to understand Matsumoto's contribution to the foundation of Southeast Asian studies.

2.1. Significance of Matsumoto Nobuhiro's research trip to French Indochina

This section examines the importance of Matsumoto's research trip to French Indochina for Matsumoto's career as a pioneer in

---

11. Itō, Seiji "Matsumoto Nobuhiro to gakumon," Keiō gijuku *daigaku gengo kenkyūjo hōkokushū*, Keiō gijuku daigaku, dai 24 kan, 1992, p. 18-19. "Matsumoto Nobuhiro sensei wo shinonde," *Minzoku kenkyū*, dai 46 kan, dai 1 gō, Nihon minzoku gakkai, 1981, p. 126.
12. Iwai, Daie "Nagata Yasukichi shūshū Annam bon mokuroku," *Shigaku*, dai 14 kan, dai 2 gō, Mita Shigakkai, 1935, pp. 101-109 (283-291); Yamamoto, Tatsurō "Betonamu kenkyū shiryō no shōkai to shuppan," *Nihon bunka no kigen*, dai 3 kan, Geppō dai 3 gō, Kōdansha, 1978, pp. 3-5; Wada, Hironari "Matsumoto Nobuhiro kyōju jūrai no Vetonamu shahon sanshu ni tsuite - Nihon-Chūgoku no kindaika to Vetonamu," *Shigaku*, dai 35 kan, dai 4 gō, Mita Shigakkai, 1963, pp. 431-434; *Keiō gijuku toshokan zō Matsumoto bunko mokuroku*, Keiō gijuku daigaku Mita jōhō sentā, 1991; Wada, Masahiko "Matsumoto Nobuhiro hakase jūrai no Annan hon ni tsuite - Keiō gijuku toshokan Matsumoto bunko shozō Annan hon kaidai" (Jō), *Shigaku*, dai 62 kan, dai 1/2 gō, Mita Shigakkai, 1992, pp. 165-183; Wada, Masahiko "Matsumoto Nobuhiro hakase jūrai no Annan hon ni tsuite - Keiō gijuku toshokan Matsumoto bunko shozō Annan hon kaidai" (Ka), *Shigaku*, dai 63 kan, dai 1/2 gō, Mita Shigakkai, 1993, pp. 165-183; Hayashi, Masako "Betonamu hon ni tsuite - Tōyō bunko zō Betonamu hon shomoku' ni miru Nihon tono kakawari," *Atomi gakuen joshi daigaku bungaku fōramu*, 9, Atomi gakuen joshi daigaku, 2011, pp. 188-127.
13. Shimao, Minoru "Betonamu. Tōnan Ajiashi he no teii to tenkai," *Tōnan Ajia shi. Kenkyū no hatten*, Tōnan Ajia Gakkai 40 shūnen, Kinen jigyō iinkai, Yamakawa shuppansha, 2009, p. 110.
14. Roustan, Frédéric "From Oriental Studies to South Pacific Studies: The Multiple Origins of Vietnamese Studies," *Journal of Vietnamese Studies*, Vol. 6, Issue 1, 2011, p. 13.

Southeast Asian studies. First, it discusses the experience and the knowledge that Matsumoto acquired through this research trip. Furthermore, it elucidates he contribution of Matsumoto brought to the Japanese academic circles from his research trip to French Indochina.

2.1.1. Matsumoto Nobuhiro's research trip to French Indochina

Matsumoto Nobuhiro's trip to French Indochina represented an important watershed in his studies of Southeast Asia because he directly experienced Indochinese culture and acquired a wealth of research material on Indochina. He visited Vietnam, specifically the research institutions and museums established by the French government. He aimed to collect research material on Southeast Asia, which was lacking in Japan. This suggests that Matsumoto aimed to establish Southeast Asian studies in Japan through this travel.

Matsumoto visited French Indochina in summer 1933. Originally, he had a chance to go to China, but he decided to go to French Indochina instead.[15] This was because he became interested in Indochina under the influence of Przyluski during his studies at Sorbonne University in 1924–1928. Moreover, Matsumoto's friend Émile Gaspardone (1895–1982) was a researcher at the École Française d'Extrême-Orient (EFEO) in Hanoi at the time; thus, Matsumoto was working under the best conditions to fullfil his purpose in Indochina. With Gaspardone's help, Matsumoto visited EFEO facilities in Vietnam and brought back to Japan Western works on Southeast Asia and a collection of Vietnamese books. In EFEO in Hanoi, Matsumoto also met the Korean scholar Kim Yung-kun (金永鍵, born in Japan in 1910) who worked there as an assistant in 1932–1940.[16] Kim presented many works on the Vietnamese culture and Vietnam's relations with abroad, including the history of the Japanese people in Vietnam.[17] However, Matsumoto

---

15. Interview with Chikamori Masashi, 23 August 2012, Keio University, Tokyo. Itō, Seiji "Matsumoto Nobuhiro – 'Nampōsetsu' no kaitakusha," *Bunka jinruigaku gunzō*, Nihonhen (3), Akademia shuppankai, Kyōto, 1988, p. 233.
16. Yun, De-yon "1930–1940 nendai no Kin Ei-ken to Betonamu kenkyū," *Tōnan Ajia kenkyū*, dai 48 kan, dai 3 gō, Kyōto daigaku tōnan Ajia kenkyū sentā, 2010, pp. 317, 320.

mentioned about Kim only once when he introduced his writing about the Vietnamese drifted to Japan in 1936.[18]

Matsumoto departed from Kobe on July 29, 1933, and arrived at Haiphong on August 8, 1933.[19] He considered his study in the library of the EFEO in Hanoi to be the best time of his research trip: "Approximately for one month and a half, I was researching through the Annamese [=Vietnamese][20] books, being helped by kind Annamese public servants in the reading room where the fan was turned on. This was the most wonderful memory of my voyage."[21] Matsumoto's impressions reveal that his delight came from being able to attain his main goal in Indochina, which was the acquisition of the written sources.

Furthermore, Gaspardone took Matsumoto on a trip by car to Cao Bằng Province in Tonkin on September 2, 1933.[22] Matsumoto observed there people of various ethnic minorities, such as Thái (Tho), Mèo, and Mán, especially in their natural environment.[23]

Then, Matsumoto went to Huế by train. He visited the royal palace with the historical archive and royal tombs there.[24] In the historical archives, he started negotiating with authorities to acquire copies of the *Annals of the Đại Nam* (Đại Nam Thực lục, 大南實錄), which were the much coveted annals of the last Vietnamese dynasty Nguyễn: "The Annals of the Đại Nam is a precious writing that has not been even partially introduced in Japan, and the goal of my trip was to bring

---

17. Ibid., pp. 314-333.
18. Matsumoto, Nobuhiro "Tsuiki," *Minzokugaku kenkyū*, dai 2 kan, dai 1 gō, Minzokugakkai, 1936, pp. 66-69.
19. Matsumoto, Nobuhiro "Indoshina inshōki (I)," *Mita hyōron*, dai 437 gō, Mita hyōron hakkōjo, 1934, pp. 24-25.
20. Annam is an old naming for Vietnam. Annamese means Vietnamese.
21. Matsumoto, Nobuhiro "Indoshina inshōki (I)," *Mita hyōron*, dai 437 gō, Mita hyōron hakkōjo, 1934, p. 27.
22. Matsumoto, Nobuhiro "Indoshina inshōki (II)," *Mita hyōron*, dai 440 gō, Mita hyōron hakkōjo, 1934, p. 24.
23. Ibid., p. 25.
24. Matsumoto, Nobuhiro "Indoshina inshōki (III)," *Mita hyōron*, dai 445 gō, Mita hyōron hakkōjo, 1934, pp. 10-11.

a part of them to Japan. I negotiated directly with Phạm Quỳnh, but I got the answer that they would only permit me to print only a section of the introduction."[25] In Huế, Matsumoto also visited the Association des Amis du Vieux Huế with its small library and the Khải Định Museum in the royal palace.[26] Finally, Matsumoto went by car to Đà Nẵng (Tourane) and Hội An (Faifo) on September 17. He stopped at Đà Nẵng to see the Cham museum. Then, he visited the Japanese bridge and the Japanese graves in Hội An, which had a Japanese town.[27] He could visit them because he learnt about them from Kim Yung-kun who described Japan-related places in his writings.[28] In short, Matsumoto visited museums, archives, and places related to Japan in Southern Vietnam.

Matsumoto was among the few Japanese who travelled to Vietnam of French Indochina at that time. Since Matsumoto was fluent in French due to his studies in Paris, he had no problems in communicating with the French and the French-speaking Vietnamese. During his stay in Vietnam, Matsumoto could see the French quarters, meet Vietnamese intellectuals who received French education, and witness the lives of the everyday folk in Vietnam, an experience important to Matsumoto because the commoners were the ones that preserved their traditional customs. In addition, he observed ethnic minorities living in the mountains of Tonkin. Matsumoto's experience was unique among Japanese scholars because he was probably the first Japanese to visit Indochina for academic purposes. Unfortunately, Matsumoto's notes from Indochina reveal little about his ideas concerning the native people of Indochina whose culture interested him. It is probably because Matsumoto was not a field worker by nature and, therefore, did not have the habit of noting his observations. Consequently, the most visible output of Matsumoto's trip to Indochina were the West-

---

25. Ibid., pp. 12-13.
26. Ibid., p. 13.
27. Ibid., pp. 13-16.
28. Yun, De-yon "1930-1940 nendai no Kin Ei-ken to Betonamu kenkyū," *Tōnan Ajia kenkyū*, dai 48 kan, dai 3 gō, Kyōto daigaku tōnan Ajia kenkyū sentā, 2010, pp. 326-327.

ern writings and Vietnamese books that he brought back to Japan and subsequently introduced to Japanese readers.

2.1.2. Significance of Matsumoto's research trip to French Indochina

This section explores why Matsumoto's research trip to Indochina had crucial importance for Matsumoto's career as the founder of the Southeast Asian studies in Japan. It shows that owing to this travel, Matsumoto made available knowledge of Indochina in various forms to the Japanese people, and this contribution made him one of the two founders of Southeast Asian studies. The section discusses three of Matsumoto's contributions to Japanese academic circles. First, Matsumoto collected research material on Indochina and Southeast Asia and brought them back to Japan. Second, Matsumoto introduced Western research (mainly of French and German scholars) on Indochina to Japanese readers in his writings. Third, Matsumoto brought back the latest information on the situation in Indochina through his writings.

First, Matsumoto contributed to the Japanese academic circles by physically bringing Western works on Indochina, Vietnamese books, and stoneware fragments excavated in Indochina to Japan. The books were stored in the library of Keio University in Toyo Bunko, and the archaeological specimens were preserved in Oyama Research Institute of Prehistory in Shibuya Ward in Tokyo.[29] The list of books brought by Matsumoto formed an important part of *The Bibliography of South Seas: the Collection of Keio University Library* that he published with his colleague Hosaka Saburo in 1942.[30] Thus, Matsumoto's trip to Indochina had significance not only for Keio University, but also for other institutions in Japan.

Matsumoto collected not only Western books on Southeast Asia but also Vietnamese annals that were rare in Japan at that time. Originally, Matsumoto was not interested in Vietnamese books, but former

---

29. Matsumoto, Nobuhiro "Jōdai Indoshina no kōkogakuteki kenkyū ni tsuite - Korani joshi kizō dozoku hyōhon wo chūshin ni" (1937), *Indoshina minzoku to bunka*, Iwanami shoten, 1942.11, p. 161.
30. Matsumoto, Nobuhiro; Hosaka, Saburō, *Nan'yō bunken mokuroku: keiōgijuku toshokan shozō*, Keiō gijuku Mochidzuki Shina kenkyū kikin, 1942.

Consul General in Hanoi Nagata Yasukichi suggested Matsumoto to buy them in Vietnam. Matsumoto confessed his ignorance after hearing Nagata's advice: "I felt I was stupid for being satisfied with the existing Chinese documents and French studies in the history of Annam."[31]

Consequently, Matsumoto supported Nagata's effort in importing books written in classic Chinese by the Vietnamese authors to Japan. They managed to bring 92 Vietnamese books, of which 40 were collected by Matsumoto.[32] These books were donated to Toyo Bunko. In this manner, the Vietnamese books that Matsumoto brought to Japan became part of the first collection of Vietnamese books in Japan.

The news of this unique collection was reported in the Japanese academic circles. Iwai Daie, an employee of Toyo Bunko, described the circumstances of the donation and presented a list of the donated Vietnamese books in his paper *The Catalogue of Nagata Yasukichi's Collection of the Vietnamese Books* in 1935.[33] Iwai also mentioned Matsumoto's role in the donation of the books: "... last year [1934], by the mediation of Professor of Keio Gijuku University, and a respected friend, Matsumoto Nobuhiro and former Consul General in Hanoi, Indochina, Nagata Yasukichi (research fellow at Ministry of Foreign Affairs at present), we got a donation of 92 volumes and 550 pieces of the Annamese books."[34] Thus, Matsumoto's and Nagata's contribution in providing the Vietnamese books was acknowledged by the Japanese academia.

These Vietnamese annals became significant especially during the Vietnam War when it was impossible to access the documents in

---

31. Matsumoto, Nobuhiro "Annan ryokōki (daiisshin)," *Minzokugaku*, dai 5 kan, dai 5 gō, Minzokugakkai, 1933, p. 87.
32. Matsumoto, Nobuhiro "Indoshina inshōki (I)," *Mita hyōron*, dai 437 gō, Mita hyōron hakkōjo, 1934, p. 27. List of the books in: Iwai, Daie "Nagata Yasukichi shūshū Annam bon mokuroku," *Shigaku*, dai 14 kan, dai 2 gō, Mita Shigakkai, 1935, pp. 105- 109 (286-291).
33. Iwai, Daie "Nagata Yasukichi shūshū Annam bon mokuroku," *Shigaku*, dai 14 kan, dai 2 gō, Mita Shigakkai, 1935, pp. 101- 109 (283-291).
34. Ibid., p. 102 (284).

Vietnam. Matsumoto contributed to their availibility in Japan and made effort to their publication especially after his retirement from Keio University.[35] In 1941, Indochina Research Society founded by Matsumoto published *The Annals of Đại Nam*（大南一統志, Đại Nam nhất thống chí).[36] Then, the Keio University Linguistic Institute put in print various Vietnamese annals[37] such as six volumes of *The Chronicles of Đại Nam*（大南實錄, Đại Nam thực lục) in 1961-1972[38] and three volumes of *Complete Annals of Đại Việt*（大越史記全書, Đại Việt sử ký toàn thư) in 1984-1986.[39] Several Japanese scholars close to Matsumoto, including those unrelated to Vietnmese studies, cooperated on their publication.[40] The edition of *The Chronicles of Đại Nam* and *Complete Annals of Đại Việt* was realized owing to Trần Kinh Hoà（陳荊和, Chin Kei Wa, 1917-1995), a Vietnamese scholar born in Taiwan who worked for EFEO in Hanoi in 1943-1945 and was one of the leading scholars of Vietnamese studies in Japan.[41]

---

35. Kawamoto, Kunie "'Dainan jitsuroku' chimei sakuin - Jo narabi ni hanrei," *Dainan jitsuroku chimei sakuin*, Keiō gijuku daigaku gengo bunka kenkyūjo, 2002, p. iii.
36. *Dainan ittō shi*, Dai1shū, Dai2shū, Indoshina kenkyūkai, 1941.
37. Kawamoto, Kunie "Jo narabi ni hanrei," *Dainan jitsuroku chimei sakuin*, Keiō gijuku daigaku gengo bunka kenkyūjo, 2002, p. iii.
38. *Dainan jitsuroku*, 1-6, Keiō gijuku daigaku gogaku kenkyūjo, 1961, 1963, 1968, 1962, 1971, 1972.
39. *Daietsu shiki zensho: kōgōbon*, jō, chū, ka, Tōkyō daigaku Tōyō bunka kenkyūjo fuzoku Tōyōgaku bunken sentā kankō iinkai, 1984-1986. Ōsawa, Kazuo "Dainan jitsuroku to Matsumoto Nobuhiro," *Ine-fune-matsuri: Matsumoto Nobuhiro sensei tsuitō ronbunshū*, Kyōshuppan, 1982, pp. 686-688.
40. Takeda Ryuji, Ito Seiji, Maejima Shinji, Makino Shinya, Wada Hironari, Shimizu Shunzo, Esaka Teruya, Osawa Kazuo, Kawamoto Kunie, Wada Masahiko, etc. Ōsawa, Kazuo "Dainan jitsuroku to Matsumoto Nobuhiro," *Ine-fune-matsuri: Matsumoto Nobuhiro sensei tsuitō ronbunshū*, Kyōshuppan, 1982, pp. 687-690.
41. "Chin Kei Wa zenshochō keireki, kenkyū jisseki ichiran," *Sōdai Ajia kenkyū*, dai 15 gō, Sōka daigaku Ajia kenkyūjo, 1994, p. 148. Kawamoto, Kunie "Shiki ni mukau keigan - Chin Kei Wa hakushi wo itamu," *Keiō gijuku daigaku gengo bunka kenkyūjo kiyō*, dai 28 gō, Keiō gijuku daigaku gengo bunka kenkyūjo, 1996, pp. 13-14.

Matsumoto reported about his trip to Indochina and the books at a research meeting of the Japan Historical Society and Mita Historical Society.[42] In addition, he introduced Vietnamese books in his papers in *Historical Science*, the journal of the Mita Historical Society First, he published a list of the books stored in Vietnam in "Appendix (A Catalogue of the Annamese Books Stored in EFEO in Hanoi)" and "Appendix (A Catalogue of the Annamese Books in the Imperial Archive of Viet Nam)."[43] Then, he introduced the *Annals of Đại Nam* and Gaspardone's work in *The General Catalogue of Đại Nam thực lục* and *Two Materials on the Annamese History - The Annals of Đại Nam and Annamese Bibliography*.[44] According to Kawamoto Kunie, these Vietnamese books written in Chinese characters served as a stepping stone for the establishment of Vietnamese studies in Japan, especially when it was difficult to study the Vietnamese language although many scholars could read Chinese.[45] Thus, Matsumoto's introduction of the Vietnamese books to the Japanese academic circles in 1934-1935 contributed to the foundation of Southeast Asian studies in Japan.

Furthermore, Matsumoto brought the archaeological specimens of Indochina stoneware to Japan. Owing to his friendship with Émile Gaspardone, a research fellow at the EFEO, Matsumoto met famous French archaeologist Madeleine Colani (1866-1943). He managed to obtain some archaeological specimens excavated by Colani as an official donation by the EFEO. From the perspective of Japanese archaeology, it was a significant contribution since he brought new artifacts to Japan. Matsumoto claimed as follows: "The stoneware dated to the so

---

42. Matsumoto, Nobuhiro "Annam ryokōdan," *Shigaku zasshi*, dai 45 kan, dai 2 gō, Shigakkai, 1934, pp. 255-257.
43. Matsumoto, Nobuhiro "Hanoi Futsukoku kyokutō gakuin shozō Annan hon shomoku dōtsuiki," *Shigaku*, dai 13 kan, dai 4 gō, Mita Shigakkai, 1934, pp. 785-786 (203-204). "Tsuiki (Betonamu ōshitsu shozō Annan honshomoku)," *Shigaku*, dai 14 kan, dai 2 gō, Mita Shigakkai, 1935, pp. 337-341.
44. Matsumoto, Nobuhiro "Annan shijō no nijishiryō: Đại Nam thực lục to Bibliographie Annamite," *Shigaku*, dai 15 kan, dai 1 gō, Mita Shigakkai, 1936, pp. 111-132.
45. Kawamoto, Kunie *Dainan jitsuroku chimei sakuin*, 1, Keiō gijuku daigaku gengobunka kenkyūjo, 2007, pp. xi-xiii.

called Bac Sonian and Hoa Binhian periods which have been used for the first time by Ms. Colani and could not have been seen in Japan until now."[46] Matsumoto presented a paper on these fragments of stonewares at a research meeting held by the Japan Anthropological Society.[47] Also, he introduced them in his paper "On Archaeological Research of Ancient Indochina - with Focus on the Folk Specimens Donated by Ms. Colani."[48]

Second, Matsumoto introduced Western works in Indochina. He described the history and work of the EFEO in Hanoi in *The French Research of Indochina*.[49] Furthermore, he summarized the Western writings about the history and culture of Indochina in the following papers: *The Korean Legend of the Old Otter and Its Annamese Variante*,[50] *On Bronze Drums of Indochina*,[51] *The Vietnamese Materials 2,3 on Bronze Drums*,[52] *The Annamese Tooth Blackening*,[53] *The Culture of Indochina*,[54] *The Genealogy of Indochina Languages*,[55] *The Peoples of Indochina*,[56] *A Supplement to Akashi Teiichi's On Relation of Magical*

---

46. Matsumoto, Nobuhiro "Jōdai Indoshina no kōkogakuteki kenkyū ni tsuite - Korani joshi kizō dozoku hyōhon wo chūshin ni" (1937), *Indoshina minzoku to bunka*, Iwanami shoten, 1942, p. 161.
47. Ibid., p. 161.
48. Ibid., pp. 161–187.
49. Matsumoto, Nobuhiro "Furansujin indoshina kenkyū," *Tōa*, Sangatsugō, Tōa keizai chōsakyoku, 1934, pp. 109–118.
50. Matsumoto, Nobuhiro "Rōnorachi densetsu no Annan iden," *Minzokugaku*, dai 5 kan, dai 12 gō, Minzokugakkai, 1933, pp. 1010–1019.
51. Matsumoto, Nobuhiro "Indoshina no dōki ni tsuite" (1933) *Nihon minzoku bunka no kigen III: Tōnan Ajia to Nihon*, Kōdansha, 1978, pp. 253–454.
52. Matsumoto, Nobuhiro "Dōki ni kan suru ni, San no Betonamu shiryō" (1935), *Nihon minzoku bunka no kigen III: Tōnan Ajia to Nihon*, Kōdansha, 1978, pp. 255–257.
53. Matsumoto, Nobuhiro "Annanjin no ohaguro," *Shigaku*, dai 12 kan, dai 4 gō, Mita Shigakkai, 1933, p. 676.
54. Matsumoto, Nobuhiro "Indoshina no bunka jō," *Iwanami kōza Tōyō shichō*, I, Iwanami shoten, 1934, pp. 1–44. "Indoshina no bunka ge," *Iwanami kōza Tōyō shichō*, 9/4, Iwanami shoten, 1935, pp. 49–95.
55. Matsumoto, Nobuhiro "Indoshina gengo no keitō," *Iwanami kōza Tōyō shichō*, I (Tōyō gengo no keitō), Iwanami shoten, 1934, pp. 1–44.

Objects and Astronomy in 'the Annamese Variation of the Legend of the Old Otter',[57] and Languages of Indochina.[58] Summarizing Western researches on Indochina, these papers became pioneer works of Southeast Asian studies in Japan. Later, the majority of the papers were republished in Matsumoto's book *The Peoples and Cultures of Indochina* (1942), which Suenari Michio listed among the first and foremost sources of cultural anthropology on Vietnam in *The Anotated Bibliography of the Cultural Anthropology of Vietnam. A Perspective from Japan*.[59]

Third, Matsumoto published several travel records on French Indochina in *Impressions from French Indochina, Travel Records from Annam, I have Seen Indochina* and *A Talk about the Travel to Annam* during 1933–1934.[60] Matsumoto referred to the places that he visited, followed by a short explanation of their history. He specifically focused on the monuments related to Japan, such as a Japanese bridge and Japanese graves in Hội An.[61] Interestingly, he did not write much

---

56. Matsumoto, Nobuhiro "Indoshina minzoku," *Iwanami kōza Tōyō shichō*, I (Tōyō no minzoku, Tōyō no shakai), Iwanami shoten, 1935, pp. 1-49.
57. Matsumoto, Nobuhiro "Akashi Teikichi 'Rōnorachi densetsu no Annan den' no reibutsu to tenmon no kankei, tsuiki" (1935), *Tōa minzoku bunkaronkō*, Seibundō shinkōsha, 1968, pp. 153-155.
58. Matsumoto, Nobuhiro "Indoshina go," *Ajia mondai kōza*, dai 8 kan, Sōgensha, 1939, pp. 385-399.
59. Suenari, Michio *Betonamu bunka jinruigaku. Bunken kaidai. Nihon kara shiten*, Fūkyōsha, 2009, p. 224.
60. Matsumoto, Nobuhiro "Indoshina inshōki (I)," *Mita hyōron*, dai 437 gō, Mita hyōron hakkōjo, 1934, pp. 24-27. "Indoshina inshōki (II)," *Mita hyōron*, dai 440 gō, Mita hyōron hakkōjo, 1934, pp. 22-25. "Indoshina inshōki (III)," *Mita hyōron*, dai 445 gō, Mita hyōron hakkōjo, 1934, pp. 10-16. "Annan ryokōki (daiisshin)," *Minzokugaku*, dai 5 kan, dai 5 gō, Minzokugakkai, 1933, pp. 86-87. "Annan ryokōki (dainishin)," *Minzokugaku*, dai 5 kan, dai 5 gō, Minzokugakkai, 1933, pp. 829-831. "Annan ryokōki (daisanshin)," *Minzokugaku*, dai 5 kan, dai 10 gō, Minzokugakkai, 1933, pp. 931-936. "Indoshina wo mite," *Gaikō jihō*, dai 703 gō, Gaikō jihōsha, 15.03.1934, pp. 131-138. "Annam ryokōdan," *Shigaku zasshi*, dai 45 kan, dai 2 gō, Shigakkai, 1934, pp. 255-257.
61. Matsumoto, Nobuhiro "Indoshina inshōki (III)," *Mita hyōron*, dai 445 gō, Mita hyōron hakkōjo, 1934, pp. 14-16.

about the ethnic minorities in Vietnam although he claimed that he was deeply impressed by them: "But in this region [Cao Bằng], I am interested more in various ethnic groups than in the historical sites."[62] It was his first trip to Indochina, so he probably aimed at collecting general information than conducting a specific research project. Furthermore, Matsumoto found it easier to describe the information on Vietnam that he obtained from books than to develop his ideas based on his own observation of the local people.

In addition, he criticized the economic situation of contemporary Indochina in his paper *I have Seen Indochina* printed in *The Diplomatic Revue*.[63] Matsumoto argued that Japan should assist France in the development of backward Indochina. In this sense, his opinion was in line with the official policy of Japan's Southern advance since he visited Indochina shortly after the conclusion of the Japan-French Trade Agreement.[64] Matsumoto's paper reflected the ambitions of Japan's economic expansion in Indochina.

Moreover, Matsumoto also wrote a paper *The First Crossing of Indochina Peninsula by the Japanese People*.[65] In this paper, he described Iwamoto Chizuna's exploration trip to Indochina in the late 19th century. This paper indicated that Matsumoto became interested in the history of the relations between Japan and Indochina.

2.2. Significance of Matsumoto Nobuhiro's research trip to Southern Pacific Islands

This section examines the significance of Matsumoto's trip to the

---

62. Matsumoto, Nobuhiro "Indoshina inshōki (II)," *Mita hyōron*, dai 440 gō, Mita hyōron hakkōjo, 1934, p. 25.
63. Matsumoto, Nobuhiro "Indoshina wo mite," *Gaikō jihō*, dai 703 gō, Gaikō jihōsha, 15.03.1934, pp. 131–138.
64. Ibid.
65. Matsumoto, Nobuhiro "Nihonjin saisho no Indoshina hantō ōdan (I)," *Shigaku*, dai 14 kan, dai 1 gō, Mita Shigakkai, 1935, p. 68. "Nihonjin saisho no Indoshina hantō ōdan (II)," *Shigaku*, dai 14 kan, dai 1 gō, Mita Shigakkai, 1935, p. 156. "Nihonjin saisho no Indoshina hantō ōdan (III)," *Shigaku*, dai 14 kan, dai 1 gō, Mita Shigakkai, 1935, p. 164.

Southern Pacific Islands for his academic career as the founder of Southeast Asian studies. It focuses on the manner in which the trip supported Matsumoto's ethnologist career and its contribution to the Japanese academic circles.

2.2.1. Matsumoto Nobuhiro's research trip to the Southern Pacific Islands

While Matsumoto Nobuhiro focused on acquiring books on his research trip to French Indochina, he sought to conduct ethnographical research in his trip to the Southern Pacific Islands in July and August 1937.[66] Matsumoto could go on this ethnographical tour owing to his relationship with Nanyo Kohatsu K. K. This relationship developed when Matsumoto and his colleages classified of the ethnographical objects owned by this company.[67]

Nanyo Kohatsu K. K. cultivated sugarcane in the Mariannas Islands of Saipan, Tenian, and Rota from the early 1920s.[68] Matsue Haruji, the director of Nanyo Kohatsu K. K., became interested in ethnography as a result of his business activities on these islands since collecting ethnographical objects was popular in that period. Consequently, Matsue with his employes acquired a large number of these ethnographic objects in New Guinea in July 1932. Furthermore, in 1935, he purchased an ethnographic collection from Komine Isokichi, a Japanese man who lived on the Southern Pacific Islands. Unfortunately, the exact place of origin of Komine's ethnographical objects was unknown, but it was clear that they came from Melanesia.[69] Hence, due to director Matsue, a substantial number of ethnographical objects

---

66. *Ine-fune-matsuri: Matsumoto Nobuhiro sensei tsuitō ronbunshū*, Rokkōshuppan, 1982, p. 694.
67. Matsumoto, Nobuhiro *Nyū Ginia dozokuhin zushū: Nan'yō kōhatsu kabushiki gaisha shūshū*, jōkan, Minami no kai hen, Nan'yō kōhatsu, 1937, pp. 3-4. Yawata, Ichirō "Kaisetsu," *Nihon minzoku bunka no kigen: Tōnan Ajia bunka to Nihon*, dai 3 kan, geppō dai 3 gō, Kōdansha, 1978, pp. 1-3.
68. Matsumoto, Nobuhiro "Waga Nan'yō wo miru," *Mita hyōron*, dai 483 gō, Mita hyōron hakkōjo, 1937, p. 6.
69. Matsumoto, Nobuhiro *Nyū Ginia dozokuhin zushū: Nan'yō kōhatsu kabushiki gaisha shūshū*, jōkan, Minami no kai hen, Nan'yō kōhatsu, 1937, pp. 3-4.

from the Southern Pacific Islands were transported to Japan.

Matsumoto learnt about the ethnographic collection of Nanyo Kohatsu K. K. from Matsue Ichirō, Matsue Haruji's son, at Keio University in 1934. After Matsue Haruji bought Komine's collection, he needed scholars to organize and classify the ethnographical objects. Therefore, he asked Matsumoto and his colleagues to do this professional work. On this occasion, the Japan Society of Oceanian Ethnography (*Minami no kai,* 南の会)[70] was established by ethnologists of various universities such as Matsumoto Nobuhiro, Oka Masao, Kobayashi Tomoo, Sugiura Ken'ichi, Nakano Tomoaki, and Yawata Ichiro. These scholars began classifying the artifacts in May 1935. Their working quarters was situated in a research room provided by Fukuyama Industry Library.[71] After the completion of the classification work, Nanyo Kohatsu K. K. sponsored the publication of *The Illustrated Catalogue of the Ethnographical Objects from Melanesia* (composing of two volumes: one in 1937 and the other in 1940). This became the first ethnographical catalogue of the Southern Pacific culture in Japan. Matsumoto wrote its preface in addition to the preface by director Matsue.[72] This suggests that Matsumoto was regarded as an authority in ethnography. In short, owing to Nanyo Kohatsu K. K., Matsumoto could join an ethnographical research of objects from the Southern Pacific Islands in Japan with other Japanese ethnologists.

The founding of the Japan Society of Oceanian Ethnography followed the establishment of the Japan Ethnological Society in January 1935.[73] Among the Japanese ethnologists of that time, Oka Masao was

---

70. Literary translation of 南の会 is "The Society of South," however the affiliated scholars themselves translated it into English as "The Japan Society of Oceanian Ethnography" which was also mentioned in Matsumoto, Nobuhiro *Nyū Ginia dozokuhin zushū: Nan'yō kōhatsu kabushiki gaisha shūshū*, jōkan, Minami no kai hen, Nan'yō kōhatsu, 1937.
71. Matsumoto, Nobuhiro *Nyū Ginia dozokuhin zushū: Nan'yō kōhatsu kabushiki gaisha shūshū*, jōkan, Minami no kai hen, Nan'yō kōhatsu, 1937, pp. 3, 5.
72. Ibid., p. 3.
73. "Nihon minzoku gakkai setsuritsu shuisho," *Minzokugaku kenkyū*, dai 1 kan, dai 1 gō, Nihon minzoku gakkai, Sanseidō, 1935, pp. 219–222.

especially important because he was Yanagita's student like Matsumoto and because he studied diffusionist ethnology under Schmidt in Vienna from 1929 to 1935.[74] This means that Oka joined the Japan Society of Oceanian Ethnography shortly after his return to Japan where he was seen as an authority in ethnology due to his doctoral degree from Schmidt. Oka's importance was visible in May 1935 when Schmidt conducted his lecture on ethnology in Tokyo.[75] Thus, Matsumoto's participation in the ethnographical research for Nanyo Kohatsu K. K. reflected the rising activity of the Japanese ethnological circles under the influence of diffusionist ethnology.

As a result of the cooperation with Nanyo Kohatsu K. K., Matsumoto went on an ethnographical research trip to the Southern Pacific Islands in summer 1937. The trip was organized by the Japan Society of Oceanian Ethnography, and Matsumoto joined it together with Yawata Ichiro, Sugiura Ken'ichi, and Nakano Tomoaki.[76] They spent four nights on a ship of the Nippon Yusen Kaisha Line from Japan before they reached Saipan in Micronesia.[77] First, they visited Saipan and Tenian where Nanyo Kohatsu K. K. had its buildings and sugar cane plantations. Then, they went to Palau, where the Japanese administration of the South Seas was located, and to Yap. In Saipan and Palau, they witnessed the Japanization of the local people as a result of the Japanese colonization.[78] Finally, they visited Dutch New Guinea, which Matsumoto considered to be important for further Japanese economic expansion, and advocated for the Japanese-Dutch cooperation there.[79] The statement that Matsumoto made corresponded with Matsue Har-

---

74. Ōbayashi, Taryō "Kaisetsu," *Ijin sonota: hoka jūni hen Oka Masao ronbunshū*, Iwanami shoten, 1994, pp. 267–278.
75. "Nihon minzoku gakkai setsuritsu shuisho," *Minzokugaku kenkyū*, dai 1 kan, dai 1 gō, Nihon minzoku gakkai, Sanseidō, 1935, pp. 219–222.
76. *Minzokugaku kenkyū*, dai 4 kan, dai 1 gō, Nihon minzoku gakkai, Sanseidō, 1938, p. 199. Yawata, Ichirō "Kaisetsu," *Nihon minzoku bunka no kigen: Tōnan Ajia bunka to Nihon*, dai 3 kan,geppō dai 3 gō, Kōdansha, 1978, p. 2.
77. Matsumoto, Nobuhiro "Waga Nan'yō wo miru," *Mita hyōron*, dai 483 gō, Mita hyōron hakkōjo, 1937, p. 6.
78. Ibid., p. 8
79. Ibid., p. 11.

uji's wish in his preface to *The Illustrated Catalogue of the Ethnographical Objects from Melanesia*, which was a "contribution to the understanding and friendship between Holland and Japan though the medium of ethnography."[80] Thus, Matsumoto's ethnographic trip to the Southern Pacific Islands reflected Japanese economic ambitions there.

2.2.2. Significance of Matsumoto Nobuhiro's research trip to the Southern Pacific Islands

This section examines the significance of Matsumoto Nobuhiro's trip to the Southern Pacific Islands by analyzing Matsumoto's contribution to the Japanese academia resulting from this trip. After his return to Japan, Matsumoto reported on this travel to the Japanese academia. First, he discussed his trip at the meeting of the Mita Historical Society on September 28, 1937.[81] Then, he delivered a presentation together with Yawata Ichiro, Sugiura Kenichi, and Nakano Tomoaki at a meeting of the Japan Etnological Society on November 8, 1937.[82] The content of Matsumoto's presentations is unknown. Furthermore, Matsumoto wrote papers *Seeing Our South Seas* and *Travel Diary to Southern Islands* (Saipan, Yap, Palau, New Guinea) in 1937.[83]

In these writings, Matsumoto gave a general overview on the South Seas from his observation and what he heard from the people that he met there. In contrast, Matsumoto did not provide any details about the culture of the local people or the ethnographical objects that he collected although he obviously observed the native people of the Southern Pacific Islands. The aspect of native culture that inter-

---

80. Matsumoto, Nobuhiro *Nyū Ginia dozokuhin zushū: Nan'yō kōhatsu kabushiki gaisha shūshū*, jōkan, Minami no kai hen, Nan'yō kōhatsu, 1937, p. 2.
81. "Mita shigaku kenkyūkai reikai hōkoku," *Shigaku*, dai 18 kan, dai 1 gō, Mita Shigakkai, 1939, p. 171.
82. *Minzokugaku kenkyū*, dai 4 kan, dai 1 gō, Nihon minzoku gakkai, Sanseidō, 1938, p. 199.
83. Matsumoto, Nobuhiro "Waga Nan'yō wo miru," *Mita hyōron*, dai 483 gō, Mita hyōron hakkōjo, 1937, pp. 6–12. "Nan'yō guntō ryokō nisshi," *Shigaku*, dai 16 kan, dai 3 gō, Mita Shigakkai, 1937, pp. 77a-109.

ested him most as an ethnologist was limited to requesting for better protection of the native culture, which was endangered by the industrialization of the islands by Japanese.[84] In other words, despite Matsumoto's participation in this ethnographical project, Matsumoto's writings about South Seas dealt with general information on the contemporary situation in Micronesia and New Guinea and did not mention anything regarding ethnographical research there. The reason for this was probably the same as in the case of his travels to French Indochina — Matsumoto was not a note taker and did not record data from his observations that a field researcher would normally do.

Since Matsumoto did not collect any research works that he could summarize and publish, he did not present any ethnographical research reports on the Southern Pacific Islands. Thus, Matsumoto's only academic work on the Southern Pacific Islands in this period was his cooperation in producing *The Illustrated Catalogue of the Ethnographical Objects from Melanesia*, a work detailing the ethnographical collection of Nanyo Kohatsu K. K. In addition to his writings from the trip and his contribution to the catalogue, he presented a one-page article *A Study on the Name of Sampan* (1936) in which he argued that the origin of the word sampan was in the South Seas.[85] Hence, his publication on Southern Pacific Islands in the 1930s was very small. In retrospect, it can be said that the trip to Southern Pacific Islands mainly served in developing Matsumoto's ideas regarding the Southern culture.

In summary, in comparison with the research trip to Indochina, Matsumoto's trip to the Southern Pacific Islands seems less significant. Matsumoto produced an academic work on Southern Pacific Islands only because he was involved in the organization of the ethnographic collection owned by Nanyo Kohatsu K. K. This means that this trip was an observatory tour rather than a research trip. In his

---

84. Matsumoto, Nobuhiro "Waga Nan'yō wo miru," *Mita hyōron*, dai 483 gō, Mita hyōron hakkōjo, 1937, p. 7. "Nan'yō guntō ryokō nisshi," *Shigaku*, dai 16 kan, dai 3 gō, Mita Shigakkai, 1937, p. 86.
85. Matsumoto, Nobuhiro "Sanpan meigi kō" (1936), *Tōa minzoku bunka ronkō*, Seibundō shinkōsha, 1968, p. 781.

writings about the Southern Pacific Islands, Matsumoto did not mention about Southeast Asia. In this light, the trip did not directly bestow the Japanese academic circles with new knowledge except for a general overview on the Southern Pacific Islands. Nevertheless, Matsumoto's exposure to the local environment in the Southern Pacific Islands can be regarded as one of the building blocks for the gestation of his future ideas.

2.3. Significance of Matsumoto Nobuhiro's research trips to China

This section examines the importance of Matsumoto's research trips to China in the summer of 1938 and in the winter of 1939 for his career as the founder of Southeast Asian studies based on his contribution to the Japanese academic circles. First, it discusses about the trip itself. Then, it discusses the connection of the trip with Matsumoto's ideas regarding Southeast Asia and the significance of Matsumoto's writings published from these trips.

2.3.1. Matsumoto Nobuhiro's research trips to China

First, Matsumoto Nobuhiro was in China from May to September 1938 after the escalation of the Second Sino-Japanese War.[86] He went to Shanghai, Nanking and Hangzhou as a member of an archaeological mission of Keio Gijuku University to the Chinese continent. This first mission comprised three teams, and Matsumoto's team included Hosaka Saburo and Nishioka Hideo.[87]

The first mission aimed at the excavation of relics in Kutang in Hangzhou Province because Matsumoto and his colleagues wanted to verify that the relics there came from the Neolithic period.[88] Matsu-

---

86. *Ine-fune-matsuri: Matsumoto Nobuhiro sensei tsuitō ronbunshū*, Rokkōshuppan, 1982, p. 694.
87. *Kōnan tōsa. Shōwa 13-nendo*, Keiō gijuku daigaku bungakubu shigakka kenkyū hōkoku; kōshu, dai 1 satsu, Mita Shigakkai, 1941, p. 1.
88. Matsumoto, Nobuhiro "Senseki junrei," *Mita hyōron*, dai 492 gō, Mita hyōron hakkōjo, 1938, p. 36. "Kōnan hōkoki," *Shigaku*, dai 17 kan 4 gō, Mita Shigakkai, 1939, p. 3. Matsumoto, Nobuhiro "Kōnan hōkoki," *Shigaku*, dai 17 kan 4 gō, Mita Shigakkai, 1939, p. 44.

moto considered the relics to be important because similar relics were found in many places in the South Seas, including Hong Kong and Indochina.[89] He assumed the existence of a connection between Southeast Asia and China since he read theories by Western scholars that argued that the ancestors of the Indochinese people migrated from China.[90] He believed in the value of relics as evidence of ancient culture.[91] Thus, he expected that the connection could be proved if there was a similarity between the specimens of Southeast Asia and China since this comparative method was used by Western scholars, such as Robert Heine-Geldern.[92] Therefore, Matsumoto's archaeological trip to China formed an important part of his research on Southeast Asia.

Matsumoto left Nagasaki on a ship called Nagasakimaru on May 13, 1938, and arrived in Shanghai on May 15, 1938.[93] First, Matsumoto and his group visited the Japanese army headquarters to explain their academic mission and ask for permission to travel. Then, they made a tour of historical sites in Shanghai with an army suite. They also stopped at the Shanghai Research Institute of Natural Sciences where they met Shinjo Shinzo, the director of the institute. Shinjo asked them to help in the study of specimens from Chinese museums that came under Japanese control, or as he put it, "rescue the historical and archaeological specimens from the dust."[94] As a result, Matsumoto and his colleagues changed their mind and decided to join Shinjo on his requisition trip.[95]

89. Matsumoto, Nobuhiro "Kōnan hōkoki," *Shigaku*, dai 17 kan 4 gō, Mita Shigakkai, 1939, p. 64.
90. Matsumoto, Nobuhiro "Indoshina wo mite," *Gaikō jihō*, dai 703 gō, Gaikō jihōsha, 15.03.1934, p. 133.
91. Matsumoto, Nobuhiro "Kodai bunkaron" *Gendai shigaku taikei*, Kyōritsusha shoten, 1932, p. 138.
92. Matsumoto, Nobuhiro "Indoshina no bunka jō," *Iwanami kōza Tōyō shichō*, I, Iwanami shoten, 1934, p. 20.
93. Matsumoto, Nobuhiro "Senseki junrei," *Mita hyōron*, dai 490 gō, Mita hyōron hakkōjo, 1938, pp. 35, 36. "Kōnan hōkoki," *Shigaku*, dai 17 kan 4 gō, Mita Shigakkai, 1939, p. 10.
94. Matsumoto, Nobuhiro "Kōnan hōkoki," *Shigaku*, dai 17 kan 4 gō, Mita Shigakkai, 1939, p. 4.

Chapter 3: Visiting the South Seas during 1933–1940   153

After negotiating with the army headquarters to organize this trip, Matsumoto and his group went by train to Nanking on May 17, 1938. They witnessed the war damages from the train window. In Nanking, they worked on classifying the specimens and the research reports in the History and Linguistic Institute of the Central Academy.[96] In short, as a result of meeting with Shinjo in Shanghai, Matsumoto's main work during his research trip in China became the study of archaeological specimens and research reports scattered in various Chinese museums occupied by the Japanese army.

After Nanking, Matsumoto went on a research trip to Hangzhou from June 9, 1938.[97] In Hangzhou, he worked on classifying the artifacts in the Department of History and Culture of the West Lake Museum.[98] In this museum, Matsumoto was fascinated by the room that presented Zhejiang (浙江) culture. He described the room as follows: "…the most interesting thing to us was the room of the ancient Zhejiang culture. … The room was small …, on the walls, there were pictures of historical records of Zhejiang and tables of important persons of each part of the Zhejiang history and Zhejiang excavation objects were lined up in the glass boxes."[99] Among the exhibited specimens in the room, Matsumoto mostly focused on the stone axes since similar axes were found in Southeast Asia and Japan.[100]

Furthermore, Matsumoto participated in excavations in Hangzhou for 10 days. However, the excavation was difficult due to the rainy season.[101] As Matsumoto stated, the excavations sought to uncover relics from the Neolithic period.[102] However, the majority of the unearthened

---

95. Matsumoto, Nobuhiro "Senseki junrei," *Mita hyōron*, dai 490 gō, Mita hyōron hakkōjo, 1938, p. 36.
96. Ibid., dai 491 gō, Mita hyōron hakkōjo, 1938, pp. 35.
97. Matsumoto, Nobuhiro "Kōnan hōkoki," *Shigaku*, dai 17 kan 4 gō, Mita Shigakkai, 1939, p. 39.
98. Ibid., p. 40.
99. Ibid., p. 41.
100. Ibid., pp. 69–71.
101. Matsumoto, Nobuhiro "Senseki junrei," *Mita hyōron*, dai 492 gō, Mita hyōron hakkōjo, 1938, p. 36.

objects were fragments of porcelain produced by the Southern Song Dynasty of the Zhejiang Province.[103] Therefore, Matsumoto's archaeological excavation in Hangzhou did not meet his research objectives.

Matsumoto went to China for the second time in January 1939 for research on Chinese specimens.[104] This time, his Keio colleagues in this mission were Matsumoto Yoshio, Shibata, Hosaka Saburo, Kitagawa, Mazaki Manri, and Mori.[105] They arrived in Shanghai on January 3, 1939. In Shanghai, they visited the Shanghai Research Institute of Natural Sciences. On January 6, they went to Nanking where they researched the specimens.[106] Matsumoto was in charge of the ethnological objects.[107] He also made two survey trips to Hangzhou.[108] In summary, Matsumoto again visited Shanghai, Nanking, and Hangzhou on his second trip and continued his research on Chinese specimens.

From the contents of the two trips made by Matsumoto in 1938 and 1939, it is obvious that Matsumoto got access to many Chinese archaeological artifacts and research reports during his stay in Shanghai, Nanking, and Hangzhou. These materials, especially specimens similar to those of Southeast Asia and Japan, supported his argument that central China had connections with Southeast Asia and Japan.

2.3.2. Significance of Matsumoto Nobuhiro's research trips to China

This section examines the significance of Matsumoto's research trips to China for his ideas regarding Southeast Asia and for his career as a pioneer in Southeast Asia studies. First, it demonstrates the con-

---

102. Ibid., p. 36. "Kōnan hōkoki," *Shigaku*, dai 17 kan 4 gō, Mita Shigakkai, 1939, p. 3. "Kōnan hōkoki," *Shigaku*, dai 17 kan, dai 4 gō, Mita Shigakkai, 1939, p. 44.
103. *Kōnan tōsa. Shōwa 13-nendo*, Keiō gijuku daigaku bungakubu shigakka kenkyū hōkoku; kōshu, dai 1 satsu, Mita Shigakkai, 1941, p. 159.
104. *Ine-fune-matsuri: Matsumoto Nobuhiro sensei tsuitō ronbunshū*, Rokkōshuppan, 1982, p. 694.
105. Matsumoto, Yoshio "Chūshi yūki," *Shigaku*, dai 18 kan, dai 1 gō, Mita Shigakkai, 1939, pp. 145, 160, 163.
106. Ibid., pp. 147–152.
107. Ibid., p. 152.
108. Ibid., pp. 153, 160.

nection of Matsumoto's ideas regarding China with his ideas regarding Southeast Asia. Then, it evaluates the significance of these travels from the perspective of academic contribution to Southeast Asian studies.

From his research trips to China, Matsumoto published travel records, research reports, and research papers. First, Matsumoto wrote about his travel records under the title *Pilgrimage around the Battlefields* in 1938.[109] Then, he rewrote these records with some additions in *Old Records from the Visit of Jiangnan* in 1939.[110] In these writings, Matsumoto decribed his impressions from the research and from China's cultural heritage affected by war damages. He mentioned about the similarity between the Chinese specimens and the specimens discovered in Southeast Asia.[111]

This similarity between the Chinese and Southeast Asian specimens was indicated in his research reports on the Chinese artifacts. Matsumoto introduced the excavated objects that he observed during his work on their classification in China in *Two Examples of Specimens of Ancient Chinese Culture in Nanking, The Outline of the Archaeological Survey in Central China, The Catalogue of Archaeological Speciments Collected by Matsumoto's Team on the Academic Mission in China, The Report of the Archaeological Team of the Academic Mission in China, The Illustrated Catalogue of Collection of Matsumoto's Team in Central China from the Academic Mission in China,* and *Archeological Studies at Nanking and Hangzhou.*[112] As a co-author of the report *Archeological Studies at Nanking and Hangzhou*, Matsumoto indicated the similarity between the Chinese stone axes and those excavated in Thanh Hoá (Vietnam) and the similarity between the Chinese porce-

---

109. Matsumoto, Nobuhiro "Senseki junrei," *Mita hyōron*, dai 490 gō - dai 493 gō, Mita hyōron hakkōjo, 1938.
110. Matsumoto, Nobuhiro "Kōnan hōkoki," *Shigaku*, dai 17 kan 4 gō, Mita Shigakkai, 1939, pp. 529–612.
111. Ibid., pp. 64, 69–71.
112. *Ine-fune-matsuri: Matsumoto Nobuhiro sensei tsuitō ronbunshū*, Rokkōshuppan, 1982, p. 708. *Kōnan tōsa. Shōwa 13-nendo*, Keiō gijuku daigaku bungakubu shigakka kenkyū hōkoku; kōshu, dai 1 satsu, Mita Shigakkai, 1941.

lain and the Vietnamese one.[113] Thus, Matsumoto contributed to the Japanese academic circles by bringing information about the Chinese specimens; simultaneously, he presented his idea regarding the connection between the ancient Chinese and Southeast Asian culture based on the similarity of the artifacts.

This idea regarding the connection between Southeast Asia and China in ancient times inspired him to write a research paper *Issues Concerning the Shouldered Axes* in 1938. The main sources of inspiration came from stone axes exhibited in Hangzhou, Robert Heine-Geldern's papers on stone axes, and Yanagita's ideas regarding metal tools. Undoubtedly, when Matsumoto saw the stone axes in Hangzhou, he recollected Heine-Geldern's work *A Contribution to the Chronology of the Neolithic Age in Southeast Asia* (1928).[114] Matsumoto adopted an argument from Heine-Geldern's works *A Contribution to the Chronology of the Neolithic in Southeast Asia* and *Homeland and Earliest Migrations of Austronesian*. These works claimed the connection of the Mon-Khmer language family (of Austroasiatic languages) with shouldered axes in Austronesia, especially Malay Peninsula, and suggested that the distribution of the shouldered axes approximately corresponds to that of the Austroasiatic languages.[115]

Matsumoto connected Heine-Geldern's theory with his ideas regarding the metal farming tools, which he developed from Yanagita's theory on the diffusion of the metal tools.[116] Matsumoto's paper *The Tale of Potato Digger Millionaire* demonstrated that Matsumoto was

---

113. *Kōnan tōsa. Shōwa 13-nendo*, Keiō gijuku daigaku bungakubu shigakka kenkyū hōkoku; kōshu, dai 1 satsu, Mita Shigakkai, 1941, p. 90.
114. Matsumoto, Nobuhiro "Yūken sekifu no shomondai," *Shigaku*, dai 18 kan, dai 2/3 gō, Mita Shigakkai, 1939, p. 298. Heine-Geldern, Robert "Ein Beitrag zur Chronologie des Neolithikums in Südostasien," St. Gabriel-Mödling bei Wien, *Anthropos*-Administration,[ca. 1924], pp. 809-843.
115. Heine-Geldern, Robert "Ein Beitrag zur Chronologie des Neolithikums in Südostasien," St. Gabriel-Mödling bei Wien, *Anthropos*-Administration,[ca. 1924], pp. 809-843. "Urheimat und früheste Wanderungen der Austronesier," *Anthropos* (XXVII), 1932, pp. 543-619. Matsumoto, Nobuhiro "Yūken sekifu no shomondai," *Shigaku*, dai 18 kan, dai 2/3 gō, MitaShigakkai, 1939, pp. 298, 303.

interested in Yanagita's hypothesis in Japan in 1930: "If the old belief of Hachimangū has a deep relation with peddlers of metal crafts, as Mr. Yanagita presumes, we may consider that such myths and legends were imported to Japan together with the technology that arrived from the continent."[117]

In his paper *Issues Concerning the Shouldered Axes*, Matsumoto combined the argument of shouldered stone axes with his ideas regarding the development of stone tools in relation to central China: "... many metal tools discovered recently have the ancestral form of stone tools in the past. The metal tools of the hoe in ancient China were developed from similar stone tools of hoe; thus we can imagine that the shouldered axes have a close relation to their ancestral form. In confirming this assumption, it is necessary to engage in more excavations in Central China from now."[118] This quotation indicates that Matsumoto linked the shoulder stone axes in Southeast Asia with those in China as a result of his research trip to China where he witnessed stone axes in the Zhejiang culture room in Hangzhou. The paper *Issues Concerning the Shouldered Axes* proved that Matsumoto's trips to China were important for his ideas regarding Southeast Asia represented by the Austroasiatic language family. The introduction of the connection between the ancient Chinese and Southeast Asian culture was Matsumoto's only contribution to the Japanese academic circles from this paper.

The significance of Matsumoto's trip to China for his ideas regarding Southeast Asia is apparent also from his paper *Issues Concerning the Shouldered Axes*. First, Matsumoto presented his paper *Primitive Farming Tools in Southeast Asia* at a research meeting held by the Mita Historical Society on October 31, 1939.[119] Then, he included it in his book *The Peoples and Cultures of Indochina*.[120]

---

116. Itō, Seiji "Matsumoto Nobuhito to imohori chōsha no hanashi," *Nihon bunka no kigen*, dai 3 kan, Geppō dai 3 gō, 1978, p. 6.
117. Matsumoto, Nobuhiro "Imohori chōsha" (1930), *Nihon minzoku bunka no kigen I: shinwa-densetsu*, Kōdansha, 1978, pp. 309-310.
118. Matsumoto, Nobuhiro "Yūken sekifu no shomondai," *Shigaku*, dai 18 kan, dai 2/3 gō, MitaShigakkai, 1939, p. 325.

Thus, Matsumoto's papers related to his trip to China indicated that Matsumoto tried to establish a connection between China and Southeast Asia through the similarity of the archaeological specimens. This was probably a result of the diffusionist influence since Matsumoto used the diffusionist terms "distribution" (*bumpu*, 分布) and "Southern genealogy" (*Nampōkei*, 南方系) in his writings about China. For example, he wrote about the distribution of shouldred axes and the distribution of Austroasiatic languages in his paper *Issues Concerning the Shouldered Axes*.[121]

To sum it up, Matsumoto's participation in the archaeological mission to China was important for Matsumoto's ideas regarding Southeast Asia because it enabled him to establish the evidential basis for his belief in the connection between Southeast Asia and China. As a result of his encounter with Shinjo Shinzo in Shanghai, Matsumoto could observe many Chinese artifacts in the History and Linguistic Institute of the Central Academy in Nanking and the West Lake Museum in Hangzhou. Hence, although his excavation survey in Kutang in the summer of 1938 was not successful, Matsumoto obtained research material on the Chinese ancient culture that he introduced to Japan in his research reports. Owing to this acquired material, he could indicated the similarities between the Chinese and Southeast Asian specimens, which became the evidence to support his claims regarding the connection between China and Southeast Asia in ancient times. These similarities could be interpreted by both evolutionism and diffusionism. However, Matsumoto did not present any interpretation on them. Though Matsumoto's trip did not directly contribute to Matsumoto's career as the founder of Southeast Asian studies, it developed his ideas regarding Southeast Asia.

---

119. "Mita shigaku kenkyūkai reikai hōkoku," *Shigaku*, dai 18 kan, dai 4 gō, Mita Shigakkai, 1939, p. 777.
120. Matsumoto, Nobuhiro "Yūken sekifu no shomondai," *Indoshina no minzoku to bunka*, Iwanami shoten, 1942, pp. 189–223.
121. Matsumoto, Nobuhiro "Yūken sekifu no shomondai," *Shigaku*, dai 18 kan, dai 2/3 gō, Mita Shigakkai, 1939, p. 297–298.

3. Conclusion

During 1933–1939, Matsumoto became the founder of Southeast Asian studies and developed his ideas regarding Southeast Asia through his research trips to French Indochina, the Southern Pacific Islands, and China. The analysis of the significance of Matsumoto's research trips showed that Ito Seiji's hypothesis that the trip to French Indochina was highly significant correct. Among his research trips, his travel to French Indochina mostly contributed to Matsumoto's formation as the founder of Southeast Asian studies because it enabled him to bring back a big volume of data on Southeast Asia to Japan and to present them in Japanese to the Japanese academic circles. This contribution was intentional because he chose to focus on Indochina instead of going to China owing to his friendship with the French scholars of the EFEO in Hanoi. Furthermore, his trips to the Southern Pacific Islands and China were related to his ideas regarding Southeast Asia because he perceived these regions to be connected with Southeast Asia due to the influence of diffusionist ethnology (especially Heine-Geldern's theories) that prevailed in the 1930s. This fact was proven in Matsumoto's writings about archaeological artifacts from China wherein he emphasized the similarity between the Chinese artifacts and objects found in Southeast Asia and Japan.

Chapter 4:
Ideas for establishing Southeast Asian studies during 1933–1945

1. Introduction

The previous chapter showed that Matsumoto came into direct contact with the people and culture of Southeast Asia and received a large volume of data related to Southeast Asia. He built up his knowledge about Indochina through his trip to Vietnam and Western works on Southeast Asia in the 1930s. This led him to develop his ideas regarding Southeast Asia after 1939. He was able to lay foundations of Southeast Asian studies because ethnology had been officially acknowledged as an academic discipline in Japan and because the Japanese penetration into Southeast Asia had been increasing.

The establishment of ethnology as an academic discipline in Japan in 1935 enabled Matsumoto to introduce Southeast Asia in his new course of ethnology at Keio University. He started teaching ethnology in 1938.[1] Although the detailed content of his lectures remains unknown, it most likely included Indochinese people. It can be assumed that Matsumoto presented an overview of various ethnic groups, which Chikamori Masashi (*1935) learnt in Matsumoto's class of ethnology in the 1950s.[2] Thus, Matsumoto probably incorporated his new knowledge from materials that he collected in French Indochina in his lectures on ethnology.

---

1. Kawakita, Nobuo "Keiō gijuku daigaku bungakubu kyōin tantō kamoku ichiran," *Shigaku*, dai 60 kan, dai 2/3 gō, Mita Shigakkai, 1991, p. 205 (379).
2. Interview with Chikamori Masashi, 23 August 2012, Keio University, Tokyo.

During the same period, Matsumoto maintained his relationship with Yanagita, who was a leader of Japanese folklore studies. Thus, despite the separation of ethnology and folklore studies in 1935, Matsumoto continued his participation both in ethnological and folkloristic circles. This is also apparent from the fact that Matsumoto published two papers on Japanese myths although he was busy with writing various papers on Indochina in 1934.[3] Furthermore, in the article *A Supplement to Akashi Teiichi's On Relation of Magical Objects and Astronomy in 'the Annamese Variation of the Legend of the Old Otter*, Matsumoto shared Yanagita's opinion on the diffusion of the legends.[4]

Moreover, in the late 1930s, Tokyo government formulated the strategy for the Southern advance as a part of the national policy. (See Chapter 5, Section 2) Under these new circumstances, the so-called "Southward Theory" became popular during the Asia-Pacific War after being neglected in comparison with the main-stream "Northward Theory" in previous years.[5] In this new light, Matsumoto's works indicating the similarity between Southeast Asia and Japan were seen as beneficient because they corresponded to the Pan-Asianist argument emphasizing comonnalities between the Japanese and other Asian peoples for the construction of a common Asian identity. (See Chapter 5 Section 3) This fuelled the academic career of Matsumoto who was gradually profiled as the founder of Southeast Asian studies.

In 1939, Matsumoto became a research fellow at the Research Institute for South Asian Culture (*Minami Ajia Kenkyūjo*, 南亜細亜研究所) under governmental auspice.[6] The Ministry of Foreign Affairs es-

---

3. Matsumoto, Nobuhiro "Nihon shinwa no kanken" (1934), *Tōa minzoku bunkaronkō*, Seibundō shinkōsha, 1968, pp. 311–319. "Nihon shinwa ni tsuite," *Iwanami kōza Nihon rekishi*, Iwanami shoten, 1934, pp. 1–44.
4. Matsumoto, Nobuhiro "Akashi Teikichi 'Rōnorachi densetsu no Annan den' no reibutsu to tenmon no kankei, tsuiki" (1935), *Tōa minzoku bunkaronkō*, Seibundō shinkōsha, 1968, pp. 153–155.
5. Itō, Seiji "Hito to gakumon, Matsumoto Nobuhiro," *Shakai jinruigaku nenpō*, Tōkyō toritsu daigaku shakai jinrui gakkai, dai 12 kan, 1986, p. 123.
6. Roustan, Frédéric "From Oriental Studies to South Pacific Studies: The Multiple Origins of Vietnamese Studies," *Journal of Vietnamese Studies*, Vol. 6, Issue 1, 2011, pp. 17–18.

tablished this institute with the cooperation of the Intelligence Bureau and the Government of Taiwan. Shiratori Kurakichi (1865-1942), famous ethnologist and the professor of Oriental history at Tokyo Imperial University, was appointed as the director of the institute. Matsumoto worked there as the director of the Indochina history project together with Yamamoto Tatsuro (1910-2001), who graduated in Oriental history at Tokyo Imperial University and conducted research on the Vietnamese history.[7]

This was an important step in Matsumoto's career because he joined scholars of different institutions researching on Southeast Asia. According to his opinion in his paper *Chinese Research in France*, Matsumoto considered the joint research of various scholars as the first step in the progress of the Japanese scholarship to catch up with the French level.[8] From this point of view, Matsumoto's wish for the mutual cooperation of the Japanese specialists from different institutions was somewhat realized 11 years after his return from Sorbonne University.

However, the achievements of the institute suggested that the cooperation between its scholars there was not intensive. The institute published only two volumes of *Southern Asian Research Report* (one in 1943 and the other in 1944) since its establishment in 1939.[9] Matsumoto only presented one paper *Betel Palm and Banana - A Research in Names of Southward Products and Plants* in the first volume of *Southern Asian Research Report*.[10] Therefore, it can be assumed that the scholars of this institute worked mainly for their original institutions. This implies that the establishment of the Research Institute for South Asian Culture did not spur the cooperation of the Japanese scholars

---

7. *Minami Ajia gakuhō*, Minami Ajia bunka kenkyūjo, dai 1 gō, 1943.
8. Matsumoto, Nobuhiro "Furansu ni okeru Shina kenkyū" in *Shina kenkyū*, Iwanami shoten, 1930, p. 386.
9. *Minami Ajia gakuhō*, Minami Ajia bunka kenkyūjo, dai 1 gō, 1943; dai 2 gō, 1944.
10. Matsumoto, Nobuhiro "Binrō to bashō —Nampō san shokubutsu mei no kenkyū *Minami Ajia gakuhō*, dai 1 gō, Minami Ajia bunka kenkyūjo, 1943, pp. 17-48.

from various institutions to a large extent. This is also suggested by the fact that Matsumoto criticized the lack of unity of the Japanese scholars in 1942.[11] He was also mobilized as a researcher of the Committee for Ethnic Issues collecting information on Southeast Asia in 1940,[12] but his activity there was limited as explained in Chapter 5.

In contrast, Matsumoto's work at his Alma Mater, Keio University, was more important. There, Matsumoto was assigned a leading position in the Linguistic Institute (*Gogaku kenkyūjo*, 語学研究所) and the Asia Research Institute (*Ajia kenkyūjo*, 亜細亜研究所), which he established in October 1942 and in January 1943, respectively.[13] The Linguistic Institute was closed after the war in 1945, but Matsumoto contributed to its re-establishment as the Keio University Institute of Cultural and Linguistic Studies in July 1962. It became one of the Japanese centers for Southeast Asian studies.[14] According to Kawamoto, Matsumoto decided to establish the institute in 1941 because similar institutions were opened at Tokyo Imperial University and Kyoto Imperial University in 1940 and 1939, respectively.[15] The first article of the Linguistic Institute regulations from 1942 reflects the direct connection between the establishment of the institute and the Greater East Asia Co-Prosperity Sphere: "the Keio University Linguistic Institute has aim to realize the Greater East Asia building by conducting linguistic research of East Asian, European and American languages."[16] The institute had 23

---

11. Especially in Matsumoto, Nobuhiro "Nampō bunka seisaku to minzokugaku," *Gaikō jihō*, dai 885 gō, Gaikō jihōsha, 15.10.1941, p. 79.
12. Yatsugi, Kazuo *Shōwa dōran shishi*, chū, Keizai ōraisha, 1971, p. 207.
13. *Ine-fune-matsuri: Matsumoto Nobuhiro sensei tsuitō ronbunshū*, Rokkō-shuppan, 1982, p. 694. Kawamoto, Kunie "Gengo bunka kenkyūjo sanjūnen," *Keiō gijuku daigaku gengo bunka kenkyūjo hōkokushū*, Keiō gijuku daigaku gengo bunka kenkyūjo, dai 24 gō, 1992, pp. 1-2.
14. *Ine-fune-matsuri: Matsumoto Nobuhiro sensei tsuitō ronbunshū*, Rokkō-shuppan, 1982, p. 695. Kawamoto, Kunie "Gengo bunka kenkyūjo sanjūnen," *Keiō gijuku daigaku gengo bunka kenkyūjo hōkokushū*, Keiō gijuku daigaku gengo bunka kenkyūjo, dai 24 gō, 1992, pp. 2-3.
15. Kawamoto, Kunie "Gengo bunka kenkyūjo sanjūnen," *Keiō gijuku daigaku gengo bunka kenkyūjo hōkokushū*, Keiō gijuku daigaku gengo bunka kenkyūjo, dai 24 gō, 1992, pp. 1-4.

language departments, including languages of Vietnam, Sanskrit, Pali, and so on.[17] Here, Matsumoto had a Vietnamese assistant Trần Kinh Hoà (陳荊和, Chin Kei Wa, 1917-1995) who later became a specialist in Vietnamese history and did the editing work for the publication of *Complete Annals of Đại Việt* (*Đại Việt sử ký toàn thư*) in Japan.[18]

Finally, Matsumoto was active in various research organizations related to Southeast Asia and the Southern Pacific, such as Indochina Research Society (*Indoshina kenkyūkai*, 印度支那研究会),[19] South Seas Association (*Nan'yō kyōkai*, 南洋協会),[20] Pacific Association (*Taiheiyō kyōkai*, 太平洋協会),[21] and so on.

From these points, it is clear that Japan's Southern advance facilitated Matsumoto's activities toward the establishment of Southeast Asian studies in Japan. Therefore, it is not surprising to find the Japan's Southern Advance Theory and Pan-Asianism in Matsumoto's works. This political influence is examined in the next chapter. This chapter focuses on Matsumoto's ideas regarding Southeast Asia during 1933-1945. First, it examines Matsumoto's adoption of the Western geographical concept of Southeast Asia, in addition to the Japanese and Chinese geographical concepts of the South Seas. Second, it clarifies the influence of diffusionist ethnology on Matsumoto's works. Third, it discusses Orientalism in Matsumoto's ideas regarding the

---

16. Ibid., pp. 3-4.
17. Ibid., p. 5.
18. Kawamoto, Kunie "Shiki ni mukau keigan – Chin Kei Wa hakushi wo itamu," *Keiō gijuku daigaku gengo bunka kenkyūjo kiyō*, dai 28 gō, Keiō gijuku daigaku gengo bunka kenkyūjo, 1996, pp. 11-20.
19. Matsumoto, Nobuhiro *Annango nyūmon. Bunpōhen*, Indoshina kenkyūkai, 1942, p. 2. *Annango nyūmon. Kaiwahen*, Indoshina kenkyūkai, 1942, p. 2. Itō, Seiji "Matsumoto Nobuhiro to gakumon," Keiō gijuku *daigaku gengo kenkyūjo hōkokushū*, Keiō gijuku daigaku, dai 24 kan, 1992, p. 18. Yamamoto, Tatsurō "Betonamu kenkyū shiryō no shōkai to shuppan," *Nihon minzoku bunka no kigen*, dai 3 kan, Geppō dai 3 gō, Kōdansha, 1978, p. 3.
20. Matsumoto, Nobuhiro "Futsuryō Indoshina no minzoku," *Nan'yō*, dai 27 kan, dai 7 gō, 1940, pp. 26-33.
21. Matsumoto, Nobuhiro "Annanjin no kigen," *Taiheiyō ken*, jōkan, Kawade shobō, 1944, p. 1 (319).

people of Southeast Asia and the Southern Pacific. Fourth, it investigates the influence of the climate theory in his ideas regarding Southeast Asia.

2. Concepts of South Seas and Southeast Asia

During 1933-1939, Matsumoto continued using both the Chinese and the Japanese terms *Nan'yō* (南洋) and *Nankai* (南海) for the South Seas, in addition to the Western term Austroasiatic (オーストロアジア) in relation to Southeast Asia and Indochina. For example, he used *Nan'yō* (南洋) in his paper *Annamese Tooth Blackening* wherein he wrote that chewing areca nuts by indigenous people was considered to be a "South Seas habit" (*Nan'yō no fūzoku*, 南洋の風俗) in Japan and that European travelers learnt about "this Annamese habit" for the first time when they visited Indochina.[22] He mentioned about *Nankai* (南海) in his paper *The Genealogy of Indochina Languages*: "Therefore, it is surely not a bold attempt to claim that there is a close relation between the South Seas races [*Nankai minzoku*, 南海民族] and Indochina, and that the origin of their languages was situated in Indochina."[23]

In addition, he started using the term "Southeast Asia" (*Tōnan Ajia*, 東南アジア) in relation to Indochina. His writing *Culture of Indochina* suggested that he perceived Indochina as a part of Southeast Asia: "Indochina is a large peninsula that juts out in the South East of the Asian Continent and is positioned between the Bengal Bay and China Sea, high mountains that start from Tibetan large plateau and go south, divide in fan shape and embrass river valleys of Irrawaddy, Salween, Menam, Mekong, Red River etc."[24] Matsumoto adopted this concept of Indochina as a part of Southeast Asia from the Western scholars. For example, Matsumoto referred to Heine-Geldern for the

---

22. Matsumoto, Nobuhiro "Annanjin no ohaguro," *Shigaku*, dai 12 kan, dai 4 gō, Mita Shigakkai, 1933, pp. 96 (676).
23. Matsumoto, Nobuhiro "Indoshina gengo no keitō," *Iwanami kōza Tōyō shichō*, I (Tōyō gengo no keitō), Iwanami shoten, 1934, p. 38.

ethnological data on Southeast Asia in his writing *Culture of Indochina*: "This Geldern's theory has extreme importance for the history of migration of Southeast Asian races [*Tōnan Ajia no jinshu*, 東南アジアの人種]."[25] Furthermore, Matsumoto mentioned regarding Southeast Asia in his references to arguments made by many Western scholars, such as Aymonier,[26] Golubev,[27] Wilhelm Schmidt, and De Hevesy.[28] Historian Shimizu Hajime claimed that the term "Southeast Asia" appeared in Japanese geography textbooks for the first time in 1917.[29] However, this term reflected Japanese colonialist ambition toward Southeast Asia. In contrast, in 1933, Matsumoto adopted and used the concept of Southeast Asia from Western scholars as a result of his interest in the culture of Southeast Asian people. In sum, during 1933–1939, Matsumoto employed the Western concept of Southeast Asia and the Japanese and Chinese concepts of the South Seas without defining them.

3. Influence of diffusionist ethnology on Matsumoto's works

As argued in Chapter 3, Matsumoto's ideas regarding Southeast Asia during 1933–1945 were strongly influenced by diffusionism. This was because diffusionism became the mainstream of ethnology in the 1930s both in the world and in Japan. The first congress of the International Anthropological and Ethnological Society in London in the

---

24. Matsumoto, Nobuhiro "Indoshina no bunka jō," *Iwanami kōza Tōyō shichō*, I, Iwanami shoten, 1934, p. 3.
25. Ibid., p. 20.
26. Matsumoto, Nobuhiro "Chamu no yashizoku to 'yashi no mi' setsuwa," *Minzokugaku*, dai 5 kan, dai 6 gō, 1933, pp. 457–458.
27. Matsumoto, Nobuhiro "Indoshina no bunka jō," *Iwanami kōza Tōyō shichō*, I, Iwanami shoten, 1934, p. 24.
28. Matsumoto, Nobuhiro "Indoshina gengo no keitō," *Iwanami kōza Tōyō shichō*, I (Tōyō gengo no keitō), Iwanami shoten, 1934, pp. 3–4, 38
29. Shimizu, Hajime "Kindai Nihon ni okeru 'Tōnan Ajiya' chiiki gainen no seiritsu (I)," (Shō-chūgakkō chiri kyōkasho ni miru), *Ajia keizai*, 28/6, Ajia kenkyūjo, 1987, p. 26.

summer of 1934 showed that diffusionism dominated the world's ethnological circles.[30] Following this event, the Japan Ethnological Society was established on the basis of diffusionist principles in January 1935.[31] Moreover, Schmidt, the leader of the Vienna Diffusionist School, visited Tokyo in May 1935 and delivered a lecture advising the Japanese scholars to reject evolutionist ethnology and implement the diffusionist research methods in ethnology.[32] Schmidt mentioned regarding the difficulty in spreading diffusionist methods throughout France since evolutionist methods were overwhelmingly more popular there.[33] This means that a great part of ethnology that Matsumoto learnt at the Sorbonne University was strongly criticized. Therefore, Matsumoto had to give priority to diffusionism. This explains why he published only one paper containing evolutionist and sociologist ideas in this period — On Banko Legend."[34]

Another limitation came with the growing Japanese nationalism preaching sacred origins of the Japanese people. In this political environment, it became dangerous to discuss the Japanese myths as "myths" because the chronicles, compraising them, were officially considered to be documents on the early history of Japan. Matsumoto lamented that there were many taboos in the research in that era.[35] As a result, he published his last papers on the Japanese imperial myths

---

30. "Nihon minzoku gakkai setsuritsu shuisho," *Minzokugaku kenkyū*, dai 1 kan, dai 1 gō, Nihon minzoku gakkai, Sanseidō, 1935, pp. 219-220.
31. Ibid., pp. 219-222.
32. Schmidt, Wilhelm *Nihon no minzokugakuteki chii tankyū he no atarashiki michi*, Kokusai bunka shinkōkai, 1935, (translated to Japanese by Oka, Masao), p. 3.
33. Schmidt, Wilhelm *The Culture Historical Method of Ethnology. The Scientific Approach to the Racial Question*, translated by S. A. Sieber, New York: Fortuny's, 1939, p. 75. (*Handbuch der Methode der kulturhistorischen Ethnologie*, 1937)
34. Matsumoto, Nobuhiro "Banko densetsu ni tsuite" *Tōkyō jinrui gakkai Nihon minzoku gakkai rengō taikai dai 4-kai kiji*, Tōkyō jinrui gakkai Nihon minzoku gakkai rengō taikai jimusho, 1939, pp. 108-112.
35. Arima, Makiko "Hito, Matsumoto Nobuhiroshi," *Kikan jinruigaku*, 5-1, Shakaishisōsha, 1974, p. 158.

in the prewar period in 1934.[36] In this light, it is clear that Matsumoto could not use important Japanese material, and therefore, he could not compare the Japanese and Southeast Asian myths to investigate the Southern influence on the ancient Japanese culture. Thus, we cannot find an elaborated diffusionist study in Matsumoto's writings in contrast to those of his younger colleague Yamamoto Tatsuro. Yamamoto made a comparative analysis of Indochinese myths with Chinese, Indian and Islamic old documents and identified the native elements of the belief in dragon and foreign elements imported from the higher Chinese, Indian, and Islamic cultures.[37]

Under this constraint, Matsumoto adopted the diffusionist ideas of Heine-Geldern (1885-1968), one of the best known students of Schmidt. As it has been already explained, Heine-Geldern hypothesized that the ancestors of the present Southeast Asian people came from the territory of ancient China and that they caused some of original inhabitants of Southeast Asia to move to the islands of Southeast Asia and Southern Pacific. Matsumoto claimed the importance of these hypotheses in 1934: "This Heine-Geldern's theory has extreme importance for the history of migration of Southeast Asian races."[38] Heine-Geldern's influence on Matsumoto writings during 1933-1939 has been already discussed in Section 2.3.2. The significance of Matsumoto's research trips to China (Chapter 3) and its relevance to Orientalism is addressed in Section 4 of this chapter.

This section examines the diffusionist influence (including that of Heine-Geldern) in Matsumoto's ethnological research and linguistic research on Southeast Asia. First, it discusses his ideas regarding Indochinese peoples' origins in China. Second, it clarifies his ideas regarding Southeast Asian peoples' relation with Japan. Third, it exam-

---

36. Matsumoto, Nobuhiro "Nihon shinwa no kanken" (1934), *Tōa minzoku bunkaronkō*, Seibundō shinkōsha, 1968, pp. 311-319. "Nihon shinwa ni tsuite," *Iwanami kōza Nihon rekishi*, Iwanami shoten, 1934, pp. 1-44.
37. Yamamoto, Tatsurō "Indoshina no kenkoku setsuwa," *Tōsei kōshō shiron*, Jōkan, Fuzanbō 1939, pp. 261-314.
38. Matsumoto, Nobuhiro "Indoshina no bunka jō," *Iwanami kōza Tōyō shichō*, I, Iwanami shoten, 1934, pp. 20.

ines his research on Southeast Asian languages.

3.1. Matsumoto's ideas regarding Indochinese peoples' origins in China

The previous chapter revealed that Matsumoto closely noted Indochinese peoples' origins in China due to the influence of Western diffusionist theories in the 1930s. In his paper *The Genealogy of Ancient Southern Culture of China* in 1943, Matsumoto wrote as follows: "...researching Southern China that was the residence area of these Indochinese peoples has great importance for clarifying the origins of cultures in Indochina and the South Seas, as well as for examining characteristics of ancient cultures in Northern China, Manchuria, Korea, and Japan."[39] Since Matsumoto considered Indochinese peoples' residence area to be different from Indochina, it means that he did not clearly differentiate between Indochinese people in Indochina and their ancestors in Southern China. This was because he believed in the theory of remnants according to which some elements of ancestors' culture were preserved in the culture of the next generations. In this manner, Matsumoto emphasized the culture of Indochinese peoples' ancestors in China in several writings in the first half of the 1940s.[40]

However, he discussed more about the people than the culture. In his paper *The Ancient Culture of Jiangnan*, he theoretized that Chinese people originally only resided the middle stream of Huanghe River and the valleys of its branches and that the other territory of contem-

---

39. Matsumoto, Nobuhiro "Shina Nampō kodai bunka no keitō," *Nihon shogaku shinkō iinkai kenkyū hōkoku*, Dai jū ichi hen (rekishi gaku) kyōgakukyoku, 1941, p. 209.
40. Matsumoto, Nobuhiro "Nampō san dōshokubutsu honpōmei no kenkyū," *Shigaku*, dai 18 kan, dai 1 gō, Mita Shigakkai, 1940, pp. 165-166. "Futsuryō Indoshina no minzoku," *Nan'yō*, dai 27 kan, dai 7 gō, 1940, p. 26. "Oobu to iu moji ni tsuite" (1941), *Tōa minzoku bunkaronkō*, Seibundō shinkōsha, 1968, p. 771. "Kōnan no kobunka" (1941), pp. 295-296. *Indoshina no minzoku to bunka*, Iwanami shoten, 1942. "Shina Nampō kodai bunka no keitō," *Nihon shogaku shinkō iinkai kenkyū hōkoku*, Dai jū ichi hen (rekishi gaku) kyōgakukyoku, 1941, pp. 203-204. "Ban meigi kō" (1944), *Tōa minzoku bunkaronkō*, Seibundō shinkōsha, 1968, p. 1.

porary China was occupied by people called "barbarians" who were different from Chinese but similar to the contemporary people Meò, Mán, and Lolo.[41] Matsumoto knew that Meò, Mán, and Lolo lived in China and Indochina. Thus, Matsumoto imagined that the territory of China used to be occupied by various people who were different from Han people and who were similar to the contemporary Indochinese people, such as Meò, Mán, and Lolo.

From these points, Matsumoto thought that Indochinese peoples' ancestors were among the people called "barbarians" by Chinese. In his paper *Peoples and Cultures of French Indochina*, Matsumoto assumed that Meò, Mán, and Khmer peoples' ancestors, who had common origin with Mongoloid people, used to live in Southern China, separated from the mainstream of Mongoloid people and migrated to Southeast Asia and to Oceania, and their power reached to Assam in India in the ancient times; thus, their Mongoloid features were not so distinctive.[42] Austroasiatic speakers currently live in Southeast Asia and India, and Austronesian speakers are dispersed in Oceania. Therefore, Matsumoto argument revealed that he did not differentiate between Austroasiatic speakers in Southeast Asia and Austronesian speakers in Oceania. Moreover, he associated these people with Mongoloid people in China. Briefly, Matsumoto ascribed origins in China to many contemporary people living in Southeast Asia, Oceania, and India and surmised that these people were Mongoloid people's relatives.

In addition, he developed a hypothesis that some of Indochinese peoples' ancestors were known as "the Hundred Yue" (Bai Yue, 百越), which is the term generally used for Vietnamese ancestors.[43] In his paper *Theories of Annamese People*, Matsumoto argued as follows: "I

---

41. Matsumoto, Nobuhiro "Kōnan no kobunka" (1941), *Indoshina no minzoku to bunka*, Iwanami shoten, 1942, pp. 295-296.
42. Matsumoto, Nobuhiro "Futsuryō *Indoshina no minzoku to* bunka," *Sosei futsuryō Indoshina no zenbō*, Aikoku shinbunsha shuppanbu, 1941, pp. 59-60.
43. Matsumoto, Nobuhiro "Annan minzoku ron," *Dai Nihon takushoku gakkai nenpō*, dai 1 gō, Nihon hyōronsha, 1943, pp. 281-282. "Annanjin no kigen," *Taiheiyō ken*, jōkan, Kawade shobō, 1944, p. 16.

think that peoples like Yue [越] were a tribe stream called the Hundred Yue, thus, there also were [peoples of] Thai genealogy, Mon-Khmer genealogy and Tibeto-Burmese genealogy, Lolo genealogy among them; these peoples went south, and exerted important influence especially on the creation of the Annamese people."[44] Matsumoto imagined that various Indochinese peoples' ancestors, including Austroasiatic speakers, were among people called "the Hundred Yue." This idea probably came from his study of Vietnamese people's origins in China that he presented in papers *A Study on Yue*,[45] *Theories of Annamese People*[46], and *The Origin of Annamese People*[47] wherein he wrote about the Hundred Yue as Vietnamese ancestors in China.

Although Matsumoto often did not mention the source of his arguments, it seems that Matsumoto's ideas regarding Indochinese peoples' origins were a combination of various scholars' arguments. Migration of Southeast Asian people was decribed by Heine-Geldern in his paper *A Contribution to the Chronology of the Neolithic Age in Southeast Asia*[48] as mentioned in the previous chapter. Origins of Vietnamese people were discussed by Léonard Aurousseau,[49] Cl. Madrolle,[50] Henri Maspero,[51] and Sugimoto Naojiro.[52] Therefore, Matsumoto only presented a patchwork of other scholars' ideas, focusing on Indo-

---

44. Matsumoto, Nobuhiro "Annan minzoku ron," *Dai Nihon takushoku gakkai nenpō*, dai 1 gō, Nihon hyōronsha, 1943, pp. 281–282.
45. Matsumoto, Nobuhiro "Etsujin kō," *Shigaku zasshi*, dai 53 kan, dai 7 gō, 1942, p. 7/133 (887).
46. Matsumoto, Nobuhiro "Annan minzoku ron," *Dai Nippon takushoku gakkai nempō*, Nippon hyōronsha, dai 1 gō, 1943, pp. 279–285.
47. Matsumoto, Nobuhiro "Annanjin no kigen," *Taiheiyōken*, jōkan, Kawade shobō, 1945, pp. 3–23 (321–341).
48. Matsumoto, Nobuhiro "Yūken sekifu no shomondai," *Shigaku*, dai 18 kan, dai 2/3 gō, Mita Shigakkai, 1939, p. 298. Heine-Geldern, Robert *Ein Beitrag zur Chronologie des Neolithikums in Su˝dostasien*, St. Gabriel-Mödling bei Wien: "Anthropos"-Administration, [ca. 1924], pp. 809–843.
49. Aurousseau, Léonard "La premiére conquête chinoise des pays annamites (IIIe siècle avant notre ère), Apendice, Note sur les origins due people annamite, *BEFEO*, XXIII. Matsumoto, Nobuhiro "Annanjin no kigen," *Taiheiyō ken*, jōkan, Kawade shōbō, 1944, p. 321.

chinese peoples' ancestors, and did not bring up any original opinion.

Nonetheless, by focusing on Indochinese peoples' ancestors, Matsumoto opposed the Northward Theory that argued regarding North Asian peoples' significance. In his paper *The Ethnic-Historical Meaning of the Greater East Asian War*, Matsumoto emphasized that the connection between Japanese and North Asian languages could not explain how rice cultivation was introduced to Japan across the sea from Asian continent because North Asian people did not cultivate rice and had nomadic culture in contrast with South Asian people.[53] Thus, despite discussing China, Matsumoto advocated the significance of Southern people by concentrating on Indochinese peoples' ancestors who had origins in China, lived close to the sea, and cultivated rice.

In conclusion, Matsumoto focused on Indochinese peoples' origins in China. By claiming the origins of Southeast Asian people in China, Matsumoto contributed to the legitimization of Japan's Greater East Asia Co-Prosperity Sphere because he argued regarding the existence of relationships between the people of Southern genealogy with the people of Northern genealogy in the ancient times. In the 1930s, Matsumoto did not present a research on Southeast Asian peoples' origins in China despite doing field research both in Southeast Asia and China and despite learning about Southeast Asian peoples' origins in China from Heine-Geldern. This suggests that the incorporation of Southern regions into the Japanese state policy instigated Matsumoto

---

50. Madrolle, Cl. "Le Tonkin ancient, Lei-leu et les district chinois de l'époque des Han. La population. Yue-chang," *BEFEO*, XXXVII, Fasc. 2. Matsumoto, Nobuhiro "Annanjin no kigen," *Taiheiyō ken*, jōkan, Kawade shōbō, 1944, pp. 335, 341.
51. Maspero, Henri "Etudes d'histoire d'Annam, IV, Le royame de Van-lang," *BEFEO*, XVIII, IV, pp. 1-10. Matsumoto, Nobuhiro "Annanjin no kigen," *Taiheiyō ken*, jōkan, Kawade shōbō, 1944, pp. 337, 341.
52. Sugimoto, Naojirō "Annan no rekishi (II)," *Rekishi kyōiku*, dai 14 satsu, dai 1 gō, pp. 47-52. Matsumoto, Nobuhiro "Annanjin no kigen," *Taiheiyō ken*, jōkan, Kawade shōbō, 1944, pp. 337, 341.
53. Matsumoto, Nobuhiro "Daitōa sensō no minzoku shitekina igi, *Gaikō jihō*, dai 893 gō, Gaikō jihōsha, 15.02.1942, p. 54.

to bring up this topic during 1940–1945. Thus, Matsumoto's ethnological theories had political significance.

3.2. Matsumoto's ideas regarding Southeast Asian peoples' relation with Japan

Previous section mentioned that Matsumoto discussed Indochinese peoples' origins in China because he considered Indochinese peoples' culture to be important for understanding the Japanese history. In his writings during 1940–1945, Matsumoto presented two hypotheses of Japan's relations with Southeast Asia. First, he assumed the influence of Indochinese peoples' ancestors from China on the Japanese culture. Second, he surmised that the culture of ancient Southeast Asian people was transmitted through the sea to Japan.

First, Matsumoto argued that the Southern culture of Southeast Asian peoples's ancestors in China spread to Japan. This is revealed in his paper *The Genealogy of Ancient Southern Culture of China*: "…we can think that Indochinese peoples clearly used to live in more Northern Region than now, they had close relation with Chinese people, and the influence of their culture extended across the coast to Korea and Japan."[54] Again, Matsumoto's words indicated that Matsumoto did not distinguish between Indochinese peoples and their ancestors.

Second, Matsumoto imagined Southeast Asian culture transmitted to Japan as maritime culture, and therefore, he surmised that water animals played an important role in this culture. In the early 1930s, he discussed water animals, such as snake, dragon, and fish, in his research on the Japanese legends in which he mentioned regarding the Southern influence. Moreover, he encouraged scholars to compare the Japanese myths with the tales of Austroasiatic people find out the original source of legends of dragons and snakes.[55]

Matsumoto's interest in water animals also appeared in his writings in 1940–1945. For example, Matsumoto discussed the presence of

---

54. Matsumoto, Nobuhiro "Shina Nampō kodai bunka no keitō," *Nihon shogaku shinkō iinkai kenkyū hōkoku*, Dai jū ichi hen (rekishi gaku) kyōgakukyoku, 1941, pp. 209.
55. Matsumoto, Nobuhiro "Kodai bunkaron," *Gendai shigaku taikei*, Kyōritsusha shoten, 1932, p. 119.

water animals in Southeast Asian and Japanese tradition in seven pages in his writing *Southern Geneaology in the Japanese Myths*.[56] In the same paper, Matsumoto connected the tales of water animals with the migration of Southeast Asian peoples as follows: "This kind of myths just fits the races who live in the places where the highland region and delta region meet each other ... who were gradually pushed out of the highlands in central Asia and lived like peasants of paddy fields in lowland delta area; or these myth were originally developed among the tribes living similar life like them. It is told that the races living in Oceania now [originally] resided in Southeast part of Asian continent and that they gradually migrated on the sea."[57] Here again, Matsumoto did not differetiate between contemporary Southeast Asian people and ancient Southeast Asian people who migrated from Southeast Asia to Oceania. Nonetheless, Matsumoto assumed that the water animals in the Southeast Asian and Japanese myths suggested the migration of ancient Southeast Asian people across the ocean to Japan.

Matsumoto had two diffusionist hypotheses on maritime migration from Southeast Asia — 1) the migration of the Austroasiatic speakers who were surmised to originate in China and 2) the migration of the Austronesian speakers who were supposed to originate in continental Southeast Asia. However, he perceived these hypotheses as one because he confused Austroasiatic speakers with Austronesian speakers (as mentioned in Chapter 2 Section 4.1.). His mistake is obvious in his paper *Southern Elements in the Japanese Language*: "The specificity of this Austric language family [Wilhelm Schmidt's common name for Austro-Asiatic and Austronesian languages] is its distribution in unparallelly wide area. Especially, the Austronesian languages are distributed from Madagascar Island in the Far West up to the eastward of Africa, and to the Far East on the Easter Island close to American Continent. This vast area of the distribution cannot be possibly attained by other language families, and it tells us that the

---

56. Matsumoto, Nobuhiro "Nihon shinwa ni okeru Nampōkei," *Risō*, jūyonen sansatsu sangatsu gō, Risōsha, 1940, pp. 271-277.
57. Ibid. pp. 279-280.

races using these languages were sailing peoples which were rare in the world."⁵⁸, Matsumoto considered ancient Austroasiatic and Austronesian speakers to be sailors since he imagined their transoceanic migration.

Furthermore, Matsumoto's belief in the transoceanic journey of ancient Southeast Asian people to Japan is apparent in his book *Peoples and Cultures of Indochina*: "...these [islands] are connected by the tidal currents, thus, when we surmise from the history of the long-distance migrations that the South Seas peoples had migrated [from Southeast Asia] to the Pacific islands, it is not difficult to see the great number of migrations of the Southward people to the Japanese islands."⁵⁹ Thus, Matsumoto surmised the migration of ancient Southeast Asian people, Austroasiatic, and Austroneasian speakers from Southeast Asia to Southern Pacific and Japan.

In accordance with this idea regarding Southeast Asian influence on Japan, Matsumoto claimed as follows in his paper *Peoples of French Indochina*: "I think that we can back to Thai contacts with the ancient Japanese people if we will do research about ancient Thai people."⁶⁰ He expressed the same opinion in his paper *Aspects of French Indochinese people*⁶¹ wherein he mentioned the similarity between Japanese and Thai people. Thus, concordance between Japanese and Thai people invoked in Matsumoto an idea that Thai people's ancestors had contacts with Japanese people's ancestors in ancient times. However, he did not propose a hypothesis if these contacts were with Thai people's ancestors from China (Thai ancestors met with Japanese ancestors in China) or with those from Southeast Asia (Thai ancestors sailed from Southeast Asia to Japan).

---

58. Matsumoto, Nobuhiro "Wagago ni okeru Nampō yōso" (1943), *Tōa minzoku bunkaronkō*, Seibundō shinkōsha, 1968, pp. 539–540.
59. Matsumoto, Nobuhiro *Indoshina minzoku to bunka*, Iwanami shoten, 1942, p. 316.
60. Matsumoto, Nobuhiro "Futsuryō Indoshina no minzoku," *Nan'yō*, dai 27 kan, dai 7 gō, 1940, p. 31.
61. Matsumoto, Nobuhiro "Futsuryō Indoshina jin no shosō," *Gaikō jihō*, Gaikō jihōsha, dai 850 gō, 1940nen 5 gatsu, p. 143.

In this manner, Matsumoto argued regarding the migration of ancient Southeast Asian people to Japan while he also suggested contacts between ancient Thai and Japanese peoples. This can be interpreted as Matsumoto's belief in Southest Asian influence on the ancient Japanese culture because Matsumoto refused to determine the origins of the Japanese nation in Southeast Asia. He wrote the following in his book *Peoples and Cultures of Indochina*: "...the influence on Japan from the South Seas was not probably only once, these groups that arrived from Southern direction and several groups that arrived from Northern direction mixed with the local inhabitants, and the Yamato people and their culture, as we can see now, were created here; from this point the Japanese are extremely mixed race, hence, I do not conclude at all, as it is commonly thought, that there exists a central birthplace on a land outside Japan, from which large groups migrated to the Japanese islands and formed the Yamato people."[62] This opinion was similar to his argument that contemporary Vietnamese people were born by mixing of various people on the Vietnamese territory and not in China where he supposed the homeland of the Vietnamese ancestors.[63] Hence, Matsumoto considered origins of the Japanese and Vietnamese people to be within the territory of Japan and Vietnam, respectively.

The above-mentioned proclamation shows that Matsumoto shared Yanagita's rule of "One-Country Folklore Studies" by excluding foreign origins from the discussion on the Japanese origins.[64] The quotation demonstrates that Matsumoto did not wish to be identified with the scholars of Southern genealogy argued regarding Japanese origins in the South. In other words, Matsumoto argued regarding the

---

62. Matsumoto, Nobuhiro *Indoshina minzoku to bunka*, Iwanami shoten, 1942, pp. 316–317.
63. Matsumoto, Nobuhiro "Annanjin no kigen," *Taiheiyō ken*, jōkan, Kawade shōbō, 1944, p. 21–22 (339–340).
64. Ikkoku minzokugaku (一国民俗学) Yanagita, Kunio "Ikkoku minzokugaku," *Teihon Yanagita Kunioshū*, dai 25-kan, Chikumashobō, 1964, pp. 339–357. Yanagita, Kunio "Kigenron kentō," *Minkan denshōron*, Kyōritsusha shoten, 1934, pp. 69–73.

diffusion of the Southern culture and migration of ancient Southeast Asian people to Japan, but his hypothesis was based on the Southern influence on the ancient Japanese culture and not on the Japanese origins in Southeast Asia. Therefore, his arguments were ambiguous, and he contradicted himself even within one book *Peoples and Cultures of Indochina*. Consequently, it is not possible to confirm Yamashita's hypothesis that Matsumoto sought for Japanese homeland there.[65]

3.3. Matsumoto's research on Southeast Asian languages

During 1940–1945, Matsumoto published two kinds of writings about Southeast Asian languages: 1) comparative research focusing on the similarities between Southeast Asian languages and ancient Japanese and Chinese languages, which was a continuation of his doctoral thesis on Austroasiatic languages, and 2) articles introducing these languages.

First, Matsumoto considered the study of these languages in the context of the Greater East Asia Co-Prosperity Sphere to increase the Japanese awareness of the importance of Southeast Asian languages. He claimed that the knowledge about Southeast Asian languages was an indispensable condition for creating effective cultural policy toward Southeast Asian people. In the preface to his book *Introduction to Annamese Language*, he argued as follows: "If one cooperates through the medium of the third language, it is impossible to touch the partner's heart."[66] In other words, he considered the knowledge regarding local language to be important for ethnologists and other scholars who played a central role in the formation of cultural policy. In his paper *The Southern Cultural Policy and Ethnology*, Matsumoto wrote as follows: "Here I want to emphasize that we must educate researchers who stay, in this case, in Indochina long enough to understand sufficiently the language of the country."[67]

---

65. Yamashita, Shinji "Selves and Others in Japanese Anthropology," *The Making of Anthropology in East and Southeast Asia*, Berghahn Books, New York, 2004, pp. 104–106.
66. Matsumoto, Nobuhiro *Annango nyūmon. Kaiwahen*, Indoshina kenkyūkai, 1942, p. 2.

Matsumoto's perspective in propagation of Southeast Asian languages for the Greater East Asia Co-Prosperity Sphere differed from his perspective of Southeast Asian languages in his research. This was because Matsumoto as a researcher was not interested in studying modern Southeast Asian languages although he participated in writing the textbook *Introduction to Annamese Language*.[68] In fact, he was attracted to Southeast Asian languages as a part of the study on primitive culture.

Matsumoto's ethnological approach to the significance of Southeast Asian languages did not change since 1928 when he claimed that the Austroasiatic languages played an important role in the formation of the Japanese language in his doctoral thesis at the Sorbonne University.[69] This was because he believed in similarities between these languages, but he was also aware of their differences. Thus, he argued regarding the Southern influence on the Japanese language and not about the Southern origin of the Japanese language. He repeated this opinion in his paper *The Genealogy of Indochina Languages* (1934), which was published in his book *Peoples and Cultures of Indochina* (1942): "The fact supported by evidences is only that the Southward elements played important role in the formation of the Japanese language…"[70] He also expressed the same opinion in his papers *A Research on the Japanese Names of Southward Animals and Plants*

---

67. Matsumoto, Nobuhiro "Nampō bunka seisaku to minzokugaku," *Gaikō jihō*, dai 885 gō, Gaikō jihōsha, 15.10.1941, p. 78.
68. Matsumoto, Nobuhiro *Annango nyūmon. Bunpōhen*, Indoshina kenkyūkai, 1942, p. 2. *Annango nyūmon. Kaiwahen*, Indoshina kenkyūkai, 1942, p. 2. Although Matsumoto is mentioned as an author of the textbook, from the preface to the volume of conversation (*Annango nyūmon. Kaiwahen*, p. 2), it seems that the main work was done by Muramatsu Katsu who lectured the Vietnamese language for the Indochina Research Society from 1941. Muramatsu learnt Vietnamese because she was wife of Émile Gaspardone, Matsumoto's friend, who stayed as researcher of EFEO in Hanoi.
69. Matsumoto, Nobuhiro *Le japonais et les langues austroasiatiques: étude de vocabulaire comparé*, P. Geuthner, Paris, 1928, p. 96.
70. Matsumoto, Nobuhiro *Indoshina no minzoku to bunka*, Iwanami shoten, 1942, p. 282.

(1940),[71] *Japan's Ancient Culture and the South Seas* (1942),[72] and *The Ethnic-Historical Meaning of the Greater East Asian War* (1942).[73] Thus, Matsumoto was concerned with the historical role of Southeast Asian languages in the formation of ancient Japanese language. He did not propose the hypothesis that the Japanese language played an important role in the formation of Southeast Asian languages, which means that he believed in the diffusionist hypothesis of the influence of Southeast Asian languages on the Japanese language in the ancient times.

Moreover, he thought that Southeast Asian languages influenced the Chinese language. In his paper *On the Character Ship*, Matsumoto wrote as follows: "In general, the Chinese language received influence of surrounding languages; especially it received influence of Thai, Meo, Man languages and languages of Mon-Khmer genealogy."[74] Since some of these languages belonged to the Austroasiatic languages, this argument was similar to his opinion expressed in his work *Theories of Ancient Culture* (1932) that Austroasiatic languages influenced Chinese language.[75] In other words, despite propagating the Japanese need for the knowledge of modern Southeast Asian languages, Matsumoto continued to be interested more in the historical role of Southeast Asian languages, including their influence on the Japanese and Chinese languages.

This fact is also apparent from his linguistic papers. He wrote 13 linguistic papers related to Austroasiatic and Austronesian languages during 1940–1945: *Languages of Indochina*,[76] *A Research on the Japanese*

---

71. Matsumoto, Nobuhiro "Nampō san dōshokubutsu honpōmei no kenkyū," *Shigaku*, dai 18 kan, dai 1 gō, Mita Shigakkai, 1940, p. 166.
72. Matsumoto, Nobuhiro "Nihon jōdai bunka to Nan'yō," *Indoshina no minzoku to bunka*, Iwanami shoten, 1942, pp. 315, 334
73. Matsumoto, Nobuhiro "Daitōa sensō no minzoku shitekina igi, *Gaikō jihō*, dai 893 gō, Gaikō jihōsha, 15.02.1942, p. 54.
74. Matsumoto, Nobuhiro "Oobu to iu moji ni tsuite" (1941), *Tōa minzoku bunkaronkō*, Seibundō shinkōsha, 1968, p. 778.
75. Matsumoto, Nobuhiro "Kodai bunkaron," *Gendai shigaku taikei*, Kyōritsusha shoten, 1932, p. 77.

Chapter 4: Ideas in establishing Southeast Asian studies during 1933-1945 181

Names of Southward Animals and Plants,[77] *On Ancient Name of Cotton*,[78] *On the Chinese Character 'Ship'*,[79] *A Study in Names of Crocodiles and other Reptiles*,[80] *The Annamese and Mon-Khmer languages*,[81] *A Research in Domestic Names of the Southward Products and Plants (continued)*,[82] *Betel Palm and Banana - A Research in Names of Southward Products and Plants*,[83] *Southern Elements in the Japanese Language*,[84] *Annamese Language, Malay Language, Javanese Language*,[85] and *A Study in Names of Ancient Weapons*.[86] Five of them represented the introductions of Southeast Asian languages to the Japanese readers.[87] Eight of them were attempts at research on historical linguistics.[88] Thus, Matsumoto presented more papers on the historical signifi-

---

76. Matsumoto, Nobuhiro "Indoshina go," *Ajia mondai kōza*, dai 8 kan, Sōgensha, 1939, pp. 385-399
77. Matsumoto, Nobuhiro "Nampō san dōshokubutsu honpōmei no kenkyū," *Shigaku*, dai 18 kan, dai 1 gō, Mita Shigakkai, 1940, pp. 165-202.
78. Matsumoto, Nobuhiro "Momen no komei ni tsuite" (1941) *Tōa minzoku bunkaronkō*, Seibundō shinkōsha, 1968, pp. 659-690.
79. Matsumoto, Nobuhiro "'Oobu' to iu moji ni tsuite" (1941), *Tōa minzoku bunkaronkō*, Seibundō shinkōsha, 1968, pp. 771-789.
80. Matsumoto, Nobuhiro "Wani sonota hachūrui meigi kō" (1942), *Tōa minzoku bunkaronkō*, Seibundō shinkōsha, 1968, pp. 691-720.
81. Matsumoto, Nobuhiro "Annan go to Mon-Kumeru go," *Nihongo*, 2-5, Nampō kensetsu to Nihongo, Nihongo kyōiku shinkōkai, dai 5 gō, 1942, pp. 38-44.
82. Matsumoto, Nobuhiro "Zoku Nampō san dōshokubutsu honpōmei no kenkyū" (1943), *Tōa minzoku bunkaronkō*, Seibundō shinkōsha, 1968, pp. 647-658.
83. Matsumoto, Nobuhiro "Binrō to bashō —Nampō san shokubutsu mei no kenkyū" (1943), *Tōa minzoku bunkaronkō*, Seibundō shinkōsha, 1968, pp. 721-750.
84. Matsumoto, Nobuhiro "Wagago ni okeru Nampō yōso" (1943), *Tōa minzoku bunkaronkō*, Seibundō shinkōsha, 1968, pp. 539-564.
85. Matsumoto, Nobuhiro "Annan go," "Marai go," "Jawa go," *Sekai no kotoba*, Keiō gijuku daigaku gogaku kenkyūjohen, Keiō shuppansha, 1943, pp. 73-79, 81-86, 87-90.
86. Matsumoto, Nobuhiro "Kodai kōsen gu meishō kō" (1944), *Tōa minzoku bunkaronkō*, Seibundō shinkōsha, 1968, pp. 597-614.
87. "Languages of Indochina," "The Annamese and Mon-Khmer languages," "Annamese Language," "Malay Language," "Javanese Language".

cance of Southeast Asian languages than on modern Southeast Asian languages.

In his linguistic research, Matsumoto adopted the comparative approach to the Japanese, Chinese, and Southeast Asian names of plants and animals, as the afore mentioned titles of Matsumoto's papers suggest. He applied the method of vocabulary comparison that he learnt from Przylusky in 1924-1928. For example, Matsumoto made comparison with the Austroasiatic languages in his paper *A Study in Names of Crocodiles and other Reptiles* as follows: "What is the naming of crocodile among the South Seas peoples in general? If we include Austro-Asiatic peoples of Indochina, we can mention the following examples..."[89] In this manner, his linguistic research was matching archaic Japanese and Chinese words with similar words in the Austroasiatic and Austronesian languages.

However, despite employing comparison with Southeast Asian languages in many papers, Matsumoto explicitly wrote only once that he looked for "the origins." As Matsumoto's paper *A Study in Names of Ancient Weapons* suggested, Matsumoto thought that linguistic research on the names of the Japanese weapons could clarify the origins of various words: "It is not only important to research weapons of ancient times archaeologically, but we also must study them linguistically. Namely, I believe that it is important to give hints by researching the origins of their namings together with researching their structure and their genealogy from material perspective."[90] Therefore, only this one writing demonstrated that Matsumoto's research aimed at finding

---

88. "A Research on the Japanese Names of Southward Animals and Plants," "On Ancient Name of Cotton," "On the Chinese Character 'Ship'," "A Study in Names of Crocodiles and other Reptiles," "A Research in Domestic Names of the Southward Products and Plants (Continued)," "Betel Palm and Banana – A Research in Names of Southward Products and Plants," "Southern Elements in the Japanese Language," "A Study in Names of Ancient Weapons."
89. Matsumoto, Nobuhiro "Wani sonota hachūrui meigi kō" (1942), *Tōa minzoku bunkaronkō*, Seibundō shinkōsha, 1968, p. 695.
90. Matsumoto, Nobuhiro "Kodai kōsen gu meishō kō" (1944), *Tōa minzoku bunkaronkō*, Seibundō shinkōsha, 1968, pp. 597-614.

"the origins." He specified the origins as "the origins of the namings," not "the origins of the languages." Since Matsumoto only compared the vocabulary and argued regarding the Southern influence on the ancient Japanese and Chinese cultures, it can be assumed that by the word "origins," he meant borrowings from the vocabulary of Southeast Asian languages to the ancient Japanese and Chinese languages.

In summary, the significance of Matsumoto's work in linguistic studies for Southeast Asian studies lied in propagating the study of Southeast Asian languages and in the study of Southeast Asian languages. He contributed to the study of Southeast Asian languages at Keio University. However, Matsumoto did not put effort in acquiring knowledge of these contemporary forms of language.

4. Orientalism in Matsumoto's ideas regarding the people of Southeast Asia

We can find Orientalism in Matsumoto's ideas regarding Southeast Asia because Orientalism was common ideational framework of the Japanese scholars in the prewar era. In 2004, Japanese cultural anthropologist Yamashita Shinji mentioned the theory of Japanese Orientalism used by Japanese ethnologists researching the South Seas and argued that these scholars perceived the South Seas as both similar and distant.[91] However, Yamashita discussed the works of Japanese ethnologists in general and did not mention any concrete examples of Orientalist expressions. Therefore, this section examines Matsumoto's writings to provide the evidencial basis for his claims of Orientalism and underline its presence in Matsumoto's ideas regarding Southeast Asia.

The term "Orientalism" was popularized by Palestinian scholar Edward W. Saïd (1935-2003) in his book *Orientalism* (1978).[92] He criticized that the framework that Western scholars used to perceive the

---

91. Yamashita, Shinji "Selves and Others in Japanese Anthropology," *The Making of Anthropology in East and Southeast Asia*, New York: Berghahn Books, 2004, p. 106.
92. Saïd, Edward W. *Orientalism*, Pantheon Books, New York, 1978.

Orient was biased, especially since it reflected a colonial power's attitude toward its subjugated people. In his work, Saïd introduced dichotomies existing in Orientalism: the dichotomy of the West and the East as "we" and "the others", the rulers and the ruled, and the civilized and the barbarians.[93] Saïd also argued that Orientalists were dictated by preconceived ideas about the West's colonial possessions in the Orient, where Western attitudes brought about romanticized notions on the exquisite beauty of the region.[94] Furthermore, Saïd indicated the inherent fear that the West had toward the Orient, especially over the possibility that the power balance between the Orient and the Western World could tip in favor of the former.[95] To further expand on the matter, Saïd developed an interpretation of the Orientalist perspective wherein the West saw the Orient as a conglomeration of exotic barbarian countries ruled by Western people that might destroy the West some day.

Saïd's concept of Orientalism was introduced to Japan. First, his book *Orientalism* was translated into Japanese in 1986.[96] Then, in the 1990s, Saïd's concept of Orientalism was applied by Japanese scholars for the interpretation of the Japanese perspective of the Asian and Oceanian people before the end of World War II. For example, in the paper *Mass Orientalism and Awareness of Asia* (1993), Kawamura Minato argued that Japanese Orientalism spread among the Japanese public through adventurous stories in comics and journals in the Taishō and Shōwa eras.[97] Kang Sang Jung presented his theory of modernity thinking beyond Japanese Orientalism in his book *Beyond Orientalism: Modern Culture Criticism* (1996).[98] In reaction to this trend of interpreting the Japanese attitude to prewar Asia as Orientalism, in the book *Prospects of Colonial Anthropology*, Nakao Natsumi et all.

---

93. Ibid., pp. 2, 5, 7, 49, 57, 95, etc.
94. Ibid., pp. 57, 60, 252, etc.
95. Ibid., p. 251.
96. Saïd, Edward W. *Orientarizumu*, transl. by Imazawa, Noriko; Itagaki, Yūzō and Sugita Hideaki, Heibonsha, 1986.
97. Kawamura, Minato "Taishū Orientarizumu to Ajia ninshiki," *Bunka no naka no shokuminchi*, Iwanami shoten, 1993, pp. 107–136.

(2000) discussed the prewar ethnological works (especially of field workers) to positionate the war and the colony in the formation of Japanese ethnology.[99] Furthermore, in his paper *Selves and Others in Japanese Anthropology* (2004), Yamashita Shinji argued that Japanese people, including scholars such as Yanagita, applied Orientalism to the South Seas.[100]

Matsumoto was exposed to the Orientalist perspective in his childhood. This was because he loved adventurous stories that occurred in various exotic locations where a hero came in contact with the primitive people. For instance, Matsumoto read journals such as *The World of Adventures* (*Bukyō sekai*, 武侠世界) and *The World of Explorations* (*Tanken sekai*, 探検世界).[101] Later, Matsumoto's Orientalist thinking was developed by his adoption of evolutionism and by his study of Oriental history and ethnology. This was because Orientalism was based on social Darwinian theories of the struggle for survival and cultural evolutionism in its dichotomies between "the powerful" and "the weak" and "the civilized" and "the barbarian."

Orientalism can be discerned from the presence of dichotomies in Matsumoto's writings. The following two sections show that Matsumoto employed the dichotomy of the powerful and the weak and the civilized and barbarian in his ideas regarding Southeast Asia. The third section discusses Matsumoto's feelings regarding Southeast Asia's exoticity and similarities with Japan. Regarding the latter, the argument highlighted its specificity to Japanese Orientalism, drawing a contrast with Western Orientalism that saw the Orient only for its differences.

---

98. Kansan, Jun *Orientarizumu no kanata he: kindai bunka hihan*, Iwanami shoten, 1996.
99. Nakao, Katsumi *Shokuminchi jinruigaku no tembō*, Fūkyōsha, 2000.
100. Yamashita, Shinji "Selves and Others in Japanese Anthropology," *The Making of Anthropology in East and Southeast Asia*, New York: Berghahn Books, 2004, p. 106.
101. Matsumoto, Nobuhiro *Matsumoto Nobuhiro shinpen zakki*, Matsumoto Chie, 1982, p. 37.

4.1. Matsumoto's hierarchy of Southeast Asian people based on the dichotomy of the powerful and the weak

This section discusses the dichotomy of the powerful and the weak concerning Matsumoto's ideas about Southeast Asia. It reconstructs Matsumoto's hierarchy of the Southeast Asian people, especially with the people in Indochina.

Matsumoto adopted the dichotomy from the theory of the survival of the fittest in social Darwinism, which spread alongside the dominance of diffusionist ethnology both in the world and Japan in the 1930s. Since diffusionist scholars considered contacts among various ethnic groups to be an important condition for the transmission of cultural influence, they focused on the history of migration and conflicts of ethnic groups. Consequently, they proposed theories explaining cultural influences on different ethnic groups as a result of foreign invasions. In particular, Matsumoto adopted Heine-Geldern's migration theories on the movement of people to and from continental Southeast Asia in ancient times.[102] As a result of this diffusionist influence, Matsumoto interpreted contacts among different races through the lens of the Darwinist theory of struggle for survival, in which the powerful won over the weak.

In this manner, Matsumoto perceived the history of Indochina from a social Darwinist perspective wherein a cycle of victory and defeat of various Southeast Asian people underlined their struggle for survival since times immemorial.[103] In his paper *The Genealogy of In-*

---

102. Matsumoto, Nobuhiro "Indoshina no bunka jō," *Iwanami kōza Tōyō shichō*, I, Iwanami shoten, 1934, pp. 20, 34, 35. "Indoshina gengo no keitō," *Iwanami kōza Tōyō shichō*, I (Tōyō gengo no keitō), Iwanami shoten, 1934, pp. 38, 39. "Furansu ni okeru minzokugakuteki kenkyū," *Nihon minzokugaku kenkyū*, (ed. by Yanagita), Iwanami shoten, Tokyo, 1935, p. 385. "Jōdai Indoshina no kōkogakuteki kenkyū ni tsuite - Korani joshi kizō dozoku hyōhon wo chūshin ni" (1937), *Indoshina minzoku to bunka*, Iwanami shoten, 1942.11, pp. 167, 183, 184. "Yūken sekifu no shomondai," *Shigaku*, dai 18 kan, dai 2/3 gō, Mita Shigakkai, 1939, p. 298. "Kōnan hōkoki," *Shigaku*, dai 17 kan, dai 4 gō, Mita Shigakkai, 1939, p. 69. "Indoshina go," *Ajia mondai kōza*, dai 8 kan, Sōgensha, 1939, p. 391.

dochina Languages, Matsumoto argued as follows: "If we study about the genealogy of Indochina languages, we can learn about the rise and fall of cultures of peoples living on this peninsula."[104] He assumed that weak Southern people in Indochina were defeated by stronger Northern people who invaded there. (This hypothesis of weak Southern peoples is further examined in Section 5.) Matsumoto also interpereted the Japanese ancient history as a struggle for territory in his writing *An Opinion on the Japanese Myths*: "...this migration was not in order to occupy a completely uninhabited land; it was a migration to break into a similar race that occupied the land earlier: to conquer it, assimilate it, and form a new state."[105] Therefore, he surmised that migrations always involved an armed conflict between a powerful foreign invader and the local people.

First, Matsumoto accepted the Western diffusionist theories about the competition of the original inhabitants of continental Southeast Asia with foreign invaders. Through Matsumoto's writings *The Peoples of Indochina, I have Seen Indochina, Travel Records from Annam* and *Ancient Indochina*, it can be discerned that he considered Negritos, Indonesians, and Austronesians as original inhabitants of this area in the stone age period.[106] He argued that Negritos were originally spread over a vast territory of Indochina but were expelled by the invasion of Indonesian tribes speaking the Austroasiatic languages.[107] In his paper

---

103. Matsumoto, Nobuhiro "Indoshina no bunka jō," *Iwanami kōza Tōyō shichō*, I, Iwanami shoten, 1934, p. 5.
104. Matsumoto, Nobuhiro "Indoshina gengo no keitō," *Iwanami kōza Tōyō shichō*, I (Tōyō gengo no keitō), Iwanami shoten, 1934, p. 3.
105. Matsumoto, Nobuhiro "Nihon shinwa no kanken" (1934), *Nihon minzokugaku no kigen I: shinwa-densetsu*, Kōdansha, 1978, p. 314.
106. Matsumoto, Nobuhiro "*Indoshina minzoku*," *Iwanami kōza Tōyō shichō*, I (Tōyō no minzoku, Tōyō no shakai), Iwanami shoten, 1935, pp. 3, 26. "Indoshina wo mite," *Gaikō jihō*, dai 703 gō, Gaikō jihōsha, 15.03.1934, p. 132. "Annan ryokōki (daisanshin)," *Minzokugaku*, dai 5 kan, dai 10 gō, Minzokugakkai, 1933, p.101. "Jōdai Indoshina," *Tōyō bunkashi taikei*, Kodai Shina to Indo, Seidōbunkadō shinkōsha, 1938, pp. 243-245.
107. Matsumoto, Nobuhiro "Jōdai Indoshina," *Tōyō bunkashi taikei*, Kodai Shina to Indo, Seidōbunkadō shinkōsha, 1938, p. 244.

Languages of Indochina, Matsumoto wrote as follows: "The earliest wave of the races was Mon-Khmer, one of the Austroasiatic tribes, and they entered from the North."[108] Consequently, Matsumoto thought that tribes speaking Austroasiatic languages (and Austronesian languages since Matsumoto tended to use these languages interchangeably) defeated the aboriginal Negritos of Southeast Asia. Based on this theory, Matsumoto theorized that Negrito tribes in the Malay Mountains of Sedang and Senoi speak the Austroasiatic languages because they adopted them from their invaders.[109] Thus, Matsumoto considered Indonesians speaking Austroasiatic and Austronesian languages to be more powerful than Negritos.

Matsumoto accepted Western diffusionist theories about the invasion of Mongoloid races over Indochina from China in the North during the Neolitic era. This opinion was presented in Matsumoto's papers *I have Seen Indochina, Travel Records from Annam, The Genealogy of Indochina Languages* and *Ancient Indochina*.[110] Matsumoto believed that the Mongoloid tribes expelled the aborigine inhabitants by driving them to the mountains or out of Indochina altogether and forced them to migrate to maritime Southeast Asia. Therefore, he called Indochina "an outlet through which peoples made their way from Middle Asia and spread towards the South Seas"[111] and "a gateway from the continent to the South Seas islands."[112] Therefore, he assumed that the Indonesian tribes who were oppressed by the Mongoloid tribes had

---

108. Matsumoto, Nobuhiro "Indoshina go," *Ajia mondai kōza*, dai 8 kan, Sōgensha, 1939, p. 385.
109. Ibid., p. 387.
110. Matsumoto, Nobuhiro "Annan ryokōki (daisanshin)," *Minzokugaku*, dai 5 kan, dai 10 gō, Minzokugakkai, 1933, p. 97. "Indoshina wo mite," *Gaikō jihō*, dai 703 gō, Gaikō jihōsha, 15.03.1934, p. 132. "Indoshina gengo no keitō," *Iwanami kōza Tōyō shichō*, I (Tōyō gengo no keitō), Iwanami shoten, 1934, p. 4. "Jōdai Indoshina," *Tōyō bunkashi taikei*, Kodai Shina to Indo, Seidōbunkadō shinkōsha, 1938, p. 246.
111. Matsumoto, Nobuhiro "Indoshina minzoku," *Iwanami kōza Tōyō shichō*, I (Tōyō no minzoku, Tōyō no shakai), Iwanami shoten, 1935, p. 3.
112. Matsumoto, Nobuhiro "Indoshina gengo no keitō," *Iwanami kōza Tōyō shichō*, I (Tōyō gengo no keitō), Iwanami shoten, 1934, p. 3.

close relations with the contemporary people of Indonesian and Melanesian genealogy living on the islands of the South Seas.[113] In other words, Matsumoto believed that Mongoloid tribes that invaded from the North in the Neolithic period gradually occupied Indochina and won over the previous inhabitants who spoke Austroasiatic and Austronesian languages. This means that Matsumoto thought that the Mongoloid race was more powerful than the Austroasiatic and Austronesian speakers.

However, Matsumoto also believed that the Mongoloid tribes who invaded Indochina assimilated with the aborigine inhabitants to some extent. Matsumoto mentioned the case of assimilating Vietnamese ancestors from the North with the local inhabitants of Indochina in his paper *The peoples of Indochina*: "...the territory of these previous inhabitants was attacked from the North and the peoples of Mongolian race ...grasped the power in Indochina; they mixed with the people in the Eastern plains and gave birth to the Annamese people."[114] In short, he thought that the Vietnamese were a mixture of the Mongoloid race and the Indonesian people[115] or, in other words, Mon-Khmer people who were Austroasiatic speakers.[116] Therefore, Matsumoto considered that the Vietnamese were born from the mixing of the superior Mongoloid race with the inferior Indonesian race speaking Austroasiatic languages. This explains his statement in his paper *I Have Seen Indochina* that the Vietnamese belonged to the most inferior people of the Mongoloid race.[117]

Furthermore, Matsumoto considered the Vietnamese to be inferi-

---

113. Matsumoto, Nobuhiro "Jōdai Indoshina," *Tōyō bunkashi taikei*, Kodai Shina to Indo, Seidōbunkadō shinkōsha, 1938, p. 245. "Indoshina go," *Ajia mondai kōza*, dai 8 kan, Sōgensha, 1939, pp. 390–391.
114. Matsumoto, Nobuhiro "Indoshina minzoku," *Iwanami kōza Tōyō shichō*, I (Tōyō no minzoku, Tōyō no shakai), Iwanami shoten, 1935, p. 3.
115. Matsumoto, Nobuhiro "Indoshina no bunka jō," *Iwanami kōza Tōyō shichō*, I, Iwanami shoten, 1934, p. 34.
116. Matsumoto, Nobuhiro "Indoshina go," *Ajia mondai kōza*, dai 8 kan, Sōgensha, 1939, p. 391.
117. Matsumoto, Nobuhiro "Indoshina wo mite," *Gaikō jihō*, dai 703 gō, Gaikō jihōsha, 15.03.1934, p. 132.

or among Mongoloid people because the Vietnamese people were under Chinese political influence from the beginning of their history. First, Matsumoto believed that Vietnamese ancestors were among the Mongoloid tribes expelled from their homeland by the expansion of Han settlements. This is largely based on the fact that Matsumoto accepted the opinion of Western scholars that the migration of the Mongoloid tribes to Indochina was caused by expansion of the Han people in China.[118] Second, Matsumoto knew that Vietnam had been a Chinese colony for thousand years.[119] Third, Matsumoto knew about the political influence of China in Vietnam before the establishment of French Indochina.[120] From these points, it can be said that the historical facts provided Matsumoto with the evidential basis for his belief in the superiority of Chinese people over Vietnamese people from the social Darwinist perspective.

Nevertheless, within the scope of Indochina Peninsula, Matsumoto considered Vietnamese and Thai people to be powerful. This was because he agreed with the French opinion that these people played an important role in contemporary Indochina.[121] The Vietnamese population was largest among the people of Indochina, and Vietnam was most successful in its expansion of power over the Indochina Peninsula before the French aggression. In his paper *Ancient Indochina*, Matsumoto wrote as follows: "The most powerful race in the present Indochina is Annamese people. Their population is 15 million... Their

---

118. Matsumoto, Nobuhiro "Indoshina gengo no keitō," *Iwanami kōza Tōyō shichō*, I (Tōyō gengo no keitō), Iwanami shoten, 1934, p. 4. "Kōnan no kobunka" (1941), *Indoshina no minzoku to bunka*, Iwanami shoten, 1942, p. 295.

119. Matsumoto, Nobuhiro "Indoshina no bunka jō," *Iwanami kōza Tōyō shichō*, I, Iwanami shoten, 1934, pp. 49–54, 57–58.

120. Matsumoto, Nobuhiro "Indoshina wo mite," *Gaikō jihō*, dai 703 gō, Gaikō jihōsha, 15.03.1934, p. 136.

121. Matsumoto, Nobuhiro "Indoshina no bunka jō," *Iwanami kōza Tōyō shichō*, I, Iwanami shoten, 1934, p. 41. "Indoshina minzoku," *Iwanami kōza Tōyō shichō*, I (Tōyō no minzoku, Tōyō no shakai), Iwanami shoten, 1935, pp. 3, 27. "Indoshina gengo no keitō," *Iwanami kōza Tōyō shichō*, I (Tōyō gengo no keitō), Iwanami shoten, 1934, p. 4. "Jōdai Indoshina," *Tōyō bunkashi taikei*, Kodai Shina to Indo, Seidōbunkadō shinkōsha, 1938, p. 237.

homeland is in Red River Valley and Annam, they expanded South and conquered Cham territory in Central and Southern Annam, and occupied the plains of Cochinchina from Cambodians. If there had been no intervention by France, [Annamese] territory would have been extended more to the West."[122]

Furthermore, he emphasized the Thai people's importance as follows: "The next influential people after the Annamese are the Thai people."[123] This was most likely because the ethnic group of Thai people was numerous and because Thai people had the only independent state in Indochina Peninsula.[124] Nonetheless, Matsumoto considered the Vietnamese people to be more important than the Thai people although the Vietnamese people, being part of French Indochina under French rule, lost their independence while the Thai people retained theirs.

Matsumoto's opinion can be explained through historical facts before the establishment of the French rule in Vietnam. This was because Vietnam continuously attacked Siam.[125] This fact was recorded in Matsumoto's paper *Peoples of Indochina*: "Also the Western neighbors, the Thai ethnic group, received unceasing pressure of the Annamese and their borders were invaded."[126]

However, Matsumoto simply adopted the opinion of the French scholars. This French opinion reflected the fact that the Vietnamese people occupied an important position in the French administration of French Indochina, while the people of Thai genealogy did not play a significant role in French Indochina. Moreover, Matsumoto did not mention any theories explaining the emergence of the Thai people. He

---

122. Matsumoto, Nobuhiro "Jōdai Indoshina," *Tōyō bunkashi taikei*, Kodai Shina to Indo, Seidōbunkadō shinkōsha, 1938, p. 237.
123. Ibid., p. 237.
124. Matsumoto, Nobuhiro "Indoshina minzoku," *Iwanami kōza Tōyō shichō*, I (Tōyō no minzoku, Tōyō no shakai), Iwanami shoten, 1935, pp. 27, 34.
125. Matsumoto, Nobuhiro "Indoshina gengo no keitō," *Iwanami kōza Tōyō shichō*, I (Tōyō gengo no keitō), Iwanami shoten, 1934, p. 27.
126. Matsumoto, Nobuhiro "Indoshina minzoku," *Iwanami kōza Tōyō shichō*, I (Tōyō no minzoku, Tōyō no shakai), Iwanami shoten, 1935, p. 4.

did not mention whether Thai people in Indochina assimilated with Indonesians.

In addition, Matsumoto assumed that the Japanese were more powerful than the Chinese in the struggle for survival. He came to this conclusion because he believed in the success of Japanese military power in the Second Sino-Japanese War newspapers as well as his own observations during his research trips to China in 1938 and 1939. In his paper *Pilgrimage around the Battlefields*, he compared the inferior position of the Chinese with that of the Japanese in the war as "a mouse in front of a cat."[127] In short, contemporary circumstances provided Matsumoto with "evidences" of Chinese inferiority from the perspective of military and political power.

Finally, Matsumoto considered the Europeans as the most powerful race. His paper *I Have Seen Indochina* stated that he considered French to be the most powerful race in French Indochina because they ruled over the local people.[128] In this manner, according to Matsumoto, the European people occupied the top position in the hierarchy of the people in Southeast Asia.

In summary, Matsumoto developed an Orientalist perspective of people in Southeast Asia based on the social Darwinist theory in which only the fit is selected for victory. By adopting the dichotomy of the powerful and the weak, Matsumoto constructed his hierarchy of people in Indochina in terms of their military strength in the known history of Indochina as follows: Negritos, Indonesians (=Austroasiatic and Austronesian speakers), Mongoloid, and European people from inferior to superior order. Matsumoto's hierarchy of Mongoloid people included Thai, Vietnamese, Chinese, and Japanese from inferior to superior order. Thus, Matsumoto placed the Europeans on the top of mankind and the Japanese on the top of Asian people. This bias suggests that as a Japanese, Matsumoto had an inferiority complex toward

---

127. Matsumoto, Nobuhiro "Senseki junrei," *Mita hyōron*, dai 490 gō, Mita hyōron hakkōjo, 1938, p. 37.
128. Matsumoto, Nobuhiro "Indoshina wo mite," *Gaikō jihō*, dai 703 gō, Gaikō jihōsha, 15.03.1934, p. 134. "Indoshina no bunka ge," *Iwanami kōza Tōyō shichō*, IX, Iwanami shoten, 1935, p. 95.

Europeans while having a superiority complex toward different Asian people. This thinking was common for the Japanese people in Matsumoto's era. However, due to the adoption of the diffusionist theories, Matsumoto was convinced that his Orientalist ideas were supported scientifically by ethnology.

4.2. Matsumoto's hierarchy in Indochina based on the dichotomy of the civilized and the primitive

This section examines the dichotomy of the civilized and the primitive in Matsumoto's writings about Southeast Asia. From this perspective, it reconstructs Matsumoto's hierarchy of cultures in Southeast Asia, focusing on Indochina.

Matsumoto had an Orientalist bias in his judgement about the culture of Southeast Asian people. He looked into the aspect of civilization in his ideas about the struggle of people in Indochina. This fact can be proved by his writing *The Incident and the Universities*. This paper presented his opinion about the Second Sino-Japanese War: "I do not know how it was in the barbarian period, but in the present, when a race fights another race, we have to give it significance like the fight of cultures."[129] This suggests that he believed that the level of cultural development determined the outcome of the fight for survival. Consequently, Matsumoto held a bias that a civilized race was always the winner in an armed confrontation with a primitive race.

This idea became especially pronounced after his visit to the Southern Pacific Islands where he could witness the dominance of the Japanese people over the aboriginal inhabitants. Matsumoto clearly expressed this opinion in his paper *Seeing Our South Seas*: "When civilized men and primitive men come into contact, it is unavoidable by the laws of the nature that the latter are gradually oppressed. Even in the case of our South Seas, with the development of the Japanese business there, it is accompanied by a difficult fact that the islanders are gradually threatened."[130] In short, Matsumoto assumed that the Japa-

---

129. Matsumoto, Nobuhiro "Jihen to daigaku," *Shigaku*, dai 17 kan, dai 3 gō, Mita Shigakkai, 1938, p. 444.

nese who were the winners over the native islanders were holders of a superior culture. Therefore, Matsumoto's hierarchy of Indochinese people can be reconsidered from the cultural evolutionist perspective of the dichotomy between the civilized and the barbarian.

Among the people of Indochina, Matsumoto was most interested in the speakers of the Austroasiatic languages as representatives of an important civilization of Southeast Asia during the stone age and the bronze age eras. He thought that the culture of Austroasiatic speakers before the invasion of Mongoloid tribes to Indochina was the primeval culture of Indochina.[131] In relation to this, Matsumoto accepted Heine-Geldern's theory that the shouldered stone ax was a typical element of the culture of people speaking Austroasiatic languages.[132] Furthermore, Matsumoto surmised that Austroasiatic speakers produced megalithic sculptures[133] and distributed the famous bronze drums in Southeast Asia and Southern China.[134] Based on these scientific arguments related to Austroasiatic speakers, Matsumoto claimed that Mon-Khmer languages were most interesting among the languages of Indochina since he considered them to be typical Austroasiatic languages.[135] Furthermore, under the influence of the theory of remnants, he thought that the study of contemporary Moi people, whose language belonged to Mon-Khmer languages, could provide further insight on the ancient culture of Indochina: "This primitive culture of Moi people probably indicates the condition of culture before the influx of the Chinese and

---

130. Matsumoto, Nobuhiro "Waga Nan'yō wo miru," *Mita hyōron*, dai 483 gō, Mita hyōron hakkōjo, 1937, p. 8.
131. Matsumoto, Nobuhiro "Jōdai Indoshina," *Tōyō bunkashi taikei*, Kodai Shina to Indo, Seidōbunkadō shinkōsha, 1938, p. 237.
132. Matsumoto, Nobuhiro "Furansu ni okeru minzokugakuteki kenkyū," *Nihon minzokugaku kenkyū*, (ed. by Yanagita), Iwanami shoten, 1935, p. 385.
133. Matsumoto, Nobuhiro "Jōdai Indoshina," *Tōyō bunkashi taikei*, Kodai Shina to Indo, Seidōbunkadō shinkōsha, 1938, p. 246.
134. Matsumoto, Nobuhiro "Indoshina no bunka jō," *Iwanami kōza Tōyō shichō*, I, Iwanami shoten, 1934, pp. 35, 36. "Furansu ni okeru minzokugakuteki kenkyū," *Nihon minzokugaku kenkyū*, (ed. by Yanagita), Iwanami shoten, 1935, p. 385.
135. Matsumoto, Nobuhiro "Indoshina gengo no keitō," *Iwanami kōza Tōyō shichō*, I (Tōyō gengo no keitō), Iwanami shoten, 1934, p. 4.

Indian civilizations to Indochina."[136] Thus, since Matsumoto was captivated by Austroasiatic culture as the primeval culture that existed before the transmisson of the Chinese and Indian cultures, he thought that the Sinicized or Indianized cultures of Indochinese people were more advanced than the Austroasiatic culture without Chinese or Indian influence.

However, he did not mention his interpretation of the relation between the culture of Austroasiatic speakers and Negritos. This means that he ignored the culture of Negritos who were conquered by the Austroasiatic speakers (Indonesians). Thus, Matsumoto considered the Austroasiatic speakers to be the holders of the first civilization in Indochina. Therefore, he designated Mon-Khmer languages as "languages of civilization" (*bunmeigo*, 文明語) in his paper *The Genealogy of Indochina Languages*.[137] Therefore, Matsumoto probably assumed that the Negritos did not have any significant culture.

Matsumoto focused on the Chinese and Indian influence in his evaluation of the culture of Indochinese people. He accepted the theory that the culture of people in Indochina Peninsula was influenced by the Chinese civilization from the North and the Indian civilization from the West.[138] Among the people of Indochina, he considered the Vietnamese people to be "the representatives of the Chinese culture"[139] because they were Sinicized during Chinese colonization and followed the Chinese model of the state.[140] Matsumoto learnt historical facts that Sinicized Vietnam conquered Champa and colonized a part of

---

136. Matsumoto, Nobuhiro "Jōdai Indoshina," *Tōyō bunkashi taikei*, Kodai Shina to Indo, Seidōbunkadō shinkōsha, 1938, p. 242.
137. Matsumoto, Nobuhiro "Indoshina gengo no keitō," *Iwanami kōza Tōyō shichō*, I (Tōyō gengo no keitō), Iwanami shoten, 1934, p. 26.
138. Matsumoto, Nobuhiro "Chamu no yashizoku to 'yashi no mi' setsuwa," *Minzokugaku*, dai 5 kan, dai 6 gō, 1933, p. 463. "Indoshina no bunka jō," *Iwanami kōza Tōyō shichō*, I, Iwanami shoten, 1934, p. 4. "*Indoshina minzoku*," *Iwanami kōza Tōyō shichō*, I (Tōyō no minzoku, Tōyō no shakai), Iwanami shoten, 1935, p. 4. "Jōdai Indoshina," *Tōyō bunkashi taikei*, Kodai Shina to Indo, Seidōbunkadō shinkōsha, 1938, p. 237.
139. Matsumoto, Nobuhiro "Indoshina minzoku," *Iwanami kōza Tōyō shichō*, I (Tōyō no minzoku, Tōyō no shakai), Iwanami shoten, 1935, p. 4.

Cambodia, whereas the latter was an Indianized state.[141] He also knew that states of Thai people, such as Siam and Laos, which were attacked by the Vietnamese, adopted Indian culture.[142] Thus, Matsumoto believed that Sinicized people (Vietnamese) were stronger than Indianized people (Cambodians, Cham, Thai, Laotians, etc.), and he considered Sinicized people to be more civilized than Indianized people.

Matsumoto's opinion probably reflects a Sinocentric perspective of the Japanese interpretation of Asian history because the Japanese themselves belonged to the Asian people who received strong Chinese influence. Hence, because of Matsumoto's cultural background and knowledge, it was easy for Matsumoto to agree to the concept that Sinicized culture was superior to Indianized culture.

Furthermore, Matsumoto considered Chinese people to be more civilized than the Sinicized people of Indochina. Since Matsumoto followed diffusionist theory, he considered the influenced people to be less civilized than the people who exerted the cultural influence. He wrote in his paper *I Have Seen Indochina* that the contemporary Vietnamese were slightly less advanced in the cultural stage than the contemporary Chinese despite almost belonging to the same race as the Chinese.[143] In Vietnam, Matsumoto was "surprised by the immense power of the Chinese culture."[144] He found "the Chinese style" of the Vietnamese architecture less majestic than that of the Chinese architecture he knew of from his visit to China in 1918.[145] Futhermore, he

---

140. Matsumoto, Nobuhiro "Indoshina no bunka jō," *Iwanami kōza Tōyō shichō*, I, Iwanami shoten, 1934, p. 43. "Indoshina no bunka ge," *Iwanami kōza Tōyō shichō*, IX, Iwanami shoten, 1935, pp. 52, 65.
141. Matsumoto, Nobuhiro "Indoshina minzoku," *Iwanami kōza Tōyō shichō*, I (Tōyō no minzoku, Tōyō no shakai), Iwanami shoten, 1935, p. 4. "Jōdai Indoshina," *Tōyō bunkashi taikei*, Kodai Shina to Indo, Seidōbunkadō shinkōsha, 1938, p. 237.
142. Matsumoto, Nobuhiro "Indoshina minzoku," *Iwanami kōza Tōyō shichō*, I (Tōyō no minzoku, Tōyō no shakai), Iwanami shoten, 1935, p. 4.
143. Matsumoto, Nobuhiro "Indoshina wo mite," *Gaikō jihō*, dai 703 gō, Gaikō jihōsha, 15.03.1934, p. 135.
144. Matsumoto, Nobuhiro "Annan ryokōki (dainishin)," *Minzokugaku*, dai 5 kan, dai 5 gō, Minzokugakkai, 1933, p. 831.

considered books written in Vietnamized characters Chữ Nôm to be inferior to books written in Chinese characters.[146] Matsumoto evaluated the Vietnamese culture as lower in comparison with Chinese culture probably because he had discovered that the Vietnamese local culture contained elements of the Southern specificity or the Southern style.[147] He explained that in his paper *Culture of Indochina*: "Annamese arts and crafts are China's extension, but they were cultivated in a specific climate that was in contact with Indian culture in the West and the South, so they gradually developed their peculiar look …"[148] Therefore, Matsumoto assumed that the climate of Indochina and Indian influence made Vietnamese culture less advanced than the Chinese culture.

However, Matsumoto considered the Chinese to be less civilized than the Japanese although the Japanese were also Sinicized people. In his writing *Travel Diary to Southern Islands (Saipan, Yap, Palau, New Guinea)*, he disclosed his satisfaction that the superiority of the Japanese over the Chinese was acknowledged by New Guinean people: "In general, I found a pleasant thing when I came to New Guinea, even more than in our South Seas; when aborigines see a Japanese, they greet him 'Hello, Sir.' It seems they never greet the Chinese by calling them 'Sir.' It is because they have learnt the excellence of the Japanese."[149] This reveals that in the case of Japan, Matsumoto did not follow the diffusionist theory that Sinicized culture is inferior to the Chi-

---

145. Matsumoto, Nobuhiro "Indoshina inshōki (II)," *Mita hyōron*, dai 440 gō, Mita hyōron hakkōjo, 1934, p. 23. "Indoshina inshōki (III)," *Mita hyōron*, dai 445 gō, Mita hyōron hakkōjo, 1934, pp. 12, 13, 22. "Indoshina no bunka ge," *Iwanami kōza Tōyō shichō*, IX, Iwanami shoten, 1935, p. 95.
146. Matsumoto, Nobuhiro "Indoshina no bunka ge," *Iwanami kōza Tōyō shichō*, IX, Iwanami shoten, 1935, p. 94.
147. Matsumoto, Nobuhiro "Indoshina inshōki (III)," *Mita hyōron*, dai 445 gō, Mita hyōron hakkōjo, 1934, p. 22. "*Indoshina minzoku*," *Iwanami kōza Tōyō shichō*, I (Tōyō no minzoku, Tōyō no shakai), Iwanami shoten, 1935, p. 28.
148. Matsumoto, Nobuhiro "Indoshina no bunka ge," *Iwanami kōza Tōyō shichō*, IX, Iwanami shoten, 1935, p. 95.
149. Matsumoto, Nobuhiro "Nan'yō guntō ryokō nisshi," *Shigaku*, dai 16 kan, dai 3 gō, Mita Shigakkai, 1937, p. 95.

nese culture.

Obviously, Matsumoto considered the Japanese to be more civilized than the Chinese because the Japanese were more westernized. This is visible in Matsumoto's opinion on the level of modern Chinese research: "Chinese archaeological research of earthenware is still in its early infant stage."[150] Since archaeology was an academic discipline developed by the Western people, Matsumoto criticized Chinese archaeology for its insufficient adoption of the Western culture. In other words, he considered the Chinese culture to be less westernized and inferior to the Japanese culture.

Moreover, Matsumoto thought that the further advance of the contemporary Vietnamese culture was hindered by the French rule in Indochina. In his paper *Impressions from Indochina*, Matsumoto wrote as follows: "But under the French rule, the Annamese, too, cannot sufficiently expand their original culture. Many of them live in misery, sinking in the naivity not different from the past."[151] This citation suggests that Matsumoto was aware that contemporary French policy did not sufficiently contribute to the development of Vietnamese people. To solve this problem, he suggested that the Vietnamese should learn modern culture from the Japanese under the influence of Japan's Southern Advance Theory (The influence of Japan's Southern Advance Theory is discussed in Chapter 5 Section 2). In this sense, Matsumoto admitted that the Japanese westernized culture did not reach the level of Western culture.

Indeed, after his return from his studies at Sorbonne University, Matsumoto described the high qualities of the French universities in his writings.[152] In his paper *Present Oriental Studies in France (1930)*,

---

150. Matsumoto, Nobuhiro "Prehistoric Pottery in China, by G. D. Wu, London, 1938," *Shigaku*, dai 18 kan, dai 4 gō, MitaShigakkai, 1940, p. 221.
151. Matsumoto, Nobuhiro "Indoshina inshōki (III)," *Mita hyōron*, dai 445 gō, Mita hyōron hakkōjo, 1934, p. 16.
152. Matsumoto, Nobuhiro "Gendai Furansu ni okeru Tōyōgaku," *Fuansu no shakaigakka. Gendai ni okeru shokeikō*, Fransu gakkai, 1930, pp. 553-599. "Furansu ni okeru Shina kenkyū," *Shina kenkyū*, Keiō gijuku Mochidzuki Kikin Shina kenkyūkai-hen, Iwanamishoten, 1930, pp. 375-397.

Matsumoto claimed that "France still maintains superiority in Oriental Researches."[153] In 1933, the high level of French Oriental studies was the reason for Matsumoto's trip to Vietnam where he focused on the collection of Western writings. After visiting the EFEO in Hanoi, Matsumoto admitted that "French researchers are a little bit ahead in Oriental studies."[154] Thus, on the basis of his experience as a scholar, Matsumoto considered French culture to be superior to the Japanese culture because he thought that westernized Japanese culture did not reach the same level as the French culture.

Matsumoto was also aware of the European cultural superiority during his trip to French Indochina. His feelings about his visit of the royal gardens in Huế showed that he believed that Europeans were the most excellent race. He described it in his writing *Impressions from Indochina* as follows: "But still, I feel really thankful that I was permitted to enter such a very interesting place equally like Europeans for the reason of being a citizen of the first-class nation."[155] In other words, although Matsumoto thought that the Japanese were the most superior out of the Asian people, he considered Europeans to be the most superior out of all races and wished that the Japanese were treated like Europeans.

Matsumoto's thinking also reflected Japanese efforts for racial equality with Western people in that time. Indeed, in 1933, Japan withdrew from the League of Nations in reaction to the Western protest against the Japanese occupation of Manchuria. In addition, Western powers refused its request to acknowledge the racial equality of all people. In this context, Japan's inferiority complex in relation to the West impacted Matsumoto's ideas regarding Japanese relations with Southeast Asian peoples.

In summary, from the dichotomy of the civilized and the barbar-

---

153. Matsumoto, Nobuhiro "Gendai Furansu ni okeru Tōyōgaku," *Fuansu no shakaigakka. Gendai ni okeru shokeikō*, Fransu gakkai, 1930, p. 553.
154. Matsumoto, Nobuhiro "Futsujin no Indoshina kenkyū," *Tōa*, Tōa keizai chōsakyoku, March 1934, p. 118.
155. Matsumoto, Nobuhiro "Indoshina inshōki (III)," *Mita hyōron*, dai 445 gō, Mita hyōron hakkōjo, 1934, p. 12.

ian and the powerful and the weak in Matsumoto's writing, it is possible to reconstruct Matsumoto's cultural hierarchy of the people in Indochina Peninsula (see Table 4 below): Austroasiatic and Austronesian culture without Indian and Chinese influence, Indianized culture, Sinicized culture, Chinese culture, Japanese culture, and European culture from inferior to superior order. Consequently, his cultural hierarchy of contemporary people in Indochina was as follows: Negritos (Senoi, Sedang) without any significant culture, non-Indianized, non-Sinicized, and non-westernized Indonesians or Austroasiatic and Austronesian speakers (Moi,); Indianized Indonesians or Austroasiatic and Austronesian speakers (Cham, Cambodians, etc.); Indianized and less-westernized Mongoloid people (Thai); Sinicized and less-westernized Mongoloid people (Vietnamese); more-westernized and most-Sinized Mongoloid people (Chinese); Sinicized and most-westernized Mongoloid people (Japanese) and most-westernized Western people (French) from the barbarian to the civilized. In this light, Matsumoto put Japanese people on the top of Asian (Oriental) people because they were most westernized.

Matsumoto's concept of cultural hierarchy was based on cultural evolutionism preaching the superiority of Western civilization over Oriental civilization. In addition, it clearly reflected diffusionist theory in which a culture that imposes its influence on a different culture is considered to be superior to the different culture that it influences. Therefore, contrary to the nationalistic myth of the Japanese people in terms of history of imperial family, Matsumoto's idea regarding the Japanese cultural superiority did not come from the belief that the Japanese was a nation chosen by gods. (The difference of Matsumoto's ideas regarding the Japanese people and the nationalist concept is discussed in Chapter 5 Section 3.) Moreover, Matsumoto applied the idea regarding the Japanese leadership in Asia from Japanese propaganda to his writings to claim the importance of his ideas regarding Indochina. Since he considered Southeast Asian people to be culturally inferior to the Japanese people from his ethnological research, the idea regarding the Japanese leadership over the Southeast Asian peoples came to him naturally.

Table 4: Matsumoto Nobuhiro's hierarchy of people in East Asia according to his evaluation of their power and culture

Hierarchy	Culture	Races	Ethnic group
Powerful and civilized ↑	Western culture	European	French
	Sinicized and most westernized	Mongoloid	Japanese
	Most Sinicized and less westernized		Chinese
	Sinicized and less westernized		Vietnamese
	Indianized and less westernized		Thai
	Indianized, non-Sinicized non-westernized	Austro-Asiatic and Austronesian (Indonesian)	Cham, Cambodians
	Non-Indianized, non-Sinicized, non-westernized	Austro-Asiatic and Austronesian (Indonesian)	Moi
Weak and barbarian	No significant culture	Negritos	Senoi, Sedang

4.3. Exotism and similarity in Matsumoto's ideas regarding Southeast Asian and Southern Pacific people

Yamashita claimed that the feeling of similarity was typical for Japanese Orientalism in sharp contrast with Western Orientalists who did not find the Orient similar.[156] This section discusses aspects of exotism and similarity in Matsumoto Nobuhiro's Orientalist ideas regarding Southeast Asia and the Southern Pacific. First, it examines why Matsumoto considered Southeast Asia to be exotic. Second, it inquires why Matsumoto considered Southeast Asia to be similar to Ja-

---

156. Yamashita, Shinji "Selves and Others in Japanese Anthropology," *The Making of Anthropology in East and Southeast Asia*, Berghahn Books, 2004, p. 107.

pan. Third, it explores the implication of Matsumoto's attention to similarities between Japan and Southeast Asia.

4.3.1. Exotism

Matsumoto perceived Indochina and Southern Pacific Islands as exotic during his stay there. In his paper *The Impressions from Indochina*, Matsumoto wrote that he was impressed by the exotic appearance of the tropical flora.[157] He also described the same feeling in *Travel Records from Annam*: "Also the landscape of the tropical forest is rare to me, in addition to the design of the hamlet with a gate surrounded by a bamboo forest."[158] He had the same attitude toward the lands of Southern Pacific Islands, as he wrote in his paper *Seeing Our South Seas*: "For us, the South Seas are associated with coconut trees; the island without coconut trees seems lonely."[159] Thus, Matsumoto saw the exoticity of Southeast Asia and Southern Pacific Islands in the tropical flora, which was a typical Japanese image of the region called the South Seas.

However, many Japanese of Matsumoto's era perceived the South Seas as an exotic but a dangerous region. For example, Kawamura Minato's paper on mass Orientalism in Japan showed that the Japanese people of the Taishō and Shōwa eras imagined the South Seas as a dangerous tropical region where the barbarian race of cannibals and predatory animals lived in the deep forest.[160]

The existence of this Japanese stereotype of the South Seas can be assumed also from Matsumoto's writings, but Matsumoto disagreed with this kind of prejudice. First, he denied the extremely exaggerated negative image of Indochina in his writing *Impressions from Indochina*:

---

157. Matsumoto, Nobuhiro "Indoshina inshōki (I)," *Mita hyōron*, dai 437 gō, Mita hyōron hakkōjo, 1934, p. 26.
158. Matsumoto, Nobuhiro "Annan ryokōki (dainishin)," *Minzokugaku*, dai 5 kan, dai 5 gō, Minzokugakkai, 1933, p. 829.
159. Matsumoto, Nobuhiro "Waga Nan'yō wo miru," *Mita hyōron*, dai 483 gō, Mita hyōron hakkōjo, 1937, p. 7.
160. Kawamura, Minato "Taishū Orientarizumu to Ajia ninshiki," *Bunka no naka no shokuminchi*, Iwanami shoten, 1993, pp. 107–111.

"When I came to these mountains [in Tonkin], I became acutely aware that I do not feel like arriving to a land of malaria or to the territory of barbarians at all. Of course, I drunk quinine as prevention towards malaria, but the nature is milder than I thought and the inhabitants are surely not primitive, but holders of a considerable culture and are gentler than Annamese and childish."[161] Second, Matsumoto also found New Guinea different from the general Japanese image of the South Seas. In his paper *Seeing Our South Seas*, Matsumoto argued that North of New Guinea is really not such a barbarian place.[162] There was not so much danger of infectious diseases[163], and there were no predatory animals or poisonous snakes.[164] In other words, contrary to many Japanese people, Matsumoto rejected the negative aspects of exoticity of Southeast Asia and Southern Pacific.

In summary, owing to his trips to Indochina and the Southern Pacific, Matsumoto's exotism of the South Seas was different from the Japanese stereotype of the South Seas in his era. Matsumoto preferred to have a positive image of the South Seas. He did not find the local people primitive. However, he also did not consider them to be sufficiently civilized as was shown in the previous section.

4.3.2. Similarity

Matsumoto perceived Southeast Asia in a more positive way than many Japanese because he was interested in the similarities between Japan and Southeast Asia as it is apparent from the beginning of his ethnological research. In his writings about Indochina, Matsumoto indicated the cultural closeness with old Japan. In his *Travel Records from Annam*, Matsumoto wrote as follows: "... the manner and customs of the Annamese people make me think of Japan's dynastical era, it soothes my nerves..."[165] He specitically focused on the similar custom

---

161. Matsumoto, Nobuhiro "Indoshina inshōki (II)," *Mita hyōron*, dai 440 gō, Mita hyōron hakkōjo, 1934, p. 24.
162. Matsumoto, Nobuhiro "Waga Nan'yō wo miru," *Mita hyōron*, dai 483 gō, Mita hyōron hakkōjo, 1937, p. 10.
163. Ibid., p. 11.
164. Ibid., p. 12.

of tooth blackening: "When I think that Annamese dye their teeth black, it reminds me of the old custom of our ancestors."[166] He also learnt that Vietnamese used similar material for tooth blackening like the Japanese in their past.[167] These similarities invoked in Matsumoto an impression that the Vietnamese royal capital Huế resembled the old Japanese capital Heiankyō: "...many women walking in the street have beautiful white faces with black teeth. The stream of the Perfume River makes me think of the Kamo River, thus everything remind me of Heiankyō."[168] In other words, Matsumoto felt the nostalgia of old Japan in Vietnam because the custom of tooth blackening still existed in Vietnam while it had disappeared in Japan.

Matsumoto noticed the architectonic similarity between some houses in Indochina and Japan. During his visit to Indochina, Matsumoto observed that local people built houses supported by pillars. In his paper *Impressions from Indochina*, Matsumoto wrote as follows: "Thai people...live in houses supported by pillars with forked roof finals like the Japanese Shintoist shrine."[169] Matsumoto mentioned in his writing *The Peoples of Indochina* that the houses on pillars were built by many races of Indochina, such as Tho,[170] White and Black Thai,[171] Laotians,[172] Shans,[173] Lolo,[174] Palaun, Wa, Tchin,[175] Siamese,[176] Cham,[177]

---

165. Matsumoto, Nobuhiro "Annan ryokōki (dainishin)," *Minzokugaku*, dai 5 kan, dai 5 gō, Minzokugakkai, 1933, p. 829.
166. Ibid., p. 831.
167. Matsumoto, Nobuhiro "Indoshina inshōki (I)," *Mita hyōron*, dai 437 gō, Mita hyōron hakkōjo, 1934, p. 26.
168. Matsumoto, Nobuhiro "Indoshina inshōki (III)," *Mita hyōron*, dai 445 gō, Mita hyōron hakkōjo, 1934, p. 10.
169. Matsumoto, Nobuhiro "Indoshina inshōki (III)," *Mita hyōron*, dai 445 gō, Mita hyōron hakkōjo, 1934, p. 24.
170. Matsumoto, Nobuhiro "Indoshina minzoku," *Iwanami kōza Tōyō shichō*, I (Tōyō no minzoku, Tōyō no shakai), Iwanami shoten, 1935, p. 28.
171. Ibid., p. 29.
172. Ibid., p. 33.
173. Ibid., p. 35.
174. Ibid., p. 40.
175. Ibid., pp. 41, 42, 44.
176. Ibid., p. 34

and by Vietnamese in some cases.[178] In this manner, Matsumoto found the Southeast Asian culture close to the Japanese culture because he saw houses supported by pillars in Indochina, which reminded him of the Japanese traditional shrine.

Matsumoto was drawn to the concordance in religious customs when he visited a Vietnamese communal house, Đình Bảng. He discovered that the communal house had functions like the Japanese Shinto shrine and that its festivals included portable shrines and secret rituals in the night.[179] Therefore, he suggested a comparative research in his writing *Impressions from Indochina*: "It is very interesting to compare these points with our primitive Shintoism."[180] Since Shintoism was considered to be an original Japanese belief, Matsumoto probably believed that he found similarities between Southeast Asian and Japanese culture before the Chinese influence. Thus, he hoped that the proposed research would help him reconstruct the primitive culture in which he was interested in.

In summary, Matsumoto was captured by similarities between contemporary Indochina and old Japan, such as tooth blackening, the landscape of the city, the architecture of the houses, and religious customs. Matsumoto's focus on its resemblances to Southeast Asian culture was associated with his opinion on Southeast Asia's backwardness in comparison with Japan because he was reminded of the old Japanese culture on seeing the contemporary Southeast Asian culture. This is clear from his paper *Rise and Fall of the Ethnics in Indochina*: "The cities, where the main transport mean is rickshaw, are not different from our cities in early Meiji Period. As for the situation of the peasants living at the fields, it is not probably different from our countryside during Tokugawa Period. ... This country needs education so that ... it enables the economic and political building of an indepen-

---

177. Ibid., p. 10
178. Matsumoto, Nobuhiro "Indoshina inshōki (III)," *Mita hyōron*, dai 445 gō, Mita hyōron hakkōjo, 1934, p. 22.
179. Matsumoto, Nobuhiro "Indoshina inshōki (II)," *Mita hyōron*, dai 440 gō, Mita hyōron hakkōjo, 1934, p. 22.
180. Ibid., p. 23.

dent state."[181] This suggests the dichotomy of the civilized and the barbarian with regard to Matsumoto's ideas regarding the relations between Japan and Southeast Asia.

4.3.3. Significance of similarity between Japan and Southeast Asia

Cultural anthropologist Yamashita proposed a theory that Matsumoto and other Japanese ethnologists attempted to present Southeast Asia as Japan's homeland by pointing out the similarity between Southeast Asia and Japan.[182] Furthermore, mythologist Hirafuji wrote that Matsumoto searched for the origins of the Japanese people in the South.[183] Ito Seiji suggested that Matsumoto considered the research on Southeast Asia to be important for clarifying the process of formation of the Japanese ethnic culture.[184] However, Chikamori said that Matsumoto did not believe in the Southern origin of the Japanese people.[185] From these points, this section examines the significance of similarity between Japan and Southeast Asia in Matsumoto's writings.

Chapter 2 demonstrated that Masumoto argued regarding Southern influence on Japan under the diffusionist influence during 1924–1932. From this perspective, Matsumoto's focus on the resemblance of Southeast Asian culture with the Japanese traditional culture can be interpreted, as Yamashita and Hirafuji suggested.

However, during 1933–1945, Matsumoto did not publish any interpretations on the significance of these similarities between Japan and Southeast Asia in his writings. As mentioned in Chapter 2 Section 4.3.2., Matsumoto was reluctant to claim the foreign origin of the Japa-

---

181. Matsumoto, Nobuhiro "Indoshina ni okeru minzoku no kōbō," *Shin Ajia*, Mantetsu Tōa keizai chōsakyoku, Nampō bunka tokugō, 1940, 1gatsu, p. 65.
182. Yamashita, Shinji "Selves and Others in Japanese Anthropology," *The Making of Anthropology in East and Southeast Asia*, Berghahn Books, New York, 2004, pp. 104–106.
183. Hirafuji, Kikuko "Shokuminchi teikoku Nihon no shinwagaku," *Shūkyō to fashizumu*, Suiseisha, 2010, p. 327.
184. Itō, Seiji "Matsumoto Nobuhiro - 'Nampōsetsu' no kaitakusha," *Bunka jinruigaku gunzō*, Nihonhen (3), Kyōto: Akademia shuppankai, 1988, p. 240.
185. Interview with Chikamori Masashi, 23 August 2012, Keio University, Tokyo.

nese culture because he was scolded by Yanagita who insisted on a nationalistic interpretation of the Japanese tradition and criticized the search for the Japanese origins abroad. Yanagita believed in the diffusion of Southern culture in Japan. However, he thought that this culture spread from the Southern parts of the Japanese Empire. Consequently, Yanagita's scope of Southern culture was smaller than that of Matsumoto. Under these circumstances, even if Matsumoto proposed a hypothesis of the Japanese origins in Southeast Asia, he could not have claimed it due to his relationship with Yanagita.

Moreover, the previous chapter showed that despite the diffusionist influence, Matsumoto kept his evolutionist belief in the universality of the primitive mind. This is also visible from the fact that in 1939, Matsumoto mentioned about the similarities among stone axes found in Southeast Asia, Japan, India, and America, as shown in Section 2.3.[186] Therefore, Matsumoto still may have believed in the common primitive culture of the Japanese, Southeast Asian, and Chinese people although he did not present them in his writings.

In addition, in the late 1930s, Matsumoto focused on concordances between the Chinese culture and the Japanese culture during his research trip to China. From his writing *Records from the Visit of Old Jiangnan*, he found similarities in the architectonical features: "The scenery of Hangzhou is like Kyoto and Ōtsu together made me feel pleasant and happy like looking at the scenery of my native land."[187] Thus, the Chinese traditional architecture invoked Matsumoto's nostalgia for Japanese places famous for its traditional architectonical architectural beauty. Furthermore, Matsumoto suggested the need to research about the Japanese connection with Central China because he noticed resemblances in the farming life: "The style of peasants near Hanzhou was a Japanese style; it invoked my serious feeling that we should academically research more about the deep relation between Central China and our country."[188] Therefore, Matsumoto had the feel-

---

186. Matsumoto, Nobuhiro "Kōnan hōkoki," *Shigaku*, dai 17 kan, dai 4 gō, MitaShigakkai, 1939, pp. 69-71.
187. Ibid., p. 40.

ing of cultural closeness not only toward Indochina but also toward China. In this light, it cannot be argued that Matsumoto considered only Southeast Asia to be Japan's homeland.

In conclusion, due to lack of evidence and Matsumoto's complex background, it cannot be concluded that Matsumoto focused on the similarities between Japan and Southeast Asia for the reason that he searched the origins of the Japanese culture in Southeast Asia. Therefore, Yamashita's interpretation of Matsumoto's opinions on these similarities is incorrect. However, Chikamori's opinion that Matsumoto did not believe in the Southern origins of the Japanese culture can not be confirmed because Matsumoto did not mention evolutionism in his conclusion. Thus, Ito's argument expressed at best Matsumoto's position of comprehending both the diffusionist and evolutionist perspectives. Nevertheless, it is clear that by noting the similarities closely, Matsumoto considered contemporary Southeast Asian culture to be less civilized than contemporary Japanese culture because it reminded him of the Japanese traditional culture before the influence of the Chinese and Western culture. Consequently, Matsumoto's opinion of similarity contained the Orientalist dichotomy of the civilized and the barbarian and the superior attitude toward Southeast Asia.

5. Influence of the climate theory on Matsumoto's ideas regarding the people of Indochina

This section discusses the influence of climate theory on Matsumoto's ideas regarding the people of Indochina. The significance of the climate theory in Matsumoto's discussion was indicated by Matsumoto's colleague and cultural anthropologist Iwata Keiji (1922-2013) who wrote in his commentary to Matsumoto's collection of papers: "The first one [approach in Matsumoto's writings] is the climatic approach [*fūdoteki apurōchi*, 風土的アプローチ] to the Southern Region, that is present in continental and maritime Southeast Asia."[189] Iwata

---

188. Matsumoto, Nobuhiro "Kōnan hōkoki," *Shigaku*, dai 17 kan, dai 4 gō, MitaShigakkai, 1939, p. 39.

presented his hypothesis that this approach probably came from the influence of the French School of Sociology on Matsumoto's ideas.[190]

As a matter of fact, the French School of Sociology based on unilinear evolutionism focused on the influence of the natural environment on culture. The impact of this sociologist theory can be seen in Matsumoto's writings in the 1920s. In this period, Matsumoto discussed the seasonal festivals that are celebrated due to the people's close relation with the nature. He expressed this influence of the climate on culture in his book *The Research of the Japanese Myths*: "Myths of a nation are a specific product of its country; it has a close relation with the seasonal festivals of the region inhabited by this nation; therefore, it is easily influenced by its climate."[191] In short, in the 1920s, like the French scholars, Matsumoto argued that the climate of each country influenced the formation of national culture.

However, he began claiming the negative influence of climate on the people during his trip to French Indochina in 1933. This was a shift from the 1920s when he did not evaluate the influence of the natural environment as positive or negative. This suggests that Matsumoto's argument of the negative influence of the climate was not the result of his study under the French scholars. He borrowed this argument from Watsuji Tetsuro's *Climate Theory* that was well known in the ethnological circles at the time. Moreover, Matsumoto knew Watsuji well because he taught "the study of the classics" (*koten kenkyū*, 古典研究) at Keio University from 1922–1927,[192] so Matsumoto most likely knew Watsuji in person and was familiar with his research. Therefore, this thesis examines the influence of Watsuji Tetsuro's climate theory on Matsumoto's writings in 1933–1939.

First, this section discusses Watsuji Tetsuro's climate theory. Second, it examines Matsumoto's application of climate theory to his ideas

---

189. Iwata, Keiji "Kaisetsu," *Nihon minzoku bunka no kigen: Tōnan Ajia bunka to Nihon*, Kōdansha, 1978, p. 448.
190. Ibid., p. 448.
191. Matsumoto, Nobuhiro *Nihon shinwa no kenkyū*, Dōbunkan, 1931, p. 177.
192. Kawakita, Nobuo "Keiō gijuku daigaku bungakubu kyōin tantō kamoku ichiran," *Shigaku*, dai 60 kan, dai 2/3 gō, Mita Shigakkai, 1991, p. 193 (367).

regarding Indochina. It will also explore contradictions in Matsumoto's interpretation of Indochina by climate theory including its relation to political propaganda.

5.1. Watsuji Tetsuro's climate theory

The theory of the influence of climate on the development of the people was based on evolutionism which claimed the general impact of the natural environment on the people. In Japan, the climate theory was especially advocated by philosopher Watsuji Tetsuro (1889-1960) who was active in the ethnological and folkloristic circles. Watsuji began developing his climate theory (*fūdoron*, 風土論) on the basis of Martin Heidegger's work *Being and Time* in the summer of 1927.[193] Consequently, Watsuji's climate theory was discussed in the Japanese academic circles at the time when Matsumoto returned from his studies at Sorbonne University in Paris in 1928.

In his climate theory, Watsuji distinguished three types of climate zones: monsoon, dessert, and pasture.[194] Watsuji characterized the monsoon zone as a zone with high humidity and high temperature and claimed that the monsoon climate made people weak in comparison with other types of climate.[195] In his book *The Climate Theory - a Scientific Study of Mankind*, he wrote as follows: "... the people in the monsoon zone are weaker in strength to oppose nature even in comparison with the people from cold countries or people from the dessert. They do not even have a single strength in place where double strength is required."[196] Thus, Matsumoto learnt from Watsuji that the monsoon environment made people weak in comparison with people from other climatic zones.

---

193. Watsuji, Tetsurō *Fūdoron — ningen kagakuteki kōsatsu*, Iwanami shoten, 1936, p. 1.
194. Watsuji, Tetsurō *Fūdoron — ningen kagakuteki kōsatsu*, Iwanami shoten, 1936, pp. 31-197.
195. Ibid., pp. 32-33.
196. Ibid.

5.2. Matsumoto's application of the climate theory for interpretation about Indochinese people

The appearance of the climate theory in Matsumoto's writings about Indochina in 1933 showed that Matsumoto became an advocator of this theory during his visit in Vietnam in the summer of 1933. Vietnam lies in the monsoon zone, thus Matsumoto could easily recollect Watsuji's climate theory that he probably learnt in the late 1920s. Since Matsumoto went to Vietnam in summer, he experienced hot and humid weather and observed the physical weakness of some people there. First, he observed the lack of energy among people in Vietnam. Second, he assumed that Indochina history could be interpreted by the climate theory.

First, Matsumoto observed that even French people in Vietnam lacked energy. In his writing *The Impression from Indochina*, he wrote as follows: "They [French] do not have the same vivid color of the face as when they stay in Europe. Many of them here are lethargic, lazy and unhealthy. It seems that any excellent race finally changes into an inferior race due to the climate of this land with its heat and high humidity. Now, when I came to Indochina, I can deeply feel the correlation of the climate [*fūdo*, 風土] and the people."[197] Furthermore, Matsumoto concluded that it was difficult for French to adapt to the climate, and the French residing in Indochina went back to France during holidays "to refresh their vital energy."[198] In other words, under the influence of Watsuji's climate theory, Matsumoto's misinterpreted his observation in Indochina in the sense that hot and humid climate of Indochina made Indochinese people weak.

This opinion on the negative influence of climate on the French people in Indochina was also presented by Takegoshi Yosaburo in his book *Records from Southern Countries*. Takegoshi wrote that the

---

197. Matsumoto, Nobuhiro "Indoshina inshōki (I)," *Mita hyōron*, dai 437 gō, Mita hyōron hakkōjo, 1934, p. 27. "Annam ryokōdan," *Shigaku zasshi*, dai 45 kan, dai 2 gō, Shigakkai, 1934, p. 256.
198. Matsumoto, Nobuhiro "Indoshina no bunka jō," *Iwanami kōza Tōyō shichō*, I, Iwanami shoten, 1934, p. 5.

French needed to go back to France for recovery.[199] In this sense, Matsumoto's observation of the French in Indochina was similar to that of Takegoshi although Matsumoto visited French Indochina 24 years later than Takegoshi. This suggests that this opinion was common for many Japanese visitors to French Indochina. However, there was a difference because Takegoshi argued that the Chinese in Indochina were unaffected by the hot climate,[200] while Matsumoto did not mention regarding the Chinese in relation to the climate at all.

Furthermore, Matsumoto specified the negative effects of the climate on people in Indochina. In his writing *Culture of Indochina*, Matsumoto wrote as follows: "The tropical climate makes a refined mental ability dull …makes these races, which were active, lazy and weak; this is the strong cause why races of Annam, Thai and Burma who went south were daunted."[201] Thus, Matsumoto believed that people in Indochina became mentally and physically weak because of the tropical climate.

Second, Matsumoto interpreted the history of Indochinese people through the climate theory. In his writing *Culture of Indochina*, Matsumoto wrote as follows: "If we trace back the decline of Champa, Khmer and Mon which used to flourish in this peninsula, we cannot but help thinking about the important role that the influence of the climate played in their eclipse."[202] He wrote about Khmer's decline in his paper *Languages of Indochina*: "…once they [Khmer] built a monumental architecture of Angkor Vat, but then they lost their vigour…"[203] Both Cham and Khmer people inhabited the Southern part of Indochina Peninsula and lost the fight against the Vietnamese and Thai peo-

---

199. Takegoshi, Yosaburō *Nankokuki*, Nippon hyōronsha, 1942 (1st edition 1910), pp. 262.
200. Matsumoto, Nobuhiro "Indoshina no bunka jō," *Iwanami kōza Tōyō shichō*, I, Iwanami shoten, 1934, p. 265.
201. Ibid., p. 5.
202. Matsumoto, Nobuhiro "Indoshina no bunka jō," *Iwanami kōza Tōyō shichō*, I, Iwanami shoten, 1934, p. 5.
203. Matsumoto, Nobuhiro "Indoshina go," *Ajia mondai kōza*, dai 8 kan, Sōgensha, 1939, p. 387.

ple occupying the Northern part of the peninsula. From these points, it seemed to Matsumoto that the climate theory could explain the fall of people in Southern Indochina.

These arguments appear logically sound in the light of theories of Western historians and ethnologists. Matsumoto read in Western books that Indochina was gradually occupied by races who invaded from the North, such as Mongoloid tribes in the Neolithic period.[204] (These theories were discussed in Section 4) In this manner, equiped with these historical facts, Matsumoto assumed that people from colder zones were stronger than people occupying hot and humid zone, as explained in the climate theory.

In summary, the analysis of Matsumoto's writings showed that Matsumoto surmised that the weakeness of people was due to the tropical climate in Indochina, and his deduction was based on the weak appearance of the people and from the history of their struggle in Indochina. It means that he combined the climate theory with social Darwinism wherein he attributed the weakness that led to the defeat of a people by a stronger invader to the climate. This theory seemed to work because the history of Indochina had many cases wherein people from the North dominated people in the South.

5.2.1. Contradictions in Matsumoto's application of the climate theory on Vietnamese people

The previous section showed that Matsumoto borrowed Watsuji's argument of the negative influence of the monsoon zone in explaining the weakness of the people in Indochina. However, in contrast to Watsuji, Matsumoto did not present an analysis of the weakness of people in Indochina by explaining the concrete effects of the climate on the people in Indochina. Since he simply added Watsuji's argument of peoples' weakness to his ideas, there are many contradictions in his thinking. First, Matsumoto mentioned various causes for the weakness

---

204. Matsumoto, Nobuhiro "*Indoshina minzoku,*" *Iwanami kōza Tōyō shichō*, I (Tōyō no minzoku, Tōyō no shakai), Iwanami shoten, 1935, p. 3. "Indoshina gengo no keitō," *Iwanami kōza Tōyō shichō*, I (Tōyō gengo no keitō), Iwanami shoten, 1934, p. 38.

of the Vietramese people. Second, he praised Vietnamese power and discussed the reasons for Vietnamese vigour.

First, Matsumoto claimed that the Vietnamese were weak for various reasons, and it was not only due to the monsoon climate. The first reason was that the Vietnamese were ruled by the French. In his writing *Peoples of Indochina*, Matsumoto mentioned the first reason: "In the nineteenth century, they [Vietnamese] fell under French rule and their growth has been hindered in this point; but their population rose to 15,000,000, and we do not think that their national vitality was completely exhausted."[205] The second reason was that Matsumoto considered the physical appearance of Vietnamese to be inferior. Matsumoto described his observation of the Vietnamese people in his paper *I Have Seen Indochina*: "They [Vietnamese] are a yellow race of low stature, with fragile limbs and high cheekbones. They probably belong to the most inferior race among Mongoloid species."[206] He expressed a similar opinion in his paper *Impressions from French Indochina*: "The physical constitution of the Annamese is smaller than the Japanese; moreover their balance is bad and inferior on the whole."[207] Thus, Matsumoto associated the lack of spiritual energy of the Vietnamese with their loss of independence and their weak-looking appearance. However, he did not explain if and how these reasons were connected with the monsoon climate of Indochina Peninsula.

Second, despite these reasons for the Vietnamese weakness, Matsumoto still argued that the Vietnamese vitality had not been completely exhausted. He even claimed that Vietnamese were "the most important nation of Indochina."[208] Matsumoto also praised Vietnamese national power. In his writing *Culture of Indochina*, he claimed as

---

205. Matsumoto, Nobuhiro "*Indoshina minzoku*," *Iwanami kōza Tōyō shichō*, I (Tōyō no minzoku, Tōyō no shakai), Iwanami shoten, 1935, p. 4.
206. Matsumoto, Nobuhiro "Indoshina wo mite," *Gaikō jihō*, dai 703 gō, Gaikō jihōsha, 15.03.1934, p. 132.
207. Matsumoto, Nobuhiro "Indoshina inshōki (I)," *Mita hyōron*, dai 437 gō, Mita hyōron hakkōjo, 1934, p. 27.
208. Matsumoto, Nobuhiro "Jōdai Indoshina," *Tōyō bunkashi taikei*, Kodai Shina to Indo, Seidōbunkadō shinkōsha, 1938, p. 237.

follows: "We should admire the energy of spiritual power of the Annamese nation whose independence was threatened by Mongols - founders of a great empire in Europe and Asia. The Trần dynasty was successful not only in the North, but also in the South where it defeated Champa..."[209] Despite Matsumoto's recognition of Vietnamese power, he did not mention that this case contradicted the climate theory because Vietnamese in the South defeated Mongolians coming from the colder region in the North. Thus, when Matsumoto adopted Watsuji's argument of negative influence of monsoon climate, he did not consider the cases in which Watsuji's climate theory was inapplicable. This means he used Watsuji's argument on the monsoon climate only for the explanation of the cases of decline.

Instead of denying the climate theory, Matsumoto provided an explanation for the Vietnamese victory over the Mongols. In the writing *Culture of Indochina* Matsumoto also praised the Vietnamese hero Trần Hưng Đạo who battled the Mongols expressing that he "demonstrated a great national spirit."[210] From his argument, it seems that Matsumoto was convinced that Vietnamese spiritual power had its source in the Vietnamese culture: "As the Trần Dynasty raised its national spirit, Vietnamized Chinese characters Chữ Nôm were in use when its self-consciousness was strong."[211] Thus, Matsumoto surmised that the Vietnamese could repulse Mongolian attacks owing to their spiritual energy coming from their Vietnamese culture. Consequently, his evolutionist opinion on the Vietnamese power based on the Vietnamese culture was in contradiction with his argument of the Vietnamese weakness due to the monsoon climate.

In another argument, Matsumoto explained the source of the Vietnamese power from the adoption of a foreign culture. In his writing *Culture of Indochina*, Matsumoto claimed as follows: "After the loss of suzerainty, Annam lost its ancient vigour that it had developed by absorbing Han culture, yet absorbing French culture is impossible

---

209. Matsumoto, Nobuhiro "Indoshina no bunka ge," *Iwanami kōza Tōyō shichō*, IX, Iwanami shoten, 1935, p. 65.
210. Ibid., p. 67.
211. Ibid., p. 68.

too."[212] In other words, Matsumoto argued that the adoption of the Chinese culture made the Vietnamese strong, but it was not enough to repulse the French aggression. Matsumoto considered the Sinization of Vietnamese people to be insufficient for their struggle against the French people because he believed that Western civilization was superior to Oriental civilization based on cultural evolutionism. However, even if he had believed that the adoption of the Chinese culture helped Vietnamese to beat Mongolian, he did not discuss why the superior Western culture did not help the French and Vietnamese to overcome the hot and humid climate of Indochina. Rationally, if the climate made Vietnamese weak, then it made no sense for the Vietnamese to adopt any culture.

These afore mentioned opinions of Matsumoto based on evolutionism show that Matsumoto thought that Vietnamese original culture and the adoption of Chinese culture made the Vietnamese people stronger. Simultaneously, he argued that the monsoon climate made Vietnamese people weak. In this manner, Matsumoto's ideas regarding Vietnamese people were inconsistent.

Moreover, Matsumoto claimed that there were people with excellent spiritual power who overcame the obstacles of nature. He suggested that these people were Japanese since he encouraged the graduates of Keio Gijuku to work in the Southern Pacific in his paper *Seeing Our South Seas*: "Climate [in the South Seas] is monotonous during one year, without any stimulation, so there is some fear that one loses his vitality. But even this is not anything that cannot be overcome by the spiritual power. I never stop wishing that more and more promising young men advance to the South Seas and contribute to the acquisition of our interests."[213] Since Matsumoto mentioned only Japanese people as an example of such excellent people, he implied that Japanese were a unique nation that did not become weak under the influence of the hot and humid climate.

---

212. Matsumoto, Nobuhiro "Indoshina no bunka ge," *Iwanami kōza Tōyō shichō*, IX, Iwanami shoten, 1935, p. 93
213. Matsumoto, Nobuhiro "Indoshina no bunka jō," *Iwanami kōza Tōyō shichō*, I, Iwanami shoten, 1934, p. 2.

However, this was the only case in which Matsumoto did not use the climate theory for interpreting the decline based on the result of the struggle between two ethnic groups. In addition, this argument of the Japanese resistance to the hot climate was in contradiction with Matsumoto's argument in the interpretation of people in Indochina based on Watsuji's theory of the monsoon climate. Matsumoto claimed that superior people become weak due to the monsoon climate. He argued that even the French people in Indochina degenerated due to the monsoon climate. Therefore, the idea regarding the Japanese resistance to the hot climate was also in contradiction with Matsumoto's evolutionist opinion that the Western people were superior to the Oriental people. Matsumoto was not such a nationalist in discussing the topic of the Japanese people's uniqueness. This excluded one case wherein he borrowed the argument of the Japanese ability to resist the hot climate from the Japanese nationalist propaganda. Moreover, despite this borrowing, he did not argue that the Japanese should replace the French in the rule over Indochina because of the unique ability of the Japanese.

6. Conclusion

This chapter showed that Matsumoto's trips to Indochina, South Seas Islands, and China brought many new ideas to Matsumoto. This was not only based on the Western works on Southeast Asia but also on his direct experience of the South Seas. It revealed that although Matsumoto had real interest in Southeast Asian culture and found it similar to the Japanese culture, he perceived it through the lenses of various biased theories, such as social Darwinism, Orientalism, and the climate theory, which he linked with the theories of diffusionist ethnology. As a result of this ideational patchwork, Matsumoto constructed a racial hierarchy of people in Southeast Asia, in which he considered Southeast Asian people to be as inferior in power and culture in comparison with those of Japan. He explained the inferiority of Southeast Asian people as a result of the hot climate in Indochina.

However, his real criterion for judging the people was the extent of their westernization, which originated in the Japanese complex of inferiority toward Western people rooted in modernization movements in the Meiji era. In this sense, Matsumoto's thoughts regarding Southeast Asia reflected the Japanese effort to achieve equality with the Western people in his period.

In addition, some researchers explained Matsumoto's focus on similarities with Japan as a search for Japan's homeland in Southeast Asia. However, this argument was not proved in Matsumoto's case since he interpreted these concordances ambiguously in the context of relations between Japan and Southeast Asia. He rarely presented a diffusionist interpretation of these relations, which was the influence of Southern culture on ancient Japan.

Chapter 5:
Political influence on Southeast Asian studies during 1933-1945

1. Introduction

The previous chapters suggested that progressing Japan's involvement in Southeast Asia created favorable conditions for the establishment of Southeast Asian studies in Japan, but it also brought some restrictions on scholars. They were forced to adapt to the environment of escalating nationalism. Many of them developed some kind of cooperation with the nationalist government in exchange for chances to pursue their activities. Furthermore Matsumoto chose to use the rhetoric of the Japanese nationalist propaganda in his works on Vietnam under the pressure from the political environment. Concretely, he adopted Japan's Southern Advance Theory (*Nanshinron*, 南進論) in the 1930s and Pan-Asianism (*Han-Ajiashugi*, 汎アジア主義) in the first half of the 1940s.

There is some research on Japan's Southern Advance Theory and Pan-Asianism in relation to Southeast Asia. Japanese historians Yano Tooru and Goto Ken'ichi[1] published several books, providing an overview of the Japan's Southern advance and discussing the Southern Advance Theory in relation to Southeast Asia. In addition, Shimizu Hajime examined Japan's Southern Advance Theory in the Meiji (1868–

---

1. Yano, Tooru *Nanshin no keifu*, Chūōkōronsha, 1975. *Nihon no Nan'yō shikan*, Chūōkōronsha, 1979. Gotō, Ken'ichi *Kindai Nihon to Tōnan Ajia: Nanshin no shōgeki to isan*, Iwanami shoten, 1995. *Tōnan Ajia kara mita kingendai Nihon: Nanshin senryō datsu shokuminchika o meguru rekishi ninshiki*, Iwanami shoten, 2012.

1912) and Taisho eras (1912-1926).[2] However, Japan's Southern advance, Japan's Southern Advance Theory, and Pan-Asianism in relation to Vietnam has not been covered yet. Moreover, the influence of these theories on the works of Japanese scholars researching Southeast Asia is scarcely examined.

Matsumoto's stance of using ethnological research for the Japanese expansionist policy in the prewar period was argued by Japanese mythologist Hirafuji Kikuko[3] and ethnoarchaeologist Chikamori Masashi.[4] In particular, Hirafuji indicated this in the book *Religion and Fascism*: "Matsumoto mentioned this episode as an example of that the mythological research was oppressed by political influence, however, when seeing Matsumoto's research presented from the 1930s to 1940s, we can see that he actively argued the use of the research for colonial policy."[5] Furthermore, Hirafuji insisted that Matsumoto legitimized the policy of Southern advance by arguing regarding the similarity between the Japanese and Southern myths and by claiming the blood mixing between the Japanese and the South Sea people.[6]

However, in her research, Hirafuji did not focus on political arguments in Matsumoto's writings; therefore, she did not differentiate between Japan's Southern Advance Theory in the 1930s and Pan-Asianism in the first half of the 1940s. However, Southern Advance Theory and Pan-Asianism had different ideas. Southern Advance Theory ad-

---

2. Shimizu, Hajime "Taishō shoki ni okeru 'Nanshinron' no ichi kōsatsu – sono Ajiashugiteki henyō wo megutte," *Ajia Keizai*, 30/1, 1983, pp. 1-53. "Nanshinron: Its Turning Point in World War I," *The Developing Economies* 15/4, December 1987, pp. 386-402. "Senkanki Nihon-keizaiteki 'Nanshin' no shisōteki haikei," Sugiyama S. & Ian G. Brown *Senkanki Tōnan Ajia no Keizai masatsu. Nihon no Nanshin to Ajia-Ōbei* Dōbunkan, 1990, pp. 13-44. "Meiji chūki no 'Nanshinron' to 'Kan-Taiheiyō' shisō no genkei (I)," *Ajia Keizai*, 32/9, September 1991, pp. 2-20. "Meiji chūki no 'Nanshinron' to 'Kan-Taiheiyō' shisō no genkei," *Ajia Keizai*, 32/10, October 1991, pp. 27-44.
3. Hirafuji, Kikuko "Shokuminchi teikoku Nihon no shinwagaku," *Shūkyō to fashizumu*, Suiseisha, 2010, pp. 326-327.
4. Interview with Chikamori Masashi, 23 August 2012, Keio University, Tokyo.
5. Ibid., pp. 326-327.
6. Ibid., p. 324.

vocated Japan's expansion southward in the region of the so-called South Seas encompassing mainly islands in the Pacific Ocean and insular and continental Southeast Asia. In contrast, Pan-Asianism was linked to Japan's northward expansion on Asian continent with the center in China.

In addition, Matsumoto differentiate between these two theories because he criticized Pan-Asianism in 1934: "Rather than being driven by childish sentimentalism, having sympathy with their loss of the homeland and preaching the Revival of Asia, we should first work on making full use of the abilities of our empire, and show our heart, free of territorial ambitions towards other European colonies in Asia outside of Manchukuo and Mongolia... In reality, preaching vague Pan-Asianism towards the majority of the unreliable China-adoring Annamese, has the effect of alienating the French who are favorable to Japan. I must say that making an unwanted enemy is the worst strategy ever for Japanese foreign policy."[7] Since Matsumoto disagreed with Pan-Asianism in the 1930s, it is important to separate his discussion supporting Japan's Southern advance from his discussion advocating Pan-Asianism in his works on Southeast Asia.

This chapter first discusses Japan's Southern advance and Japan's Southern Advance Theory and analyzes the influence of this theory on Matsumoto's writings about Vietnam in the 1930s. Second, it investigates Pan-Asianism and its influence on Matsumoto's writings about Southeast Asia during 1940–1945.

2. Influence of Japan's Southern Advance Theory

2.1. Japan's Southern Advance and Southern Advance Theory

For a deeper understanding of Matsumoto Nobuhiro's relation to Japan's Southern Advance Theory, it is necessary to discuss the devel-

---

7. Matsumoto, Nobuhiro "Indoshina wo mite," *Gaikō jihō*, No. 703, 15.03.1934, pp. 137–138.

opment of Japan's Southern advance and its theory.

Japan's Southern advance began in the late 19th century. In the earlier period, Japanese had knowledge of Southeast Asia as a part of the South Seas, but they had not thought of advancing in this region yet. One of the main reasons was that Japan's attention was always directed toward China in the North; thus, the Northern Advance Theory shaped the Japanese national policy. However, the situation slightly changed during the Meiji era when Japan decided to secure its borders through colonization of Ezo (Hokkaido), in the North and annexation of Ryukyu Kingdom in the South in 1879. Then, in 1895, Japan acquired Formosa (Taiwan) from China as a result of its victory in the Sino-Japanese War. These islands became stepping stones for Japan's further advance to the South Seas, including Southeast Asia.[8]

During the Meiji era (1868-1912), the Southern Advance Theory advocating peaceful penetration to South Seas emerged in contrast to Asianism. This was based on Fukuzawa Yukichi's *Leaving-Asia Theory* (*Datsu-A Ron*, 脱亜論)[9], which aimed at making Japan a member of first-class nations in the modern imperialist order. Thus, Japan stuck to the idea of free trade in international relations while acknowledging the existing world order. In this sense, the Southern Advance Theory combined expansionism with internationality. Japan planned to promote its economic interest with the principles of international trade as an "oceanic nation" in the region it called the South Seas.[10]

---

8. Yano, Tooru *Nanshin no keifu. Nihon no Nan'yō shikan*, Chikurashobō, 2009, pp. 251-254, 263-264. Gotō, Ken'ichi *Kindai Nihon to Tōnan Ajia: Nanshin no shōgeki to isan*, Iwanami shoten, 1995, pp. 85-117.
9. *Leaving-Asia Theory* (1885) argued that Japan had not to remain underdeveloped like other Asian countries, but had to adopt Western civilization in order to survive in the modern world. In reaction to this trend, Asianism emerged to advocate the values of the Japanese tradition and its ties with Asia/Orient, especially China, emphasizing their contrast with Western civilization/ Occident.
10. Yano, Tooru *Nanshin no keifu. Nihon no Nan'yō shikan*, Chikurashobō, 2009, pp. 285-288. "Meiji chūki no 'Nanshinron' to 'Kan-Taiheiyō' shisō no genkei (I)," *Ajia Keizai*, 32/9, September 1991, pp. 2-5. "Meiji chūki no 'Nanshinron' to 'Kan-Taiheiyō' shisō no genkei," *Ajia Keizai*, 32/10, October 1991, pp. 27-44.

During the Meiji era, advocates of Japan's Southern advance considered South Seas as a separate region both from Orient (Asia) and the West (Europe and America), so they preached the theory in contradiction to the Northern advance. They also emphasized Japan's connections with the South Seas from geographical, historical, cultural, and ethnological perspectives. Doing so, they fought against the Japanese stereotypes portraying the South Seas as a completely barbarian region with dangerous nature and hot climate. Despite this, they still considered South Sea people to be uncivilized in comparison with the Japanese people.[11]

Japan's territorial expansion to South continued in the Taisho era (1912–1926) during World War I when Japan occupied the German colonies in Southern Pacific (Marshall Islands, the Carolinas, the Marianas, and the Palau Islands) and received these islands under its mandate based on its membership in the League of Nations in 1919. The islands were named as South Seas Islands (Nan'yō shotō, 南洋諸島). In addition, economic vacuum in Southeast Asia during the war facilitated Japan's advance into Southeast Asian market which boosted industrial production in the Japanese homeland.[12]

As a result of these developments, Japan proceded its Southern advance while keeping the priority of Northern advance in China after the annexation of Korea in 1910. In 1915, Japanese entrepreneurs established South Seas Association (Nan'yō kyōkai, 南洋協会) to build close economic ties with the South Seas.[13] The Japanese government founded the South Seas Bureau (Nan'yōchō, 南洋庁, 1922) for the adminis-

---

11. Yano, Tooru *Nanshin no keifu. Nihon no Nan'yō shikan*, Chikurashobō, 2009, pp. 41, 285. Shimizu, Hajime "*Nanshin-ron*: Its Turning Point in World War I," *The Developing Economies* 15/4, December 1987, pp. 386–402.
12. Shimizu, Hajime "Taishō shoki ni okeru 'Nanshinron' no ichi kōsatsu – sono Ajiashugiteki henyō wo megutte," *Ajia Keizai*, 30/1, 1983, p. 18. Shimizu, Hajime "Kindai Nihon ni okeru 'Tōnan Ajiya' chiiki gainen no seiritsu (I)," (Shō-chūgakkō chiri kyōkasho ni miru), *Ajia keizai*, 28/6, Ajia kenkyūjo, 1987, p. 10.
13. Yano, Tooru *Nanshin no keifu. Nihon no Nan'yō shikan*, Chikurashobō, 2009, p. 59. Gotō, Ken'ichi *Kindai Nihon to Tōnan Ajia: Nanshin no shōgeki to isan*, Iwanami shoten, 1995, p. 17.

tration of the South Seas.[14] In the 1920s, the Japanese migration and businessmen's investment in the South Seas gradually developed.[15] Although the Japanese government established administration in the South Seas, it did not have an elaborated economic policy, so economic activities in the South Seas were rather determined by individual Japanese entrepreneurs. One of the most significant companies was Kohatsu K. K. (Nan'yō Kōhatsu Kaisha, 南洋興発会社), which was discussed in relation to Matsumoto's trip to South Seas Islands.[16] (See Chapter 3) In this manner, through its entrepreneurs, Japan materialized its expansion in the areas of lower importance for the Western powers, so it was still in accord with the international principles.

Although Japan's advance into the South Seas, including Southeast Asia, was peaceful and of economic character, the Southern Advance Theory added some aspects of Asianism in the Taisho era. Shimizu explained that the reason was that Japan slowly shifted the emphasis from economy to defense, which was linked to the Northern direction.[17] As a result, the advocates of Southern Advance Theory stopped perceiving Japan's Southern expansion in contradiction with the Northern advance.[18] Doing so, they justified Japan's Southern expansion by the Asianist slogan of propagating a great family under the Japanese leadership (Eight Corners of One Universe, hakkō ichiu, 八紘一宇).[19] Another aspect of Taisho Southern Advance Theory was also

---

14. Yano, Tooru *Nanshin no keifu. Nihon no Nan'yō shikan*, Chikurashobō, 2009, pp. 255, 260. Shimizu, Akitoshi *Anthropology and Colonialism in Asia and Oceania*, Survey, Curzon Richmond, 1999, p. 144.
15. Yano, Tooru *Nanshin no keifu. Nihon no Nan'yō shikan*, Chikurashobō, 2009, pp. 53-60. Shimizu, Hajime "Taishō shoki ni okeru 'Nanshinron' no ichi kōsatsu – sono Ajiashugiteki henyō wo megutte," *Ajia Keizai*, 30/1, 1983, pp. 18-22.
16. Matsumoto, Nobuhiro "Waga Nan'yō wo miru," *Mita hyōron*, dai 483 gō, Mita hyōron hakkōjo, 1937, p. 6. Yano, Tooru *Nanshin no keifu. Nihon no Nan'yō shikan*, Chikurashobō, 2009, pp. 260-262.
17. Shimizu, Hajime "Taishō shoki ni okeru 'Nanshinron' no ichi kōsatsu – sono Ajiashugiteki henyō wo megutte," *Ajia Keizai*, 30/1, 1983, pp. 11, 16.
18. Yano, Tooru *Nanshin no keifu. Nihon no Nan'yō shikan*, Chikurashobō, 2009, pp. 181-183.

the call for better organization of the economic expansion that would correspond to Japan's status of first-class nation.[20]

However, in the 1930s, Japan hit the limits of its Southern advance. South Seas Islands were small compared to the territories received by the Western Powers from World War I. As indicated by Yano, the Japanese investments in the South Seas were small in comparison with those in China.[21] Simultaneously, the economic crisis made Western authorities in Asia and the Pacific cautious against the Japanese economic penetration, and they also found Japan's advance in China too aggressive. Therefore, they implemented various restrictions on the Japanese activities in the territories under their rule.[22]

Under these difficult conditions, Japan started its economic advance into French Indochina. In 1932, Japan concluded the Japan-French Trade Agreement, which facilitated Japan's relations with French Indochina.[23] In the same year, a direct connection between Japanese Kobe and Vietnamese Haiphong was established.[24] This was followed by the Customs Treaty between Japan and French Indochina in 1934.[25] Nevertheless, as the custom process was unfavorable, Japanese found it difficult to succeed. Matsumoto described this experience in his writings about Vietnam, in which he complained about "bullying

---

19. Shimizu, Hajime "Taishō shoki ni okeru 'Nanshinron' no ichi kōsatsu – sono Ajiashugiteki henyō wo megutte," *Ajia Keizai*, 30/1, 1983, pp. 2, 19, 39, 40. Shimizu, Hajime "*Nanshin-ron*: Its Turning Point in World War I," *The Developing Economies* 15/4, December 1987, pp. 386-402.
20. Shimizu, Hajime "Taishō shoki ni okeru 'Nanshinron' no ichi kōsatsu – sono Ajiashugiteki henyō wo megutte," *Ajia Keizai*, 30/1, 1983, p. 30. Yano, *Nanshin no keifu: Nihon no Nan'yō shikan*, 285.
21. Yano, Tooru *Nanshin no keifu. Nihon no Nan'yō shikan*, Chikurashobō, 2009, p. 86.
22. Gotō, Ken'ichi *Kindai Nihon to Tōnan Ajia: Nanshin no shōgeki to isan*, Iwanami shoten, 1995, pp. 56-57.
23. "Customs agreement conclusion between Japan and Indochina," National Archives of Japan, Showa Financial Historical Materials No. 4 Vol.137, Reference code: A08072515300
24. Matsumoto, Nobuhiro "Indoshina inshōki (III)," *Mita hyōron*, dai 445 gō, Mita hyōron hakkōjo, 1934, p. 24.

the foreign passengers" at the custom office[26] and criticized the prohibitive custom taxes against Japan.[27] Still, Japan was advocating its peaceful intention and will to cooperate with the Western Powers.

With the escalation of Sino-Japanese War (called "China Incident" by the Japanese), Vietnam stopped having only economic significance since provisions for the Japanese enemy in China were transported through it. In 1936, Japanese military circles began focusing on Southeast Asia.[28] At this point, Japan's Southern advance became firmly connected to its Northern Advance in the national policy. On August 1, 1940, Japanese foreign minister Matsuoka Yosuke announced the idea regarding the Greater East Asia Co-Prosperity Sphere (*Dai Tō-A kyōeiken*, 大東亜共栄圏), which also included Southeast Asia.[29] After the French capitulation to Germany in June 1940, Japan took control over French Indochina during 1940-1941. First, Japan dispatched its troops to Northern Indochina in September 1940.[30] Then, it gained control over all French Indochina by enforcing the Japan-French Protocol for Joint Defense of French Indochina (July 29, 1941).[31] Thus, Southeast Asia, on which Matsumoto concentrated, became a part of Japan's Greater East Asia Co-Prosperity Sphere before the outbreak of

---

25. "Documents relating to customs treaty between Japan and French Indochina," Diplomatic Archives of the Ministry of Foreign Affairs, Documents relating to customs treaty between Japan and French Indochina, Reference code: B04013588500.
26. Matsumoto, Nobuhiro "Indoshina inshōki (III)," *Mita hyōron*, dai 445 gō, Mita hyōron hakkōjo, 1934, p. 25.
27. Matsumoto, Nobuhiro "Indoshina wo mite," *Gaikō jihō*, dai 703 gō, Gaikō jihōsha, 15.03.1934, p137.
28. Yano, Tooru *Nanshin no keifu. Nihon no Nan'yō shikan*, Chikurashobō, 2009, pp. 294-297. Gotō, Ken'ichi *Kindai Nihon to Tōnan Ajia: Nanshin no shōgeki to isan*, Iwanami shoten, 1995, p. 24.
29. Yano, Tooru *Nanshin no keifu. Nihon no Nan'yō shikan*, Chikurashobō, 2009, pp. 308-309.
30. Hata, Ikuhiko "The Army Move into Northern Indochina," *The Fateful Choice. Japan's Advance into Southeast Asia, 1939-1941*, ed. by J. W. Morley, New York: Columbia University Press, 1980, pp. 179-180, 192.
31. Murakami, Sachiko *Japan's Thrust into French Indochina 1940-1945*, New York University, 1981, p. 337.

Asia-Pacific War.

The development of the Southern Advance Theory in the Showa era has not been sufficiently researched yet. However, the typical feature in this era was an overwhelming influence of Pan-Asianism. This means that the Pan-Asianist concept of East Asia centered on China was applied to the South Seas after this region had been encompassed into the Greater East Asia Co-Prosperity Sphere. In other words, Southeast Asia became a mere Southern extension of the continental China.[32] Yano called it voiding because the amalgamation of Southern Advance Theory with Pan-Asianism ideology lacked real content.[33]

In summary, Japan's Southern Advance Theory mainly advocated peaceful economic advance to the South Seas, but it was gradually infiltrated by Asianist ideas and finally fused into Pan-Asianism. The shift in direction of Southern Advance Theory toward Indochina in the 1930s meant favorable conditions for establishment of Southeast Asian studies in Japan. Therefore, Matsumoto could not miss this chance to promote his research.

2.2. Influence of Japan's Southern Advance Theory on Matsumoto's works

This section analyzes the influence of Japan's Southern Advance Theory on Matsumoto's writings about Indochina in the 1930s and clarifies the reasons why Matsumoto incorporated this theory.

Matsumoto started studying Southeast Asia as a result of his interest in ethnology in 1919 in the period of "Southern advance fever," but there is no trace of Japan's Southern Advance Theory in his writings in the 1920s. He researched Southeast Asia from the perspective of ethnology, so he was concerned with the primitive culture in Southeast Asia. In this light, Matsumoto's motivation to study Indochina was different from the economic ambitions of the Southern Advance Theory. Therefore, Matsumoto's interest in Southeast Asia was not the

---

32. Shimizu, Hajime "*Nanshin-ron*: Its Turning Point in World War I," *The Developing Economies* 15/4, December 1987, p. 387.
33. Yano, Tooru *Nanshin no keifu. Nihon no Nan'yō shikan*, Chikurashobō, 2009, pp. 309, 315.

result of the influence of the Southeast Advance Theory despite its wide propagation in this era, and Matsumoto cannot be considered as a representative of it.

Political influence of the Southern Advance Theory appeared in Matsumoto's writings only after his stay in Vietnam, where he went to collect research materials on Southeast Asia in 1933. Matsumoto criticized the economic situation of contemporary Indochina and argued that Japan should assist France in the development of backward Indochina.[34] He suggested that Vietnamese development was hindered by insufficient French policy: "But under the French rule, the Annamese, too, cannot sufficiently expand their original culture. Many of them live in misery, sinking in the naivity not different from the past."[35] As a solution to this problem, Matsumoto proposed the adoption of the modern (that is westernized) Japanese culture: "What the Annamese need is that we stand by their side and supply cheap goods so that we can meet their demand, and thus promote the spirit of progress in them, stimulate their luxurious heart, to develop their industry, to increase their fortune. Furthermore, they need a nation that they could emulate and that could provide them the model of civilization and production."[36] As the reason for the Japanese support, Matsumoto mentioned that: "there is a too big gap between the French and the native peoples, and the [French] culture is too dissimilar from that of Annamese people."[37] Matsumoto's stance corresponded to Japan's Southern Advance Theory in relation to Indochina, advocating Japan-French cooperation in Indochina.

By arguing for Japanese help to Vietnamese people, Matsumoto implied that the Japanese were better teachers for Vietnamese people than the French because though they were less westernized than

---

34. Matsumoto, Nobuhiro "Indoshina wo mite," *Gaikō jihō*, dai 703 gō, Gaikō jihōsha, 15.03.1934, pp. 131–138.
35. Matsumoto, Nobuhiro "Indoshina inshōki (III)," *Mita hyōron*, dai 445 gō, Mita hyōron hakkōjo, 1934, p. 16.
36. Matsumoto, Nobuhiro "Indoshina wo mite," *Gaikō jihō*, dai 703 gō, Gaikō jihōsha, 15.03.1934, pp. 135–137.
37. Ibid., pp. 135–137.

Western people, they successfully digested the Western culture. Matsumoto himself was an example of French-educated Japanese.[38] The argument suggested Japan's civilization mission to Indochina. However, it did not come from Asianist influence, but it stemmed from Matsumoto's Orientalism (See Chapter 4, Section 4), through the lens of which he considered the Japanese to be superior in culture and power to the Vietnamese and inferior to the European people.

This seems to suggest that he considered the Vietnamese as those who were unable to learn Western civilization from the French. If this was the case, then it is likely that he either chose to ignore or completely neglected the fact that there was a certain group of Vietnamese that received French education either at home or in France. Eitherways, this poses a problem with his argument especially since he had personally met with this class of Vietnamese intelligentsia both in Paris and Vietnam. He met with a Vietnamese for the first time during his studies at Sorbonne University in 1924–1928.[39] Moreover, he believed that the Vietnamese people were capable of studying Western science since he praised the Vietnamese researchers: "I am glad that recently the folkloristic research is becoming popular among young Annamese scholars."[40] In his writings about the Vietnamese culture, he drew from the research of the Vietnamese scholars of the EFEO, such as Nguyễn Văn Khoan.[41] He even wrote a review of Khoan's work, appreciating his academic level: "The author's description is always a report without any analogy and dogma and I am happy that he mentions the custom of his countrymen faithfully."[42] Therefore,

---

38. Matsumoto received doctorate degree in Oriental studies from Sorbonne University in 1928.
39. Matsumoto, Nobuhiro *Betonamu minzoku shōshi*, Iwanami shinsho, 1973 (1st ed. 1969), p. 207.
40. Matsumoto, Nobuhiro "Indoshina minzoku," *Iwanami kōza Tōyō shichō*, I (Tōyō no minzoku, Tōyō no shakai), Iwanami shoten, 1935, pp. 7, 8. "
41. Ibid., p. 7.
42. Matsumoto, Nobuhiro "Nguyen-van-Khoan, Le Repêchage de l'âme, avec une note sur les hôn et les phách d'après les croyances tonkinoises actuelles," *Shigaku kenkyū*, dai 1 kan dai 2 gō, Minzokugakkai, Sanseidō, 1935, p. 176.

Matsumoto knew that Vietnamese were able to adopt Western civilization directly from the European people. This means that he chose to follow the Japanese propaganda of Southern advance although it was in contradiction with his experience of Vietnamese intelligentsia.

Indeed, Matsumoto had three reasons for the adoption of the Southern Advance Theory. First, he promoted the Japanese advance to French Indochina because he perceived it as part of the Japanese-French economic cooperation. He explained it in his paper *I Have Seen Indochina*: "The influx of the cheap Japanese goods will bring some profit to Annamese ... On the one hand, it may suppress the French industry, but on the other hand, it will make this French colony prosper, and from the general situation it will surely benefit both Japan and France. The Japan-French friendship should not be just a useless theory, and it should be first implemented in the land of Indochina close to Japan."[43] Matsumoto established friendship with the French people during his studies in France (1924–1928), and his close relationship with the French scholar Émile Gaspardone facilitated his trip to Indochina in 1933. Therefore, it was natural for Matsumoto to preach Japan-French cooperation in Indochina.

Second, Matsumoto supported the policy of Japan's Southern advance because he believed that ethnology should work for the Japanese national interests. He had learnt the model for this in France. When he studied at Sorbonne University in Paris, he witnessed the establishment of the Institute of Ethnology with the support of the Ministry of Colonies in 1925.[44] In his article *From Paris*, he mentioned about "the necessity of ethnology for the colonial administration."[45] Therefore, following the model of the French ethnology, Matsumoto thought that it was his duty as an ethnologist to aid the Japanese policy toward Indochina. Similarly, he expressed his support for Pan-Asianism when it became the foundation of Japan's national policy in

---

43. Matsumoto, Nobuhiro "Indoshina wo mite," *Gaikō jihō*, dai 703 gō, Gaikō jihōsha, 15.03.1934, p. 137.
44. Matsumoto, Nobuhiro "Pari yori," *Minzoku*, dai 2 kan, dai 1 gō, Minzoku hakkōjo, 1926, p. 141.
45. Ibid.

the early 1940s. (See Section 3.)

Third, from the point that both ethnology and Southeast Asian studies were new disciplines to Japan, Matsumoto needed to gain support for their development. His research trip to Indochina could materialize due to the financial support from Keio University Mochidzuki Foundation, which was founded by entrepreneur Mochidzuki Gunshiro.[46] Mochidzuki Foundation mainly supported Chinese studies, as suggested by the title *First Ten Years of Mochidzuki Foundation's Chinese Research* (*Mochidzuki Shina kenkyū kikin daiichiji jūnenshi*).[47] In this sense, financing Matsumoto's stay in Indochina was an exception, but from the perspective of business opportunies, it was a logical step since Japan had just established economic relations with French Indochina while lacking information about this region. In this manner, Matsumoto grasped the opportunity brought by Japan's economic expansion in Southern direction to appeal the importance of his research and create conditions for the establishment of Southeast Asian studies in Japan.

Matsumoto's further trips to South Seas Islands and China also were financed by business circles (by Nanyo Kohatsu K. K. and Keio University Mochidzuki Foundation).[48] Fukuyama Industry Library provided a research room for him and his colleagues[49] working on the publication of *The Illustrated Catalogue of the Ethnographical Objects from Melanesia* that was sponsored by Nanyo Kohatsu K. K.[50] (See Chapter 3)

Moreover, he had contacts with many graduates of Keio Universi-

---

46. *Keiō gijuku Mochidzuki Shina kenkyū kikin daiichiji jūnenshi*, Keiō gijuku, 1937, p. 19.
47. *Keiō gijuku Mochidzuki Shina kenkyū kikin daiichiji jūnenshi*, Keiō gijuku, 1937.
48. Matsumoto, Nobuhiro "Waga Nan'yō wo miru," *Mita hyōron*, dai 483 gō, Mita hyōron hakkōjo, 1937, pp. 6-12. "Nan'yō guntō ryokō nisshi," *Shigaku*, dai 16 kan, dai 3 gō, Mita Shigakkai, 1937, pp. 77a-109. Matsumoto, Nobuhiro "Senseki junrei," *Mita hyōron*, dai 492 gō, Mita hyōron hakkōjo, 1938, p. 35.
49. Matsumoto, Nobuhiro *Nyū Ginia dozokuhin zushū: Nan'yō kōhatsu kabushiki gaisha shūshū*, jōkan, Minami no kai hen, Nan'yō kōhatsu, 1937, pp. 3, 5.
50. Ibid., p. 3.

ty who got jobs not only in the Japanese mainland but also in the territories under the Japanese rule. Matsumoto mentioned about meeting them on his trips in South Seas Islands[51] and China.[52] He advocated the idea that Keio graduates were suitable for working in companies in the South Seas[53] and expressed hope for expanding Keio authority in Central China.[54] Thus, through his affiliation with Keio University itself, he made an effort to create connections with persons of influence in economic and bureaucratic matters, which could be helpful for expanding his research.

3. Influence of Pan-Asianism on Matsumoto's research on Southeast Asia

3.1. Concept of Pan-Asianism

This section briefly introduces Pan-Asianism before progressing to the analysis of Matsumoto's works. Pan-Asianist influence on Matsumoto was limited to the period of Greater East Asia War. Moreover, the Pan-Asianist concept had been rather unrelated to Southeast Asia until this period. Therefore, this section does not cover the whole development of Pan-Asianism but focuses only on the period 1940–1945.

Pan-Asianism preached the need for deepening Japan's relations

---

51. Matsumoto, Nobuhiro "Nan'yō guntō ryokō nisshi," *Shigaku*, dai 16 kan, dai 3 gō, Mita Shigakkai, 1937, p. 109.
52. Matsumoto, Nobuhiro "Senseki junrei," *Mita hyōron*, dai 493 gō, Mita hyōron hakkōjo, 1938, p. 36.
53. "Now, people who are requested in the South Seas, especially in the forefront area, must be gentlemen who work as a member of a big company and can cooperate internationally. I must say that people like the graduates of Keio correspond to these requirements." Matsumoto, Nobuhiro "Waga Nan'yō wo miru," *Mita hyōron*, dai 483 gō, Mita hyōron hakkōjo, 1937, p. 11.
54. "But I am really happy that I could meet so many colleagues and students from Keio this summer. ... Almost nobody came from other universities. Hopefully, the authority of the Keio will advance rapidly in Central China like recently." Matsumoto, Nobuhiro "Senseki junrei," *Mita hyōron*, dai 493 gō, Mita hyōron hakkōjo, 1938, p. 36.

with Asian continent and supported Japan's expansion in the northern direction. The term Pan-Asianism was coined by Takeuchi Yoshimi (1910–1977) in his work *Asianism* (1963).⁵⁵ However, Takeuchi himself was reluctant to define it and chose to discuss its historical development starting from the Meiji period. He traced the history of Pan-Asianism from the Meiji period when Asianism emerged from the Japanese reaction to the encounter with the Western civilization. Takeuchi indicated Okakura Tenshin's ideas regarding the Japanese culture as the best of the Asian cultures and considered Japan as a leader and savior of unified Asia from the West. Furthermore, Takeuchi argued that Asianism developed into Pan-Asianism when the concept of common identity of Asian (Oriental) people and the concept of Japan's civilizing mission were adopted by the Japanese rightwing as an ideational background for the political concept of Greater East Asian Co-Prosperity Sphere. Thus, Takeuchi discussed Pan-Asianist aspects of the Japanese uniqueness, Japanese leadership (meishuron, 盟主論), common Asian identity (dōbun dōshu, 同文同種) and the Japanese civilizing mission (bunneika shukumei, 文明化宿命) in Asia.

After the publication of Takeuchi's *Asianism*, many scholars examined this problem. Generally, two aspects of Pan-Asianism were indicated: Japanese nationalism based on the idea of national polity (kokutai, 国体) and Japanese regionalism based on the idea of the Greater East Asia Co-Prosperity Sphere. The first aspect preached Japanese uniqueness coming from the sacred origin of the Japanese nation that legitimized the Japanese leadership of Asian nations. The second aspect emphasized the similarities between Japanese and Asian nations through which Japanese constructed common Asian identity in contrast to the West. From these points, many scholars, such as historians Yamamuro Shin'ichi, Sven Saaler, Christopher W. A. Szpilman, and Kimitada Miwa, argued that Pan-Asianism was an extension of the Japanese nationalism in the Asia-Pacific Region.⁵⁶

These previous researchers of Pan-Asianism explored the Japanese people's ideas regarding the region of Asia as a whole. However,

---

55. Takeuchi, Yoshimi *Ajiashugi*, Chikuma shobō, 1963.

they did not investigate Pan-Asianism of the scholars who were representatives of the Southward Theory, including Matsumoto Nobuhiro. Scholars like Matsumoto mainly wrote about Southeast Asia or about the Southern Pacific, that is the region of the South Seas. Therefore, the examination of Matsumoto's adoption of Pan-Asianism can contribute to understand how the advocates of the Southward Theory adapted their discussion on the South Seas to the context of Pan-Asianism.

From above, it is clear that Pan-Asianism was not originally associated with Southeast Asia. It began being applied to it only after Southeast Asia had been attached to East Asia in the concept of Greater East Asia Co-Prosperity Sphere when Japan fused its Northern advance to its Southern advance. Therefore, we can expect a shift in Matsumoto's arguments on Vietnam after his adoption of Pan-Asianism.

3.2. Matsumoto's reluctance toward Pan-Asianism

The incorporation of Southeast Asia into the national policy concept of Greater East Asia Co-Prosperity Sphere generated favorable conditions to further Matsumoto's work on the development of Southeast Asian studies in Japan. However, Matsumoto was originally against Pan-Asianism, so he was reluctant to fully accept it.

First, like in the case of Japan's Southern Advance Theory, he tried to negotiate with Pan-Asianism in favor of Southeast Asian studies. Therefore, he argued in favor of the need for ethnology for the improvement of Japanese policy toward Southeast Asia in his paper *Southern Cultural Policy and Ethnology*.[57] He appealed to the Japanese

---

56. Yamamuro, Shin'ichi *Shisō kadai to shiteno Ajia: kijiku-rensa-tōki*, Iwanami shoten, 2001, p. 630. *Pan-Asianism in Modern Japanese History. Colonialism, regionalism and borders*, ed. by Saaler, Sven and Koschmann, Victor J., London: Routledge Taylor & Francis Group, 2007. *Pan-Asianism*, Vol. 1 & Vol. 2, ed. by Saaler, Sven and Szpilman, Christopher W. A., New York: Rowman & Littlefield Publishers, Inc., 2011.
57. Matsumoto, Nobuhiro "Nampō bunka seisaku to minzokugaku," *Gaikō jihō*, dai 885 gō, Gaikō jihōsha, 15.10.1941, pp. 76, 78.

government that it should establish an ethnological institute and a museum to support the formation of a cultural policy.[58] He believed that ethnologists who conducted research on the local culture could mediate a true understanding of the local people: "The most necessary thing for the propagation work is to understand the other party; from this point of view, to think that the partner will immediately follow us just when we say that the partner is of the same race like us, that we are 'Asia Co-Prosperity Sphere,' that we are 'Eight Corners of One Universe,' without preparing anything more, that is a big mistake."[59] In short, Matsumoto emphasized the importance of ethnology in Southeast Asian studies for successful Japanese policy toward Southeast Asia while indicating the insufficiency of Pan-Asianist propaganda.

Furthermore, he did not accept the first aspect of Pan-Asianism — the Japanese uniqueness based on the sacred origins[60] — because, as a western-educated scholar, he considered scientific thinking as the top feature of civilization development that overcame religion based on unfounded beliefs. Matsumoto's stance is clear from his argument in his work *Theories of Ancient Culture*: "In the usual perspective, we have thinking that myths were born because man has fear of the natural forces and personifies the nature, that an interpretation of natural phenomena is the basis of myths; and there is also an idea that man believes in immortal soul, therefore he worships great men after their death as gods; thus, we can divide persons in myths to natural gods and human gods."[61] Thus, Matsumoto thought that myths and belief in supernatural power originate due to the human fear of natural phe-

---

58. Matsumoto, Nobuhiro "Nampō bunka seisaku to minzokugaku," *Gaikō jihō*, dai 885 gō, Gaikō jihōsha, 15.10.1941, pp. 76, 78.
59. Ibid., p. 77.
60. The belief in the sacred origin claimed the descent of Japanese Emperor from the Sun Goddess (Amaterasu Ōmikami) which was extended into an argument of superiority of the Japanese nation. This Pan-Asianist discourse claimed its credibitily by referring to the Japanese annals *Kojiki* (古事記) and *Nihonshoki* (日本書紀) from the eighth century.
61. Matsumoto, Nobuhiro "Kodai bunkaron," *Gendai shigaku taikei*, Vol. 10, Kyōritsusha shoten, 1932, p. 148.

nomena and death; therefore, he did not believe in the sacred origins in general.

Futhermore, as a comparative ethnologist, Matsumoto was not concerned about the Japanese uniqueness since he focused on common elements between ancient Japanese culture and other cultures. For example, in his book *The Research of the Japanese Myths*, he indicated the similarity between the Japanese and Korean myths on a sun deity and claimed the origin of the Japanese myth in Korea: "From the above mentioned legend, we can judge that the origin of Amanohiboko [a Japanese Sun Deity] is in Korea. In Korea, there are many legends where a king was miraculously born due to an influence of the sun, and the tale of Amanohiboko is one of them."[62] In this case, Matsumoto argued regarding the Korean cultural influence on the Japanese myth. However, in general, Matsumoto interpreted the resemblances as a result of the Southern influence or universal primitive culture. Therefore, by emphasizing the similarities between the Japanese and non-Japanese myths, Matsumoto showed that the story of imperial ancestors' sacred origin from the sun is not specific to Japanese but a common myth among many people.

Nonetheless, as it was already mentioned above, Matsumoto could not discuss the Japanese myths as "myths" because of the political pressure. He could observe growing aversion against the academic discussion on the Japanese myths that undermined the belief in the Japanese people's sacred origin in the case of the so-called Tsuda Incident. In 1940, historian Tsuda Sokichi (1873-1961) was criticized and even imprisoned for denying the credibility of the chronicles *Kojiki* and *Nihonshoki* containing the myths of imperial ancestors.[63] This incident considerably impacted Matsumoto because Matsumoto's teacher Yanagita maintained a close relationship with Tsuda from the 1910s, when they research the Japanese tradition.[64] Therefore, it is easy to understand why Matsumoto chose not to present his opinions regard-

---

62. Matsumoto, Nobuhiro *Nihon shinwa no kenkyū*, Dōbunka, 1931, p. 258.
63. Yusa, Michiko *Zen and Philosophy: An Intellectual Biography of Nishida Kitarô*, University of Hawai'i Press, Honolulu, 2002, p. 305.

ing the imperial origins and avoided the discussion on the Japanese imperial myths in the 1940s.

Therefore, he came up with a different argument of the Japanese uniqueness that seemed to be scientific. In his paper *The Ethnic-Historical Meaning of the Greater East Asian War*, he claimed as follows: "There is no doubt that there was a peculiar ethnic group (*koyū minzoku*, 固有民族) residing in our Yamato Shimane from prehistory, two elements of Southern and Northern Asia arrived to this [ethnic group], and formed here our nation. In short, both from the cultural perspective and from the constitution, our nation contains both elements of Southern and Northern Asia together, so it has sufficient adaptability to develop northward and southward."[65] Therefore, Matsumoto provided the legitimization for the Japanese expansion in Asia-Pacific through an ethnological interpretation of foreign influence on the Japanese nation instead of legitimizing it by the Japanese sacred origin.

Matsumoto's ethnological interpretation of the Japanese origins reflected the Pan-Asianist concept of common Asian identity because it argued regarding the inclusion of South Asian and North Asian elements. However, since Matsumoto did not explain about the peculiar ethnic group residing in Yamato Shimane, the above-mentioned quotation in *The Ethnic-Historical Meaning of the Greater East Asian War* does not contain Matsumoto's opinion on the Japanese uniqueness. In general, he rarely discussed contemporary Japan in his writings and mainly looked into the similarities between Japan and other regions, especially with Indochina. Therefore, Matsumoto's writings reveal about Japan's similarities with Indochina, but they lack information about the Japanese uniqueness. This implies that he only believed in

---

64. Yusa, Michiko *Zen and Philosophy: An Intellectual Biography of Nishida Kitarô*, Honolulu: University of Hawai'i Press, 2002, p. 305.
   Masuo, Shinichirō "Reimei-ki no Kiki shinwa kenkyū o meguru dōkō : Tsuda Sōkichi to Takagi Toshio, Yanagita Kunio wo chūshin ni," *Shiryō to shite no "Nihonshoki": Tsuda Sōkichi o yomi naosu*, Bensei shuppan, 2011, pp. 406–422.
65. Matsumoto, Nobuhiro "Daitōa sensō no minzoku shitekina igi, *Gaikō jihō*, dai 893 gō, Gaikō jihōsha, 15.02.1942, p. 55–56.

the Japanese superiority and considered the Japanese to be the most westernized among Asian people, under the influence of Orientalism.

3.3. Pan-Asianist elements in Matsumoto's works on Indochina

In Matsumoto's writings about Indochina, we can mainly find the second aspect of Pan-Asianism — Japanese regionalism — preaching Japanese leadership, Japan's civilizing mission, and common Oriental identity.

First, Matsumoto promoted Pan-Asianist propaganda by claiming the need for the Japanese leadership over Indochinese people. For example, he mentioned about the leadership toward the primitive people: "Moi people residing in Southern mountains of Indochina are Austro-Asiatic people; they are not Indianized like residents of plains; they continue protecting primitive culture. ... I met Moi people who came from mountains of Hue; they were naked with red loincloth, they were completely primitive children. ... They are people completely outside the political authority; thus their education and leading must be regarded as very problematic at first."[66]

He also insisted on Japan's leadership of more civilized Burmese and Vietnamese. In his paper *Rise and Fall of the Ethnics in Indochina*, he stated as follows: "Burmese are 1m 62–63 high people, of robust constitution, middle headed with docile character; they are a promising nation: if they receive good leadership as soldiers, they will become the first-class soldiers; we can expect much of them in the future."[67] He also recommended Japan's leadership to the Vietnamese in his paper *Southern Cultural Policy and Ethnology*: "When I looked at the textbooks which they, the Annamese, use, I was surprised that their political conscience is completely removed and their national feeling is castrated. Therefore, it is only natural that the Annamese do not understand what is to love homeland and they are apathetic and blind. ...thus, a plan should be considered to make them flourish in the

---

66. Matsumoto, Nobuhiro "Futsuryō Indoshina no minzoku," *Nan'yō*, dai 27 kan, dai 7 gō, 1940, p. 33.
67. Matsumoto, Nobuhiro "Indoshina ni okeru minzoku no kōbō," *Shin Ajia*, Mantetsu Tōa keizai chōsakyoku, Nampō bunka tokugō, 1940, 1gatsu, p. 67.

East Asia Co-Prosperity Sphere."[68]

However, Matsumoto's opinion collides with his knowledge that the Vietnamese had patriotic movements led by nationalist leaders, such as Phan Bội Châu,[69] or Communist leaders, such as Nguyễn Ái Quốc, that he mentioned in his papers.[70] In this light, the adoption of Pan-Asianist rhetoric made Matsumoto compromise with his own ideas regarding Indochina.

Second, he continued to advocate Japan's civilizing mission to Vietnamese people. Nonetheless, he changed his interpretation of the civilizing mission from the one he had borrowed from Japan's Southern Advance Theory in the 1930s. Under the influence of Pan-Asianism, he avoided mentioning Japanese-French friendship; in addition to recommending the teaching of westernized Japanese culture to the Vietnamese, he insisted that the Vietnamese should learn Sinicized culture from the Japanese. He wrote as follows: "For the revival of the Annamese people as a part of the East Asia Co-Prosperity Sphere, Annamese should learn the Chinese writing again to some extent, understand the political perspective, the attitude to the life from the Oriental morality and they need to have a significant understanding about the past of their ancestors."[71] This shift in his argument clearly reflected the Pan-Asianist concept of common Asian identity based on

---

68. Matsumoto, Nobuhiro "Nampō bunka seisaku to minzokugaku," *Gaikō jihō*, dai 885 gō, Gaikō jihōsha, 15.10.1941, p. 79.
69. "Confucianist Phan Bội Châu came to Japan, met with interested figures outside the government in order to gathered like-minded persons, learn progress from Japan and ask for [Japanese] help for attaining Annam's independence." Matsumoto, Nobuhiro "Futsuryō Indoshina no minzoku to bunka" *Sosei futsuryō indoshina no zenbō*, Aikoku shinbunsha shuppanbu, 1941, p. 45.
70. "When talking about the Communist movement, we must not forget Nguyễn Ái Quốc. He became sailor in 18, went to France, became communist revolutionary, his famous petition that is requirement of Annamese people [for the independence] was distributed to Lloyd George, Wilson, Clemenceau, etc." Matsumoto, Nobuhiro "Futsuin no minzoku mondai," *Shin Ajia*, Mantetsu Tōa keizai chōsakyoku, 1940, 8gatsu, p. 35.
71. Matsumoto, Nobuhiro "Annan go to Mon-Kumeru go," *Nihongo*, 2-5, Nampō kensetsu to Nihongo, Nihongo kyōiku shinkōkai, dai 5 gō, 1942, p. 41.

the idea of Greater East Asia Co-Prosperity Sphere, which gave more importance to East Asia, represented by the Chinese cultural sphere, than to Southern regions.

Matsumoto's words express this application of the concept of China-centered Oriental identity on Vietnamese people: "It is necessary to say that if Annamese shall truly extend their individuality, they need to learn from Japan that is of the same culture and same race, and that adopted Chinese culture like them."[72] This kind of argumentation was atypical for Matsumoto who concentrated on similarities between Southeast Asian culture and Japanese culture before they were influenced by Chinese and Indian civilizations. Thus, under Pan-Asianist influence, Matsumoto adjusted his argument on Japan's civilizing mission so that it fits the concept of common Oriental identity centered on Sinicized culture.

This Pan-Asianist argument is not logical because Matsumoto knew from his trip to Indochina (1933) that the majority of the Vietnamese people still kept their traditional Sinicized culture. Moreover, he knew that only Vietnamese who received French education were westernized, as it can be seen from his argument in his paper *French Indochinese peoples* (1940): "...such Asian intelligentsia broke up with the Asian tradition, was educated according to the European thinking and feeling and gave a weak feeling of being out of their environment."[73] Therefore, it is clear that Matsumoto argued regarding the transmission of the Sinicized culture from Japan to Vietnam because he wanted to put his discussion on Vietnam in the Pan-Asianist context.

Matsumoto recommended the Vietnamese people to learn Chinese writings from the Japanese people because he knew about the significance of the Chinese writing in the Vietnamese history.[74] He

---

72. Matsumoto, Nobuhiro "Futsuin no minzoku mondai," *Shin Ajia*, Mantetsu Tōa keizai chōsakyoku, 1940, 8gatsu, p. 37.
73. Matsumoto, Nobuhiro "Futsuryō Indoshina no minzoku," *Nan'yō*, dai 27 kan, dai 7 gō, 1940, p. 29.
74. Matsumoto, Nobuhiro "Annan go," *Sekai no kotoba*, Keiō gijuku daigaku gogaku kenkyūjohen, Keiō shuppansha, 1943, pp. 74, 78.

thought that the Vietnamese should be able to read Chinese writing to connect with their roots: "Now the Annamese newspapers, journals, paper backs, and all the Annamese books are recorded in *quốc ngữ*.[75] But, stopping the use of Chinese characters is definitely not a good thing for the Annamese; all kinds of literature and arts, such as important history, geography, politics, law in their past documents, were recorded in the Chinese characters; the young Annamese who cannot read them are completely cut off from their past and sadly lost their cultural tradition."[76]

Furthermore, Matsumoto presented the revival of the Oriental civilization, i. e., Sinicized civilization, as a first step in the development of the Asian nations. He suggested that "Orientals first must awaken to their own tradition before they adopt the products of the Western civilization"[77] and, that they must "based themselves on the Asian tradition" and then "input the Western European culture."[78] This argument contradicts the logic of evolutionism in which Matsumoto believed. He considered the Western civilization to be the highest stage of the cultural evolution. Therefore, he should not have felt the need to revive the Oriental civilization because it should have been replaced by superior Western civilization. In addition, the argument of the revival of the Oriental civilization was not present in Matsumoto's writings in the 1930s, which means that he borrowed it from Pan-Asiniasm in the first half of the 1940s.

Simultaneously, Matsumoto also criticized the diffusion of the Japanese civilization to primitive Asian-Pacific people. Matsumoto's opinion appeared in his writings in 1937. It came from his experience of the Japanization of aborigine peoples in the Southern Pacific, which he could observe during his trip to Saipan in 1937. He learnt that Japanized islanders of Palau could not show their traditional dance any-

---

75. Quốc ngữ = Latinized Vietnamese writing.
76. Matsumoto, Nobuhiro "Annan go," *Sekai no kotoba*, Keiō gijuku daigaku gogaku kenkyūjohen, Keiō shuppansha, 1943, p. 78.
77. Matsumoto, Nobuhiro "Futsuryō Indoshina no minzoku," *Nan'yō*, dai 27 kan, dai 7 gō, 1940, p. 52.
78. Ibid., pp. 29–30.

more.[79] In his paper *Seeing Our South Seas*, he stated as follows: "...they [the Japanese in Palau] continue painful effort to teach them [the Southern Pacific peoples] the Japanese language; but when I think that the islanders will forget their tradition as a result of this complete assimilative education, and that this will accelerate the disassemblement of the social structure, it makes me sad."[80] Therefore, Matsumoto began criticizing Japan's civilizing mission in the Southern Pacific because he was against the disappearance of the islanders' local tradition.

Matsumoto's wish for the preservation of the local culture was visible in his paper *Travel Diary to Southern Islands (Saipan, Yap, Palau, New Guinea)*: "I have heard in Tokyo that Abai[81] of all the Palau Island are protected as monuments by the South Sea Office, but in reality, only Abai in Koror island is protected, I am truly sorry that the other places are disregarded. ...I really want to ask the South Sea Office to keep in mind the protection of the monuments of local culture."[82]

As a result of his experience in the Southern Pacific in 1937, Matsumoto criticized the forced transmission of the Japanese civilization to the Southeast Asian people in the first half of the 1940s. In his writing *The Southern Cultural Policy and Ethnology*, he disagreed with the existing Japanese way of civilizing indigenous peoples: "... I truly regret to hear about the tragedy that sanctuaries from ancient times have been recently destroyed in our colonies in the name of 'the Movement of the Imperial Nationalization' [kōminka undo, 皇民化運動], ... please let them [local people] to have at least what they have been worshipping as aborigines for centuries; this sympathizing com-

---

79. Matsumoto, Nobuhiro "Waga Nan'yō wo miru," *Mita hyōron*, dai 483 gō, Mita hyōron hakkōjo, 1937, p. 8.
80. Ibid.
81. Abai is meeting house where people join to talk internal affairs and lodge visitors.
82. Matsumoto, Nobuhiro "Waga Nan'yō wo miru," *Mita hyōron*, dai 483 gō, Mita hyōron hakkōjo, 1937, pp. 6-12. "Nan'yō guntō ryokō nisshi," *Shigaku*, dai 16 kan, dai 3 gō, Mita Shigakkai, 1937, pp. 77.

plaint is heard in the classrooms of ethnology at universities."[83] Furthermore, he wrote in the same paper as follows: "The harmony of the ruler and the ruled ones is possible only if the customs of the [ruled] nation are respected and if the sufficient consideration is paid to its habits and thinking."[84] From these quotations, it is obvious that Matsumoto thought that the transmission of the Japanese culture to the Southeast Asian people was undesirable.

In this light, Matsumoto's writings in the 1930s and 1940s revealed that Matsumoto had different opinions on the Japanese civilizing mission toward the Vietnamese people and toward the Southern Pacific islanders. From the evolutionist perspective, the Vietnamese were semi-civilized people and the Southern Pacific islanders were barbarians. These islanders were holders of the primitive culture that Matsumoto researched as an ethnologist. Matsumoto's writing in 1937 demonstrated his attitude toward the local people in the Southern Pacific as his research objects. He called the Southern Pacific Islands "a treasury for racial and ethnological studies."[85] Apparently, he strongly wished for the preservation of the living culture of the primitive people for the research purpose and advocated Japan's civilizing mission to semi-civilized people whose contemporary culture was not the target of his ethnological interest.

However, Matsumoto was aware of this dilemma between the preservation of tradition and the import of new civilization. This is expressed in his paper *Travel Diary to Southern Islands (Saipan, Yap, Palau, New Guinea)*: "My idea is that it is necessary to keep their tradition for them to some extent, but when speaking from experience of the practical person, it is not simple, it seems that we cannot clearly attain both keeping the old habits and improvement."[86] Thus, Matsumoto had doubts concerning the transmission of the Japanese culture

---

83. Matsumoto, Nobuhiro "Nampō bunka seisaku to minzokugaku," *Gaikō jihō*, dai 885 gō, Gaikō jihōsha, 15.10.1941, p. 75.
84. Ibid., p. 75.
85. Matsumoto, Nobuhiro "Nan'yō guntō ryokō nisshi," *Shigaku*, dai 16 kan, dai 3 gō, Mita Shigakkai, 1937, p. 77.
86. Ibid., p. 108.

in relation to the primitive people. In this way, some Pan-Asianist arguments were acceptable to Matsumoto to some extent.

3.4. Matsumoto's contribution to the Pan-Asianist policy toward Southeast Asia

Matsumoto's ethnological and linguistic research emphasizing the similarities between the Japanese and Indochinese cultures was useful for the Pan-Asianist propaganda of common Asian identity. However, since it focused on primitive culture, its use for Pan-Asianist policy toward Southeast Asia was questionable. Therefore, this section explores which Matsumoto's works were useful for the Japanese policy toward Southeast Asia.

Matsumoto was among the Japanese scholars who were mobilized by the Japanese Pan-Asianist government. Yatsugi Kazuo, who examined the history of research activities for the state policy, listed Matsumoto among scholars in the Committee for Ethnic Issues (*Minzoku mondai iinkai*, 民族問題委員会), collecting information on the contemporary situation in Southeast Asia and discussing Japanese measures for it.[87]

Chapter 4 demonstrated that Matsumoto propagated the study of Southeast Asian languages for building the Greater East Asia Co-Prosperity Sphere. He presented papers introducing Southeast Asian languages to the Japanese readers. In particular, his book *Introduction to the Annamese Language* was significant because it was the first Japanese textbook of the Vietnamese language.[88] Matsumoto's linguistical writings about Southeast Asian languages were useful for the Pan-Asianist policy because they provided the knowledge of these languages in a situation when Japan gradually took control over Southeast Asia.

In addition, Matsumoto contributed to the Japanese policy by presenting three papers on contemporary Indochina: *Aspects of Indochi-*

---

87. Yatsugi, Kazuo *Shōwa dōran shishi*, chū, Keizai ōraisha, 1971, p. 207.
88. Matsumoto, Nobuhiro *Annango nyūmon. Bunpōhen*, Indoshina kenkyūkai, 1942, p. 2. *Annango nyūmon. Kaiwahen*, Indoshina kenkyūkai, 1942.

nese peoples,[89] *The Problem of Peoples of French Indochina*,[90] and *Peoples and Cultures of French Indochina*.[91] This is a small number in comparison with his publications on linguistic and ethnological research. This reflects that Matsumoto lacked enthusiasm to deal with contemporary issues, which were a priority for Pan-Asianist government. This was because Matsumoto focused on primitive people.

In his papers on contemporary Indochina, Matsumoto focused on the Vietnamese people's situation. He focused on the connection between the Vietnamese peasants' problems and the growing influence of Communism. He discussed the topic in his paper *Aspects of Indochinese peoples*: "... the gap between the poor peasants and rich people promotes the encroachment of Communism. In early 1929, the Communist Party secretly emphasized the inequality of Indochinese people and plotted the revolution movement."[92] He also described the spread of Communism in Vietnam in his paper *The Problem of Peoples of French Indochina*: "Annamese village is a kind of autonomy, the village administration is managed by the elderly class called notables, and many of leaders are nationalists so they retained neutrality towards the Communist movement. The Communist Party capitalizes on it, provides dissatisfied elements in the countryside with the propaganda documents in the Romanized writing quốc ngữ which is now used in Annam..."[93]

Furthermore, Matsumoto also wrote an article about the new Vietnamese religion, Caodaism. He discussed Caodaism on four pages in his paper *Peoples and Cultures of French Indochina*.[94] After summa-

---

89. Matsumoto, Nobuhiro "Futsuryō Indoshina jin no shosō," *Gaikō jihō*, Gaikō jihōsha, dai 850 gō, May 1940.
90. Matsumoto, Nobuhiro "Futsuin no minzoku mondai," *Shin Ajia*, Mantetsu Tōa keizai chōsakyoku, 1940, 8gatsu.
91. Matsumoto, Nobuhiro "Futsuryō Indoshina no minzoku to bunka," *Sosei futsuryō Indoshina no zenbō*, Aikoku shinbunsha shuppanbu, 1941, pp. 64–67.
92. Matsumoto, Nobuhiro "Futsuryō Indoshina jin no shosō," *Gaikō jihō*, Gaikō jihōsha, dai 850 gō, May 1940, p. 138.
93. Matsumoto, Nobuhiro "Futsuin no minzoku mondai," *Shin Ajia*, Mantetsu Tōa keizai chōsakyoku, 1940nen 8gatsu, pp. 35–36.

rizing the growing popularity of Cao Đài sect in Vietnam, Matsumoto expressed sympathy for this new religion: "In this vibrant time when trying to understand the society and the form of government of one country and make them reform, this kind of the religion always flourishes in the Oriental state, if those things [like Caodaism] are not used, it is impossible to make the ignorant masses move. At this point, Caodaism is a religious movement which surely cannot be disregarded in present French Indochina; we can say that it has revolutionary significance."[95] In this manner, Matsumoto presented Caodaism as a beneficial tool of Japanese control over the Vietnamese people.

From these writings, it is apparent that Matsumoto followed the news of the contemporary situation in Indochina. He had access to the news from French Indochina most likely because of his relations with the EFEO and his knowledge of the French language. The choice of Communism and Caodaism suggests that Matsumoto discussed topics that were at the center of Japanese attention in relation to Indochina. It is because the Communist movement hindered the Japanese interests there. In contrast, Caodaism was regarded positively because its followers cooperated with the Japanese Army. Hence, Matsumoto discussed the contemporary problems of Indochina that were most attractive from the perspective of the Japanese official policy in Indochina.

Within this context of the Japanese interest in Indochina, Matsumoto emphasized contemporary China and Manchuria. For example, he indicated the threat of Chinese Communism for Indochina in his paper *Rise and Fall of Peoples in Indochina*: "Also the Chinese themselves will probably enter Indochina if they are pushed from north. In particular, if they follow the Kublai route, the power of the Communist Party may infiltrate Indochina. I remember that French publicists at the time of the Manchurian Incident discussed the spread of Communism in Asia and said that the Japan's activity in Manchuria was

---

94. Matsumoto, Nobuhiro "Futsuryō Indoshina no minzoku to bunka," *Sosei futsuryō Indoshina no zenbō*, Aikoku shinbunsha shuppanbu, 1941, pp. 64–67.
95. Ibid., p. 67.

against the Red imperialism, and thus defended Asia."[96] Except from this opinion, there is basically no mention of contemporary China and Manchuria in Matsumoto's writings. Thus, as a representative of the Southward Theory, Matsumoto rarely discussed China and Manchuria although they formed the core of the Greater East Asia Co-Prosperity Sphere together with Japan. In summary, Matsumoto's contribution to Japan's policy in the period 1940–1945 was limited due to his specialization in the ethnology of Southeast Asia.

4. Conclusion

This chapter examined the influence of Japan's Southern Advance Theory and Pan-Asianism on Matsumoto's writings during 1933–1945. The analysis showed that Matsumoto borrowed some arguments from these theories. However, he cannot be considered as their representative because his main purpose was to make use of them for the propagation of Southeast Asian studies in Japan.

In accord with Japan's Southern Advance Theory, he advocated Japan's economic expansion to Indochina with French cooperation and the transmission of the Japanese westernized culture to the Vietnamese. He had three reasons for it. He was pro-French oriented, followed the French model of an ethnologist who works for the country, and wanted to gain support for his research on Southeast Asia. Thus, he was indebted to Japanese enterpreneurs and other people, who were involved in Japanese advance in South Seas and China. According to Shimizu, the Southern Advance Theory in this period had some Asiatic influence, but this cannot be seen in Matsumoto's works. Indeed, Matsumoto expressed his disagreement with Pan-Asianism in the 1930s.

However, during 1940–1945, he was forced to accept the Pan-Asianist arguments of the Japanese leadership over Indochinese peo-

---

96. Matsumoto, Nobuhiro "Indoshina ni okeru minzoku no kōbō," *Shin Ajia*, Mantetsu Tōa keizai chōsakyoku, Nampō bunka tokugō, 1940, 1gatsu, p. 68.

ple and transmission of Japanese Sinicized culture to Vietnamese people based on the concept of common Oriental identity. This signified a shift in comparison with his opinions coming from the Southern Advance Theory. At the same time, he advocated the preservation of primitive culture and never supported the sacred origin of the Japanese. The shift was caused by the fact that these theories were originally based on different geographical and cultural concepts and that they contained different approaches to Japan's expansion.

In addition, as indicated by Sakurai Yumio, Matsumoto distanced himself from his support to the Southern Advance Theory and Pan-Asianism in 1971 when he defined Southeast Asian studies as an antithesis of colonialism and Oriental studies based on ancient documents.[97] This means that Matsumoto abandoned his advocation of ethnology for the colonial policy in the postwar period. This is because he became aware that the world criticized the ethnologists' connection to colonialism, especially when he witnessed that one of his close fellow researchers, Pan-Asianist Ōkawa Shūmei, was prosecuted as a class-A war criminal by Tokyo War Crimes Tribunal after the war.[98]

Nevertheless, Matsumoto's works did not impact the formation of Japan's policy although he explained to military men that ethnology was important for effective cultural policy toward Southeast Asia. His advices were never put in practice.[99] It is questionable to what extent his research would have improved the policy because it focused on primitive culture and was biased by evolutionism and Orientalism.

---

97. Sakurai, Yumio "Tōnan Ajia shi no yonjūnen," *Tōnan Ajia shi. Kenkyū no hatten*, Tōnan Ajia Gakkai 40 shūnen, Kinen jigyō iinkai, Yamakawa shuppansha, 2009, pp. 12-13.
98. Chikamori said that Matsumoto appreciated Ōkawa Shūmei as a researcher in Islam and therefore he was strongly affected by Ōkawa's persecution and worried about his own life. Interview with Chikamori Masashi, 23 October 2012, Keio University, Tokyo.
99. National Museum of Ethnology (Kokuritsu Minzoku Hakubutsukan, 国立民族博物館 was not established until 1974, and moreover in Osaka, not in Tokyo, which meant big disappointment for Matsumoto who developed huge effort for its establishing for many years.

Moreover, Japanese advance into Southeast Asia was useful for his research, so he was motivated to follow the change in the political environment, especially when some advance-oriented enterpreners provided him with financial and other resources for his academic activities. Nevertheless, it is true that Matsumoto's effort in establishing Southeast Asian studies in Japan did not spring from economic or political reasons but from real interest in primitive Southeast Asian culture.

Conclusion

The case of the Japanese scholar Matsumoto during 1919–1945 showed that his prewar perspective of Southeast Asia focused on Southeast Asian culture and was shaped by many theories more or less connected to ethnology and Oriental history. This study traced his growing interest in Southeast Asian culture, which culminated in establishing Southeast Asian studies in Japan during 1933–1945. It was found out that Matsumoto made use of the Japanese economical and political ambitions for the propagation and development of Southeast Asian studies in the same period. In other words, Matsumoto's aim in Southeast Asia was its culture, and Japan's economical and political advance into the same region spurred the expansion of his academic activities.

The overview of the formation and development of Matsumoto's ideas regarding Southeast Asian culture during 1919–1945 is presented in Table 5 below. The table indicates that Matsumoto started studying about the Southeast Asian people as a result of his study of evolutionist ethnology in the early 1920s and began focusing on Southeast Asia as a part of the Japanese geographical concept of the South Seas in the second half of the 1920s owing to the diffusionist influence during his study in France. Upon his return to Japan, he became the founder of Southeast Asian studies in the 1930s when he adopted the Western geographical concept of Southeast Asia from Western research materials that he brought from French Indochina in 1933. He presented many papers on Southeast Asian culture and history, taught regarding Southeast Asian people in his classes of ethnology at Keio University, and further developed Southeast Asian studies at the same university during 1933–1945. To propagate the new disciplines of ethnology and

Table 5: Summary of Matsumoto Nobuhiro's ideas regarding Southeast Asia during 1919–1945

Period, location	Theories in Matsumoto's writings	Geographical names related to Southeast Asia
1919–1923, Japan, China, Korea, Manchuria	Unilinear evolutionism based on universalism, animism, totemism, theory of magic	No geographical name (only names of Southeast Asian peoples)
1924–1932, Japan, France	Multilinear evolutionism, unilinear evolutionism based on universalism, sociology (theory of gift and potlatch, etc.), totemism, diffusionism	The South Seas
1933–1939, Japan, Indochina, the Southern Pacific Islands, China	Multilinear evolutionism, social Darwinism, diffusionism, Orientalism, Climate Theory	The South Seas, Southeast Asia,
1940–1945, Japan	Multilinear evolutionism, social Darwinism, diffusionism, Orientalism, Climate Theory, Pan-Asianism	The South Seas, Southeast Asia

Southeast Asian studies, he borrowed some arguments from Japan's Southern Advance Theory and Pan-Asianism, which consequently gave political significance to his works written during 1933–1945.

In this manner, Matsumoto incorporated multiple theories in his writings about Southeast Asia, which resulted in many contradictions in his opinions. Some contradictions sprang from the fact that these theories were imperfect and that Matsumoto's adoption of these theories was rather superficial. Some other inconsistences were caused by Matsumoto's effort to receive support for Southeast Asian studies by advocating contemporary policies. Consequently, Matsumoto's ideas regarding Southeast Asian and Indochina, as they can be reconstructed from his writings, are ambiguous and reflect prejudices of contemporary Japanese people toward the region. Matsumoto's case shows that scholars of minor disciplines can be vulnerable to political and social pressures.

Matsumoto's ideas regarding Southeast Asia were influenced by various schools of ethnology — evolutionist, sociologist, and diffusionist ethnology. Table 5 shows that Matsumoto was an evolutionist ethnologist in the beginning before adopting sociologist and diffusionist theories from 1924, but he transformed somewhat into a diffusionist ethnologist during 1924–1945 since diffusionism gradually prevailed in Japanese ethnology. This finding is in contradiction with previous research (namely Hirafuji) that characterized Matsumoto mainly as a representative of sociologist ethnology in Japan. Moreover, the analysis of Matsumoto's writings demonstrated that his ideas regarding Southeast Asian culture did not exhibit a sufficient sociologist approach because he did not focus on Southeast Asian society but on Southeast Asian culture.

Matsumoto chose to follow diffusionist ethnology because he wanted to join the discourse on Southeast Asia, which was developed by Western diffusionist ethnologists, and because diffusionist ethnology became the mainstream in Japanese ethnology in the 1930s and the 1940s. This enabled him to become the founder of Southeast Asian studies in Japan. The significance of diffusionism based on multilinear evolutionism and social Darwinism for his establishment of Southeast Asian studies is apparent from Table 5, where evolutionist and sociological theories (totemism, theory of the gift, etc.) disappeared from Matsumoto's writings during 1933–1945 (except one paper *On Banko Legend*[1]) when Matsumoto concentrated on Southeast Asia under the diffusionist influence.

The diffusionist approach to Southeast Asia made Matsumoto an advocator of Southward Theory that preached the significance of the

---

1. Matsumoto, Nobuhiro "Banko densetsu ni tsuite" *Tōkyō jinrui gakkai Nihon minzoku gakkai rengō taikai dai 4-kai kiji*, Tōkyō jinrui gakkai Nihon minzoku gakkai rengō taikai jimusho, 1939, pp. 108–112.

South Seas for Japan. Inspired by Western and Japanese scholars (Przyluski, Rivet, Yanagita, etc.), Matsumoto sometimes argued regarding the Southern influence on the Japanese culture. Previous researchers interpreted this as Matsumoto's search for the Japanese origins in Southeast Asia or Matsumoto's advocation of Southern genealogy in the Japanese culture. This book demonstrated that Matsumoto did not argue about the Japanese origins in the South and claimed close relations between Japan and Southeast Asia. Moreover, it was shown that Matsumoto's argument of Japan's connection with Southeast Asia was the result of the diffusionist influence.

Despite this importance of diffusionism, Matsumoto's conclusion on Japan's relation with Southeast Asia was not based on the Japanese origins in Southeast Asia because he shared Yanagita's argument that similarities between two cultures do not mean foreign origins for one of the compared cultures. Moreover, Matsumoto did not always argue regarding Southern influence on the Japanese culture when indicating similarities between Japan and Southeast Asia. This reveals that although Matsumoto began focusing on Southeast Asia as a result of diffusionist influence and adopted diffusionist theories on Southeast Asia, Matsumoto's ideas regarding Southeast Asia were not purely diffusionist. He reached a compromise among diffusionist, evolutionist, and sociologist approaches, which was comparing of the similarities between Japan and Southeast Asia without drawing a conclusion on their meaning.

Matsumoto focused on the similarities between Japanese and Southeast Asian cultures from the very beginning when he started his academic career as an evolutionist ethnologist. Although his interpretations of these similarities were ambiguous, it seems clear that he believed in their deep significance. This belief drove his effort to develop Southeast Asian studies in the postwar period when he urged his students to research Southeast Asia. His students, such as Kawamoto or Chikamori, did not conduct their research on Southeast Asia based on Matsumoto's findings but rather on his direct instigation. According to Roustan, Kawamoto admitted that Matsumoto's recommendation to study about Southeast Asia played an important role in his decision to specialize on Vietnam.[2] Furthermore, Matsumoto provided Kawamoto with sufficient conditions for his Vietnamese study by inviting him to become a full-time researcher at the Keio Institute of Cultural and Linguistic Studies.[3]

Furthermore, Chikamori said that Matsumoto asked him to do research on Cambodian culture.[4] For example, Chikamori examined the ritual in which a shaman presented mountain products to the Cambodian king Sihanouk.[5] Matsumoto was keen to know about this ritual because he learnt about it from Frazer's book *The Golden Bough* wherein Frazer described the shaman as king-magician who had a similar religious-political role like priests in ancient Japan.[6] Furthermore, Matsumoto observed the progress of the excavation of the ancient boats in Japan, which he considered to be important for his theories on the sea route connection between Japan and Southeast Asia.[7] Chikamori recollected the time Matsumoto asked him during the excavation works of the boats if they had found a boat similar to the boats engraved on Đông Sơn drums in Vietnam.[8]

Matsumoto delegated research tasks to his students since he himself did not do field work. According to Chikamori, Matsumoto did not know how to conduct ethnological field work or archaeological

---

2. Roustan, Frédéric "From Oriental Studies to South Pacific Studies: The Multiple Origins of Vietnamese Studies," *Journal of Vietnamese Studies*, Vol. 6, Issue 1, 2011, p. 20.
3. Interview with Chikamori Masashi, 23 August 2012, Keio University, Tokyo.
4. Ibid.
5. Ibid.
6. Matsumoto, Nobuhiro "Annan shiryō ni arawareru Indoshina sanchi minzoku," *Andō kyōju kanreki Shukuga kinenronbunshū*, Andō kyōju kanreki Shukuga kinenkaihen, Sanseidō, 1940, p. 1010.
7. Shimizu, Junzō "Kaisetsu," *Nihon minzoku bunka no kigen II: kodai no fune, Nihongo to Nampōgo* Kōdansha, 1978, pp. 403–408.
   Mabuchi, Tōichi "Odayaka de fukutsu no daisempai," *Nihon minzoku bunka no kigen*, dai 2 kan, geppō dai 2 gō, Kōdansha, 1978, p. 3.
8. Chikamori, Masashi "Minzokugaku kōkogaku kenkyūshitsu no Kujūkuri chōsa," *Keiō gijuku daigaku daigakuin shakaigaku kenkyū kiyō. Ningen to shakai no tankyū. Kujūkuri chōsa*, Keiō gijuku daigaku daigakuin shakaigaku kenkyūka, 2013, p. 236.

excavations and was not willing to learn it.[9] Matsumoto preferred to keep a distance and stay in the observer's position although he advocated the preservation of the native culture of primitive people. For example, he refused to greet Polynesians by their custom of rubbing the noses when he visited Chikamori during an ethnoarchaeological research on Rennel Island.[10] Hence, Matsumoto's efforts to collect evidence for his hypotheses of Japan's connection with Southeast Asia from his students' field research resulted in the development of Southeast Asian studies. In this sense, Matsumoto is rightfully remembered as an initiator of many projects at Keio University.

Another feature of Matsumoto's research on Southeast Asia is that he almost remained silent about Islam. He mentioned it only in a few cases: when he indicated the adoption of Islam by Cham people[11] and the Islamic influence in Malaysia[12] and when he wrote about Arabic influence and struggles between Muslims and Portuguese in the trade in Southeast Asia.[13] It is because he considered Islam as a higher culture than the primitive one, which was his main research target. In addition, Islam was the speciality of Izutsu Toshikiho (1914-1993), who worked in the same department at Keio University with Matsumoto.[14] Therefore, Matsumoto was also reluctant to interfere in the sphere of Izutsu's interest.

In the postwar period, Matsumoto continued to focus on Japan's connection with Southeast Asia in cooperation with Yanagita. As Chikamori emphasized, Matsumoto's opinion that "Ancient Japanese

---

9. Interview with Chikamori Masashi, 13 October 2012, Keio University, Tokyo.
10. Ibid.
11. Matsumoto, Nobuhiro "Indoshina minzoku," *Iwanami kōza Tōyō shichō*, I (Tōyō no minzoku, Tōyō no shakai), Iwanami shoten, 1935, p. 10. "Indoshina go," *Ajia mondai kōza*, dai 8 kan, Sōgensha, 1939, p. 398. *Indoshina no minzoku to bunka*, Iwanami shoten, 1942, p. 10. Matsumoto, Nobuhiro "Nampō chiiki," *Tōa sekaishi* (2), Sekaishi kōza (4), Kōbundō shobō, 1944, p. 28 (136).
12. Matsumoto, Nobuhiro "Marai go," *Sekai no kotoba*, Keiō gijuku daigaku gogaku kenkyūjohen, Keiō shuppansha, 1943, p. 86.
13. Matsumoto, Nobuhiro "Nampō chiiki," *Tōa sekaishi* (2), Sekaishi kōza (4), Kōbundō shobō, 1944, pp. 28 -30 (136-138), 25 (143).
14. Interview with Chikamori Masashi, 23 August 2012, Keio University, Tokyo.

culture resembles the cultural sphere of the Austro-Asiatic languages" boded well with Yanagita's hypothesis that "The Japanese brought rice from the South."[15] Due to their hypothesis of migration from the South, Matsumoto and Yanagita were interested in boats excavated in Chiba Prefecture in 1947, which practically coincided with the time Heyerdahl set sail on his famed expedition from America to the Pacific islands.[16] In the 1950s, Matsumoto was an active member of Yanagita's New Harvest Research Society (*Niiname kenkyūkai*, 新嘗研究会), exploring agricultural rituals.[17] Inspired by the society's activities, Matsumoto led a research mission to Indochina Peninsula for conducting a comprehensive survey of rice cultivation culture of Southeast Asian people in 1956-1957.[18] Obviously, both Matsumoto and Yanagita conjectured about the migration (diffusion) of Southeast Asian people to Japan in the ancient times, and therefore, they hoped to find similarities between the Japanese and Southeast Asian boats and rice cultivation culture in Japan and Southeast Asia.

Matsumoto discussed these diffusionist ideas regarding Southeast Asia in the theoretical framework borrowed from Yanagita and from Mauss' student André Varagnac. From Yanagita, Matsumoto adopted the theory of basic culture, and he combined it with Varagnac's concept of archeocivilization.[19] Yanagita developed his theory of basic culture (*kisō bunka*, 基層文化) from German folklorists, such as Hans Naumann, arguing that the basic culture is the old culture preserved

---

15. Chikamori, Masashi "Minzokugaku kōkogaku kenkyūshitsu no Kujūkuri chōsa," *Keiō gijuku daigaku daigakuin shakaigaku kenkyū kiyō. Ningen to shakai no tankyū. Kujūkuri chōsa*, Keiō gijuku daigaku daigakuin shakaigaku kenkyūka, 2013, p. 232.
16. Ishii, Kenji "Kodai suitei fune yasei gō no omoide," *Nihon minzoku bunka no kigen*, dai 2 kan, geppō dai 2 gō, Kōdansha, 1978, pp. 3-6.
17. Matsumoto, Nobuhiro "Yanagita Kunio 'Kainan shōki' to 'Kaijō no michi' - minzoku to minzoku ni tsuite" *Nihonminzokubunka no kigen I: shinwa-densetsu*, Kōdansha, 1978, p. 339. Matsumoto, Nobuhiro "Indoshina no nōkō girei," *Niiname no kenkyū, I.*, Sōgensha, 1953, pp. 156-163.
18. Matsumoto, Nobuhiro *Tōnan Ajia no inasaku bunka no sōgō chōsa shuisho*, Nihon minzoku kyōkai, 1957. Iwata, Keiji "Kaisetsu," *Nihon minzoku bunka no kigen: Tōnan Ajia bunka to Nihon*, Kōdansha, 1978, pp. 447-454.

among contemporary common people.[20] This opinion clearly comes from Tylor's theory of remnants claiming continuity of ancient cultural elements in the modern era.

Varagnac's concept of archaeocivilization was based on Tylor's theory since André Varagnac was a scholar of the French School of Sociology who was inspired by Frazer.[21] Varagnac criticized the research on the cultural evolution, with its focus on changes in achieved progress. On the contrary, he focused on the continuity in the evolution and defined archaeocivilization as cultural phenomena (technics, beliefs, institutions) that persist for a longtime.[22]

These new concepts in the 1950s enabled Matsumoto to return back to the ethnological style influenced by sociology, which he was forced to give up in the 1930s when diffusionism dominated in ethnology. As a result, Matsumoto could again concentrate on cultural phenomena that he considered to have persisted from ancient times. On this basis, he developed his hypothesis of rice cultivation culture (*Inasaku bunka*, 稲作文化) encompassing cultures of Japan, Southeast Asia, and Southern China, which represented an amalgamation of diffusionist, sociologist, and evolutionist theories. It assumed the exis-

19. "At present, the people of the new generation are active in the Parisian academic circles. For example, the people who listened to Mauss's lectures, such as Varagnac, etc., they advocate a new academic discipline "archeo-civilization," indicating the direction towards which the folkloristic should advance." Matsumoto, Nobuhiro "Hashigaki," *Nihon no shinwa*, Ibundō, 1956.
20. "In the popular tradition [studies], there are people arguing for cultural sedimentation (gesunkene Kultur) that was proposed by German Naumann etc. Namely, that the culture of the upper class gradually sunk into the layer of common people and is spread among the entire people of the country. This fact surely exists. On the contrary, basic culture is taken in consideration; in fact the flows of these two cultures are constantly negotiating with each other." Yanagita, Kunio "Minkan denshō," *Minzokugaku jiten*, 1969 (first edition 1951), p. 579. Itō, Seiji "Hito to gakumon, Matsumoto Nobuhiro," *Shakai jinruigaku nenpō*, Tōkyō toritsu daigaku shakai jinrui gakkai, dai 12 kan, 1986, p. 13. Ōbayashi, Taryō "Kaisetsu," *Nihon minzokugaku no kigen I: shinwa-densetsu*, Kōdansha, 1978, p. 402.
21. Varagnac, André, *Définition du folklore*, Société d'éditions géographiques, maritimes et coloniales, Paris, 1938, p. 2.

tence of ancient rice cultivation culture as a common basic culture of these regions. It was the natural outcome of his cooperation on Yanagita's project researching rice culture through the New Harvest Research Society.[23] According to Ito Seiji, Matsumoto's concept received attention as an argument competing with the theory of Laurel-Forest Culture (Shōyō jurin bunkaron, 照葉樹林文化論) among Japanese cultural anthropologists and ethnologists in the 1970s.[24] Thus, Matsumoto's arguments on Southeast Asian culture received a certain amount of recognition among researchers of the common culture in Japan.

However, from the standards of academic research, it is necessary to notify the reader that Matsumoto's research did not produce findings supported by clear evidence. As Ito Seiji has indicated, Matsumoto's writing style was "literature style" inspired by Yanagita and the French School of Sociology.[25] Ito said that: "...he did not hasten to reach a conclusion, thus his approach probably lost the quality of being based on evidence."[26] In short, although Matsumoto was an ethnol-

22. "on ne peut aucunement pretender que le passage d'un statut technique à un autre statut technique, bien que suscitant ces véritables phénomènes de volcanisme humain que nous avons appelés « techno-biologic », fasse en quelque sorte table rase dans la nature humaine, et abolisse brutalement au fond de nous-mês le très vieil homme des lointains genres de vie. ... Nous avons donc proposé de les appeler du terme nouveau d'*archéocivilisation*, entendant par là l'ensemble des longues persistances culturelles, et sans d'ailleurs attacher à ces phénomènes de persistance aucune jugement de valeur favorable ou défavorable." Varagnac, André "Les phénomènes d'archéocivilisation," *De la préhistoire au monde modern. Essai d'une anthropodynamique*, Librarie Plon, Paris, 1954, pp. 164, 166.
23. Matsumoto, Nobuhiro "Yanagita Kunio 'Kainan shōki' to 'Kaijō no michi' - minzoku to minzoku ni tsuite" *Nihonminzokubunka no kigen I: shinwa-densetsu*, Kōdansha, 1978, p. 339. Matsumoto, Nobuhiro "Indoshina no nōkō girei," *Niiname no kenkyū, I.*, Sōgensha, 1953, pp. 156-163.
24. Itō, Seiji "Matsumoto Nobuhiro - 'Nampōsetsu' no kaitakusha," *Bunka jinruigaku gunzō*, Nihonhen (3), Akademia shuppankai, Kyōto, 1988, p. 238. Iwata, Keiji "Kaisetsu," *Nihon minzoku bunka no kigen: Tōnan Ajia bunka to Nihon*, Kōdansha, 1978, pp. 447-454.
25. Itō, Seiji "Matsumoto Nobuhiro - 'Nampōsetsu' no kaitakusha," *Bunka jinruigaku gunzō*, Nihonhen (3), Akademia shuppankai, Kyōto, 1988, p. 240.

ogist investigating Southeast Asia, many of his writings might not be regarded as academic due to his literary style and, the lack of evidence in supporting his arguments.

Matsumoto's interest in Southeast Asia led him to sympathize with the Vietnamese people in their war with the United States of America. Chikamori mentioned that Matsumoto disliked America.[27] During the Vietnam War, Matsumoto wrote the book *Small History of the Vietnamese People*.[28] He also contributed to the publication of several Vietnamese annals written in Chinese characters, which became a precious research material because all the Vietnamese documents were unaccessible due to the war in Vietnam.[29] Despite this effort, Matsumoto believed in the superiority of the Western culture since he claimed that "The Vietnamese are a very proud nation, they do not submit although they are beaten; they are similar to us, the Japanese, in the point they are quick in imitating and responding. Under the French rule, they have well adopted the French culture; their elites have acquired the French education. Today, they feel strong rivalry against America, but we expect that they will be active as trasmitters of the European culture in Southeast Asia in the distant future."[30] This quotation is in contrast with his opinions in 1933–1945 when he criticized Vietnamese insufficient westernization under the influence of Japan's Southern Advance Theory and Pan-Asianism. Still, it clearly shows that Matsumoto's evolutionist and Orientalist attitude to see the Vietnamese traditional culture as inferior to the Western culture did not change.

---

26. Ibid., p. 234.
27. Chikamori, Masashi "Matsumoto Nobuhiro no 'Genmin no kenkyū'," Keiō gijuku *daigaku daigakuin shakaigaku kenkyū kiyō. Ningen to shakai no tankyū. Kujūkuri chōsa*, Keiō gijuku daigaku daigakuin shakaigaku kenkyūka, 2013, pp. 236.
28. Matsumoto, Nobuhiro *Betonamu minzoku shōshi*, Iwanami shinsho, 1973 (1st ed. 1969).
29. Chin, Kei Wa "Maegaki,"*Daietsu shiki zensho: kōgōbon*, jō, Tōkyō daigaku Tōyō bunka kenkyūjo fuzoku Tōyōgaku bunken sentā kankō iinkai, 1984, p. 1.
30. Matsumoto, Nobuhiro *Betonamu minzoku shōshi*, Iwanami shinsho, 1973 (1st ed. 1969), pp. 206–207.

Bibliography

Matsumoto Nobuhiro 松本信広（works in the chronological order）

1919

"Sayama kikō," *Tōkōkō*, I, Keiō gijuku taiikukai sangakubu nenpō, Shuppan kagaku sōgō kenkyūjo, 1919, pp. 123-127.「狭山紀行」『登高行』I‐慶應義塾體育會山岳部年報, 出版科学総合研究所, 1919. ("Records from Journey to Sayama," *Tōkōkō*, I, Keiō gijuku taiikukai sangakubu nenpō, Shuppan kagaku sōgō kenkyūjo, 1919.)

1920

"Iwate no Kōgen yori" (1920), *Nihon minzoku bunka no kigen I: shinwa - densetsu*, Kōdansha, 1978, pp. 364-373.「岩手の高原より」(1920)『日本民族文化の起源Ｉ：神話・伝説』講談社, 1978. ("From Kōgen in Iwate" (1920), *The Origins of the Japanese Ethnic Culture I: Myths, Legends*, Kōdansha, 1978.)

"Fudoki ni arawaretaru santake densetsu," *Tōkōkō*, II, Keiō gijuku taiikukai sangakubu nenpō, Shuppan kagaku sōgō kenkyūjo, 1920, pp. 23-40.「風土記に現れたる山岳伝説」『登高行』II, 慶應義塾體育會山岳部年報, 出版科学総合研究所, 1920. ("The Mountain Legends in Fudoki," *Tōkōkō*, II, Keiō gijuku taiikukai sangakubu nenpō, Shuppan kagaku sōgō kenkyūjo, 1920.)

1921

"Taizan no kenkyū," *Tōkōkō*, III, Keiō gijuku taiikukai sangakubu nenpō, Shuppan kagaku sōgō kenkyūjo, 1921, pp. 34-40.「泰山の研究」『登高行』III, 慶應義塾體育會山岳部年報, 出版科学総合研究所, 1921. ("The Research of Mount Tai," *Tōkōkō*, III, Keiō gijuku taiikukai sangakubu nenpō, Shuppan kagaku sōgō kenkyūjo, 1921.)

"Shina kodai seishi no kenkyū" (1921), *Tōa minzoku bunka ronkō*, Seibundō shinkōsha, 1968, pp. 411-452.「支那古代姓氏の研究」(1921)『東亜民族文化論攷』誠文堂新光社, 1968. ("The Research of the Family in Ancient China" (1921), *The Collections of Papers on Culture of East Asian People*, Seibundō shinkōsha, 1968.)

"Shina kosei to tōtemizumu" (1921-1922), *Tōa minzoku bunka ronkō*, Seibundō shinkōsha, 1968, pp. 453-490.「支那古姓とトーテミズム」(1921-1922)『東亜民族文化論攷』誠文堂新光社, 1968. ("The Family in Ancient China and Totemism" (1921-1922), *The Collections of Papers on Culture of East Asian People*, Seibundō shinkōsha, 1968.)

1922

"Kodai Shina minzoku no sosen saishi," *Shigaku*, dai 1 kan, dai 4 gō, Mita Shigakkai, 1922, pp. 49-71.「古代支那民族の祖先祭祀」『史学』第1巻, 第4号, 三田史学会, 1922. ("The Ancestor Worship of People in Ancient China," *The Historical Science*, Vol. 1, No. 4, Mita Historical Society, 1922.)

"Marcel Granet; La Polygynie sororale et la Sororate dans la Chine féodale: Études sur les former anciennes de la polygamie chinoise, Paris, 1920," *Shigaku*, dai 1 kan, dai 4 gō, Mita Shigakkai, 1922, pp. 625-626. "Marcel Granet; La Polygynie sororale et la Sororate dans la Chine féodale: Études sur les former anciennes de la polygamie chinoise, Paris, 1920,"『史学』第1巻, 第4号, 三田史学会, 1922. ("Marcel Ranet; Sororal Polygyny and Sororate in Feudal China: Studies on the Ancient Formes of Chinese Polygamy, Paris, 1920," *The Historical Science*, Vol. 1, No. 4, Mita Historical Society, 1922.)

"Shashoku no kenkyū" (1922), *Tōa minzoku bunka ronkō*, Seibundō shinkōsha, 1968.「社稷の研究」(1922)『東亜民族文化論攷』誠文堂新光社, 1968, pp. 493-513. ("The Research of the Shrine and the Millet" (1922), *The Collections of Papers on Culture of East Asian People*, Seibundō shinkōsha, 1968.)

1923

"Tanaka hakushi wo itamu," *Mita hyōron*, dai 316 gō, Mita hyōron hakkōjo, December 1923, pp. 26-27.「田中博士を悼む」『三田評論』第316号, 三田評論発行所, 1923年10月, pp. 26-27. ("Mourning for Doctor Tanaka," *Mita hyōron*, No. 316, Mita hyōron hakkōjo, December 1923, pp. 26-27)

1926

"Pari yori," *Minzoku*, da 2 kan, dai 1 gō, Minzoku hakkōjo, 1926, pp. 141-142.「巴里より」『民族』第2巻, 第1号, 民族発行所, 1926. ("From Paris," *Ethnos*, Vol. 2, No. 1, Minzoku hakkōjo, 1926.)

1928

Essai sur la mythologie Japonaise, P. Geuthner, Paris, 1928. (An Essay on the Japanese Mythology, P. Geuthner, Paris, 1928.)

Le japonais et les langues austroasiatiques: étude de vocabulaire comparé, P. Geuthner, Paris, 1928. (*The Japanese and the Austro-Asiatic Languages: a Comparative Study of Vocabulary*, P. Geuthner, Paris, 1928.)

1929

"Nihongo to Ōsutoroajiago," *Shigaku zasshi*, dai 40 kan, dai 1 gō, Shigakkai, January 1929, pp.111-113.「日本語とオーストロアジア語」『史学雑誌』第40巻, 第1号, 史学会, 1929. ("The Japanese and the Austro-Asiatic Languages," *Journal of Historical Science*, Vol. 40, No. 1, Historical Society of Japan, 1929.)

"Ōshūjin no Kyokutō kenkyū (I)," *Shigaku*, dai 8 kan, dai 1 gō, Mita Shigakkai, 1929, pp. 1-26.「欧州人の極東研究(Ⅰ)」『史学』第 8 巻, 第 1 号, 三田史学会, 1929. ("European Research of the Far East (I)," *The Historical Science*, Vol. 9, No. 1, Mita Historical Society, 1929.)

"Ōshūjin no Kyokutō kenkyū (II)," *Shigaku*, dai 8 kan, dai 3 gō, Mita Shigakkai, 1929, pp. 43 (365)-60 (382).「欧州人の極東研究(Ⅱ)」『史学』第 8 巻, 第 3 号, 三田史学会, 1929. ("European Research of the Far East (II)," *The Historical Science*, Vol. 9, No. 3, Mita Historical Society, 1929.)

1930

"Ainu no potoracchi" (1930), *Nihon minzoku bunka no kigen I: shinwa-densetsu*, Kōdansha, 1978, pp. 327-330.「アイヌのポトラッチ」(1930)『日本民族文化の起源Ⅰ：神話・伝説』講談社, 1978. ("Ainu's Potlatch" (1930), *The Origins of the Japanese Ethnic Culture I: Myths, Legends*, Kōdansha, 1978.)

"Furansu ni okeru Shina kenkyū," *Shina kenkyū*, Keiō gijuku Mochidzuki Kikin Shina kenkyūkai-hen, Iwanamishoten, 1930, pp. 375-397.「仏蘭西に於ける支那研究」『支那研究』慶応義塾望月貴金支那研究会編, 岩波書店, 1930. ("Chinese Studies in France," *Chinese Studies*, Mochidzuki Foundation, Chinese Studies, Iwanami Publishing, 1930.)

"Gaisha kantai densetsu kō," *Shigaku*, Mita Shigakkai, dai 9 kan, dai 1 gō, 1930.「外者款待伝説考」『史学』第 9 巻, 第 1 号, 三田史学会, 1930, p. 1-26. ("A Study of a Legend of Hospitality towards Strangers," *The Historical Science*, Vol. 9, No. 1, Mita Historical Society, 1930.)

"Gendai Furansu ni okeru Tōyōgaku," *Furansu no shakai kagaku*, Gendai ni okeru sho keikō, Furansu gakkai-hen, 1930, pp. 553-599.「現代フランスに於ける東洋学」『フランスの社会学科学』―現代における諸傾向―, フランス学会編, 1930. ("Oriental Studies in present France," *French Social Sciences*, Present Trends, French Studies Association, 1930.)

"Imohori chōsha" (1930), *Nihon minzoku bunka no kigen I: shinwa-densetsu*, Kōdansha, 1978, pp. 308-310.「芋掘長者」(1930),『日本民族文化の起源Ⅰ：神話・伝説』講談社, 1978. ("Potato Digger Millionaire" (1930), *The Origins of the Japanese Ethnic Culture I: Myths, Legends*, Kōdansha, 1978.)

1931

Nihon shinwa no kenkyū, Dōbunkan, 1931.『日本神話の研究』同文館, 1931 (*The Research of the Japanese Myths*, Dōbunkan, 1931.)

"Ōsutorikku gozoku ha hatashite sonzai nasuya," *Shigaku*, dai 10 kan, dai 1 gō, Mita Shigakkai, 1931, p. 96.「オーストリック語族は果たして存在なすや」『史学』第 10 巻, 第 1 号, 三田史学会, 1931. Vol. 10, No. 1, 1931. ("Does the Austrisch Language Family Really Exist?" *The Historical Science*, Vol. 10, No. 1, Mita Historical Society, 1931.)

1932

"Kodai bunkaron," *Gendai shigaku taikei*, Kyōritsusha shoten, 1932.「古代文化論」『現代史学大系』共立社書店, 1932. ("Theories of Ancient Culture," *Present History System*, Kyōritsusha shoten, 1932.)

"Warazaru onna" (1932), *Nihon minzoku bunka no kigen III: Tōnan Ajia to Nihon*, Kōdansha, 1978, pp. 423-426.「笑わざる女」(1932)『日本民族文化の起源 III：東南アジア文化と日本』講談社, 1978. ("Woman That Does Not Laugh" (1932), *The Origins of the Japanese Ethnic Culture III: Southeast Asian Culture and Japan*, Kōdansha, 1978.)

1933

"Annanjin no ohaguro," *Shigaku*, dai 12 kan, dai 4 gō, Mita Shigakkai, 1933, p. 96 (676).「安南人のおはぐろ」『史学』第12巻, 第 4 号, 三田史学会, 1933. ("The Annamese Tooth Blackening," *The Historical Science*, Vol. 12, No. 4, Mita Historical Society, 1933.)

"Annan ryokōki (daiisshin)," *Minzokugaku*, dai 5 kan, dai 5 gō, Minzokugakkai, 1933, pp. 86-87 (721-722).「安南旅行記（第一信）」『民俗学』第 5 巻, 第 5 号, 民俗学会, 1933. ("Travel Records from Annam I," *Folklore Studies*, Vol. 5, No. 5, Society of Folklore Studies, 1933.)

"Annan ryokōki (daisanshin)," *Minzokugaku*, dai 5 kan, dai 8 gō, Minzokugakkai, 1933, pp. 829-831.「安南旅行記（第二信）」『民俗学』第 5 巻, 第 8 号, 民俗学会, 1933. ("Travel Records from Annam II," *Folklore Studies*, Vol. 5, No. 8, Society of Folklore Studies, 1933.)

"Annan ryokōki (daisanshin)," *Minzokugaku*, dai 5 kan, dai 10 gō, Minzokugakkai, 1933.「安南旅行記（第三信）」『民俗学』第 5 巻, 第10号, 民俗学会, 1933, pp. 97-102 (931-936). ("Travel Records from Annam III," *Folklore Studies*, Vol. 5, No. 10, Society of Folklore Studies, 1933.)

"Chamu no yashizoku to 'yashi no mi' setsuwa," *Minzokugaku*, dai 5 kan, dai 6 gō, Minzoku gakkai, 1933, pp. 449-465.「チャムの椰子族と「椰子の実」説話」『民俗学』第 5 巻, 第 6 号, 民俗学会, 1933. ("The Clan 'Coconut tree' and the Popular Tale 'Coconut' of Cham People," *Folklore Studies*, Vol. 5, No. 6, Society of Folklore Studies, 1933.)

"Indoshina no dōki ni tsuite" (1933) *Nihon minzoku bunka no kigen III: Tōnan Ajia to Nihon*, Kōdansha, 1978, pp. 253-454.「インドシナの銅鼓について」(1933)『日本民族文化の起源 III：東南アジア文化と日本』講談社, 1978. ("On Bronze Drums of Indochina," (1933) *The Origins of the Japanese Ethnology III: Southeast Asian Culture and Japan - legends*, Kōdansha, 1978.)

"Miao zoku no haru no matsuri to hashira," *Minzokugaku*, dai 5 kan, dai 3 gō, Minzokugakkai, 1933, pp. 190-192.「苗族の春の祭と柱」『民俗学』第 5 巻, 第 3 号, 民俗学会, 1933. ("Miao People's Festival of Spring and the Pillar," *Folklore Studies*, Vol. 5, No. 3, Society of Folklore Studies, 1933.)

"Minzokugaku no kōyō," *Minzokugaku*, Minzokugakkai, dai 5 kan, dai 1 gō, 1933, p. 16. 「民俗学の効用」『民俗学』第 5 巻, 第11号, 民俗学会, 1933. ("The Utility of the Folklore Studies," *Folklore Studies*, Vol. 5, No. 11, Society of Folklore Studies, 1933.)

"Rōnorachi densetsu no Annan iden," *Minzokugaku*, dai 5 kan, dai 12 gō, Minzokugakkai, 1933, pp. 1-10 (1010-1019). 「老獺稚伝説の安南異伝」『民俗学』第 5 巻, 第 12号, 民俗学会, 1933. (The Annamese Variante of the Old Otter Legend," *Folklore Studies*, Vol. 5, No. 12, Society of Folklore Studies, 1933.)

1934

"Annam ryokōdan," *Shigaku zasshi*, dai 45 kan, dai 2 gō, Shigakkai, 1934, pp. 255-257. 「安南旅行談」『史学雑誌』第45巻, 第 2 号, 史学会, 1934. ("A Talk about Travel to Annam," *Journal of Historical Science*, Vol. 45, No. 2, Historical Society of Japan, 1934.)

"Futsujin no Indoshina kenkyū," *Tōa*, Tōa keizai chōsakyoku, 1934nen, 3gatsu gō, pp. 109-118. 「佛人の印度支那研究」『東亜』東亜経済調査局, 1934年 3 月号. ("The French Research of Indochina," *East Asia*, Eas Asia Survey Office, March 1934.)

"Hanoi Futsukoku kyokutō gakuin shozō Annan hon shomoku dōtsuiki," *Shigaku*, dai 13 kan, dai 4 gō, Mita Shigakkai, 1934, pp. 785-786 (203-204). 「河内仏国極東学院所蔵安南本書目　同追記」『史学』第13巻, 第 4 号, 三田史学会, 1934. ("Appendix ('A Catalogue of the Annamese Books Stored in EFEO in Hanoi')," *The Historical Science*, Vol. 13, No.4, Mita Historical Society, 1934.)

"Indoshina no bunka jō," *Iwanami kōza Tōyō shichō*, I, Iwanami shoten, 1934, pp. 1-44. 「印度支那の文化(上)」『岩波講座東洋思潮』第 1 巻13, 岩波書店, 1934. ("The Culture of Indochina," Vol. 1, *Iwanami kōza Lecture: Oriental thinking*, Vol. 1, 13, Iwanami shoten, 1934.)

"Indoshina inshōki (Ⅰ)," *Mita hyōron*, dai 437 gō, Mita hyōron hakkōjo, 1934, pp. 24-27. 「佛領印度支那印象記(Ⅰ)」『三田評論』第437号, 三田評論發行所, 1934. ("Impressions from French Indochina (Ⅰ)," *Mita hyōron*, No. 437, Mita hyōron hakkōjo, 1934)

"Indoshina inshōki (Ⅱ)," *Mita hyōron*, dai 440 gō, Mita hyōron hakkōjo, 1934, pp. 22-25. 「佛領印度支那印象記(Ⅱ)」『三田評論』第440号, 三田評論發行所, 1934. ("Impressions from French Indochina (Ⅱ)," *Mita hyōron*, No. 440, Mita hyōron hakkōjo, 1934)

"Indoshina inshōki (Ⅲ)," *Mita hyōron*, dai 445 gō, Mita hyōron hakkōjo, 1934, pp. 10-16. 「佛領印度支那印象記(Ⅲ)」『三田評論』第445号, 三田評論發行所, 1934. "Impressions from French Indochina (Ⅲ)," *Mita hyōron*, No. 445, Mita hyōron hakkōjo, 1934.)

"Indoshina gengo no keitō," *Iwanami kōza Tōyō shichō*, Ⅱ (Tōyō gengo no keitō), Iwanami shoten, 1934, pp. 1-44. 「印度支那言語の系統」『岩波講座東洋思潮』第 2 巻(東洋言語の系統)岩波書店, 1934. ("Genealogy of Indochina Languages," *Iwanami Lecture: Oriental Thinking*, Vol. 2, (Genealogy of Oriental Languages),

Iwanami shoten, 1934.)

"Indoshina wo mite," *Gaikō jihō*, dai 703 gō, Gaikō jihōsha, 15.03.1934, pp. 131-138.「佛領印度支那を観て」『外交時報』第703号, 外交時報社, 1934年3月15日. ("I have Seen Indochina," *Diplomatic Review*, No. 703, Gaikō jihōsha, 15.03.1934.)

"Nihon shinwa ni tsuite," *Iwanami kōza Nihon rekishi*, Iwanami shoten, 1934.「日本神話に就いて」『岩波講座　日本歴史』岩波書店, 1934. ("On the Japanese Myths," *Iwanami Lecture: Japanese History*, Iwanami shoten, 1934.)

"Nihon shinwa no kanken" (1934), *Tōa minzoku bunka ronkō*, Seibundō shinkōsha, 1968, pp. 311-319.「日本神話の管見」(1934)『東亜民族文化論攷』誠文堂新光社, 1968. ("An Opinion on the Japanese Myths" (1934) *The Collections of Papers on Culture of East Asian People*, Seibundō shinkōsha, 1968.)

1935

"Akashi Teikichi 'Rōnorachi densetsu no Annan den' no reibutsu to tenmon no kankei, tsuiki" (1935), *Tōa minzoku bunka ronkō*, Seibundō shinkōsha, 1968, pp. 153-155.「明石貞吉「老獺稚伝説の安南傳」の霊物と天文との関係について, 附記」(1935)『東亜民族文化論攷』誠文堂新光社, 1968. ("Supplement to Akashi Teikichi's 'On the Relation of Astronomy and Spiritual Things in the Vietnamese Legend on Old Otter'," *The Collections of Papers on Culture of East Asian People*, Seibundō shinkōsha, 1968.)

"Dōki ni kan suru ni, san no Betonamu shiryō" (1935), *Nihon minzoku bunka no kigen III: Tōnan Ajia to Nihon*, Kōdansha, 1978, pp. 255-257.「銅鼓に関する二, 三のベトナム資料」(1935)『日本民族文化の起源 III : 東南アジア文化と日本』講談社, 1978. ("The Vietnamese Materials 2,3 on Bronze Drums," (1935) *The Origins of the Japanese Ethnology III: Southeast Asian Culture and Japan*, Kōdansha, 1978.)

"Furansu ni okeru minzokugakuteki kenkyū," Yanagita Kunio, *Nihon minzokugaku kenkyū*, Iwanami shoten, 1935, pp. 363-375.「フランスに於ける民俗学的研究」柳田国男『日本民俗学研究』岩波書店, 1935. ("The Folklore Studies in France" in Yanagita, Kunio, *The Japanese Folklore Studies*, Iwanami shoten, 1935)

"Indoshina no bunka ge," *Iwanami kōza Tōyō shichō*, 9/4, Iwanami shoten, 1935, pp. 49-95.「印度支那の文化（下）」『岩波講座東洋思潮』第9巻4, 岩波書店, 1935. ("The Culture of Indochina," Vol. 2, *Iwanami Lecture: Oriental Thinking*, Vol. 9, 4, Iwanami shoten, 1935.)

"Indoshina minzoku," *Iwanami kōza Tōyō shichō*, I (Tōyō no minzoku, Tōyō no shakai), Iwanami shoten, 1935, pp. 1-49.「印度支那民族」『岩波講座東洋思潮』第1巻, (東洋の民族・東洋の社会), 岩波書店, 1935. ("Peoples of Indochina," *Iwanami Lecture: Oriental Thinking*, Vol. 1, (Peoples and Society of Orient), Iwanami shoten, 1935.)

"Nguyen-van-Khoan, Le Repêchage de l'âme, avec une note sur les hôn et les phách d'après les croyances tonkinoises actuelles," *Shigaku kenkyū*, dai 1 kan dai 2 gō, Minzokugakkai, Sanseidō, 1935, pp. 175-176.「Nguyen-van-Khoan, Le Repêchage de l'âme, avec une note sur les hôn et les phách d'après les croyances tonkinoises actualles」『民族学研究』第 1 巻, 第 2 号, 民族学会, 三省堂, 1935. ("Nguyen-van-Khoan, Invocation of Soul with a Note about Hôn and Phách in Contemporary Tonkin Belief," *Ethnological Research*, Vol. 1, No. 2, Japanese Society of Ethnology, Sanseidō, 1935.)

"Nihonjin saisho no Indoshina hantō ōdan (Ⅰ)," *Shigaku*, dai 14 kan, dai 1 gō, Mita Shigakkai, 1935, p. 68.「日本人最初の印度支那半島横断(Ⅰ)」『史学』第14巻, 第 1 号, 三田史学会, 1935. ("The First Crossing of Indochina Peninsula by the Japanese people (Ⅰ)," *The Historical Science*, Vol. 14, No. 1, Mita Historical Society, 1935.)

"Nihonjin saisho no Indoshina hantō ōdan (Ⅱ)," *Shigaku*, dai 14 kan, dai 1 gō, Mita Shigakkai, 1935, p. 156.「日本人最初の印度支那半島横断(Ⅱ)」『史学』第14巻, 第 1 号, 三田史学会, 1935. ("The First Crossing of Indochina Peninsula by the Japanese people (Ⅱ)," *The Historical Science*, Vol. 14, No. 1, Mita Historical Society, 1935.)

"Nihonjin saisho no Indoshina hantō ōdan (Ⅲ)," *Shigaku*, dai 14 kan, dai 1 gō, Mita Shigakkai, 1935, p. 164.「日本人最初の印度支那半島横断(Ⅲ)」『史学』第14巻, 第 1 号, 三田史学会, 1935. ("The First Crossing of Indochina Peninsula by the Japanese people (Ⅲ)," *The Historical Science*, Vol. 14, No. 1, Mita Historical Society, 1935.)

"Tsuiki (Betonamu ōshitsu shozō Annan honshomoku)," *Shigaku*, dai 14 kan, dai 2 gō, Mita Shigakkai, 1935, pp. 155-159 (337-341).「追記(越南王室所蔵安南本書目)」『史学』第14巻, 第 2 号, 三田史学会, 1935. ("Appendix (A Catalogue of the Annamese Books in the Imperial Archive of Viet Nam)," *The Historical Science*, Vol. 14, No. 2, Mita Historical Society, 1935.)

1936

"Annan shijō no nijishiryō: *Dainan jitsuroku* to *Bibliographie Annamite*," *Shigaku*, dai 15 kan, dai 1 gō, Mita Shigakkai, 1936, pp. 111 - 132.「安南史上の二資料」(大南寔録と*Bibliography Annamite*)『史学』第15巻, 第 1 号, 三田史学会, 1936. ("Two Materials on the Annamese History: *The Annals of Đại Nam* and *Bibliography Annamite*," *The Historical Science*, Vol. 15, No. 1, Mita Historical Society, 1936.)

"Sanpan meigi kō" (1936), *Tōa minzoku bunka ronkō*, Seibundō shinkōsha, 1968, p. 781.「サンパン名義考」(1936)『東亜民族文化論攷』誠文堂新光社, 1968. ("A Study on the Name of Sampan," *The Collections of Papers on Culture of East Asian People*, Seibundō shinkōsha, 1968.)

"Tsuiki," *Minzokugaku kenkyū*, dai 2 kan, dai 1 gō, Minzokugakkai, 1936, pp. 66-69.「追記」『民族学研究』第 2 巻, 第 1 号, 民族学会, 三省堂, 1936, pp. 66-69. ("Postscript," *The Japanese Journal of Ethnology*, Vol. 2, No. 1, Japanese Society of Ethnology, Sanseidō, 1936.)

1937

"Jōdai Indoshina no kōkogakuteki kenkyū ni tsuite - Korani joshi kizō dozoku hyōhon wo chūshin ni" (1937), *Indoshina minzoku to bunka*, Iwanami shoten, 1942, p. 161-187.「上代印度支那の考古学的研究に就て―コラニ女史寄贈土俗標本を中心に」(1937)『印度支那の民族と文化』岩波書店, 1942. ("On Archaeological Research of Ancient Indochina - with Focus on the Folk Specimens Donated by Ms. Colani." (1937) *Peoples and Cultures of Indochina*, Iwanami shoten, 1942.)

"Nan'yō guntō ryokō nisshi," *Shigaku*, dai 16 kan, dai 3 gō, Mita Shigakkai, 1937, pp. 77a-109（405a-437）.「南洋群島旅行日誌」『史学』第16巻, 第3号, 三田史学会, 1937. ("Travel Diary to Southern Islands (Saipan, Yap, Palau, New Guinea)," *The Historical Science*, Vol. 16, No. 3, Mita Historical Society, 1937.)

"Waga Nan'yō wo miru," *Mita hyōron*, dai 483 gō, Mita hyōron hakkōjo, 1937, pp. 6-12.「我南洋を見る」『三田評論』No. 483, October 1937. ("Seeing Our South Seas," *Mita hyōron*, No. 483, Mita hyōron hakkōjo, 1937.)

Nyū Ginia dozokuhin zushū: Nan'yō kōhatsu kabushiki gaisha shūshū, jōkan, Minami no kai hen, Nan'yō kōhatsu, 1937.『ニューギニア土俗品圖集：南洋興發株式會社蒐集』上巻, 南の会 編, 南洋興発, 1937. (*The Illustrated Catalogue of the Ethnographical Objects from Melanesia*, the Japan Society of Oceanian Ethnography, Nanyo Kohatsu K. K., 1937.)

1938

"Jihen to daigaku," *Shigaku*, dai 17 kan, dai 3 gō, Mita Shigakkai, 1938, p. 444.「事変と大学」『史学』第17巻, 第3号, 三田史学会, 1938, p. 444. ("Incident and the Universities," *Historical Science*, Vol. 17, No. 3, Mita Historical Society, 1938, p. 444.)

"Jōdai Indoshina," *Tōyō bunkashi taikei*, Kodai Shina to Indo, Seidōbunkadō shinkōsha, 1938, pp. 236-250.「上代インド支那」『東洋文化史大系』古代支那及びインド, 誠文堂新光社, 1938. ("Ancient Indochina," *System of Cultural History of Orient*, Ancient China and India, Seidōbunkadō shinkōsha, 1938.)

"Senseki junrei," *Mita hyōron*, dai 490 gō, Mita hyōron hakkōjo, 1938nen 6gatsu, pp. 35-36.「戦跡巡礼」『三田評論』第490号, 三田発行所, 1938年6月. ("Pilgrimage around the Battlefields," *Mita hyōron*, No. 490, Mita hyōron hakkōjo, June 1938.)

"Senseki junrei," *Mita hyōron*, dai 491 gō, Mita hyōron hakkōjo, 1938nen 7gatsu, pp. 35-38.「戦跡巡礼」『三田評論』第491号, 三田発行所, 1938年7月. ("Pilgrimage around the Battlefields," *Mita hyōron*, No. 491, Mita hyōron hakkōjo, July 1938.)

"Senseki junrei," *Mita hyōron*, dai 492 gō, Mita hyōron hakkōjo, 1938nen 8gatsu, pp. 36-38.「戦跡巡礼」『三田評論』第492号, 三田発行所, 1938年8月. ("Pilgrimage around the Battlefields," *Mita hyōron*, No. 492, Mita hyōron hakkōjo, August 1938.)

"Senseki junrei," *Mita hyōron*, dai 493 gō, Mita hyōron hakkōjo, 1938nen 9gatsu, pp. 34-36.「戦跡巡礼」『三田評論』第493号, 三田発行所, 1938年9月. ("Pilgrimage around the Battlefields," *Mita hyōron*, No. 493, Mita hyōron hakkōjo, September

1938.)

1939

"Indoshina go," *Ajia mondai kōza*, dai 8 kan, Sōgensha, 1939, pp. 385-399.「印度支那語」『アジア問題講座』第 8 巻, 創元社, 1939. ("Languages of Indochina," Vol. 8, *Lecture of Asia Issues*, Sōgensha, 1939.)

"Kōnan hōkoki," *Shigaku*, dai 17 kan, dai 4 gō, Mita Shigakkai, 1939, pp. 529-612.「江南訪古記」『史学』第17巻, 第 4 号, 三田史学会, 1939. ("Old Records from the Visit of Jiangnan," *The Historical Science*, Vol. 17, No. 4, Mita Historical Society, 1939.)

"Yūken sekifu no shomondai," *Shigaku*, dai 18 kan, dai 2/3 gō, Mita Shigakkai, 1939, pp. 483-514.「有肩石斧の諸問題」『史学』第18巻, 第 2 / 3 号, 三田史学会, 1939. ("Issues Concerning the Shouldered Axes," *Historical Science*, Vol. 18, No. 2/3, Mita Historical Society, 1939.)

1940

"Annan shiryō ni arawareru Indoshina sanchi minzoku," *Andō kyōju kanreki Shukuga kinenronbunshū*, Andō kyōju kanreki Shukuga kinenkaihen, Sanseidō, 1940, pp. 1009-1013.「安南資料に表はれたる印度支那山地民族」『安藤教授還暦祝賀記念論文集』安藤教授還暦記念会編, 三省堂, 1940. ("Indochina Mountain Peoples in Annamese Materials," *Papers Collection to Celebrate the Sixtieth Birthday of Professor* Andō, Andō kyōju kanreki Shukuga kinenkaihen, Sanseidō, 1940.)

"Futsuin no minzoku mondai," *Shin Ajia*, Mantetsu Tōa keizai chōsakyoku, 1940nen 8gatsu, pp. 26-37.「仏印の民族問題」『新亜細亜』満鉄東亜経済調査局, 1940年 8 月. ("Problems of French Indochinese peoples," *New Asia*, Manchurian Railway Economic Survey Office, August 1940.)

"Futsuryō Indoshina jin no shosō," *Gaikō jihō*, Gaikō jihōsha, dai 850 gō, 1940nen 5 gatsu, p. 134-145.「仏印印度支那人の諸相」『外交時報』第850号, 外交時報社, 1940年 5 月. ("Aspects of French Indochinese peoples," *Diplomatic Revue*, Gaikō jihōsha, No. 850, May 1940.)

"Indoshina ni okeru minzoku no kōbō," *Shin Ajia*, Mantetsu Tōa keizai chōsakyoku, Nampō bunka tokugō, 1940nen, 1gatsu, pp. 60-69.「印度支那に於ける民族の興亡」『親亜細亜』南方文化特号, 満鉄東亜経済調査局, 1940年 1 月. ("Rise and Fall of Peoples in Indochina," *New Asia*, Special Number on South Seas Culture, Manchurian Railway Economic Survey Office, January 1940.)

"Nampō san dōshokubutsu honpōmei no kenkyū," *Shigaku*, dai 18 kan, dai 1 gō, Mita Shigakkai, 1940, pp. 165-202.「南方産動植物本邦名の研究」『史学』第18巻, 第 1 号, 1940. ("A Research on the Japanese Names of Southward Animals and Plants," *Historical Science*, Vol. 18, No. 1, Mita Historical Society, 1940.)

"Futsuryō Indoshina no minzoku," *Nan'yō*, dai 27 kan, dai 7 gō, Nan'yō Kyōkai, 1940, pp. 26-33.「仏領印度支那の民族」『南洋』第27巻, 第 7 号, 南洋協会, 1940. ("Peoples of French Indochina," *South Seas*, Vol. 27, No. 7, South Seas Society, 1940.)

"Nihon shinwa ni okeru Nampōkei," *Risō*, jūyonen sansatsu sangatsu gō, Risōsha, 1940, pp. 33-44 (271-282).「日本神話に於ける南方系」『理想』14年3冊3月号, 理想社, 1940. ("Southern Geneaology in the Japanese Myths," *Ideal*, the 14th Year, Vol. 3, March, Risōsha, 1940.)

"Prehistoric Pottery in China, by G. D. Wu, London, 1938," *Shigaku*, dai 18 kan, dai 4 gō, Mita Shigakkai, 1940, p. 783.「Prehistoric Pottery in China, by G. D. Wu (呉金鼎) London, 1938」『史学』第18巻, 第4号, 三田史学会, 1940. ("Prehistoric Pottery in China, by G. D. Wu, London, 1938," *Historical Science*, Vol. 18, No. 4, Mita Historical Society, 1940.)

1941

"Futsuryō Indoshina no minzoku to bunka," *Sosei futsuryō Indoshina no zenbō*, Aikoku shinbunsha shuppanbu, 1941, pp. 37-67.「佛領印度支那の民族と文化」『甦生佛領印度支那の全貌』愛国新聞社出版部, 1941. ("Peoples and Cultures of French Indochina," *The Full Picture of Revived French Indochina*, Aikoku shinbunsha shuppanbu, 1941.)

"Kōnan no kobunka" (1941), *Indoshina no minzoku to bunka*, Iwanami shoten, 1942, pp. 295-313.「江南の古文化」(1941)『印度支那の民族と文化』岩波書店, 1942. ("Ancient Culture of Jiangnan" (1941), *Peoples and Cultures of Indochina*, Iwanami shoten, 1942.)

Kōnan tōsa. Shōwa 13-nendo, Keiō gijuku daigaku bungakubu shigakka kenkyū hōkoku; kōshu, dai 1 satsu, Mita Shigakkai, 1941.『江南踏査. 昭和13年度』慶応義塾大学文学部史学科研究報告; 甲種, 第1冊; 三田史学会, 1941. (*Exploration of Jiangnan. 1938*, The Keio University Faculty of Letters, Research Reports, Department of History, Vol. 1, Mita Historical Society, 1941.)

"Momen no komei ni tsuite" (1941), *Tōa minzoku bunka ronkō*, Seibundō shinkōsha, 1968, pp. 659-690.「木綿の古名に就いて」(1941)『東亜民族文化論攷』誠文堂新光社 Seibundō shinkosha 1968. ("On Ancient Name of Cotton" (1941), *The Collections of Papers on Culture of East Asian People*, Seibundō shinkōsha, 1968.)

"Nampō bunka seisaku to minzokugaku," *Gaikō jihō*, dai 885 gō, Gaikō jihōsha, 15.10.1941, pp. 74-58.「南方文化政策と民族学」『外交時報』第885号, 外交時報社, 1941年10月15日. ("Southern Cultural Policy and Ethnology," *Diplomatic Revue*, No. 885, Gaikō jihōsha, 15.10.1941.)

"Oobu to iu moji ni tsuite" (1941), *Tōa minzoku bunka ronkō*, Seibundō shinkōsha, 1968, pp. 771-789.「舶と云う文字に就いて」(1941)『東亜民族文化論攷』誠文堂新光社, 1968 ("On the Character Ship" (1941), *The Collections of Papers on Culture of East Asian People*, Seibundō shinkōsha, 1968.)

"Shina Nampō kodai bunka no keitō," *Nihon shogaku shinkō iinkai kenkyū hōkoku*, dai jū ichi hen (rekishi gaku), Kyōgakukyoku, 1941, p. 203-213.「支那南方古代文化の系統」『日本諸学振興委員会研究報告』第十一篇(歴史学), 教学局, 1941. ("Genealogy of Southern Ancient Culture in China," *Japan Academic Promotion Com-*

mittee Research Report, Vol. 11 (History) Kyōgakukyoku, 1941.)

1942

"Daitōa sensō no minzoku shitekina igi, *Gaikō jihō*, dai 893 gō, Gaikō jihōsha, 15.02.1942, pp. 51-58.「大東亜戦争の民族史的な意義」『外交時報』第893号, 外交時報社, 1942年2月15日. ("The Ethnic-Historical Meaning of the Greater East Asian War," *Diplomatic Revue*, No. 893, Gaikō jihōsha, 15.02.1942.)

Indoshina minzoku to bunka, Iwanami shoten, 1942.『印度支那の民族と文化』岩波書店, 1942. (*Peoples and Cultures of Indochina*, Iwanami shoten, 1942.)

Matsumoto, Nobuhiro; Hosaka, Saburō, *Nan'yō bunken mokuroku: Keiō gijuku toshokan shozō*, Keiō gijuku Mochidzuki Shina kenkyū kikin, 1942. 松本信廣, 保坂三郎『南洋文獻目録：慶應義塾圖書館所藏』慶應義塾望月支那研究基金, 1942. (*The Bibliography of South Seas: the Collection of Keio University Library*, Keiō gijuku Mochidzuki Shina kenkyū kikin, 1942.)

Annango nyūmon. Bunpōhen, Indoshina kenkyūkai, 1942.『安南語入門 文法篇』印度支那研究会, 1942. (*Introduction to the Vietnamese Language. Grammar*, Indochina Research Society, 1942.)

Annango nyūmon. Kaiwahen, Indoshina kenkyūkai, 1942.『安南語入門 会話篇』印度支那研究会, 1942. (*Introduction to the Vietnamese Language. Conversation*, Indochina Research Society, 1942.)

"Annan go to Mon-Kumeru go," *Nihongo*, 2-5, Nampō kensetsu to Nihongo, Nihongo kyōiku shinkōkai, dai 5 gō, 1942, pp. 38-44.「安南語とモン・クメル語」『日本語』2-5, 南方建設と日本語, 日本語教育振興会, 第5号, 1942. ("Annamese Language and Mon-Khmer Languages," *Japanese Language*, 2-5, South Seas Building and Japanese Languages, Society for Promotion of the Japanese Language Education, No. 5, 1942.)

"Etsujin kō," *Shigaku zasshi*, dai 53 kan, dai 7 gō, Shigakkai, 1942, p. 133 (887).「越人考」『史学雑誌』史学会, 第53巻, 第7号, 1942. ("A Study on Yue People," *Journal of Historical Science*, Vol. 53, No. 7, Historical Society of Japan, 1942.)

"Nihon jōdai bunka to Nan'yō," *Indoshina no minzoku to bunka*, Iwanami shoten, 1942, pp. 315-336.「日本上代文化と南洋」『印度支那民族と文化』岩波書店, 1942. ("The Japanese Ancient Culture and the South Seas," *Peoples and Cultures of Indochina*, Iwanami shoten, 1942.)

"Wani sonota hachūrui meigi kō" (1942), *Tōa minzoku bunka ronkō*, Seibundō shinkōsha, 1968, pp. 691-720.「和邇其他爬蟲類名義考」(1942)『東亜民族文化論攷』誠文堂新光社, 1968. ("A Study on the Meaning of Name of Crocodile and Other Reptiles" (1942), *The Collections of Papers on Culture of East Asian People*, Seibundō shinkōsha, 1968.)

1943

"Annan go," "Marai go," "Jawa go," *Sekai no kotoba*, Keiō gijuku daigaku gogaku kenkyūjohen, Keiō shuppansha, 1943, pp. 73-79, 81-86, 87-90.「安南語、マライ語、ジャワ語」『世界の言葉』慶應義塾大学語学研究所編, 慶應出版社, 1943. ("Annamese Language," "Malay Language," "Javanese Language," *World and Languages*, Keio University Linguistic Institute, Keiō shuppansha, 1943.)

"Annan minzoku ron," *Dai Nihon takushoku gakkai nenpō*, dai 1 gō, Nihon hyōronsha, 1943.「安南民族論」『大日本拓殖学会年報』第1号, 日本評論社, 1943, pp. 279-285. ("Theory of Annamese People," *Annual Report of Great Japan Colonization Society*, Vol. 1, Nihon hyōronsha, 1943.)

"Binrō to bashō —Nampō san shokubutsu mei no kenkyū," *Minami Ajia gakuhō*, dai 1 gō, Minami Ajia bunka kenkyūjo, 1943, pp. 721-750.「檳榔と芭蕉―南方産植物名の研究」『東亜アジア学報』第1号, 東亜アジア文化研究所, 1943. ("Betel Palm and Banana - A Research in Names of Southward Products and Plants," *Southern Asian Research Report*, Vol. 1, Research Institute for South Asian Culture, 1943.)

"Wagago ni okeru Nampō yōso" (1943), *Tōa minzoku bunka ronkō*, Seibundō shinkōsha, 1968, pp. 539-564.「我国語に於ける南方要素」(1943)『東亜民族文化論攷』誠文堂新光社, 1968. ("Southern Elements in the Japanese Language" (1943), *The Collections of Papers on Culture of East Asian People*, Seibundō shinkōsha, 1968.)

"Zoku Nampō san dōshokubutsu honpōmei no kenkyū" (1943), *Tōa minzoku bunka ronkō*, Seibundō shinkōsha, 1968, pp. 647-658.「続南方動植物本邦名の研究」(1943)『東亜民族文化論攷』誠文堂新光社, 1968. ("A Research on the Japanese Names of Southward Animals and Plants. Continued" (1943), *The Collections of Papers on Culture of East Asian People*, Seibundō shinkōsha, 1968.)

1944

"Annanjin no kigen," *Taiheiyō ken*, jōkan, Kawade shōbō, 1944, pp. 3-23 (321-341).「安南人の起源」『太平洋圏』上巻, 河出書房, 1944. ("Origins of Vietnamese People," *Pacific Sphere*, Vol. 1, Kawade shōbō, 1944.)

"Ban meigi kō" (1944), *Tōa minzoku bunka ronkō*, Seibundō shinkōsha, 1968, p. 1-45.「夷蛮名義考」(1944)『東亜民族文化論攷』誠文堂新光社, 1968. ("Barbarians' Names" (1944), *The Collections of Papers on Culture of East Asian People*, Seibundō shinkōsha, 1968.)

"Kodai kōsen gu meishō kō" (1944), *Tōa minzoku bunka ronkō*, Seibundō shinkōsha, 1968, pp. 597-614.「古代攻戦具名称考」(1944)『東亜民族文化論攷』誠文堂新光社, 1968. ("A Study in Names of Ancient Weapons" (1944), *The Collections of Papers on Culture of East Asian People*, Seibundō shinkōsha, 1968.)

"Nampō chiiki," *Tōa sekaishi* (2), Sekaishi kōza (4), Kōbundō shobō, 1944, pp. 3-41 (111-149).「南方地域」『東亜世界史』(2), 世界史講座 (4), 弘文堂書房, 1944. ("Southern Region," *World History of East Asia* (2), Lecture of World History (4), Kōbundō shobō, 1944.)

1951

"Furansu daigaku," *Sanshokuki*, dai 42 gō, Keiō Gijuku Daigaku tsūshin kyōikubu, 1951, pp. 1-4.「フランスの大学」『三色旗』第42号，慶應義塾大学通信教育部, 1951. ("French University, *Three Color Flague*, Vol. 42, Keiō gijuku daigaku tsūshin kyōikubu, 1951.)

1953

"Indoshina no nōkō girei," *Niiname no kenkyū*, I., Sōgensha, 1953, pp. 156-163.「インドシナの農耕儀礼」『新嘗の研究』創元社, 1953. ("Agricultural Rites of Indochina," *The Research of New Harvest*, I., Sōgensha, 1953.)

1956

"Hashigaki," *Nihon no shinwa*, Ibundō, 1956.「はしがき」『日本の神話』至文堂, 1956. ("Preface," *The Japanese Myths*, Ibundō, 1956.)

"Ko Orikuchi Shinobu hakase to 'kodai kenkyū'," *Nihon oyobi Nihonjin*, 7(9), Kanaobun'endō, 1956-09, pp. 100-105.「故折口信夫博士と「古代研究」」『日本及び日本人』, 7(9), 金尾文淵堂, 1956-09 pp. 100-105. (Late Dr. Orikuchi Shinobu and 'Ancient Studies'," *Japan and the Japanese*, 7(9), Kanaobun'endō, 1956-09, pp. 100-105.

Nihon shinwa kenkyū, Ibundō, 1956.『日本の神話』至文堂, 1956. (*The Japanese Myths*, Ibundō, 1956, 2nd edition)

1957

"Ko Hashimoto Masukichi kyoju no tsuioku," *Shigaku*, dai 219 kan, dai 4 go, Mita Shigakkai, 1957, pp. 102-106（466-470）.「故橋本増吉教授の追憶」『史学』第219巻, 第4号, 三田史学会, 1957. ("Reminiscences of Late Professor Hashimoto Masukichi," *The Historical Science*, Vol. 219, No. 4, Mita Historical Society, 1957.)

Tōnan Ajia no inasaku bunka no sōgō chōsa shuisho, Nihon minzoku kyōkai, 1957.『東南アジアの稲作民族文化の綜合調査趣意書』日本民族学協会, 1957. (*The Prospectus of the Comprehensive Study of Rice Ethnic Cultures of Southeast Asia*, The Japanese Ethnological Society, 1957.)

1962

"Tōhoku no tabi," *Teihon Yanagita Kunioshū*, Geppō 1, Chikumashobō, 1962, pp. 360-363.「東北の旅」『定本柳田国男集』月報１, 筑摩書房, 1962. ("The Trip to Tōhoku," *Yanagita Kunio's Authentic Writings Collection*, Monthly Report 1, Chikumashobō, 1962.)

1969

Betonamu minzoku shōshi, Iwanami shinsho, 1973 (1st ed. 1969).『ベトナム民族小史』岩波新書, 1973. (*Small History of the Vietnamese People*, Iwanami shinsho, 1973

(1st ed. 1969).)

1971

"Kaisetsu," *Nihon bunka no kigen*, dai 3 kan, "Minzokugaku 1," Matsumoto Nobuhiro hen, Heibonsha, 1971, pp. 3-59.「解説」『日本文化の起源』第3巻「民族学1」松本信広編集, 平凡社, 1971. (*"Commentary," The Origins of Japanese Culture*, Vol. 3, "Ethnology 1," edited by Matsumoto Nobuhiro, Heibonsha, 1971.)

1973

Betonamu minzoku shōshi, Iwanami shinsho, 1973 (1st ed. 1969).『ベトナム民族小史』岩波新書, 1973. (*Small History of Vietnamese People*, Iwanami shinsho, 1973 (1st ed. 1969).)

"Mita no Orikuchi Shinobu" (zadankai), *Mita hyōron*, dai 730 gō, Mita hyōron hakkōjo, October 1973.「三田の折口信夫」座談会『三田評論』第730号, 三田評論発行所, 1973. ("Orikuchi Shinobu of Mita" (panel discussion), *Mita hyōron*, No. 730, Mita hyōron hakkōjo, October 1973.)

"Orikuchi san no koto," *Kokubungaku*, 18/1, 1973nen 1gatsu.「折口さんのこと」『国文学』解釈と教育の研究, 18-1, 1973. ("On Mr. Orikuchi," *National Literature*, 18/1, January 1973.)

"Shigakusha to shite Tanaka Suiichirō sensei," *Shigaku* 45/4, Mita Shigakkai, 1973, p. 49 (409)-61 (421).「史学者としての田中萃一郎先生」『史学』第45巻, 第4号, 三田史学会, 1973. ("Teacher Tanaka Suiichirō as a Historian," *The Historical Science*, Vol. 45, No. 4, Mita Historical Society, 1973.)

1978

"Yanagita Kunio 'Kainan shōki' to 'Kaijō no michi' - minzoku to minzoku ni tsuite," *Nihon minzoku bunka no kigen I: shinwa-densetsu*, Kōdansha, 1978, pp. 331-359.「柳田国男『海南小記』と『海上の道』―民族と民俗について」『日本民族文化の起源 I：神話・伝説』講談社, 1978. ("Yanagita Kunio's 'Notes from South Sea' and 'The Sea Route' - about the Race and the Folklore," *The Origins of the Japanese Ethnic Culture I: Myths, Legends*, Kōdansha, 1978.)

1982

Matsumoto Nobuhiro shinpen zakki, Matsumoto Chie, 1982.『松本信廣身辺雑記』松本千枝, 1982. (*Matsumoto Nobuhiro's Miscellaneous Writings*, Matsumoto Chie, 1982.)

Other authors (works in alphabetic order)

A

Arima, Makiko "Hito, Matsumoto Nobuhiroshi," *Kikan jinruigaku*, 5-1, Shakaishisōsha, 1974, pp. 155-160. 有馬真喜子「ひと, 松本信広氏」『季刊　人類学』5‐1, 京都大学人類学研究会, 社会思想社, 1974. ("People, Mr. Matsumoto Nobuhiro," *Quarterly Anthropology*, 5-1, Shakaishisōsha, 1974.)

Aurousseau, Léonard "La premiére conquête chinoise des pays annamites (IIIe siècle avant notre ère), Apendice, Note sur les origins due people annamite, *BEFEO*, XXIII. ("The First Chinese Conquest of Annamese Countries" (3rd century BC), *BEFEO*, XXIII.)

C

Chavannes, Édouard *Le T'ai chan: essai de monographie d'un culte chinois: appendice: Le dieu du sol dans la Chine antique*, E. Leroux, Paris, 1910. (*Mount Tai: a Monographic Essay on Chinese Cult: Appendix: The God of the Earth in Ancient China*, Paris: E. Leroux, 1910.)

Chavannes, Édouard *Les mémoires historiques de Se-Ma Ts'ien*, Société asiatique, Ernest Leroux, Paris, 1895. (*Sima Qian's Historical Memoirs*, Asian Sociaty, Ernest Leroux, Paris, 1895.)

Chikamori, Masashi "Matsumoto Nobuhiro no 'Genmin no kenkyū'," *Keiō gijuku daigaku daigakuin shakaigaku kenkyū kiyō. Ningen to shakai no tankyū. Kujūkuri chōsa*, Keiō gijuku daigaku daigakuin shakaigaku kenkyūka, 2013, pp. 235-239. 近森正「松本信広の『源民の研究』」『慶應義塾大学大学院社会学研究紀要　人間と社会の探究　九十九里調査』慶應義塾大学大学院社会学研究科, 2013. ("Matsumoto Nobuhiro's 'Research of Genmin'," *Keio University Graduate School Sociological Research Bulletin. Human and Society Exploration. Survey of Kujūku Village*, Keio University Graduate School Sociology Department, 2013.)

Chin, Kei Wa "Maegaki," *Daietsu shiki zensho: kōgōbon*, jō, Tōkyō daigaku Tōyō bunka kenkyūjo fuzoku Tōyōgaku bunken sentā kankō iinkai, 1984. 陳荊和「まえがき」『大越史記全書：校合本』(上), 東京大学東洋文化研究所附属東洋学文献センター刊行委員会, 1984. (Trần Kinh Hoà [Chen Ching Ho], Foreword, *Đại Việt sử ký toàn thư* [Complete Annals of Đại Việt], Vol. 1, Tokyo University Oriental Culture Research Institute, Publishing Committee of the Center for Oriental Documents, 1984.)

"Chin Kei Wa zenshochō keireki, kenkyū jisseki ichiran," *Sōdai Ajia kenkyū*, dai 15 gō, Sōka daigaku Ajia kenkyūjo, 1994, pp. 148-155.「陳荊和前所長経歴・研究実績一覧」『創大アジア研究』第15号, 創価大学アジア研究所, 1994. ("Former Director Trần Kinh Hoà's [Chen Ching Ho's] Life History and Research Achievements Overview," *Sōdai Ajia kenkyū*, dai 15 gō, Sōka daigaku Ajia kenkyūjo, 1994.)

Clémentine-Ojha, Catherine and Manguin, Pierre-Yves *A Century in Asia. The History of École française d'Extrême-Orient 1898-2006*, Edition Didier Millet, EFEO, 2007.

D

Daietsu shiki zensho: kōgōbon, jō, chū, ge, Tōkyō daigaku Tōyō bunka kenkyūjo fuzoku Tōyōgaku bunken sentā kankō iinkai, 1984. 『大越史記全書: 校合本』(上, 中, 下), 東京大学東洋文化研究所附属東洋学文献センター刊行委員会, 1984. (*Đại Việt sử ký toàn thư* [Complete Annals of Đại Việt], Tokyo University Oriental Culture Research Institute, Publishing Committee of the Center for Oriental Documents, 1984.)

Dainan ittō shi, dai1shū, dai2shū, Indoshina kenkyūkai, 1941. 『大南一統志』第1輯, 第2輯, 印度支那研究会, 1941. (*Đại Nam nhất thống chí* [The Annals of the Đại Nam], 1, 2 Indochina Research Association, 1941.)

Dainan jitsuroku, 1-6, Keiōgijuku daigaku gogaku kenkyūjo, 1961, 1963, 1968, 1962, 1971, 1972. 『大南寔錄』1-6, 慶応義塾大学語学研究所, 1961, 1963, 1968, 1962, 1971, 1972. (*Đại Nam thực lục* [The Chronicles of Đại Nam], 1-6, Keio University Linguistic Institute, 1961, 1963, 1968, 1962, 1971, 1972.)

David, Nicolas and Kramer, Carol *Ethnoarchaeology in Action*. Cambridge World Archaeology, Cambridge University Press, 2001.

Dixon, Roland Burrage *Oceanic*, Boston: Marshall Jones, 1916.

The Dictionary of Anthropology, edited by Barfield, Thomas, Cambridge, Mass.: Blackwell Publishers, 1997.

E

Encyclopedia of Cultural Anthropology, Vol. 2, edited by Levinson, David and Ember, Melvin, New York: Henry Holt and Company, 1996.

Esaka, Teruya "Matsumoto Nobuhiro sensei tono chōsa kaiko," "Matsumoto Nobuhiro sensei wo shinobu," Kodaigaku Jānaru, dai 194 gō, Nyū saiensusha, 1981, p. 27-28. 江坂輝彌「松本信廣先生との調査回顧」「松本信廣先生をしのぶ」『考古学ジャーナル』第194号, ニュー・サイエンス社, 1981. ("Retrospective Study with Teacher Matsumoto Nobuhiro," "Remembering Teacher Matsumoto Nobuhiro," *Archaeological Journal*, No. 194, New Science Company, 1981.)

Esaka, Teruya "Mita no kōkogaku" (Dainikai zadankai, Mitashigaku no hyakunen wo kataru), *Shigaku*, dai 60 kan, dai 2/3 gō, Mita Shigakkai, 1991, p. 69-78 (243-252). 江坂 輝弥「三田の考古学」(第二回座談会, 三田氏学の百年を語る)第60巻, 第2・3号, 三田史学会, 1991. ("Mita Archaeology" (Symposium on a Hundred Years Historical School of Keio University), *The Historical Science*, Vol. 60, No. 2/3, Mita Historical Society, 1991.)

F

Frazer, Jamese George, *Totemism and Exogamy*, Vol. I, Edinburgh, 1910 (first edition 1887).

Fukuta, Ajio *Yanagita Kunio no minzokugaku*, Yoshikawa kōbunkan, 1992. 福田アジオ『柳田国男の民俗学』吉川弘文館, 1992. (Fukuda, Ajio "Yanagita Kunio's Folklore Studies," Yoshikawa kōbunkan, 1992.)

Fukuzawa, Yukichi *An Outline of a Theory of Civilization*, Columbia University Press, New York, 2008.

Furuno, Kiyoto "Nihon shinwagaku no shinkenkyū - Matsumoto Nobuhiro shi no kingyō shōkai," *Minzoku*, dai 4 kan, dai 1 gō, Minzoku hakkōjo, 1928, p. 153-164. 古野清人「日本神話学の新研究―松本信広氏の近業紹介」『民族』第 4 巻, 第 1 号, 民族発行所, 1928. ("New Research in the Japanese Mythology - Introducing Matsumoto Nobuhiro's Latest Work," *Ethnos*, Vol. 4, No. 1, Minzoku hakkōjo, 1928.)

G

Gaillard, Gérald "III The turn of the century. The Diffusionist Schools," *The Routledge Dictionary of Anthropologists*, London, Routledge, New York, 1997, pp. 40-41.

Gengo bunka kenkyūjo sōritsu 50 shūnen kinen kōenkai - kinen shimpojiumu, Keiō Gijuku Daigaku, 2012nen 10gatsu 13nichi, (symposium).『言語文化研究所創立50周年記念講演会―記念シンポジウム』慶應義塾大学, 2012年10月13日. (*Lectures and Symposium at the Occasion of the 50th Anniversary of the establishment of Institute of Cultural and Linguistic Studies*, Keio University, 13 October 2012.)

"Granet, Marcel," Encyclopedia of religion, second edition, Macmillan Reference USA, Detroit, 2005, pp. 3654-3655.

Granet, Marcel *Danses et légendes de la Chine ancienne*, Les Presses universitaires de France, Paris, 1926. (*Dances and Legends of Ancient China*, Les Presses universitaires de France, Paris, 1926.)

Granet, Marcel *Fêtes et chanson anciennes de la Chine*, second edition, Librarie Ernest Leroux, Paris, 1929 (first edition 1919). (*Festivals and Songs of Ancient China*, second edition, Librarie Ernest Leroux, Paris, 1929.)

Granet, Marcel *La Polygénie sororale et le sororat dans la Chine féodale*, Leroux, Paris, 1920. (*Sororal Polygyny and Sororate in Feudal China*, Paris: Leroux, 1920.)

Gurane, Maruseru (translation by Tsuda Itsuo), *Shina kodai no sairei to kayō*, Kōbundō shobō, 1938. マルセル・グラネ(内田智雄 訳)『支那古代の祭礼と歌謡』弘文堂書房, 1938. (Granet, Marcel (translated by Tsuda Itsuo), *Festivals and Songs of Ancient China*, Kōbundō shobō, 1938.)

H

Hashimoto, Masukichi *Tōyōshi kōza ikki*, Jitaiko gokanmatsu, Ji taiko, Kokushi kōshūkai, 1926. 橋本増吉『東洋史講座第一期』自太古至後漢末, 国史講習会, 1926.

(*Lecture in Oriental History - Semester 1*, From ancient times to the end of Later Han, Kokushi kōshūkai, 1926.)

Hata, Ikuhiko "The Army Move into Norhern Indochina," *The Fateful Choice. Japan's Advance into Southeast Asia, 1939-1941*, Edited by Morley, James William, Columbia University Press, New York, 1980.

Hayashi, Masako "Betonamu hon ni tsuite - Tōyō bunko zō Betonamu hon shomoku' ni miru Nihon tono kakawari," *Atomi gakuen joshi daigaku bungaku fōramu*, 9, Atomi gakuen joshi daigaku, 2011, pp.118 - 127. 林正子「越南本について―『東洋文庫蔵越南本書目』にみる日本とのかかわり―」跡見学園女子大学文化フォーラム9, 跡見学園女子大学, 2011. ("About Vietnamese Books - Relations with Japann Seen in 'The Catalogue of Vietnamese Books Stored in Oriental Library'," *Atomi gakuen joshi daigaku bungaku fōramu*, 9, Atomi gakuen joshi daigaku, 2011.)

Heine-Geldern, Robert "Ein Beitrag zur Chronologie des Neolithikums in Südostasien," St. Gabriel-Mödling bei Wien, *Anthropos*-Administration, [ca. 1924], pp. 809–843. ("A contribution to the Chronology of the Neolithic in Southeast Asia," St. Gabriel bei Wien Anthropos-Administration, [ca.1924].)

Heine-Geldern, Robert "Urheimat und früheste Wanderungen der Austronesier," *Anthropos* (XXVII), 1932, pp. 543-619. ("Home and Earliest Migration of Austronesians," Anthoropos (XXVII), 1932)

Hirafuji, Kikuko "Shakaigakuteki kenkyū - Matsumoto Nobuhiro no shinwa kenkyū ni okeru Furansu shakaigakuha no eikyō," *Shinwagaku to Nihon no kamigami*, Kōbunkan, 2004, pp. 33-41. 平藤喜久子「社会学的研究―松本信広の神話研究における フランス社会学派の影響」『神話学と日本の神々』弘文堂, 2004. ("Sociological Research - the Influence of the French School of Sociology in Matsumoto Nobuhiro's Mythological Research," *Mythology and Japan's Deities*, Kōbunkan, 2004.)

Hirafuji, Kikuko "Shokuminchi teikoku Nihon no shinwagaku," *Shūkyō to fashizumu*, 1, pp. 311-347. 平藤喜久子「植民地帝国日本の神話学」『宗教とファシズム』水声社, 2010. ("Mythology of Colonialist Imperialist Japan," *Religion and Fascisim*, Suiseisha, 2010.)

I

Ine-fune-matsuri: Matsumoto Nobuhiro sensei tsuitō ronbunshū, Rokkōshuppan, 1982. 『稲・舟・祭: 松本信広先生追悼論文集』六興出版, 1982. (*Rice, Boat, Festival: Memorial Collection of Papers for Teacher Matsumoto Nobuhiro*, Rokkōshuppan, 1982.)

Ishida, Mikinosuke *Nankai ni kansuru Shina shiryō*, Seikatsusha, 1945. 石田幹之助『南海に関する支那史料』生活社, 1945. (*Chinese Historical Records on the South Seas*, Seikatsusha, 1945.)

Ishii, Kenji "Kodai suitei fune yasei gō no omoide," *Nihon minzoku bunka no kigen*, dai 2 kan, geppō dai 2 gō, Kōdansha, 1978, pp. 3-6. 石井謙治「古代推定船野性号の

思い出」『日本民族文化の起源』第 2 巻, 月報第 2 号, 1978. ("Memoirs of the 'Wild Boat' supposed as ancient", Vol. 2, No. 2, Kōdansha, 1978.)

Ishii, Yoneo "Tōnan Ajia no shiteki ninshiki no ayumi," *Tōnan Ajia no rekishi*, Kōbundō, 1991, pp. 1-14. 石井米雄「東南アジアの史的認識の歩み」『東南アジアの歴史』弘文堂, 1991, pp. 1-14. (Ishii, Yoneo "History of Historical Awareness of Southeast Asia," *History of Southeast Asia*, Kōbundō, 1991.)

Itō, Mikiharu "Nihon shinwa to Ryūkyū shinwa," *Nihon shinwa to Ryūkyū*, Kōza Nihon no shinwa, dai 10 kan, Yūseidō shuppan, 1977, pp. 1-25. 伊藤幹治「日本神話と琉球神話」『日本神話と琉球』講座日本神話, 第10巻, 有精堂出版, 1977. ("The Japanese Myths and Ryukyu Myths," *The Japanese Myths and Ryukyu*, Lecture The Japanese Myths, Vol. 10, Yūseidō shuppan, 1977.)

Itō, Seiji "Hito to gakumon, Matsumoto Nobuhiro," *Shakai jinruigaku nenpō*, Tōkyō toritsu daigaku shakai jinrui gakkai, dai 12 kan, 1986, pp. 117-131. 伊藤清司［人と学問］「松本信廣」『社会人類学年報』東京都立大学社会人類学会, 第12巻, 1986. ([People and Scholarship] "Matsumoto Nobuhiro," *Annual Report of Social Anthropology*, Tokyo Metropolitan University Social Anthropological Society, Vol. 12, 1986.)

Itō, Seiji "Matsumoto Nobuhito to imohori chōsha no hanashi," *Nihon bunka no kigen*, dai 3 kan, Geppō dai 3 gō, Kōdansha, 1978, pp. 5-8. 伊藤清司「松本先生と芋堀長者の話し」『日本民族文化の起源』第 3 巻, 月報第 3 号, 講談社, 1978. ("Matsumoto Nobuhiro and the Tale of Potato Digger," *The Origins of the Japanese Culture*, Vol. 3, Monthly Report No. 3, Kōdansha, 1978.)

Itō, Seiji "Matsumoto Nobuhiro - 'Nampōsetsu' no kaitakusha," *Bunka jinruigaku gunzō*, Nihonhen (3), Akademia shuppankai, Kyōto, 1988, pp. 225-242. 伊藤清司「松本信広―「南方説」の開拓者『文化人類学群像』「日本編」（3）, アカデミア出版会, 京都, 1988. ("Matsumoto Nobuhiro - A Pioneer in the 'Southward Theory', *Portraits of Cultural Anthropology, Japan* (3), Akademia shuppankai, Kyoto, 1988.)

Itō, Seiji "Matsumoto Nobuhiro sensei no omoide to kodai fune no kenkyū" "Matsumoto Nobuhiro sensei wo shinobu," *Kodaigaku Jānaru*, dai 194 gō, Nyū saiensusha, 1981, p. 30 伊藤清司「松本信廣先生の思い出と古代船の研究」「松本信廣先生をしのぶ」『考古学ジャーナル』第194号, ニュー・サイエンス社, 1981. ("Memories of Teacher Matsumoto Nobuhiro and the Research of Ancient Boats," "Remembering Teacher Matsumoto Nobuhiro," *The Archaeological Journal*, No. 194, New Science Co., 1981.)

Itō, Seiji "Matsumoto Nobuhiro to gakumon," *Keiō gijuku daigaku gengo kenkyūjo hōkokushū*, Keiō gijuku daigaku, dai 24 kan, 1992, pp. 13-26. 伊藤清司「松本信廣と学問」『慶応義塾大学文化言語研究所報告集』第24巻, 慶応義塾大学, 1992. ("Matsumoto Nobuhiro and Scholarship," *Reports of the Keio Institute of Cultural and Linguistic Studies*, Vol. 24, Keio University, 1992.)

Itō, Seiji "Matsumoto Nobuhiro sensei wo shinonde," *Minzoku kenkyū*, dai 46 kan, dai 1 gō, Nihon minzoku gakkai, 1981, pp. 125-127. 伊藤清司「松本信廣先生を偲んで」『民族研究』46-1, 日本民族学会, 1981. ("In Memory of Teacher Matsumoto Nobuhiro," *Ethnological Research*, The Japanese Society of Ethnology, 1981.)

Itō, Seiji "Minzokugaku, Fōkuroa, Tōyō shigaku no hazamade" (Dainikai zadankai, Mitashigaku no hyakunen wo kataru), *Shigaku*, dai 60 kan, dai 2/3 gō, Mita Shigakkai, 1991, pp. 253-263. 伊藤清司「民族学・フォークロア・東洋史学のはざまで」(第二回座談会, 三田史学の百年を語る)『史学』第60巻, 第2・3号, 三田史学会, 1991. ("Interdisciplinary Research Tradition: Ethnology, Folklore and Oriental History" (Symposium on a Hundred Years Historical School of Keio University), *The Historical Science*, Vol. 60, No. 2/3, Mita Historical Society, 1991.)

Itō, Seiji "Sumiyaki chōsha no hanashi - Yanagita Kunio to Mastumoto Nobuhiro," *Shigaku*, dai 75 kan, dai 2/3 gō, Mita Shigakkai, 2007, pp. 211-231. 伊藤清司「炭焼き長者の話―柳田国男と松本信廣―」『史学』第75巻, 第2・3号, 三田史学会, 2007. (The Folktale of Charcoal Burner Kogorō - Yanagita Kunio and Matsumoto Nobuhiro," *The Historical Science*, Vol. 75, No. 2/3, Mita Historical Society, 2007.)

Iwai, Daie "Nagata Yasukichi shūshū Annam bon mokuroku," *Shigaku*, dai 14 kan, dai 2 gō, Mita Shigakkai, 1935, pp. 283-291. 岩井, 大慧「永田安吉氏蒐集安南本目録」『史学』第14巻, 第2号, 三田史学会, 1935. ("The Catalogue of Nagata Yasukichi's Collection of the Vietnamese Books," *The Historical Science*, Vol. 14, No. 2, Mita Historical Society, 1935.)

Iwata, Kenji, "Kaisetsu," *Nihon minzoku bunka no kigen: Tōnan Ajia bunka to Nihon*, Kōdansha, 1978, pp. 447-454. 岩田慶治「解説」『日本民族文化の起源 III：東南アジア文化と日本』講談社, 1978. ("Commentary," *The Origins of the Japanese Ethnology III: Southeast Asian Culture and Japan*, Kōdansha, 1978.)

K

Kani, Hiroaki "Matsumoto Nobuhiro sensei to Honkon kōkogaku" "Matsumoto Nobuhiro sensei wo shinobu," *Kodaigaku Jānaru*, dai 194 gō, Nyū saiensusha, 1981, pp. 27-30. 可児弘明「松本信廣先生との香港考古学」「松本信廣先生をしのぶ」『考古学ジャーナル』第194号, 1981. ("Teacher Matsumoto Nobuhiro and Archaeology in Hong Kong," "Commemorating Teacher Matsumoto Nobuhiro," *Archaeological Journal*, No. 194, 1981.)

Kawamoto, Kunie *Dainan jitsuroku chimei sakuin*, 1, Keiō gijuku daigaku gengobunka kenkyūjo, 2007. 川本邦衛『大南寔録地名索引(一)』慶應義塾大学言語文化学研究所, 2007. (*Index of Place Names in the Annals of Đại Nam*, vol. 1, Keiō gijuku daigaku gogaku kenkyūjo, 2007.)

Kawamoto, Kunie "'Dainan jitsuroku' chimei sakuin - Jo narabi ni hanrei," *Dainan jitsuroku chimei sakuin*, Keiō gijuku daigaku gengo bunka kenkyūjo, 2002, pp. i-iv. 川本邦衛「『大南寔録』地名索引―序並びに凡例」『大南寔録地名索引』慶應義塾大学言語文化学研究所, 2002. ("Index of Place Names in "the Annals of Đại

Nam - Introduction and Legend," *The Annals of Đại Nam - Index of Place names*, Keiō gijuku daigaku gogaku kenkyūjo, 2002.)

Kawamoto, Kunie "Gengo bunka kenkyūjo sanjūnen," *Keiō Gijuku daigaku gengo bunka kenkyūjo hōkokushū*, Keiō Gijuku daigaku gengo bunka kenkyūjo, dai 24 gō, 1992, pp. 1-12. 川本邦衛「言語文化言語研究所三十年」『慶応義塾大学文化言語研究所報告集』慶応義塾大学文化言語研究所, 第24号, 1992. ("Thirty Years of the Keio Institute of Cultural and Linguistic Studies," *The Keio Institute of Cultural and Linguistic Studies Report Collection*, the Keio Institute of Cultural and Linguistic Studies, No. 24, 1992.)

Kawamoto, Kunie "Shiki ni mukau keigan - Chin Kei Wa hakushi wo itamu," *Keiō gijuku daigaku gengo bunka kenkyūjo kiyō*, dai 28 gō, Keiō gijuku daigaku gengo bunka kenkyūjo, 1996, pp. 11-20. 川本邦衛「史記に対う慧眼—陳荊和博士を悼む」『慶應義塾大学言語文化研究所紀要』第28号, 慶應義塾大学言語文化研究所, 1996. ("Keen Insight in Historical Records - Mourning for Dr. Trần Kinh Hoà [Chen Ching Ho]", *Bulletin of Keio the Institute of Cultural and Linguistic Studies*, the Keio Institute of Cultural and Linguistic Studies, 1996.)

Kobayashi, Hideo "Nihongo no shozoku mondai - Matsumoto Nobuhiro shi no kingi wo yomu," *Minzoku*, dai 4 kan, dai 1 gō, Minzoku hakkōjo, 1928, pp. 159-164. 小林英夫「日本語所属の問題—松本信広氏の近업を読む」『民族』第4巻, 第1号, 民族発行所, 1928. ("The Problem of Classification of the Japanese Language - Reading Matsumoto Nobuhiro's Latest Work," *Ethnos*, Vol. 4, No. 1, Minzoku hakkōjo, 1928.)

Kōyama, Shirō "Fuhō," *Shigaku*, dai 51 kan, dai 1/2, Mita Shigakkai, 1981. 神山四郎「訃報」『史学』第51巻, 第1・2号, 三田史学会, 1981, pp. 237-238. ("News of Death," *Historical Science*, Vol. 51, No. 1/2, Mita Historical Society, 1981.)

Kanokogi, Kazunobu *Bunmei to tetsugaku seishin*, Keiō gijuku shuppankyoku, 1915. 鹿子木員信『文明と哲学的精神』慶応義塾出版局, 1915. (Kanokogi, Kazunobu, *Civilization and the Philosophical Spirit*, Keio Gijuku Publishing Office, 1915.)

Kanokogi, Kazunobu *Sentō-teki jinseikan*, Bunsendō shobō, 1943 (first edition 1917). 鹿子木員信『戦闘的人生観』文川堂書房, 1943 (1917). (*The Outlook on the Life of Fight*, Bunsendō shobō, 1943 (first edition 1917).)

Kansan, Jun *Orientarizumu no kanata he: kindai bunka hihan*, Iwanami shoten, 1996. 姜尚中『オリエンタリズムの彼方へ:近代文化批判』岩波書店, 1996. (*Beyond Orientalism: Critic of Modern Culture*, Iwanami shoten, 1996.)

Kawai, Teiichi "Daigaku no ninmu," *Mita hyōron*, dai 321 gō, Keiō gijuku daigaku, 1924, pp. 1-4. 川合貞一「大学の任務」『三田評論』第321号, 慶応義塾大学, 1924. ("The Duty of the University," *Mita hyōron*, No. 321, Keio Gijuku University, 1924.)

Kawai, Teiichi "Futatabi bunka no mondai ni suite," *Mita hyōron*, dai 314 gō, Keiō gijuku daigaku, 1923, pp. 1-18. 川合貞一「再び文化の問題に就いて」『三田評論』第314号, 慶応義塾大学, 1923. ("Again about the problem of culture," *Mita hyōron*, No.

314, Keio gijuku University, 1923.)

Kawai kyōju kanreki kinen ronbunshū, Kawaikyōju kanreki shukugakai, 1931.『川合教授還暦記念論文集』川合貞一教授還暦祝賀会編, 1931. (*Collection of Papers Published at the Occasion of Professor Kawai's Sixtieth Birthday*, Association for Celebration of Professor Kawai's Sixtieth Birthday, 1931.)

Kawai, Teiichi "Tetsugaku to kyōiku," Ōsaka kōen, Keiō gijuku shuppankyoku, 1913, pp. 118-164. 川合貞一「哲学と教育」慶応義塾『大阪講演』慶応義塾出版局, 1913. ("Philosophy and Education," *Osaka Lecture*, Keio Gijuku Publishing Office, 1913.)

Kawakita, Nobuo "Keiō gijuku daigaku bungakubu kyōin tantō kamoku ichiran," *Shigaku*, dai 60 kan, dai 2/3 gō, Mita Shigakkai, 1991, pp. 353-404. 河北展生「慶應義塾大学文学部教員担当科目一覧」『史学』第60巻, 第2・3号, 三田史学会, 1991. (Kawakita Nobuo, "Curriculum Lists of Faculty of Letters, 1890-1959," *The Historical Science*, Vol. 60, No. 2/3, Mita Historical Society, 1991.)

Kawamura, Minato "Taishū Orientarizumu to Ajia ninshiki," *Bunka no naka no shokuminchi*, Iwanami shoten, 1993, pp. 107-136. 川村湊「大衆オリエンタリズムとアジア認識」『文化のなかの植民地』岩波書店, 1993. ("Mass Orientalism and Awareness of Asia," *Colonialism in Culture*, Iwanami shoten, 1993.)

Keiō gijuku hyakunenshi. Chūkanzen. Keiō gijuku daigaku, 1960.『慶應義塾百年史』中巻前, 慶應義塾大学, 1960. (*One Hundred Years of Keio University*, Upper Middle Volume, Keio University, 1960.)

Keiō gijuku toshokan zō Matsumoto bunko mokuroku, Keiō gijuku daigaku Mita jōhō sentā, 1991.『慶應義塾図書館松本文庫目録』慶應義塾大学三田情報センター, 1991. (*A Catalogue of the Matsumoto Collection in the Keio University Library*, Keiō gijuku daigaku Mita jōhō sentā, 1991.)

Keiō gijuku Mochidzuki Shina kenkyū kikin daiichiji jūnenshi, Keiō gijuku, 1937.『慶應義塾望月支那研究基金第一次十年史』慶應義塾, 1937. (*10 Years from Establishment Keio University Mochidzuki Foundation for Chinese Studies*, Keiō gijuku, 1937.)

King, Victor T. and Wilder, William D. *The Modern Anthropology of South-East Asia. An Introduction*, London and New York: Routledge Curzon, 2005 (first edition 2003).

L

Liebersohn, Harry *The Return of the Gift*, Cambridge University Press, 2010.

Lévy-Bruhl, Lucien *Les fonctions mentales dans les société inférieures*, Librarie Félix Alcan, Paris, 1922 (7th edition) (*Mental Function in Inferior Societies*, Librarie Felix Alcan, Paris, 1922 (7th edition).)

Lowie, Robert H. *The History of Ethnological Theory*, Harrap, London, 1937.

M

Mabuchi, Tōichi "Odayaka de fukutsu no daisempai," *Nihon minzoku bunka no kigen*, dai 2 kan, geppō dai 2 gō, Kōdansha, 1978, pp. 1-3. 馬淵東一「おだやかで不屈の大先輩」『日本民族文化の起源』第2巻, 月報第2号, 講談社, 1978. ("Calm and Indominable Daisempai," *The Origins of the Japanese Culture*, Vol. 2, Monthly Report No. 2, Kōdansha, 1978.)

Madrolle, Cl. "Le Tonkin ancient, Lei-leu et les district chinois de l'époque des Han. La population. Yue-chang," *BEFEO*, XXXVII, Fasc. 2. ("Ancient Tonkin, Lei-leu and Chinese Districts in Han Era. popularion. yue-chang," *BEFEO*, XXXVII, Face. 2.)

Masuo, Shinichirō "Reimei-ki no Kiki shinwa kenkyū o meguru dōkō: Tsuda Sōkichi to Takagi Toshio, Yanagita Kunio wo chūshin ni," *Shiryō to shite no "Nihonshoki": Tsuda Sōkichi wo yominaosu*, Bensei shuppan, 2011. 増尾伸一郎「黎明期の記紀神話研究をめぐる動向: 津田左右吉と高木敏雄・柳田國男を中心に」『史料としての『日本書紀』: 津田左右吉を読みなおす』勉誠出版, 2011. ("Trends in the Research of Myths in Kojiki and Nihonshoki during the Dawn: Focused on Tsuda Sōkichi and Takagi Toshio, Yanagita Kunio," *"Nihonshoki" as a Historical Material: Rereading Tsuda Sōkichi*, Bensei shuppan, 2011.)

Maspero, Anri, "Senshin jidai no Shina ni okeru saihōbunka no eikyō", *Shina kenkyū*, Keiō Gijuku Mochidzuki kikin Shina kenkyūkai hen, Iwanami shoten, 1930, pp. 399-416 マスペロ・アンリ「先秦時代に於ける西方文化の影響」『支那研究』慶應義塾望月貴金支那研究会, 岩波書店, 1930. ("The Influence of Western Culture in Pre-Qin Period," *Chinese Studies*, Mochidzuki Foundation Chinese Studies Society, Iwanami shoten, 1930.)

Maspero, Henri "Etudes d'histoire d'Annam, IV, Le royame de Van-lang," *BEFEO*, XVIII, IV, pp. 1-10. ("Studies on History of Annam, IV, Kingdom Van-Lang, *BEFEO*, XVIII, IV.)

Matsumoto, Mikio "Yanagita Kunio no Ryūkyū tabi," *Yanagita Kunio to umi no michi: "Kainan shōki" no genkei*, Yoshikawa kōbunkan, 2003. 松本三喜夫『柳田國男と海の道』―『海南小記』の原景, 吉川弘文館, 2003. (*Yanagita Kunio and the Sea Route: The Background of the "Small Records from the Sea in South"*, Yoshikawa kōbunkan, 2003.)

Matsumoto, Yoshio "Chūshi yūki," *Shigaku*, dai 18 kan, dai 1 gō, Mita Shigakkai, 1939, pp. 145-163. 松本芳夫「中支遊記」『史学』第18巻, 第1号, 三田史学会, Mita Shigakkai, 1939. ("Central China Travel Records," *Historical Science*, Vol. 18, No. 1, Mita Historical Society, 1939.)

Matsumoto, Yoshio "Nihon shinwa no kenkyū (Matsumoto Nobuhiro cho, Dōbunkan hakkō)," *Shigaku*, dai 11 kan, dai 1 gō, Mita Shigakkai, 1932, pp. 137-138. 松本芳夫「日本神話の研究（松本信廣著, 同文館發行）」『史学』第11巻, 第1号, 三田史学会, 1932. (Matsumoto, Yoshio "The Research of Japanese Myths (by Matsumoto Nobuhiro, published by Dōbunkan), *The Historical Science*, Vol. 11,

No. 1, Mita Historical Society, 1932.)

Mauss, Marcel, Hubert, Henri, *Mélanges d'histoire des religions*, Félix Alcan, Paris, 1909. (*Mellanges of History of Religion*, Félix Alcan, Paris, 1909.)

Mauss, Marcel, *The Gift*, translated by W. D. Halls, Routledge, London, 1990.

McClain, James L., *Japan: A Modern History*, W. W. Norton & Company, New York, London, 2002.

Meillet *Les Langues du Monde*, É. Champion Paris, 1924. (*The Languages of the World*, Paris: É. Champion 1924.)

Minami Ajia gakuhō, dai 1 gō, Minami Ajia bunka kenkyūjo, 1943.『東亜アジア学報』第1号, 東亜アジア文化研究所, 1943.(*Southern Asian Research Report*, No. 1, Research Institute for South Asian Culture, 1943.)

Minami Ajia gakuhō, dai 2 gō, Minami Ajia bunka kenkyūjo, 1943.『東亜アジア学報』第2号, 東亜アジア文化研究所, 1943.(*Southern Asian Research Report*, No. 2, Research Institute for South Asian Culture, 1943.)

"Mita no shigakusha profīru," *Shigaku*, dai 60 kan, dai 2/3 gō, Mita Shigakkai, 1991, pp. 161-177（335-351）.「三田の史学者プロフィール」『史学』第60巻, 第2・3号, 三田史学会, 1991. ("The Profiles of Historians at Keio University," *The Historical Science*, Vol. 60, No. 2/3, Mita Historical Society, 1991.)

Minzokugaku kenkyū, dai 4 kan, dai 1 gō, Nihon minzoku gakkai, Sanseidō, 1938.『民族学研究』第4巻, 第1号, 日本民族学会, 三省堂, 1938. (*The Japanese Journal of Ethnology*, Vol. 4, No. 1, Japanese Society of Ethnology, Sanseidō, 1938.)

Mori, Kōichi, "Yanagita Kunio: An Interpretative Study," *Japanese Journal of Religious Studies*, 7/2-3, June-September, 1980, pp. 83-115.

Morse, Ronald A. *The Legends of Tōno*, Japan Foundation, 1975.

Mōsu, Maruseru (translated by Yamada Yoshihiko), *Taiheiyō minzoku no genshi keizai: kosei shakai ni okeru kōkan no keishiki to riyū*, Nikkōshoin, 1943. モース・マルセル（山田吉彦 訳）『太平民族の原始経済：古制社会に於ける交換の形式と理由』日光書院, 1943. (Mauss, Marcel (translation by Yamada Yoshihiko), *Primitive Economy of Pacific People: Form and Reasons of Exchange in Old-System Society*, Nikkōshoin, 1943.)

Murakami, Sachiko *Japan's Thrust into French Indochina 1940-1945*, New York University, 1981.

N

Nakao, Katsumi *Shokuminchi jinruigaku no tembō*, Fūkyōsha, 2000. 中生勝美『植民地人類学の展望』風響社, 2000. (*Prospects of Colonial Anthropology*, Fūkyōsha, 2000.)

"Nihon minzoku gakkai setsuritsu shuisho," *Minzokugaku kenkyū*, dai 1 kan, dai 1 gō, Nihon minzoku gakkai, Sanseidō, 1935, p. 219-222.「日本民族学会設立趣意書」『民族学研究』第1巻第1号, 日本民族学会, 三省堂, 1935. ("The Japanese Society of Ethnology Charter," *The Ethnological Research*, Vol. 1, No. 1, The Japanese Society of Ethnology, Sanseidō, 1935.)

O

Ōbayashi, Taryō "Kaisetsu," *Ijin sonota: hoka jūni hen Oka Masao ronbunshū*, Iwanami shoten, 1994, pp. 267-277. 大林太良「解説」『異人その他 他十二篇』岡正雄論文集, 岩波文庫, 1994. ("Commentary," *Foreigners and Others, Other Twelve Stories, Collection of Oka Masao's Papers*, Iwanami shoten, 1994.)

Ōbayashi, Taryō "Kaisetsu," *Nihon minzokugaku no kigen I: shinwa, densetsu*, Kōdansha, 1978, pp. 401-406. 大林太良「解説」『日本民族学の起源Ⅰ：神話・伝説』講談社, 1978. ("Commentary," *The Origins of the Japanese Ethnology I: Myths - Legends*, Kōdansha, 1978.)

Ōbayashi, Taryō "Nihon shinwa no kenkyū," Kokubungaku kaishaku to kanshō, 37-1, 1972, pp. 162-164. 大林太良「日本神話の研究」『国文学 解釈と鑑賞』37-1, 1972. ("The Research of the Japanese Myths," *National Literature. Commentary and Appreciation*, 37-1, 1972.)

Ōbayashi, Taryō "Sōzōgata shinwa," *Nihon shinwa no kigen*, Kadokawa shoten, 1961, pp. 58-64. 大林太良「創造型神話」『日本神話の起源』角川書店, 1961, pp. 58-64. ("Myths of the Creative Type," *The Origins of the Japanese Myths*, Kadokawa shoten, 1961.)

Ōbayashi, Taryō "Tsuranaru Tōnan Ajia, Oceania," *Shinwa no keifu: Nihon shinwa no genryū wo saguru*, Seidosha, 1986, pp. 221-315. 大林太良「つらなる東南アジア・オセアニア」『神話の系譜：日本神話の源流をさぐる』青土社, 1986, pp. 221-315. ("Extended Southeast Asia, Oceania," *The Genealogy of the Myths: Exploring the Headwaters of the Japanese Myths*, Seidosha, 1986.)

Ōsawa, Kazuo "Dainan jitsuroku to Matsumoto Nobuhiro," *Ine-fune-matsuri: Matsumoto Nobuhiro sensei tsuitō ronbunshū*, Kyōshuppan, 1982, pp. 679-691. 大澤一雄「大南大南寔録」『稲・舟・祭：松本信広先生追悼論文集』六興出版, 1982, pp. 679-691. ("Đại Nam thực lục to Matsumoto Nobuhiro," *Rice, Boat, Festival: Memorial Collection of Papers for Teacher Matsumoto Nobuhiro*, Rokkōshuppan, 1982, pp. 679-691.)

P

Pan-Asianism in Modern Japanese History. Colonialism, Regionalism and Borders, ed. by Saaler, Sven and Koschmann, Victor J., Routledge Taylor & Francis Group, London, 2007. *Pan-Asianism*, Vol. 1 & Vol. 2, ed. by Saaler, Sven and Szpilman, Christopher W. A., New York: Rowman & Littlefield Publishers, Inc., 2011.

Penny, Glenn H. *Objects of Culture. Ethnology and Ethnographic Museums in Imperial Germany*, The University of North California Press, Chapel Hill and London, 2002

Przyluski, Jean "L'or, son origine et ses pouvoirs magiques. Etude de folklore annamite," *BEFEO*, XIV, 5, Hanoi, 1911. ("Gold, Its Origin and Its Magic Powers. A

Study on Annamese Folkore, *BEFEO*, XIV, 5, Hanoi, 1911.)

Przyluski, Jean "Non-Aryan Loans in Indo-Aryan," *Pre-Aryan and Pre-Dravidian in India*, translated by Prabodh Chandra Bagchi Culcatta, Culcutta University Press, Senate House, Culcutta, 1929 (French edition in 1923).

R

Rivet, Paul *Sumérien et Océanien*, Librairie ancienne honoré champion, La Société de linguistique de Paris, Paris, 1929.

Roustan, Frédéric "From Oriental Studies to South Pacific Studies: The Multiple Origins of Vietnamese Studies," *Journal of Vietnamese Studies*, Vol. 6, Issue 1, 2011, pp. 1-42.

The Routledge Dictionary of Anthropologists, Routledge and New York, London, 1997.

S

Sakurai, Yumio "Tōnan Ajia shi no yonjūnen," *Tōnan Ajia shi. Kenkyū no hatten*, Tōnan Ajia Gakkai 40 shūnen, Kinen jigyō iinkai, Yamakawa shuppansha, 2009, pp. 4-40. 桜井由躬雄「東南アジア史の四〇年」『東南アジア史 研究の発展』東南アジア学会40年, 記念事業委員会, 山川出版社, 2009, pp. 4-40. ("40 Years of Southeast Asian History," *History of Southeast Asia. Development of the Research*, 40 Years of the Japan Society for Southeast Asian Studies, Kinen jigyō iinkai, Yamakawa shuppansha, 2009.)

Satō, Yoshiyuki "Iha Fuyū no Matsumoto Nobuhiro ate shokan. Meiji-Taishō no gengogaku, sono 9," *Gakuen*, No. 821, 2009/3, pp. 102-109. 佐藤喜之「伊波普猷の松本信広宛書簡 明治・大正の言語学 その9」『学園』第821号, 2009/3. ("Iha Fuyu's Letter to Matsumoto Nobuhiro. Linguistics of Meiji and Taishō Periods. 9," *Gakuen*, No. 821, 2009/3.)

Schmidt, Wilhelm "Die Mon-Khmer-Völker, ein Bindeglied zwischen Völkern Zentralasiens und Austronesiens," *Archiv für Anthropologie*, Braunschweig, 5, 1906, pp. 59-109. ("The Mon-Khmer peoples, a Link between Peoples of Central Asia and Austronesiens," *Archive for Anthropology*, 5, 1906.)

Schmidt, Wilhelm *Nihon no minzokugakuteki chii tankyū he no atarashiki michi*, Kokusai bunka shinkōkai, 1935. ウィルヘルム・シュミット『日本の民族学的地位探究への新しき途』国際文化振興会, 1935 (岡正雄 訳). (*Neue Wege zue Erforschung der ethnologischen Stellung Japans* [New Approaches to the Study in Ethnological Position of Japan], Kokusai bunka shinkōkai, 1935, (translated to Japanese by Oka Masao).)

Schmidt, Wilhelm *The Culture Historical Method of Ethnology. The Scientific Approach to the Racial Question*, translated by S. A. Sieber, Fortuny's, New York, 1939, p. 17. (*Handbuch der Methode der kulturhistorischen Ethnologie*, 1937.)

Shimao, Minoru "Betonamu. Tōnan Ajiashi he no teii to tenkai," *Tōnan Ajia shi*.

Kenkyū no hatten, Tōnan Ajia Gakkai 40 shūnen, Kinen jigyō iinkai, Yamakawa shuppansha, 2009, pp. 110–129. 嶋尾稔「ベトナム　東南アジア史への定位と展開」『東南アジア史　研究の発展』東南アジア学会40年, 記念事業委員会, 山川出版社, 2009. ("Vietnam. Orientation and Development to Southeast Asian History," *History of Southeast Asia. Development of the Research*, 40 Years of the Japan Society for Southeast Asian Studies, Kinen jigyō iinkai, Yamakawa shuppansha, 2009.)

Shimizu, Akitoshi *Anthropology and Colonialism in Asia and Oceania*, ed. by J. v. Bremen and A. Shimizu, Curzon, Richmond, Surrey, 1999.

Shimizu, Hajime "Kindai Nihon ni okeru 'Tōnan Ajiya' chiiki gainen no seiritsu (Ⅰ)," (Shō-chūgakkō chiri kyōkasho ni miru), *Ajia keizai*, 28/6, Ajia kenkyūjo, 1987, pp. 2–15. 清水元「近代日本における『東南アジヤ』地域概念の成立(Ⅰ)」(—小・中学校地理教科書にみる—)『アジア経済』28/6, アジア研究所, 1987. ("The Emergence of Regional Concept of 'Southeast Asia' in Modern Japan (Ⅰ): A Study Based on Geography Textbooks of Japanese Elementary and Middle Schools," *Asia Economy*, 28/6, Ajia kenkyūjo, 1987.)

Shimizu, Hajime "Meiji chūki no 'Nanshinron' to 'Kan-Taiheiyō' shisō no genkei (Ⅰ)," *Ajia Keizai*, 32/9, Ajia kenkyūjo, September 1991, pp. 2–20. 清水元「明治中期の「南進論」と「環太平洋」の構想の原型(Ⅰ)」『アジア経済』32/9, アジア研究所, September 1991. ("Southern Advance Theory" during Meiji Era and the Original Idea of the Pacific Rim (Ⅰ)," *Asia Economy*, 32/9, Ajia kenkyūjo, September 1991)

Shimizu, Hajime "Meiji chūki no 'Nanshinron' to 'Kan-Taiheiyō' shisō no genkei (Ⅱ)," *Ajia Keizai*, 32/10, Ajia kenkyūjo, October 1991, pp. 27–44. 清水元「明治中期の「南進論」と「環太平洋」の構想の原型(Ⅱ)」『アジア経済』32/10, アジア研究所, October 1991, pp. 27–44. ("Southern Advance Theory" during Meiji Era and the Original Idea of the Pacific Rim (Ⅱ)," *Asia Economy*, 32/10, Ajia kenkyūjo, October 1991, pp. 27–44.)

Shimizu, Hajime *Nanshin-ron*: Its Turning Point in World War I," *The Developing Economies* 15/4, December 1987, 386–402.

Shimizu, Hajime "Senkanki Nihon-keizaiteki 'Nanshin' no shisōteki haikei," Sugiyama S. & Ian G. Brown *Senkanki Tōnan Ajia no Keizai masatsu. Nihon no Nanshin to Ajia-Ōbei* Dōbunkan, 1990, pp. 13–44. 清水元「戦間期日本・経済的「南進」の思想的背景」杉山伸也, イアン・ブラウン編著『戦間期東南アジアの経済摩擦. 日本の南進とアジア・欧米』同文館, 1990. ("The Ideational Background of Japan's Economical 'Southern Advance' between the Wars," Sugiyama S. & Ian G. Brown *Economical Friction in Southeast Asia between the Wars. Japan's Southern Advance, Asia, Europe and America*, Dōbunkan, 1990.)

Shimizu, Junzō "Kaisetsu," *Nihon minzoku bunka no kigen II:* Kodai no Fune, Nihongo to Nampōgo, Kōdansha, 1978, pp. 403–408. 清水潤三「解説」『日本民族文化の起源Ⅱ：古代の舟・日本語と南方語』講談社, 1978 ("Commentary," *The Origins of the Japanese Ethnic Culture II: Ancient Boats* Japanese Language and Southward Language, Kōdansha, 1978.)

Suenari, Michio *Betonamu bunka jinruigaku. Bunken kaidai. Nihon kara shiten*, Fūkyōsha, 2009. 末成道男『ベトナム文化人類学』文献解題, 日本から視点, 風響堂, 2009. (*Cultural Anthropology of Vietnam*, Annotated Bibliography, Perspective from Japan, Fūkyōsha, 2009.)

Suzuki, Masataka "Chiiki kenkyū to Keiō gijuku - jinbunshakaigaku no shiza kara," *Mita Hyōron*, 10/ No. 1182, 2014, pp. 32-37. 鈴木正崇「地域研究と慶応義塾—人文社会学の視座から」『三田評論』10/ No. 1182, 2014. "Area Studies and Keio University - from the viewpoint of the Humanities and Social Sciences," *Mita Hyōron*, 10/ No. 1182, 2014.

T

Takeda, Ryūji "Indoshina no minzoku to bunka (Matsumoto Nobuhiro, Iwanami shoten shokō," *Shigaku*, dai 22 kan, dai 4 gō, Mita Shigakkai, 1943, p. 119 (489). 竹田龍兒「印度支那の民族と文化(松本信廣著, 岩波書店發行)」『史学』第22巻, 第4号, 三田史学会, 1943, p. 119 (489).

Takegoshi, Yosaburō *Nankokuki*, Nippon hyōronsha, 1942 (1st edition 1910). 竹越与三郎『南国記』日本評論社, 1942 (1st edition 1910). (*Records from Southern Countries*, Nippon hyōronsha, 1942 (1st edition 1910).)

Takeuchi, Yoshimi *Ajiashugi*, Chikuma shobō, 1963. 竹内好『アジア主義』筑摩書房, 1963. (*Asianism*, Chikuma shobō, 1963.)

Tanaka, Suiichirō "Chūkōron", *Ōsaka kōen*, Keiō Gijuku shuppankyoku, 1913, pp. 77-117. 田中萃一郎「忠孝論」慶応義塾『大阪講演』慶応義塾出版局, 1913. ("Theory of Loyalty and Filial piety," *Osaka Lecture*, Keio Gijuku Publishing Office, 1913.)

Tanaka, Suiichirō "Seiji to fujin", *Ōsaka kōen*, Keiō Gijuku shuppankyoku, 1913, pp. 336-357. 田中萃一郎「政治と婦人」『大阪講演』慶応義塾出版局, 1913. ("Politics and Ladies," *Osaka Lecture*, Keio Gijuku Publishing Office, 1913.)

Tanaka, Suiichirō *Tōhō kinseishi*, Tōhō kyōkai, 1900-1902. 田中萃一郎『東邦近世史』東邦協会, 1900-1902. (*Early Modern History of Orient*, Society for Orient, 1900-1902.)

The Dictionary of Anthropology, edited by Barfield, Thomas, Blackwell Publishers, Cambridge, Mass., 1997.

The Routledge Dictionary of Anthropologists, Routledge and New York, London, 1997.

Tōkōkō, II, Keiō gijuku taiikukai sangakubu nenpō, Shuppan kagaku sōgō kenkyūjo, 1920. 『登高行』II, 慶應義塾體育會山岳部年報, 出版科学総合研究所, 1920.

Tōnan Ajia Gakkai *Tōnan Ajia shi. Kenkyū no hatten*, Tōnan Ajia Gakkai 40 shūnen, Kinen jigyō iinkai, Yamakawa shuppansha, 2009. 東南アジア学会『東南アジア史研究の発展』東南アジア学会40年, 記念事業委員会, 山川出版社, 2009. (Japan Society for Southeast Asian Studies, *History of Southeast Asia. Development of the*

Research, 40 Years of the Japan Society for Southeast Asian Studies, Kinen jigyō iinkai, Yamakawa shuppansha, 2009.)

Tylor, Edward Burnett, *Primitive Culture. The Research into the Development of Mythology, Philosophy, Religion, Language, Art, and Custom*, Vol. 1, London: John Murray, 1929 (first edition 1871).

U

Ushijima, Iwao "Matsumoto Nobuhiro, Mishina Sōei, Oka Masao ni okeru Nihon shinwa no kenkyū," *Kokubungaku kaishaku to kanshō*, 37-1, 1972, pp. 174-177. 牛島巌「松本信広・三品彰英・岡正雄における日本神話研究」『国文学　解釈と鑑賞』37-1, 1972. ("The Research of the Japanese Myths by Matsumoto Nobuhiro, Mishina Sōei and Oka Masao," *National Literature. Commentary and Appreciation*, 37-1, 1972.)

V

Varagnac, André "Les phénomènes d'archéocivilisation," *De la préhistoire au monde modern. Essai d'une anthropodynamique*, Librarie Plon, Paris, 1954. ("Phenomen's of Archaeo-Civilisation," *From Prehistory to the Modern World, An Essay on Anthropodynamics*, Librarie Plon, Paris, 1954.)

Varagnac, André *Définition du folklore*, Société d'éditions geographiques, maritimes et coloniales, Paris, 1938. (*Definition of Folklore*, Society of Geographic, Maritime and Colonial Editions, Paris, 1938).

W

Wada, Hironari "Matsumoto Nobuhiro kyōju jūrai no Vetonamu shahon sanshu ni tsuite - Nihon - Chūgoku no kindaika to Vetonamu," *Shigaku*, dai 35 kan, dai 4 gō, Mita Shigakkai, 1963. 和田博徳「松本信廣教授従来のヴェトナム写本—日本・中国の近代化とヴェトナム」『史学』第35巻, 第4号, 1963, pp. 93-96 (431-434). ("Professor Matsumoto Nobuhiro's Existing Copies of Vietnamese Books - Modernization of Japan and China and Vietnam," *The Historical Science*, Vol. 35, No. 4, Mita Historical Society, 1963.

Wada, Masahiko "Matsumoto Nobuhiro hakase jūrai no Annan hon ni tsuite - Keiō gijuku toshokan Matsumoto bunko shozō Annan hon kaidai" (Jō), *Shigaku*, dai 62 kan, dai 1/2 gō, Mita Shigakkai, 1992, pp. 165-183. 和田正彦「松本信廣博士従来の安南本について—慶應義塾図書館・松本文庫所蔵安南本解題」(上)『史学』第62巻, 第1/2号, 三田史学会, 1992. ("About Dr. Matsumoto Nobuhiro's Annamese Books - Annamese Books Stored in Matsumoto Archive of the Keio University Library" (I) *The Historical Science*, Vol. 62, No. 1/2, Mita Historical Society, 1992.)

Wada, Masahiko "Matsumoto Nobuhiro hakase jūrai no Annan hon ni tsuite - Keiō gijuku toshokan Matsumoto bunko shozō Annan hon kaidai" (Ka), *Shigaku*, dai

63 kan, dai 1/2 gō, Mita Shigakkai, 1993, p. 125-158 (337-370). 和田正彦「松本信廣博士従来の安南本について―慶應義塾図書館・松本文庫所蔵安南本解題」(下)『史学』第63巻, 第1/2号, 三田史学会, 1993. ("About Dr. Matsumoto Nobuhiro's Annamese Books - Annamese Books Stored in Matsumoto Archive of the Keio University Library" (II) *The Historical Science*, Vol. 63, No. 1/2, Mita Historical Society, 1993.)

Watsuji, Tetsurō *Fūdoron — ningen kagakuteki kōsatsu*, Iwanami shoten, 1936. 和辻哲郎『風土論―人間科学的考察』岩波書店, 1936. (*Climate Theory - Scientific Consideration of Human*, Iwanami shoten, 1936.

Wundt, Wilhelm *Elements of Folk Psychology. Outlines of a Psychological History of the Development of Mankind*, George Allen & Unwin Ltd., London, 1916 (German edition in 1912).

Y

Yamada, Yoshihiko "Hanrei," Mōsu, Maruseru *Taiheiyō minzoku no genshi keizai: kosei shakai ni okeru kōkan no keishiki to riyū*, Nikkōshoin, 1943. 山田吉彦,「凡例」, モース・マルセル『太平洋民族の原始経済:古制社会に於ける交換の形式と理由』日光書院, 1943. (Yamada, Yoshihiko, "Introductory Remarks," Mauss, Marcel, *Primitive Economy of Pacific People: Form and Reasons of Exchange in Old-System Society*, Nikkōshoin, 1943.)

Yamamoto, Tatsurō "Indoshina no kenkoku setsuwa," *Tōsei kōshō shiron*, Jōkan, Fuzanbō 1939, pp. 261-314. 「印度支那の建国説話」『東西交渉史論』上巻, 富山房, 1939, pp. 261-314. ("Legends of Founding the States in Indochina," *Historical Theories on Contacts between the East and West*," Vol. 1, Fuzanbō 1939.)

Yamamoto, Tatsurō "Betonamu kenkyū shiryō no shōkai to shuppan," *Nihon minzoku bunka no kigen*, dai 3 kan, Geppō dai 3 gō, Kōdansha, 1978, pp. 3-5. 山本達郎「越南研究資料の紹介と出版」『日本民族文化の起源』第3巻, 月報第3号, 講談社, 1978. ("Introduction and Publication of Materials of Vietnamese Studies," *The Origins of the Japanese Culture*, Vol. 3, Monthly Report No. 3, Kōdansha, 1978.)

Yamamuro, Shin'ichi *Shisō kadai to shiteno Ajia: kijiku - rensa - tōki*, Iwanami shoten, 2001. 山室信一『思想課題としてのアジア:基軸・連鎖・投企』岩波書店, 2001. (*Asia as a Task for Thinking: Axis, Chaining, Projection*, Iwanami shoten, 2001.)

Yamashita, Shinji *The Making of Anthropology in East and Southeast Asia*, Berghahn Books, New York, 2004.

Yanagita Kunio: sasayakanaru mukashi shō kokyō shichijūnen shō, ed. by Okaya Kōji, Nihontoshosentā, 1998. 『柳田国男:さゝやかなる昔(抄)/故郷七十年(抄)』岡谷公二 編解説, 日本図書センター, 1998. (*Yanagita Kunio: Modest Former Times (Excerpt) / 70 Years of Narive Place (Excerpt)*, ed. by Okaya Koji, Nihontosho senta, 1998.)

Yanagita, Kunio "Daisshō ikkoku minzokugaku," *Teihon Yanagita Kunioshū*, dai 25 kan, Chikumashobō, 1964. 柳田国男「第一章―国民俗学」『定本柳田国男集』Vol.

25, 筑摩書房, 1964. ("Chapter One: National Folklore Studies," *Yanagita Kunio's Authentic Writings Collection*, Vol. 25, Chikumashobō, 1964.)
Yanagita, Kunio "Ethnology to ha nanika," *Teihon Yanagita Kunioshū*, dai 25 kan, Chikumashobō, 1964, pp. 232-47. 柳田国男「Ethnologyとは何か」『定本柳田国男集』第25巻, 筑摩書房, 1964. ("What is Ethnology?" *Yanagita Kunio's Authentic Writings Collection*, Vol. 25, Chikumashobō, 1964.)
Yanagita, Kunio "Ikkoku minzokugaku," *Teihon Yanagita Kunioshū*, dai 2 kan, Chikumashobō, 1964, p. 339-357. 柳田国男「一国民俗学」『定本柳田国男集』第25巻, 筑摩書房, 1964. ("Folklore Studies of One Country," *Yanagita Kunio's Authentic Writings Collection*, Vol. 25, Chikumashobō, 1964.)
Yanagita, Kunio *Kainan shōki*, Sōgensha, 1945 (first edition 1925). 柳田国男『海南小記』創元者, 1945 (1925). (*Small Records from the Sea in the South*, Sōgensha, 1945 (first edition 1925).)
Yanagita, Kunio "Kigenron kentō," *Minkan denshōron*, Kyōritsusha shoten, 1934, pp. 69-73. 柳田国男「起原論検討」『民間伝承論』共立社書店, 1934. ("Considering Theory of Origins," *Folklore Theory*, Kyōritsusha shoten, 1934.)
Yanagita, Kunio "Musashino zatsuwa," *Tōkōkō*, I, Keiō gijuku taiikukai sangakubu nenpō, Shuppan kagaku sōgō kenkyūjo, 1919, pp. 18-37. 柳田国男「武蔵野雑話」『登高行』I, 慶應義塾體育會山岳部年報, 出版科学総合研究所, 1919. ("Miscellaneous Talks on Musashino," *Tōkōkō*, I, Keiō gijuku taiikukai sangakubu nenpō, Shuppan kagaku sōgō kenkyūjo, 1919.)
Yanagita, Kunio "Nantō kenkyū no genjō," *Teihon Yanagita Kunioshū*, dai 25 kan, Chikumashobō, 1964, pp. 159-181. 柳田国男「南島研究の現状」『定本柳田国男集』第25巻, 筑摩書房, 1964. ("The Present Situation of the Research of Southern Islands," *Yanagita Kunio's Authentic Writings Collection*, Vol. 25, Chikumashobō, 1964.
Yanagita, Kunio "Nihon no Minzokugaku" (1926), *Teihon Yanagita Kunioshū*, dai 25 kan, Chikumashobō, 1964. 「日本の民俗学」(1926)『定本柳田国男集』第25巻, 筑摩書房, 1964. ("The Japanese Folklore Studies" (1926), *Yanagita Kunio's Authentic Writings Collection*, Vol. 25, Chikumashobō, 1964.)
Yanagita, Kunio "Suisu nikki" (1922), *Teihon Yanagita Kunioshū*, dai 3 kan, Chikuma shobō, 1963, pp. 251-304. 柳田国男「瑞西日記」(1922)『定本柳田国男集』第3巻, 筑摩書房, 1963. ("Diary from Switzerland" (1922), *Yanagita Kunio's Authentic Writings Collection*, Chikuma shobō, 1963.)
Yanagita, Kunio "Zoku Musashino zatsuwa," *Tōkōkō*, II, Keiō gijuku taiikukai sangakubu nenpō, Shuppan kagaku sōgō kenkyūjo, 1920, pp. 1-18. 「続武蔵野雑話」『登高行』II, 慶應義塾體育會山岳部年報, 出版科学総合研究所, 1920. ("Miscellaneous Talks on Musashino Continued," *Tōkōkō*, II, Keiō gijuku taiikukai sangakubu nenpō, Shuppan kagaku sōgō kenkyūjo, 1920.)
"Yanagita Kunio," *Kodansha Encyclopedia of Japan*, Vol. 8, Kodansha, 1983, p. 315.
Yano, Tooru *Nanshin no keifu. Nihon no Nan'yō shikan*, Chikurashobō, 2009. 矢野暢

『南進の系譜. 日本の南洋史観』千倉書房, 2009. (*Chronology of Southern Advance. Japan's Historical Perspective of the South Seas*, Chikurashobō, 2009.

Yatsugi, Kazuo *Shōwa dōran shishi*, chū, Keizai ōraisha, 1971. 矢次一夫『昭和動乱私史』中, 経済往来社, 1971. (*Personal History of Shōwa Upheavals*, II, Keizai ōraisha, 1971.)

Yawata, Ichirō "Kaisetsu," *Nihon minzoku bunka no kigen III: Tōnan Ajia bunka to Nihon*, dai 3 kan, geppō dai 3 gō, Kōdansha, 1978, pp. 1-3. 八幡一郎「解説」『日本民族文化の起源』第3巻, 月報第3号, 講談社, 1978. ("Commentary," *The Origins of the Japanese Ethnology III: Southeast Asian Culture and Japan*, Vol. 3, Monthly Report No. 3, Kōdansha, 1978.)

Yoshikai, Masato "One Century of Bronze Drum Research in Japan," *Transactions of the International Conference of Eastern Studies*, No. XLIX 2004, Vol. 419, The Tōhō Gakkai, pp. 23-40.

Yoshikai, Masato "Rekishigakusha to 'Minami Shina'," *Shōwa - Ajiashugi no jitsuzō. Teikoku Nihon to Taiwan, 'Nanyō', 'Minami Shina*, ed. by Matsuura, Masataka, Minerva shobō, 2007 pp. 54-77. 吉開将人「歴史学者と「南支那」」『昭和・アジア主義の実像. 帝国日本と台湾・「南洋」・「南支那」』松浦正孝編, ミネルヴァ書房, 2007. "Historian and the 'South China,'" *The Real Image of Showa Asianism. Imperial Japan and Taiwan, "South Seas," "South China,"* ed. by Matsuura, Masataka, Minerva shobō, 2007.

Yun, De-yon "1930-1940 nendai no Kin Ei-ken to Betonamu kenkyū," *Tōnan Ajia kenkyū*, dai 48 kan, dai 3 gō, Kyōto daigaku tōnan Ajia kenkyū sentā, 2010, pp. 314-333. ユン・デヨン「1930-40年代の金永鍵とベトナム研究」『東南アジア研究』第48巻, 第3号, 京都大学東南アジア研究センター, 2010. (Youn Daeyeong, "Kim Yung-kun's Course of Life and Vietnamese Studies in the 1930s and the 1940s", *Southeast Asia Research*, Vol. 48, No. 3, Kyoto University Southeast Asian Research Center, 2010.)

Yusa, Michiko *Zen and Philosophy: An Intellectual Biography of Nishida Kitarô*, University of Hawai'i Press, Honolulu, 2002

The list of the Japanese personal names

Chikamori Masashi	Chikamori Masashi	近森 正
Endo Ryukichi	Endō Ryūkichi	遠藤 隆吉
Esaka Teruya	Esaka Teruya	江坂 輝弥
Fukuzawa Yukichi	Fukuzawa Yukichi	福沢 諭吉
Furuno Kiyoto	Furuno Kiyoto	古野 清人
Goto Kenichi	Gotō Kenichi	後藤 乾一
Hashimoto Masukichi	Hashimoto Masukichi	橋本 増吉
Hirafuji Kikuko	Hirafuji Kikuko	平藤 喜久子
Hosaka Saburo	Hosaka Saburō	保坂 三郎
Iha Fuyu	Iha Fuyū	伊波 普猷
Ishii Yoneo	Ishii Yoneo	石井 米雄
Ito Mikiharu	Itō Mikiharu	伊藤 幹治
Ito Seiji	Itō Seiji	伊藤 清司
Izutsu Toshikiho	Izutsu Toshikiho	井筒 俊彦
Iwata Keij	Iwata Keiji	岩田 慶治
Iwai Daie	Iwai Daie	岩井 大慧
Kani Hiroaki	Kani Hiroaki	可児 弘明
Kanokogi Kazunobu	Kanokogi Kazunobu	鹿子木員信
Kato Shigeshi	Katō Shigeshi	加藤 繁
Kawai Teiichi	Kawai Teiichi	川合 貞一
Kawamoto Kunie	Kawamoto Kunie	川本 邦衛
Kitagawa	Kitagawa	北川
Kobayashi Hideo	Kobayashi Hideo	小林 英夫
Kobayashi Tomoo	Kobayashi Tomoo	小林 知生
Koyama Shiro	Kōyama Shirō	神山 四郎
Mabuchi Toichi	Mabuchi Tōichi	馬淵 東一
Matsubara Hideichi	Matsubara Hideichi	松原 秀一
Matsue Haruji	Matsue Haruji	松江 春次
Matsumoto Nobuhiro	Matsumoto Nobuhiro	松本 信広
Matsumoto Yoshio	Matsumoto Yoshio	松本 芳夫
Matsuoka Yosuke	Matsuoka Yōsuke	松岡 洋右

Mazaki Manri	Mazaki Manri	間崎 萬里
Mochidzuki Gunshiro	Mochidzuki Gunshirō	望月 軍四郎
Mori	Mōri	毛利
Nagata Yasukichi	Nagata Yasukichi	永田 安吉
Nakano Tomoaki	Nakano Tomoaki	中野 朝明
Nishioka Hideo	Nishioka Hideo	西岡 秀雄
Obayashi Taryo	Ōbayashi Taryō	大林 太良
Okakura Tenshin	Okakura Tenshin	岡倉 天心
Oka Masao	Oka Masao	岡 正雄
Onishi Yoshihisa	Ōnishi Yoshihisa	大西 吉寿
Orikuchi Shinobu	Orikuchi Shinobu	折口 信夫
Osawa Kazuo	Ōsawa Kazuo	大澤 一雄
Sakurai Yumio	Sakurai Yumio	桜井 由躬雄
Sakima Koei	Sakima Kōei	佐喜眞 興英
Sato Yoshiyuki	Satō Yoshiyuki	佐藤 喜之
Sayama Yukichi	Sayama Yūkichi	佐山 融吉
Shibata Joe	Shibata Jōe	柴田 常恵
Shimao Minoru	Shimao Minoru	嶋尾 稔
Shimizu Akitoshi	Shimizu Akitoshi	清水 昭俊
Shimizu Hajime	Shimizu Hajime	清水 元
Shimizu Junzo	Shimizu Junzō	清水 潤三
Shinjo Shinzo	Shinjō Shinzō	新城 新蔵
Shiraishi Masaya	Shiraishi Masaya	白石 昌也
Shiratori Kurakichi	Shiratori Kurakichi	白鳥 倉吉
Suenari Michio	Suenari Michio	末成 道男
Sugiura Ken'ichi	Sugiura Ken'ichi	杉浦 健一
Sugimoto Naojiro	Sugimoto Naojirō	杉本 直治郎
Suzuki Masataka	Suzuki Masataka	鈴木 正崇
Takeda Ryuji	Takeda Ryūji	竹田 龍兒
Takegoshi Yosaburo	Takegoshi Yosaburō	竹越 与三郎
Takeuchi Yoshimi	Takeuchi Yoshimi	竹内 好
Tanaka Suiichiro	Tanaka Suiichirō	田中 萃一郎
Tsuboi Shogoro	Tsuboi Shōgorō	坪井 正五郎
Tsuda Sokichi	Tsuda Sōkichi	津田 左右吉
Ushijima Iwao	Ushijima Iwao	牛島 巖

Utsushikawa Nenozo	Utsushikawa Nenozō	移川	子之蔵
Wada Hironari	Wada Hironari	和田	博徳
Wada Masahiko	Wada Masahiko	和田	正彦
Watsuji Tetsuro	Watsuji Tetsurō	和辻	哲郎
Yamada Yoshihiko	Yamada Yoshihiko	山田	吉彦
Yamamoto Tatsuro	Yamamoto Tatsurō	山本	達郎
Yamashita Shinji	Yamashita Shinji	山下	晋司
Yamamuro Shin'ichi	Yamamuro Shin'ichi	山室	信一
Yanagita Kunio	Yanagita Kunio	柳田	国男
Yano Toru	Yano Tooru	矢野	暢
Yatsugi Kazuo	Yatsugi Kazuo	矢次	一夫
Yawata Ichiro	Yawata Ichirō	八幡	一郎
Yoshikai Masato	Yoshikai Masato	吉開	将人

Index

aborigine people 243
Adam František Kolár 20
Adolf Bastian 32
Alpine Club 35
Amaterasu Ōmikami 84
American Indian 94
American people 74
ancient China 47
Ancient history 20
André Varagnac 10
Annals of Đại Nam 139, 142
Annam 214
Annamese 174
Annamese people 192
anthropology 29
archaeo-civilization 9
archaeology 7
artifacts 160
Asia Research Institute 5, 166
Asianism 235
Asia-Pacific Region 235
Asia-Pacific War 229
Association des Amis du Vieux Huế 140
Australia 112
Austric language 107
Austroasiatic cultures 108
Austroasiatic languages 95, 103, 107
Austronesians 189
Aymonier 169

Bac Sonian and Hoa Binhian periods 145
Back South Seas 19
basic culture (kisō bunka) 9, 10
Battle of Shanghai 135
Bi Shi Hong x
boats 15
Boys Junior High School 3
Bronze Drums 145
Burma 214

Cambodians 56
Cao Bằng Province 139
Cao Đài sect 248
Caodaism 247
Cham museum 140
Cham people 95
Chapa 215
Chikamori Masashi vii, x, 41
Chin Kei Wa 4, 142
China ix, 74, 224, 254
China Incident 228
China-centered Oriental identity 242

Chinese 194
Chinese ancient history 45
Chinese writing 242
Christopher W. A. Szpilman 235
Chronicles of Đại Nam 142
Chữ Nôm 218
civilizing mission 235
climate 214
climate theory 23, 211
Committee for Ethnic Issues 246
common Asian identity 235
Communism 247
comparative research 48
Complete Annals of Đại Việt 142
cultural diffusion 22
cultural evolutionism 23
cultural history 48

Đà Nẵng (Tourane) 140
De Hevesy 169
Department of History and Culture of the West Lake Museum 155
dichotomy 187, 188
Diffusionist ethnology 21
Đông Sơn culture 95

École Française d'Extrême-Orient (EFEO) 14, 68
Édouard Chavannes 45
Edward Burnett Tylor 37
Edward W. Saïd 185
EFEO 139
Émile Durkheim 47
Émile Gaspardone 14
Endo Ryukichi 53
erthnologists 45
Esaka Tetsuya 6

Essay on Japanese Mythology 84
ethnic minorities 147
ethnoarchaeological research 16
ethnographic 73
ethnology 7
ethnopsychology 29
European 194
evolutionism 25
Evolutionist ethnology 21
excavation 135
exogamy 53, 65
exoticity 187
Exotism 204
Ezo (Hokkaido) 224

Far East 75
festivals 84
field trips 133
field work 35
first-class nation 201
folklore studies 20, 35
Formosa (taiwan) 224
France 67, 254
Frédéric Roustan 1
French 228, 242
French Indchina 138
French School of Sociology 67
French sinological school 46
Front South Seas 19
Fukuyama Industry Library 149
Fukuzawa Yukichi 26
Furuno Kiyoko 129
geneology 189
geographical concepts 121

Germany 228
Gift 68, 79

goddess Demeter   100
Golden Bough   97
Golubev   169
Gotō Ken'ichi   vii, ix, 221
Greater East Asia Co-Prosperity Sphere   166

Haiphong   139
Han culture   218
Han people   136
Hangzhou   135
Hanoi   139
Hans Naumann   259
Hashimoto Masakichi   29
Hashimoto Matsukichi   xi
Hayase Shinzō   vii
Heiankyō   206
Heine-Geldern's   135
Henri Maspero   14
Hirafuji Kikuo   2
History and Linguistic Institute of the Central Academy   155
Hội An (Faifo)   140
Holland   151
homeland   208
Hong Kong Chinese University   4
Hosaka Saburo   156
houses supported by pillars   207
Huế   139
Hundred Yue   173
Hyūga   119

Iha Fuyu   119
Imperial Nationalization   244
India   114
Indian and Chinese influence   202
Indian culture   198
Indianized   202
Indnesians   189
Indochina   18, 68
Indochina Research Society   167
inferiority   220
influence of the natural environment on culture   211
Inner South Seas   19
Institute of Ethnology   232
intelligentsia   242
Islam   258
Ito Mikiharu   2
Ito Seiji   2
Iwai Daie   142
Iwamoto Chizuna   147
Iwata Keiji   211
Izutsu Toshikiho   258

James George Frazer   xi, 37
Japan Ethnological Society   3
Japan Ethnological Society   149
Japan Historical Society   144
Japan Society for Southeast Asian Historical Studies   3
Japan Society for Southeast Asian Studies Tōnan Ajia Gakkai   3
Japan Society of Oceanian Ethnography (Minami no kai, 南の会)   149
Japan Society South Asian Studies   2
Japanese and Austroasiatic language: A Comparative Study of Vocabulary   107
Japanese graves   140
Japanese leadership   203
Japanese Orientalism   204

Japanese uniqueness 235
Japan-French Trade Agreement 133
Japan's Southern Advance Theory 23, 221
Jean Przyluski xi, 14

kagai 85
Kang Sang Jung 186
Kani Hiroaki 4
Kanokogi Kazunobu 60
Kato Shigeshi xi, 29
Kawai Teiichi xi, 29
Kawamoto Kunie 1
Kawamura Minato 186
Keio Gijuku 26
Keio Institute of Cultural and Linguistic Studies 4
Keio University 3
Keio University Mochidzuki Foundation 133
Khải Định Museum 140
Khasi 121
Khmer 215
Kidaichi Kyosuke 41
Kim Yung-kun 138
Kimitada Miwa 235
king-magician 257
Kitagawa 156
Kobayashi Tomoo 149
Kobe 139
Komine Isokichi 148
Korea 225, 254
Koyama Shiro 2
Kyoto 210
Kyushu 118

Laos 198
Laotians 56
Laurel-Forest Culture 261
League of Nations 134
Leaving-Asia Theory 224
legend 94
Linguistic Institute 4, 5, 166
Lucien Lévy-Bruhl 61
Ludwig Riess 51

Mabuchi Tōichi 128
Madeleine Colani 144
magic 62
Malaysia 258
Man 182
Manchuria 254
Marcel Granet xi, 13, 45
Marcel Mauss xi, 13
Marco Polo Bridge Incident 135
maritime culture 176
Martin Heidegger 212
Matsubara Hidekichi 6
Matsue Haruji 148
Matsue Ichirō 149
Matsumoto Yoshio 156
Mazaki Manri 156
Meiji 221, 208
Melanesian 74
Meo 182
Micronesia 150
migration 189, 226
Mita Historical Society 3, 144
Moi people 196
Mon 215
Mongolians 217
Mongoloid tribes 190
Mongols 217

Mon-Khmer   122, 182
monsoon zone   213
Mori   156
mountain beliefs   40
Multilinear evolutionism   21
Munda   121
Myths   81

Nagata Yasukichi   142
naïve   59
naivity   200
Nakano Tomoaki   149
Nakao Natsumi   187
Nampō   26
Nanjing   135
Nanjing Incident   135
Nankai（南海）　121
Nanyo Kohatsu K. K.（南洋興発会社）　134
Nanyō（南洋）　18, 121
nationalism   235
Negritos   189
Neolithic period   153
Nevski   41
New Guinea   134
New Harvest Research Society   259
Nguyễn Ái Quốc   241
Nguyễn Văn Khoan   231
Nguyễnn Văn Khánh   viii
Nippon Yusen Kaisha Line   150
Nishioka Hideo   153
Northward Theory   123

Obayashi Taryo   2
Occident（Seiyō 西洋）　19
Oceania   19

Oceanian   109
Oka Masao   149
Okakura Tenshin   235
Ōkawa Shūmei   250
Okinaawa studies   120
Orient（Tōyō 東洋）　19, 225
Oriental civilization   218
Oriental history   8, 70
Oriental studies   67
Orientalism   23, 185
origins   210
Orikuchi Shinobu   41
OSK Company   133
Outer South Seas   19

Pacific Association   167
Palau   134
Pan-Asianism   23, 221
Paul Rivet   109
Peoples and Cultures of Indchina   146
Phan Bội Châu   241
Physical anthropology   20
Polynesian   74, 115
porcelain   157
potlatch   79
Poul-Louis Couchoud   100
powerful and civilized   203
priest-king   89
primitive   57
primitive culture   22
primitive people   56
primitive society   22
Princess Toyotama   100

regionalism   235
remnants   38

Research Institute for South Asian Culture 3, 164
Research of Family in Ancient China 52
Research of Japanese Myths 84
Research of the Mythology 77
Revival of Asia 223
Rice Cultivation Culture theory 15
rice-cultivation culture 260
Robert Heine-Geldern 154
Roland B. Dixon 111
Ryukyu 26, 118

sacred origin 238
Saipan 134
Sakima Kōei 119
Salmon Reinach 100
Sato Yoshiyuki 119
Sayama and Onishi 119
Science Council of Japan 5
seasonal festival (kisetsu sai) 82, 83
Second Sino-Japanese War 194, 228
Sedang 190
Senoi 190
shaman 257
shamaness 99
Shanghai 135
Shanghai Research Institute of Natural Sciences 154
Shibata 156
Shimao Minoru vii, 1, 6
Shimizu Akitoshi 2
Shimizu Hajime 169, 221
Shinjo Shinzo 154

Shintoism 207
Shintoist shrine 207
Shiraishi Masaya vii
Shiratori Kurakichi 165
shouldered stone axes 159
shōwa 186
Siam 198
similarities 187
Similarity 206
Sinicized culture 199, 202
Sinicized people 198
Sinocized civilization 243
Sino-Japanese War 224
sinologists 47
Small History of the Vietnamese People 262
Small Records from Seas in South 117
social Darwinism 23
Sociologist ethnology 21
sociologists 45
Sorbonne University 13
South Korea ix
South Sea culture 114
South Sea languages 113
South Sea people 225
South Seas 18
South Seas Association 167, 225
South Seas Bureau 26, 225
South Seas Development Company 26
South Seas Islands (Nanyō shotō 南洋諸島) 19, 69
South Seas Reagion 70
Southeast Asia 7
Southeast Asia studies 16
Southern Advance Theory 56

Southern China   260
Southern genealogy   160
Southern Pacific   121
Southern Pacific influence   111
Southern Pacific Islands   7, 70
Southern Region   26
Southward Theory (Nampōron)   122
spiritual power   97
stone axes   157
stone tools   159
stoneware   144
struggle for survival   34
Suenari Michio   1
Sugiura Ken'ichi   149
sun goddess   100
superior   203
superiority   203
survival of the fittest   43
Suzuki Masataka   2
Sven Saaler   235

taboo   96
Tachikawa Kyoichi   ix
Taihoku Imperial University   69
Taisho   186, 222
Taiwan   26
Takeda Ryuji   6
Takegoshi Yosaburo   120
Takeuchi Yoshimi   235
tale of Potato Digger Millionaire   118
Tanaka Suiichiro   xi, 42
Tenian   134
Thai   182, 214
Thai people   179, 193
Theories of Ancient Culture   124

theory of animism   62
theory of remnants   37
theory of taboo   96
theory of the gift and of the potlatch   79
theory on magic   64
Tokugawa Period   208
Tokyo Imperial University   165
Tokyo University   129
Tokyo War Crimes Tribunal   250
Tonkin   47
Tooth Blackening   168, 206
totemism   49, 62
Toyo Bunko   142
Trần Dynasty   218
Trần Hưng Đạo   217
Trần Kinh Hoà   4, 142
Tsuda Sokichi   238

uncivilized   57, 225
Unilinear evolutionism   21
uniqueness   219
unity of religious and political power   87
universalism   38
universality   209
Ushijima Iwao   8
utagaki   87
Utsushima Nenozo   29

Vegetalism   92
Vienna Diffusionist School   170
Vietnam   138
Vietnam War   142, 262
Vietnamese   56
Vietnamese annals   136
Vietnamese communal house   207

Vietnamese studies　17

water animals　176
Watsuji Tetsuro　xi, 212
Weak and barbarian　203
West　225
Western civilization　243
Western culture　203, 231
Western Powers　227
westernization　26
westernized　200, 202, 230
Wilhelm Schmidt　xi
Wilhelm Wundt　xi
World War II　ix
World War I　26

Yamada Yoshihiko　129
Yamamoto Tatsuro　x
Yamamuro Shin'ichi　235
Yamashita Shinji　2
Yamato people　179
Yanagita Kunio　xi, 29
Yano Tooru　ix, 221
Yap　150
Yatsugi Kazuo　246
Yawata Ichiro　149
Yoshikai Masato　2

Zhejiang（浙江）culture　155

Author Profile

Petra Karlová

Czech historian in Oriental studies. Ph. D. in international studies from Waseda University, Japan, Ph. D. in historical science, M. A. in Japanese studies and M. A. in Vietnamese studies from Charles University in Prague, Czech. Former lecturer in Vietnamese and Japanese studies at Charles University in Prague. Former Research Fellow in the department of East Asia at the Oriental Institute of the Czech Academy of Sciences. Former tutor of academic writing at Waseda University Writing Center. Present faculty staff at Waseda University Global Education Center. Specialist on Japan-Vietnamese relations in the first half of the 20th century, published several peer-reviewed articles on Matsumoto Nobuhiro. Contributed to the book *Dějiny Vietnamu* (History of Vietnam, published in Czech in 2008) by chapters on the Vietnamese history from the 16th century to 1945. Supports international exchange with Japan, especially in karate.

早稲田大学エウプラクシス叢書　10

Japan's Pre-War Perspective of Southeast Asia:
Focusing on Ethnologist Matsumoto Nobuhiro's Works during 1919–1945

2018 年 1 月 25 日　　初版第 1 刷発行

著　者 ……………… Petra Karlová
発行者 ……………… 島 田 陽 一
発行所 ……………… 株式会社 早稲田大学出版部
　　　　　　　　　　169-0051 東京都新宿区西早稲田 1-9-12
　　　　　　　　　　電話 03-3203-1551　　http://www.waseda-up.co.jp/
装　　丁 …………… 笠 井 亞 子
印刷・製本 ………… 株式会社 平文社

© 2018, Petra Karlová. Printed in Japan　　ISBN978-4-657-17808-4
無断転載を禁じます。落丁・乱丁本はお取替えいたします。

刊行のことば

　1913（大正2）年、早稲田大学創立30周年記念祝典において、大隈重信は早稲田大学教旨を宣言し、そのなかで、「早稲田大学は学問の独立を本旨と為すを以て　之が自由討究を主とし　常に独創の研鑽に力め以て　世界の学問に裨補せん事を期す」と謳っています。

　古代ギリシアにおいて、自然や社会に対する人間の働きかけを「実践（プラクシス）」と称し、抽象的な思弁としての「理論（テオリア）」と対比させていました。本学の気鋭の研究者が創造する新しい研究成果については、「よい実践（エウプラクシス）」につながり、世界の学問に貢献するものであってほしいと願わずにはいられません。

　出版とは、人間の叡智と情操の結実を世界に広め、また後世に残す事業であります。大学は、研究活動とその教授を通して社会に寄与することを使命としてきました。したがって、大学の行う出版事業とは大学の存在意義の表出であるといっても過言ではありません。これまでの「早稲田大学モノグラフ」、「早稲田大学学術叢書」の2種類の学術研究書シリーズを「早稲田大学エウプラクシス叢書」、「早稲田大学学術叢書」の2種類として再編成し、研究の成果を広く世に問うことを期しています。

　このうち、「早稲田大学エウプラクシス叢書」は、本学において博士学位を取得した新進の研究者に広く出版の機会を提供することを目的として刊行するものです。彼らの旺盛な探究心に裏づけられた研究成果を世に問うことが、他の多くの研究者と学問的刺激を与え合い、また広く社会的評価を受けることで、研究者としての覚悟にさらに磨きがかかることでしょう。

　創立150周年に向け、世界的水準の研究・教育環境を整え、独創的研究の創出を推進している本学において、こうした研鑽の結果が学問の発展につながるとすれば、これにすぐる幸いはありません。

2016年11月

早稲田大学